Taste of Home
quick
COOKING
ANNUAL RECIPES

Taste of Home
RDA ENTHUSIAST BRANDS, LLC • GREENDALE, WI

Taste of Home quick COOKING
ANNUAL RECIPES

■ EDITORIAL
Editor-in-Chief **Catherine Cassidy**
Creative Director **Howard Greenberg**
Editorial Operations Director **Kerri Balliet**

Managing Editor, Print & Digital Books **Mark Hagen**
Associate Creative Director **Edwin Robles Jr.**

Editor **Christine Rukavena**
Contributing Art Director **Jennifer Ruetz**
Layout Designers **Siya Motamedi, Catherine Fletcher**
Editorial Production Coordinator **Dena Ahlers**
Copy Chief **Deb Warlaumont Mulvey**
Copy Editor **Mary-Liz Shaw**
Content Operations Manager **Colleen King**
Content Operations Assistant **Shannon Stroud**
Executive Assistant **Marie Brannon**

Chief Food Editor **Karen Berner**
Food Editors **James Schend; Peggy Woodward, RD**
Associate Food Editor **Krista Lanphier**
Recipe Editors **Mary King; Annie Rundle; Jenni Sharp, RD; Irene Yeh**

Test Kitchen & Food Styling Manager
Sarah Thompson
Test Cooks **Nicholas Iverson (lead), Matthew Hass, Lauren Knoelke**
Prep Cooks **Megumi Garcia, Melissa Hansen, Nicole Spohrleder, Bethany Van Jacobson**
Food Stylists **Kathryn Conrad (senior), Leah Rekau, Shannon Roum**

Photography Director **Stephanie Marchese**
Photographers **Dan Roberts, Jim Wieland**
Photographer/Set Stylist **Grace Natoli Sheldon**
Set Stylists **Stacey Genaw, Melissa Haberman, Dee Dee Jacq**

Editor, *Simple & Delicious* **Jeanne Ambrose**
Art Director, *Simple & Delicious* **Kristen Johnson**

■ BUSINESS
General Manager, Taste of Home Cooking Schools
Erin Puariea

Vice President, Brand Marketing
Jennifer Smith

Vice President, Circulation & Continuity Marketing
Dave Fiegel

■ READER'S DIGEST NORTH AMERICA
Vice President, Business Development & Marketing
Alain Begun
President, Books & Home Entertainment
Harold Clarke
General Manager, Canada **Philippe Cloutier**
Vice President, Operations **Mitch Cooper**

Vice President, Chief Marketing Officer **Leslie Doty**
Chief Operating Officer **Howard Halligan**
Vice President, Chief Sales Officer **Mark Josephson**
Vice President, Digital Sales **Steve Sottile**
Vice President, Chief Content Officer **Liz Vaccariello**
Vice President, Global Financial Planning & Analysis
Devin White

■ THE READER'S DIGEST ASSOCIATION, INC.
President and Chief Executive Officer
Robert E. Guth

■ COVER PHOTOGRAPHY
Taste of Home Photo Studio

© 2014 RDA Enthusiast Brands, LLC
5400 S. 60th St., Greendale WI 53129

International Standard Book Number:
978-1-61765-288-2
International Standard Serial Number:
1522-6603

Component Number: 117800045H00

All rights reserved.

Taste of Home and Reader's Digest are registered trademarks of The Reader's Digest Association, Inc.

For other Taste of Home books and products, visit us at tasteofhome.com.

For more Reader's Digest products and information, visit rd.com (in the United States) or see rd.ca (in Canada).

Printed in U.S.A.
1 3 5 7 9 10 8 6 4 2

Easy MEALS for BUSY · FAMILIES ·

PICTURED ON FRONT COVER BBQ Chicken Waffle Fries (p. 102), Citrus Berry Shortcake (p. 245), French Meat Pie (p. 180), Slow Cooker Beef Vegetable Stew (p. 204) and Polish Casserole (p. 309).
PICTURED ON BACK COVER Marmalade Candied Carrots (p. 241), Family-Favorite Fried Chicken (p. 302), Easy Philly Cheesesteaks (p. 198), Ice Cream Cone Treats (p. 60) and Creamy Berry Smoothies (p. 88).
PICTURED AT LEFT Cherry Bonbon Cookies (p. 292), Spinach Pastrami Wraps (p. 133) and Orange Pecan Waffles (p. 92).

contents

HANDY ICONS IN THIS BOOK

FAST FIX Recipes are table-ready in 30 minutes or less. Discover more than 290 in all!

5 INGREDIENTS 139 dishes use 5 or fewer ingredients. Recipes may also call for water, salt, pepper, and canola or olive oil.

EAT SMART Dietitian-approved recipes are lower in calories, fat and sodium. Find 115 better-for-you choices!

LIKE US
facebook.com/tasteofhome

FOLLOW US
pinterest.com/taste_of_home

SHOP WITH US
shoptasteofhome.com

E-MAIL US
bookeditors@tasteofhome.com

TWEET US
@tasteofhome

VISIT OUR BLOG
loveandhomemaderecipes.com

SHARE A RECIPE
tasteofhome.com/submit

VISIT
tasteofhome.com
for
MORE!

Get ready for home cooking that's QUICK & EASY!

SMART COOKS KNOW that hearty meals don't have to take all day–and now they're sharing their secrets with you! This all-new edition of *Quick Cooking Annual Recipes* offers more than 600 recipes and tips for satisfying dishes that come together in a pinch.

Inside, you'll find every recipe that appeared in *Simple & Delicious* magazine over the past year, as well as 60 bonus dishes! This value-packed collection is loaded with weeknight dinners, homey casseroles, impressively easy desserts, and quick snacks and treats.

You'll even find sizzling grilled items, party foods that pop and seasonal delights that are surprisingly simple to pull off. Best of all, more than half of these family-favorite foods are table-ready in 30 minutes or less!

HIGHLIGHTS IN THIS EDITION

Weekly Menu Planner
Kick-start dinner with three weeks' worth of super-fast entrees! Complete with handy shopping lists, this popular chapter begins on page 64.

Time-Saving Specialties
Multiply your time with dozens of delicious 30-minute dinners! You'll also find easy morning starters and simmer-all-day sensations that slow cook while you're at work!

Handy New Icons
At-a-glance icons help you find the especially quick, healthy and simple recipes you're looking for. Finding the perfect recipe has never been easier! See page 3 to learn how these icons can work for you.

Contest Winners
Judged as the best by the Taste of Home Test Kitchen, these contest-winning dishes are sure to garner blue-ribbon approval from your family! Featured on pages 5 through 7, these winners include speedy dinner solutions, bake-sale goodies and crowd-pleasing appetizers.

Holiday & Seasonal Pleasers
Whip up cute Halloween treats, create new Thanksgiving traditions and make merry sweets that are a joy to share with the ideas in this popular chapter. The party starts on page 264...and you're the guest of honor!

Plus...
Readers share swift kitchen tips and speedy substitutions, as well as the strategies that help them make time for family meals. Now you can make memories at your own table, with a little help from the effortless ideas found in *Quick Cooking Annual Recipes*.

The Past Year's
RECIPE CONTESTS & THEIR WINNERS

PERFECT PARTY APPETIZERS

66 Dig into this hot one-skillet dip and enjoy the spicy kick from chorizo and pepper jack cheese. 99

—**JULIE MERRIMAN** COLD BROOK, NY

SIMPLE SIMMERED SENSATIONS

66 My husband adores this dish, and I love how good it makes the house smell as it simmers away! The tangy, sweet-salty sauce with fresh ginger and garlic is delicious with rice or noodles. 99

—**JULIE KO** ROGERS, AR

INSTANT UPGRADE: DINNER

❝ We call this dish OMG Chicken! Frozen veggies and rice make this hearty meal in one both quick and delicious, and we love the easy prep and cleanup. ❞

—WENDY GORTON OAK HARBOR, OH

SUMMER COMFORT

❝ After trying a fruit salad at a backyard barbecue, I wanted to make a rib sauce that tasted as sweet. Everyone loves the raspberry-red wine sauce combo. ❞

—STEPHEN MARINO NUTLEY, NJ

BAKE SALE BEAUTIES

66 After many tries, I finally created my own version of a doughnut muffin. It has the taste of a cake doughnut and it's a lot simpler to make. 99

—**MORGAN BOTWINICK** RICHMOND, VA

GO WITH THE DOUGH

66 We're fans of Mediterranean food, so this play on antipasto is a favorite in my family. Meat and cheese make it a nice, hearty appetizer. 99

—**PATRICIA HARMON** BADEN, PA

**Elizabeth Deguit's
Beef Tenderloin Stroganoff**
PAGE 31

30-Minute Meals

Each delicious meal on the following pages includes a family-pleasing main dish and a complementary side or sweet. And each amazing dinner is table-ready in 30 minutes or less!

Jacob Kitzman's
Steaks with Cherry Sauce
PAGE 19

Sue Schmidtke's
Fruit & Granola Crisp with Yogurt
PAGE 14

James Ockerman's
Baked Horseradish Salmon
PAGE 30

Cranberry-Kissed Pork Chops

I enjoy coming up with new recipes for my health-conscious family. I like to serve these pretty chops with cooked noodles or wild rice.
—**BETTY JEAN NICHOLS** EUGENE, OR

START TO FINISH: 25 MIN.
MAKES: 6 SERVINGS

- 6 boneless pork loin chops (5 ounces each)
- ¼ teaspoon coarsely ground pepper
- ⅓ cup jellied cranberry sauce
- 4½ teaspoons stone-ground mustard
- 3 tablespoons dried cranberries
- 2 tablespoons raspberry vinegar

1. Sprinkle pork chops with pepper. Brown chops on both sides over medium-high heat in a large skillet coated with cooking spray. Combine cranberry sauce and mustard; spoon over chops. Reduce heat; cover and cook for 4-6 minutes or until a thermometer reads 145°.
2. Remove chops and let stand for 5 minutes. Add cranberries and vinegar to skillet, stirring to loosen browned bits from pan. Bring to a boil; cook until liquid is reduced to about ½ cup. Serve with chops.
PER SERVING *229 cal., 8 g fat (3 g sat. fat), 68 mg chol., 119 mg sodium, 10 g carb., 1 g fiber, 27 g pro.* **Diabetic Exchanges:** *4 lean meat, 1 starch.*

Mashed Winter Squash

Bring a little color and a whole lot of hearty flavor to the table with this quick side. Each creamy bite has a subtle blend of cinnamon, nutmeg and ginger.
—**TASTE OF HOME TEST KITCHEN**

START TO FINISH: 20 MIN.
MAKES: 8 SERVINGS

- 4 packages (12 ounces each) frozen cooked winter squash
- ½ cup packed brown sugar
- ¼ cup butter, cubed
- 1 teaspoon salt
- ½ teaspoon ground cinnamon
- ¼ teaspoon ground nutmeg
- ⅛ teaspoon ground ginger

1. Place squash in a microwave-safe bowl. Cover and microwave on high for 7-8 minutes or until heated through, stirring after 5 minutes. Add the sugar, butter, salt, cinnamon, nutmeg and ginger; mix well.
2. Microwave, uncovered, for 2-3 minutes or until heated through.
NOTE *This recipe was tested in a 1,100-watt microwave.*
PER SERVING *119 cal., 6 g fat (4 g sat. fat), 15 mg chol., 359 mg sodium, 18 g carb., 1 g fiber, 27 g pro.*

Pistachio-Crusted Fish Fillets

The crunchy nut crust on this fish is delicious. It's a fresh and fun way to reel in your family to the dinner table.
—**MARIE STUPIN** ROANOKE, VA

START TO FINISH: 25 MIN.
MAKES: 4 SERVINGS

- 1 egg white, beaten
- ½ cup pistachios, finely chopped
- ⅓ cup dry bread crumbs
- ¼ cup minced fresh parsley
- ½ teaspoon pepper
- ¼ teaspoon salt
- 4 orange roughy fillets (6 ounces each)
- 4 teaspoons butter, melted

1. Place egg white in a shallow bowl. Combine the pistachios, bread crumbs, parsley, pepper and salt in another shallow bowl. Dip fillets in egg white, then pistachio mixture.
2. Place fish on a baking sheet coated with cooking spray. Drizzle with butter. Bake at 450° for 8-10 minutes or until fish flakes easily with a fork.

Glazed Sprouts and Carrots

Autumn veggies garner big smiles with a simple glaze of orange juice and nutmeg.
—**PAGE ALEXANDER** BALDWIN CITY, KS

START TO FINISH: 20 MIN.
MAKES: 4 SERVINGS

- ½ cup water
- 1 cup halved fresh brussels sprouts
- 2 medium carrots, sliced
- 1 teaspoon cornstarch
- ½ teaspoon sugar
- ¼ teaspoon salt, optional
- ⅛ teaspoon ground nutmeg
- ⅓ cup orange juice

1. Bring water to a boil in a large saucepan over medium heat. Add vegetables. Cover and simmer for 6-8 minutes or until almost tender; drain and return to pan.
2. Combine the cornstarch, sugar, salt if desired, nutmeg and orange juice; stir until smooth. Pour over the vegetables. Bring to a boil; cook and stir for 2 minutes or until thickened.
PER SERVING *39 cal., 0 fat (0 sat. fat), 0 chol., 18 mg sodium, 9 g carb., 0 fiber, 1 g pro.* **Diabetic Exchange:** *2 vegetable.*

CRANBERRY-KISSED PORK CHOPS
MASHED WINTER SQUASH

PISTACHO-CRUSTED FISH FILLETS
GLAZED SPROUTS AND CARROTS

DUTCH POTATOES
STEAKS WITH SHALLOT SAUCE

GREEK FISH FILLETS
EASY RICE AND PEAS

Dutch Potatoes

I like to whip up mashed potatoes with carrots and sour cream for a stick-to-your-ribs side dish. Cook it for the potato lover in your family.

—**PERLENE HOEKEMA** LYNDEN, WA

START TO FINISH: 30 MIN.
MAKES: 2 SERVINGS

- 2 **cups cubed peeled potatoes**
- 1 **cup sliced fresh carrots**
- ¼ **cup chopped onion**
- 2 **teaspoons butter**
- ¼ **cup sour cream**
- ¼ **teaspoon salt**
  Minced chives

1. Place potatoes and carrots in a large saucepan and cover with water. Bring to a boil. Reduce heat; cover and cook for 10-15 minutes or until tender. Meanwhile, saute onion in butter in a small skillet for 8-10 minutes or until golden brown.
2. Drain potatoes and carrots; mash. Beat in the onion, sour cream and salt. Sprinkle with chives.

Steaks with Shallot Sauce

My family members prefer hearty foods, and this dish is always a hit with them. It's easy to double or triple the recipe to feed your hungry bunch.

—**NANCY SUMMERS** CLIFTON, VA

START TO FINISH: 25 MIN.
MAKES: 2 SERVINGS

- ⅔ **cup sliced shallots or green onions**
- 2 **tablespoons butter, divided**
- ¼ **cup beef broth**
- 1 **tablespoon red wine vinegar**
- 2 **teaspoons Worcestershire sauce**
- 2 **beef tenderloin steaks (6 ounces each)**
- ½ **teaspoon pepper**
- ½ **teaspoon olive oil**

1. Saute shallots in 1 tablespoon butter in a small skillet until tender. Add broth; bring to a boil. Reduce heat; simmer until liquid is reduced to about 1 tablespoon.

2. Stir in vinegar and Worcestershire sauce; cook 1 minute longer. Remove from the heat. Stir in 1½ teaspoons butter. Cover and keep warm.
3. Sprinkle steaks with pepper. In a large skillet, cook steaks in oil and remaining butter until meat reaches desired doneness (for medium-rare, a thermometer should read 145°; medium, 160°; well-done, 170°). Serve with shallot sauce.

EAT SMART
Greek Fish Fillets

Olives, red onion, yogurt and feta cheese combine for a flavorful Greek topping. It works well with any mild-tasting white fish, not just tilapia. I usually serve the fish with a side of rice.

—**JENNIFER MASLOWSKI** NEW YORK, NY

START TO FINISH: 25 MIN.
MAKES: 4 SERVINGS

- 4 **tilapia fillets (4 ounces each)**
- ⅛ **teaspoon salt**
- ⅛ **teaspoon pepper**
- 2 **tablespoons plain yogurt**
- 1 **tablespoon butter, softened**
- 1½ **teaspoons lime juice**
- ½ **small red onion, finely chopped**
- ¼ **cup pitted Greek olives**
- ½ **teaspoon dill weed**
- ¼ **teaspoon paprika**
- ⅛ **teaspoon garlic powder**
- ¼ **cup crumbled feta cheese**

1. Sprinkle tilapia with salt and pepper. Place on a broiler pan coated with cooking spray.
2. Combine the yogurt, butter and lime juice. Stir in the onion, olives and seasonings. Spread down the middle of each fillet; sprinkle with feta cheese.
3. Broil 3-4 in. from the heat for 6-9 minutes or until fish flakes easily with a fork.
PER SERVING *170 cal., 7 g fat (3 g sat. fat), 67 mg chol., 344 mg sodium, 3 g carb., 1 g fiber, 23 g pro.* **Diabetic Exchanges:** *3 lean meat, 1½ fat.*

(5)INGREDIENTS
Easy Rice and Peas

Even kids (or adults) who aren't veggie lovers will gobble up this simple-to-prepare side. For a variation, sub in some other frozen veggies for the peas.

—**NANCY TAFOYA** FORT COLLINS, CO

START TO FINISH: 15 MIN.
MAKES: 4 SERVINGS

- 2 **cups water**
- 1 **tablespoon butter**
- 1 **teaspoon salt**
- 2 **cups uncooked instant rice**
- 1 **cup frozen peas**

Bring water, butter and salt to a boil in a large saucepan. Add rice and peas. Cover and remove from the heat. Let stand for 5-7 minutes or until all of the water is absorbed.

BUSY COOKS' SECRETS

Double or triple the recipe. Use extras to jump-start new meals.

I PREP EXTRA and use leftovers in new meals. For example, when I chop an onion, I chop the entire onion, use what I need and place the remainder in a sealed container. Then, when I need chopped onion, it's available! I also cook 2 to 4 pounds of potatoes at a time. Next morning, I make hash browns, chorizo and fried potatoes, potato salad or scalloped potatoes. When we have a roast for dinner, it becomes beef stroganoff or fajitas the following night. And I often use baked chicken breasts from dinner in chicken salad for lunch or chicken soft tacos the next day.

—**KAREN BAUER** LINCOLN, CA

MUSHROOM & HERB CHICKEN

Fruit & Granola Crisp with Yogurt

Here's an easy dessert you can feel good about. Blueberries and peaches are a delightful flavor combination.

—**SUE SCHMIDTKE** ORO VALLEY, AZ

START TO FINISH: 10 MIN.
MAKES: 4 SERVINGS

- 3 **cups fresh or frozen sliced peaches, thawed**
- 1 **cup fresh or frozen blueberries, thawed**
- 4 **tablespoons hot caramel ice cream topping**
- 4 **tablespoons granola without raisins**
- 2 **cups low-fat frozen yogurt**

Divide the peaches and blueberries among four 8-oz. ramekins. Top each with caramel and granola. Microwave, uncovered, on high for 1-2 minutes or until bubbly. Top each with a scoop of frozen yogurt.
NOTE *This recipe was tested in a 1,100-watt microwave.*
PER SERVING *251 cal., 3 g fat (1 g sat. fat), 5 mg chol., 133 mg sodium, 54 g carb., 4 g fiber, 7 g pro.*

FRUIT & GRANOLA CRISP WITH YOGURT

Mushroom & Herb Chicken

My easy skillet dish is a comfort food classic. It's also delicious with rice instead of noodles. No one will guess they're eating healthy with this one.

—**BETSY KING** DULUTH, MN

START TO FINISH: 30 MIN.
MAKES: 4 SERVINGS

- 4 **boneless skinless chicken breast halves (5 ounces each)**
- 1 **tablespoon butter**
- 1 **can (10¾ ounces) reduced-fat reduced-sodium condensed cream of mushroom soup, undiluted**
- 1 **cup sliced fresh mushrooms**
- ½ **cup water**
- 1 **teaspoon minced chives**
- 1 **teaspoon Dijon mustard**
- ½ **teaspoon lemon-pepper seasoning**
- ¼ **teaspoon salt**
- ¼ **teaspoon garlic salt**
- ¼ **teaspoon dried rosemary, crushed**
- ¼ **teaspoon dried thyme**
  Hot cooked egg noodles

1. Flatten chicken to ½-in. thickness. In a large skillet, brown chicken in butter. In a small bowl, combine the soup, mushrooms, water, chives, mustard, lemon-pepper, salt, garlic salt, rosemary and thyme; pour over chicken.
2. Bring to a boil. Reduce heat; cover and simmer for 8-10 minutes or until a thermometer reads 170°. Serve with noodles.
PER SERVING *228 cal., 7 g fat (3 g sat. fat), 89 mg chol., 698 mg sodium, 8 g carb., 1 g fiber, 30 g pro.* **Diabetic Exchanges:** *4 lean meat, ½ starch.*

ITALIAN CHICKEN SAUSAGE AND ORZO
SEASONED BROCCOLI SPEARS

Italian Chicken Sausage and Orzo

Your family will adore this Mediterranean one-pot dish. For less heat, omit the pepper flakes and scale back the pepper.
—**DEBRA PAQUETTE** UPTON, MA

START TO FINISH: 30 MIN.
MAKES: 5 SERVINGS

- 1 **cup uncooked orzo pasta**
- 1 **package (12 ounces) fully cooked Italian chicken sausage links, cut into ¾-inch slices**
- 3 **teaspoons olive oil, divided**
- 1 **cup chopped onion**
- 3 **garlic cloves, minced**
- ¼ **cup white wine or chicken broth**
- 1 **can (28 ounces) whole tomatoes, drained and chopped**
- 2 **tablespoons minced fresh parsley**
- 1 **tablespoon capers, drained**
- ½ **teaspoon dried oregano**
- ½ **teaspoon dried basil**
- ¼ **teaspoon crushed red pepper flakes**
- ¼ **teaspoon pepper**
- ½ **cup crumbled feta cheese**

1. Cook pasta according to package directions.
2. Meanwhile, brown the sausages in 2 teaspoons oil in a large skillet. Remove and keep warm. In the same pan, saute onion in remaining oil until tender. Add garlic and wine; cook 1 minute longer, stirring to loosen browned bits from pan.
3. Stir in the tomatoes, parsley, capers, oregano, basil, pepper flakes and pepper. Bring to a boil. Reduce heat; simmer, uncovered, for 5 minutes. Stir in orzo and sausage; heat through. Sprinkle with cheese.
PER SERVING *363 cal., 11 g fat (3 g sat. fat), 58 mg chol., 838 mg sodium, 42 g carb., 3 g fiber, 21 g pro.* **Diabetic Exchanges:** *2 starch, 2 lean meat, 2 vegetable, 1 fat.*

Seasoned Broccoli Spears

Dressing up broccoli is a snap with this recipe. We flavored fresh spears with lemon-pepper, garlic salt and thyme.
—**TASTE OF HOME TEST KITCHEN**

START TO FINISH: 10 MIN.
MAKES: 6 SERVINGS

- 1½ **pounds fresh broccoli, cut into spears**
- ¼ **cup water**
- 2 **tablespoons butter**
- 1 **teaspoon lemon-pepper seasoning**
- ½ **teaspoon garlic salt**
- ½ **teaspoon dried thyme**

Place the broccoli in a microwave-safe bowl; add water. Cover and microwave on high for 4-5 minutes or until tender; drain. Stir in the remaining ingredients.
NOTE *This recipe was tested in a 1,100-watt microwave.*
PER SERVING *66 cal., 4 g fat (2 g sat. fat), 10 mg chol., 285 mg sodium, 6 g carb., 3 g fiber, 3 g pro.* **Diabetic Exchanges:** *1 vegetable, 1 fat.*

Mixed Greens with Strawberries

So quick and easy to prepare, this recipe is a busy mom's dream. If you're in a rush, go ahead and use red wine vinaigrette instead of homemade dressing.

—MARY PERSO BROOKFIELD, WI

START TO FINISH: 15 MIN.
MAKES: 4 SERVINGS

- 1 **package (5 ounces) spring mix salad greens**
- 1 **cup sliced fresh strawberries**
- 2 **tablespoons sliced almonds, toasted**

DRESSING

- 2 **tablespoons sugar**
- 2 **tablespoons canola oil**
- 4 **teaspoons red wine vinegar**
- ¼ **teaspoon salt**
- ¼ **teaspoon ground mustard**

Combine the salad greens, strawberries and almonds in a large bowl. Whisk dressing ingredients in a small bowl; pour over salad mixture and toss to coat.

Chicken & Apple Waffle Sandwiches

Waffles don't need to be considered just a breakfast food any more! These fun and hearty sandwiches make a delicious meal any time of day.

—DEB WILLIAMS PEORIA, AZ

START TO FINISH: 20 MIN.
MAKES: 4 SERVINGS

- 8 **frozen waffles, thawed**
- 3 **tablespoons mayonnaise**
- 8 **slices sharp cheddar cheese**
- ¾ **pound thinly sliced deli chicken**
- 1 **medium apple, thinly sliced**
- 2 **tablespoons butter, softened**

1. Spread four waffles with mayonnaise; top with half of the cheese. Layer with chicken, apple and remaining cheese. Top with remaining waffles. Spread outsides of sandwiches with butter.

2. Toast sandwiches in a large skillet over medium heat for 4-5 minutes on each side or until waffles are lightly browned and cheese is melted.

top tip ⬤ Waffle Magic

For a quick treat, I cook brownie batter in my waffle iron. I serve the brownie waffles hot with ice cream, or use them as a base for strawberry shortcake.

—CLARICE S. SUN CITY, AZ

MIXED GREENS WITH STRAWBERRIES
CHICKEN & APPLE WAFFLE SANDWICHES

CREAMY MUDSLIDE PARFAITS
STOVETOP GOULASH

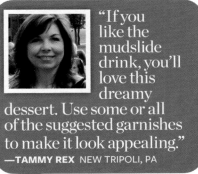

"If you like the mudslide drink, you'll love this dreamy dessert. Use some or all of the suggested garnishes to make it look appealing."
—**TAMMY REX** NEW TRIPOLI, PA

(5) INGREDIENTS

Creamy Mudslide Parfaits

START TO FINISH: 15 MIN.
MAKES: 4 SERVINGS

- 1 package (8 ounces) cream cheese, softened
- ¼ cup confectioners' sugar
- 2 tablespoons coffee liqueur
- 1½ cups whipped topping
- 10 Oreo cookies, crushed
  Optional toppings: additional whipped topping, chocolate syrup, maraschino cherries and Oreo cookie crumbs

1. Beat cream cheese and confectioners' sugar in a small bowl. Add liqueur; mix well. Fold in whipped topping.
2. Spoon half of cookie crumbs into four parfait glasses. Top with half the cream cheese mixture. Repeat layers. Refrigerate until serving. Serve with toppings of your choice.

Stovetop Goulash

I created this recipe after trying goulash at a local restaurant. The blend of spices gives it great flavor, and it's easy for a weeknight meal.
—**KAREN SCHELERT** PORTAND, OR

START TO FINISH: 25 MIN.
MAKES: 4 SERVINGS

- 1 pound ground beef
- 1 package (16 ounces) frozen mixed vegetables, thawed
- 2 cans (10¾ ounces each) condensed tomato soup, undiluted
- 1 cup water
- 1 small onion, chopped
- 2 teaspoons Worcestershire sauce
- 1 teaspoon garlic salt
- 1 teaspoon chili powder
- ½ teaspoon dried oregano
- ½ teaspoon paprika
- ⅛ teaspoon ground cinnamon
- ⅛ teaspoon pepper
- 1 package (24 ounces) refrigerated mashed potatoes

1. Cook beef in a large skillet over medium heat until no longer pink; drain. Add mixed vegetables, soup, water, onion, Worcestershire sauce and seasonings; bring to a boil. Reduce heat; simmer, uncovered, for 10 minutes or until slightly thickened.
2. Meanwhile, heat potatoes according to package directions. Serve with goulash.

SESAME ASPARAGUS SAUTE
SMOTHERED TERIYAKI CHICKEN BREASTS

Sesame Asparagus Saute

This is the prettiest side dish I've ever seen! When fresh asparagus is in season, I make it at least once a week.

—KAREN PAUMEN ANNANDALE, MN

START TO FINISH: 15 MIN.
MAKES: 4 SERVINGS

- 1 pound fresh asparagus, trimmed and cut into 1-inch pieces
- 4 green onions, thinly sliced
- 1 tablespoon butter
- 1 cup grape tomatoes
- 1 tablespoon sesame seeds, toasted
- 1 tablespoon reduced-sodium soy sauce
- 2 teaspoons lemon juice
- ¼ teaspoon sesame oil

Saute asparagus and green onions in butter in a large skillet until crisp-tender. Add remaining ingredients; cook and stir 2 minutes longer or until heated through.

Smothered Teriyaki Chicken Breasts

Wondering what to do with chicken tonight? This sweet and savory choice makes chicken dinner a winner!

—SALLY NIELSEN QUINCY, IL

START TO FINISH: 30 MIN.
MAKES: 4 SERVINGS

- 8 medium fresh mushrooms, sliced
- 1 medium onion, thinly sliced
- 2 tablespoons canola oil, divided
- ¼ cup reduced-sodium teriyaki sauce
- 1 tablespoon brown sugar
- ½ teaspoon garlic powder
- ½ teaspoon ground ginger
- 4 boneless skinless chicken breast halves (6 ounces each)
- 4 slices Muenster or Swiss cheese

1. Saute mushrooms and onion in 1 tablespoon oil in a large skillet until tender. Stir in the teriyaki sauce, brown sugar, garlic powder and ginger; heat through. Remove and keep warm.
2. Flatten chicken to ¼-in. thickness. In the same skillet over medium heat, cook the chicken in remaining oil for 2-3 minutes on each side or until no longer pink.
3. Top with mushroom mixture and cheese. Cover and let stand until cheese is melted.

Steaks with Cherry Sauce

For a special dinner, try my recipe. It stars filet mignon in a slightly sweet port wine and cherry sauce.

—JACOB KITZMAN SEATTLE, WA

START TO FINISH: 25 MIN.
MAKES: 4 SERVINGS

- ⅓ **cup dried tart cherries**
- ¾ **cup port wine**
- 2 **teaspoons butter**
- ¾ **teaspoon salt, divided**
- ⅛ **teaspoon plus ¼ teaspoon coarsely ground pepper**
- 4 **beef tenderloin steaks (4 ounces each)**
- 1 **green onion, chopped**

1. Place wine and cherries in a large saucepan. Bring to a boil; cook for 5 minutes or until liquid is reduced to ¼ cup. Stir in the butter, ¼ teaspoon salt and ⅛ teaspoon pepper.

2. Sprinkle steaks with remaining salt and pepper. Broil 4 in. from the heat for 4-6 minutes on each side or until meat reaches desired doneness (for medium-rare, a thermometer should read 145°; medium, 160°; well-done, 170°).

3. Serve steaks with cherry sauce and sprinkle with green onion.

PER SERVING *291 cal., 9 g fat (4 g sat. fat), 55 mg chol., 461 mg sodium, 15 g carb., 1 g fiber, 25 g pro.* **Diabetic Exchanges:** *3 lean meat, 1 starch, ½ fat.*

Walnut Zucchini Saute

This recipe is special to me because I can get my family to eat their veggies when I serve it.

—ANGELA STEWART WEST SENECA, NY

START TO FINISH: 15 MIN.
MAKES: 4 SERVINGS

- 2 **medium zucchini, cut into ¼-inch slices**
- ⅓ **cup chopped walnuts**
- 2 **teaspoons olive oil**
- 1 **teaspoon butter**
- 3 **garlic cloves, minced**
- ¼ **teaspoon salt**
- ¼ **teaspoon pepper**

Saute zucchini and walnuts in oil and butter in a large skillet until zucchini is tender. Add the garlic, salt and pepper; cook and stir for 1 minute.

PER SERVING *111 cal., 10 g fat (2 g sat. fat), 3 mg chol., 165 mg sodium, 5 g carb., 2 g fiber, 3 g pro.* **Diabetic Exchanges:** *2 fat, 1 vegetable.*

STEAKS WITH CHERRY SAUCE
WALNUT ZUCCHINI SAUTE

EAT SMART
Pork Medallions with Dijon Sauce

I lightened up this recipe years ago, and I've been using it ever since. I brown lean pork medallions in a skillet before stirring up a succulent sauce.

—**LOIS KINNEBERG** PHOENIX, AZ

START TO FINISH: 25 MIN.
MAKES: 3 SERVINGS

- 1 pork tenderloin (1 pound)
- ⅓ cup all-purpose flour
- ¼ teaspoon salt
- ¼ teaspoon pepper
- 1 tablespoon butter
- 3 green onions
- ⅓ cup white wine or chicken broth
- ½ cup fat-free evaporated milk
- 4 teaspoons Dijon mustard

1. Cut pork widthwise into 6 pieces; flatten to ¼-in. thickness. In a large resealable plastic bag, combine the flour, salt and pepper. Add pork, a few pieces at a time, and shake to coat. In a large nonstick skillet, brown pork in butter over medium-high heat. Remove and keep warm.

2. Slice green onions, separating the white and green portions; reserve green portions for garnish. In the same pan, saute white portions for 1 minute. Stir in wine.

3. Bring to a boil; cook until liquid is reduced to about 2 tablespoons. Add milk. Reduce heat; simmer, uncovered, for 1-2 minutes or until slightly thickened. Whisk in mustard.

4. Serve pork with Dijon sauce. Garnish with reserved green onions.

PER SERVING *323 cal., 10 g fat (4 g sat. fat), 96 mg chol., 516 mg sodium, 18 g carb., 1 g fiber, 35 g pro.* **Diabetic Exchanges:** *4 lean meat, 1 starch, ½ fat.*

EAT SMART
Cranberry Couscous

Although it looks like a grain, couscous is actually a type of pasta. The couscous pellets cook very quickly due to their small size. You'll find it near the Middle Eastern or Mediterranean foods.

—**TASTE OF HOME TEST KITCHEN**

START TO FINISH: 15 MIN.
MAKES: 6 SERVINGS

- 1 can (14½ ounces) chicken broth
- 1 tablespoon butter
- 1½ cups uncooked couscous
- ¼ cup dried cranberries, chopped
- 3 tablespoons chopped green onions

Bring broth and butter to a boil in a large saucepan. Stir in the couscous, cranberries and onions. Remove from the heat. Cover and let stand for 5 minutes or until broth is absorbed. Fluff with a fork.

PER SERVING *202 cal., 3 g fat (1 g sat. fat), 5 mg chol., 295 mg sodium, 39 g carb., 2 g fiber, 7 g pro.*

PORK MEDALLIONS WITH DIJON SAUCE
CRANBERRY COUSCOUS

PRETZEL-CRUSTED CATFISH
MAPLE-PECAN BRUSSELS SPROUTS

Pretzel-Crusted Catfish

I'm not a big fish lover, so any concoction that has me enjoying fish is a keeper in my book. This combination of flavors works for me. It's awesome served with corn muffins, butter and honey!

—KELLY WILLIAMS FORKED RIVER, NJ

START TO FINISH: 30 MIN.
MAKES: 4 SERVINGS

- 4   catfish fillets (6 ounces each)
- ½   teaspoon salt
- ½   teaspoon pepper
- 2   eggs
- ⅓   cup Dijon mustard
- 2   tablespoons 2% milk
- ½   cup all-purpose flour
- 4   cups honey mustard miniature pretzels, coarsely crushed
      Oil for frying
      Lemon slices, optional

1. Sprinkle catfish with salt and pepper. Whisk the eggs, mustard and milk in a shallow bowl. Place flour and pretzels in separate shallow bowls. Coat fillets with flour, then dip in egg mixture and coat with pretzels.

2. Heat ¼ in. of oil to 375° in an electric skillet. Fry fillets, a few at a time, for 3-4 minutes on each side or until fish flakes easily with a fork. Drain on paper towels. Serve with lemon slices if desired.

⑤ INGREDIENTS
Maple-Pecan Brussels Sprouts

I found this recipe in the local paper. I love how it puts a holiday-worthy twist on basic Brussels sprouts. Double the recipe for a memorable Thanksgiving side dish.

—MAUREEN BAISDEN CANAL WINCHESTER, OH

START TO FINISH: 20 MIN.
MAKES: 4 SERVINGS

- 1   pound fresh Brussels sprouts, halved
- 2   tablespoons butter
- 1½ teaspoons cider vinegar
- 1½ teaspoons maple syrup
- ½   teaspoon salt
- ¼   teaspoon pepper
- ⅓   cup chopped pecans, toasted

Saute Brussels sprouts in butter in a large skillet for 8-10 minutes or until tender. Add the vinegar, syrup, salt and pepper; cook and stir 1 minute longer. Sprinkle with pecans.

Summer Squash & Pepper Saute

Summer squash and orange pepper give my herby side dish fantastic color. Remember this recipe—it complements almost any main dish.

—**SHIRLEY WARREN** THIENSVILLE, WI

START TO FINISH: 20 MIN.
MAKES: 4 SERVINGS

- 2 **yellow summer squash, halved lengthwise and cut into ¼-inch slices**
- 1 **medium sweet orange pepper, cut into thin strips**
- 2 **tablespoons butter**
- 3 **green onions, chopped**
- 2 **teaspoons brown sugar**
- 2 **teaspoons lemon juice**
- ½ **teaspoon dried basil**
- ½ **teaspoon salt**
- ¼ **teaspoon pepper**

Saute squash and orange pepper in butter in a large skillet until crisp-tender. Add remaining ingredients; cook 4-5 minutes longer or until sugar is dissolved and vegetables are tender.

Ancho Chili-Spiced Tilapia

I love a little spice in my life, and with this dish, that's exactly what you get! A few pantry staples and 20 minutes are all you need for this light and flaky tilapia.

—**JENNIFER SCHAUB** CHANDLER, AZ

START TO FINISH: 20 MIN.
MAKES: 4 SERVINGS

- ½ **teaspoon salt**
- ½ **teaspoon ground ancho chili pepper**
- ½ **teaspoon cayenne pepper**
- ½ **teaspoon dried oregano**
- ¼ **teaspoon garlic powder**
- ¼ **teaspoon ground cumin**
- 4 **tilapia fillets (4 to 5 ounces each)**
- ⅓ **cup reduced-fat chipotle mayonnaise**
- 1 **teaspoon lime juice**
- ¼ **teaspoon dried oregano**

1. Combine the first six ingredients; sprinkle over fillets. Cook fillets in a large nonstick skillet coated with cooking spray over medium-high heat for 3-4 minutes on each side or until fish flakes easily with a fork.

2. Meanwhile, combine mayonnaise, lime juice and oregano in a small bowl. Serve with fillets.

SUMMER SQUASH & PEPPER SAUTE
ANCHO CHILI-SPICED TILAPIA

ITALIAN-STYLE BROCCOLI
RAVIOLI WITH SAUSAGE & TOMATO CREAM SAUCE

5 INGREDIENTS
Italian-Style Broccoli

With just a handful of ingredients, this side comes together in a jiffy. Paired with ravioli, it creates a fabulous Italian meal.

—**PHYLLIS SCHMALZ** KANSAS CITY, KS

START TO FINISH: 30 MIN.
MAKES: 4 SERVINGS

- 1 small onion, finely chopped
- 2 tablespoons olive oil
- 1 garlic clove, minced
- 1½ pounds fresh broccoli, cut into 2-inch spears
- ¼ cup water
- ½ teaspoon salt
- ¼ teaspoon chili powder

1. In a large skillet, saute onion in oil for 2-3 minutes or until tender. Add garlic; cook 1 minute longer.
2. Stir in the remaining ingredients; bring to a boil. Reduce heat; cover and cook for 8-10 minutes or until broccoli is crisp-tender.

Ravioli with Sausage & Tomato Cream Sauce

This Italian specialty is ready in just 25 minutes. Family and friends request my ravioli often.

—**CHERYL WEGENER** FESTUS, MO

START TO FINISH: 25 MIN.
MAKES: 4 SERVINGS

- 1 package (9 ounces) refrigerated cheese ravioli
- ¾ pound bulk Italian sausage
- 1 jar (24 ounces) tomato basil pasta sauce
- ½ cup heavy whipping cream
- 2 bacon strips, cooked and crumbled
- 2 tablespoons grated Parmesan cheese
  Minced fresh parsley

1. Cook ravioli according to package directions. Meanwhile, cook sausage in a large skillet over medium heat until no longer pink; drain. Stir in the pasta sauce, cream and bacon. Bring to a boil; reduce heat. Simmer, uncovered, for 2 minutes or until slightly thickened.
2. Drain ravioli; stir into sauce. Top with Parmesan cheese and parsley.

|||||||||||||||||||||||||||||||||||||||||||||||||

BUSY COOKS' SECRETS

Read recipes all the way through before you begin.

I LIKE TO STUDY SEVERAL DIFFERENT RECIPES before going out on my own and making one up. This has taught me cooking methods, seasonings that go well together, and how to make bases for different types of sauces. If I'm following a recipe, I study it before making the dish and make sure that I follow it to a T.

—**BROOKE KELLER** LEXINGTON, KY

Apple 'n' Pepper Saute

This nutritious side dish blends apple slices, red onion rings, sweet pepper strips and herbs with a touch of soy sauce.

—**EMILY GUIDRY** BREAUX BRIDGE, LA

START TO FINISH: 25 MIN.
MAKES: 6 SERVINGS

- 3 **medium sweet peppers, julienned**
- 1 **small red onion, sliced and separated into rings**
- 1 **medium apple, sliced**
- 2 **tablespoons olive oil**
- 1 **tablespoon reduced-sodium soy sauce**
- 2 **garlic cloves, minced**
- ¼ **teaspoon dried rosemary, crushed**
- ¼ **teaspoon dried basil**

Saute the peppers, onion and apple in oil in a large nonstick skillet until crisp-tender. Stir in the soy sauce, garlic, rosemary and basil. Cook and stir until heated through.
PER SERVING *83 cal., 5 g fat (1 g sat. fat), 0 chol., 103 mg sodium, 10 g carb., 2 g fiber, 1 g pro.* **Diabetic Exchanges:** *2 vegetable, 1 fat.*

"This meal is quick, easy and good. I usually have all the ingredients for it on hand. Everyone enjoys the flavor pairing of honey mustard with pork."

—**JOYCE MOYNIHAN** LAKEVILLE, MN

Honey Mustard Pork Tenderloin

START TO FINISH: 30 MIN.
MAKES: 4 SERVINGS

- 1 **pork tenderloin (1 pound)**
- **GLAZE**
- ¼ **cup honey**
- 2 **tablespoons brown sugar**
- 2 **tablespoons cider vinegar**
- 1 **tablespoon prepared mustard**
- ½ **teaspoon salt**
- ¼ **teaspoon pepper**

1. Place pork tenderloin on a greased rack in a 15-in. x 10-in. x 1-in. baking pan lined with foil. In a small bowl, combine glaze ingredients; set aside 3 tablespoons mixture for basting. Spoon remaining honey mixture over the pork.

2. Bake, uncovered, at 400° for 24-28 minutes or until a thermometer reads 145°, basting occasionally with reserved glaze. Let stand for 5 minutes before slicing.
PER SERVING *226 cal., 4 g fat (1 g sat. fat), 63 mg chol., 386 mg sodium, 25 g carb., trace fiber, 23 g pro.* **Diabetic Exchanges:** *3 lean meat, 1½ starch.*

? Did you know?

Allowing pork to stand for a few minutes after cooking (known as carry-over cooking) ensures that it has reached a food-safe temperature, and also preserves the meat's juiciness. Perfectly cooked pork will be juicy and slightly pink in the center.

APPLE 'N' PEPPER SAUTE
HONEY MUSTARD PORK TENDERLOIN

**TUNA WITH CITRUS PONZU SAUCE
SESAME TOSSED SALAD**

Tuna with Citrus Ponzu Sauce

I like this Asian-inspired tuna because it's easy to prepare, delicious and healthy. It's a favorite among my friends.

—DIANE HALFERTY CORPUS CHRISTI, TX

START TO FINISH: 20 MIN.
MAKES: 4 SERVINGS

- ½ teaspoon Chinese five-spice powder
- ¼ teaspoon salt
- ¼ teaspoon cayenne pepper
- 4 tuna steaks (6 ounces each)
- 1 tablespoon canola oil
- ¼ cup orange juice
- 2 green onions, thinly sliced
- 1 tablespoon lemon juice
- 1 tablespoon reduced-sodium soy sauce
- 2 teaspoons rice vinegar
- 1 teaspoon brown sugar
- ¼ teaspoon minced fresh gingerroot

1. Combine the five-spice powder, salt and cayenne; sprinkle over tuna steaks. In a large skillet, cook tuna in oil over medium heat for 2-3 minutes on each side for medium-rare or until slightly pink in the center; remove and keep warm.

2. Combine the orange juice, onions, lemon juice, soy sauce, vinegar, brown sugar and ginger; pour into skillet. Cook for 1-2 minutes or until slightly thickened. Serve with tuna.

PER SERVING *234 cal., 5 g fat (1 g sat. fat), 77 mg chol., 364 mg sodium, 5 g carb., trace fiber, 40 g pro.* **Diabetic Exchanges:** *5 lean meat, ½ fat.*

Sesame Tossed Salad

Crisp, crunchy, and slightly sweet, this nutritious salad is simply delightful. Feel free to double up on any of your favorite toss-ins.

—ELIZABETH PERKINS SOUTH RIDING, VA

START TO FINISH: 10 MIN.
MAKES: 4 SERVINGS

- 1 package (5 ounces) spring mix salad greens
- ½ cup sliced fresh mushrooms
- ½ cup chopped cucumber
- ½ cup canned mandarin oranges, drained
- ¼ cup sliced almonds, toasted
- ¼ cup shredded carrots
- 2 green onions, chopped
- ⅓ cup reduced-fat Asian toasted sesame salad dressing

Combine the first seven ingredients in a large bowl. Drizzle with dressing; toss to coat.

PER SERVING *87 cal., 5 g fat (trace sat. fat), 0 chol., 233 mg sodium, 9 g carb., 2 g fiber, 3 g pro.* **Diabetic Exchanges:** *1 fat, ½ starch.*

BLACKENED CHICKEN AND BEANS
CON QUESO SPIRALS

ITALIAN MIXED VEGETABLES
PROSCIUTTO-PEPPER PORK CHOPS

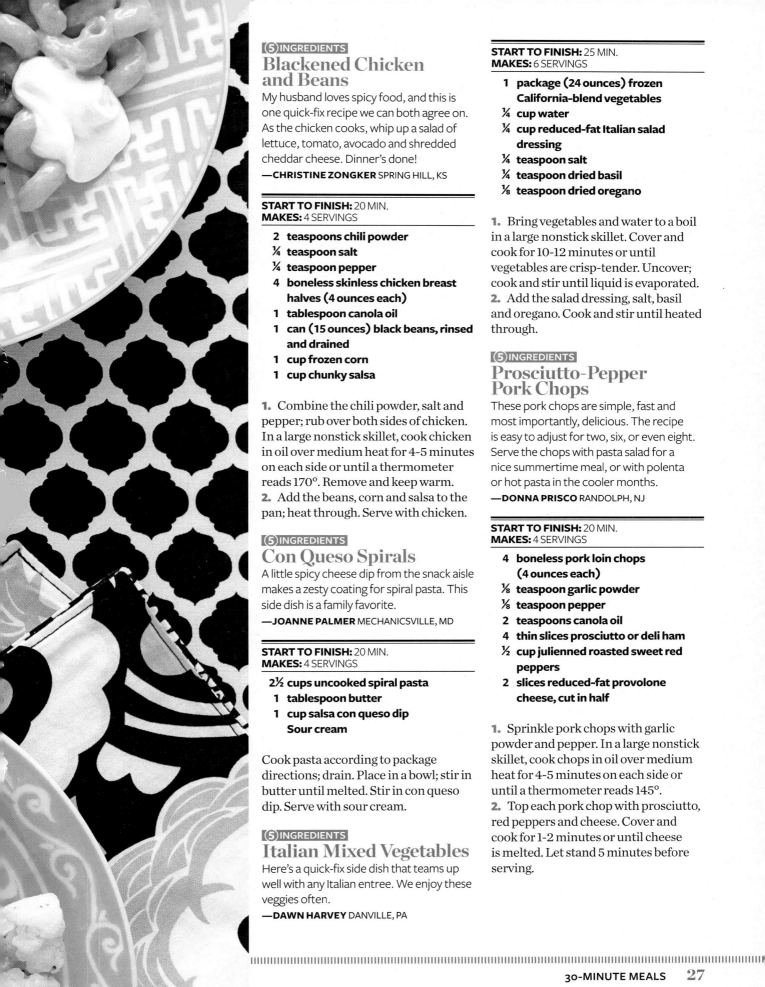

(5) INGREDIENTS
Blackened Chicken and Beans

My husband loves spicy food, and this is one quick-fix recipe we can both agree on. As the chicken cooks, whip up a salad of lettuce, tomato, avocado and shredded cheddar cheese. Dinner's done!

—**CHRISTINE ZONGKER** SPRING HILL, KS

START TO FINISH: 20 MIN.
MAKES: 4 SERVINGS

- 2 teaspoons chili powder
- ¼ teaspoon salt
- ¼ teaspoon pepper
- 4 boneless skinless chicken breast halves (4 ounces each)
- 1 tablespoon canola oil
- 1 can (15 ounces) black beans, rinsed and drained
- 1 cup frozen corn
- 1 cup chunky salsa

1. Combine the chili powder, salt and pepper; rub over both sides of chicken. In a large nonstick skillet, cook chicken in oil over medium heat for 4-5 minutes on each side or until a thermometer reads 170°. Remove and keep warm.
2. Add the beans, corn and salsa to the pan; heat through. Serve with chicken.

(5) INGREDIENTS
Con Queso Spirals

A little spicy cheese dip from the snack aisle makes a zesty coating for spiral pasta. This side dish is a family favorite.

—**JOANNE PALMER** MECHANICSVILLE, MD

START TO FINISH: 20 MIN.
MAKES: 4 SERVINGS

- 2½ cups uncooked spiral pasta
- 1 tablespoon butter
- 1 cup salsa con queso dip
  Sour cream

Cook pasta according to package directions; drain. Place in a bowl; stir in butter until melted. Stir in con queso dip. Serve with sour cream.

(5) INGREDIENTS
Italian Mixed Vegetables

Here's a quick-fix side dish that teams up well with any Italian entree. We enjoy these veggies often.

—**DAWN HARVEY** DANVILLE, PA

START TO FINISH: 25 MIN.
MAKES: 6 SERVINGS

- 1 package (24 ounces) frozen California-blend vegetables
- ¼ cup water
- ¼ cup reduced-fat Italian salad dressing
- ¼ teaspoon salt
- ¼ teaspoon dried basil
- ⅛ teaspoon dried oregano

1. Bring vegetables and water to a boil in a large nonstick skillet. Cover and cook for 10-12 minutes or until vegetables are crisp-tender. Uncover; cook and stir until liquid is evaporated.
2. Add the salad dressing, salt, basil and oregano. Cook and stir until heated through.

(5) INGREDIENTS
Prosciutto-Pepper Pork Chops

These pork chops are simple, fast and most importantly, delicious. The recipe is easy to adjust for two, six, or even eight. Serve the chops with pasta salad for a nice summertime meal, or with polenta or hot pasta in the cooler months.

—**DONNA PRISCO** RANDOLPH, NJ

START TO FINISH: 20 MIN.
MAKES: 4 SERVINGS

- 4 boneless pork loin chops (4 ounces each)
- ⅛ teaspoon garlic powder
- ⅛ teaspoon pepper
- 2 teaspoons canola oil
- 4 thin slices prosciutto or deli ham
- ½ cup julienned roasted sweet red peppers
- 2 slices reduced-fat provolone cheese, cut in half

1. Sprinkle pork chops with garlic powder and pepper. In a large nonstick skillet, cook chops in oil over medium heat for 4-5 minutes on each side or until a thermometer reads 145°.
2. Top each pork chop with prosciutto, red peppers and cheese. Cover and cook for 1-2 minutes or until cheese is melted. Let stand 5 minutes before serving.

Pizzeria Burgers

When my children were teenagers, they asked for these burgers every week! I like to fix them because they don't take much work and kids of all ages adore them.

—AMY LAPOINTE NORTH FOND DU LAC, WI

START TO FINISH: 30 MIN.
MAKES: 6 SERVINGS

- ¾ cup pizza sauce, divided
- ¼ cup dry bread crumbs
- ¼ teaspoon dried oregano
- 1 teaspoon salt
  Dash pepper
- 1½ pounds ground beef
- ¼ pound bulk pork sausage
- 6 slices part-skim mozzarella cheese
- 6 sandwich rolls, split

1. Combine ½ cup pizza sauce, bread crumbs, oregano, salt and pepper in a large bowl. Crumble beef and sausage over mixture and mix well. Shape into six patties.
2. Cook patties in a large skillet over medium heat for 5-7 minutes on each side or until a thermometer reads 160° and juices run clear. Top with remaining pizza sauce and cheese. Cover and cook 2 minutes longer or until cheese is melted. Serve on rolls.

⑤ INGREDIENTS
Seasoned Fries

Instead of preparing French fries from scratch, I reach for frozen spuds and make them my own with Parmesan cheese and Italian seasoning. They're always popular with my family.

—MARIBETH EDWARDS FOLLANSBEE, WV

START TO FINISH: 15 MIN.
MAKES: 6 SERVINGS

- 6 cups frozen shoestring potatoes
- ½ cup grated Parmesan cheese
- 2 teaspoons Italian seasoning
- ½ teaspoon salt

Place potatoes on a foil-lined baking sheet. Bake at 450° for 8 minutes. Combine remaining ingredients; sprinkle over potatoes and mix gently. Bake 4-5 minutes longer or until the potatoes are browned and crisp.

⑤ INGREDIENTS
Makeover Nutty Monkey Malts

Get all the flavor of a classic diner malt in the comfort of your own home. With yummy peanut butter and bananas, this is one drink kids will go nutty for!

—TASTE OF HOME TEST KITCHEN

START TO FINISH: 5 MIN.
MAKES: 5 SERVINGS

- ¼ cup fat-free milk
- 1 small banana, cut into chunks
- ¼ cup chocolate malted milk powder
- 2 tablespoons reduced-fat creamy peanut butter
- 2 cups fat-free frozen chocolate yogurt
  Whipped cream, optional

1. Place the milk, banana, malted milk powder and peanut butter in a blender. Cover and process for 10 seconds or until smooth. Add frozen yogurt. Cover and process 10 seconds longer or until blended. Stir if necessary.
2. Pour into chilled glasses; garnish with whipped cream if desired. Serve immediately.

Bacon Cheeseburger Pizza

Who doesn't love pizza and cheeseburgers? This recipe marries those two dishes perfectly. My grandchildren usually request pizza for supper when they visit me. They like to help me assemble the pizza, and, of course, to eat the results!

—CHERIE ACKERMAN LAKELAND, MN

START TO FINISH: 20 MIN.
MAKES: 8 SLICES

- ½ pound ground beef
- 1 small onion, chopped
- 1 prebaked 12-inch pizza crust
- 1 can (8 ounces) pizza sauce
- 6 bacon strips, cooked and crumbled
- 20 dill pickle coin slices
- 2 cups (8 ounces) shredded part-skim mozzarella cheese
- 2 cups (8 ounces) shredded cheddar cheese
- 1 teaspoon pizza or Italian seasoning

1. Cook beef and onion in a large skillet over medium heat until meat is no longer pink; drain and set aside.
2. Place crust on an ungreased 12-in. pizza pan. Spread with pizza sauce. Top with beef mixture, bacon, pickles and cheeses. Sprinkle with pizza seasoning. Bake at 450° for 8-10 minutes or until cheese is melted.

top tip
Fast Fixes From Your Kitchens

For many of us, the dinner hour quickly turns into rush hour. So we asked our Facebook friends for a few tips on dinners that are ready in half an hour (or less).

Skillet Lasagna:
Cooked ground beef, spaghetti sauce and lasagna noodles in one pan. Top with cheese and finish in the broiler for 5 minutes.
—LATONYA PASCHAL
ATLANTA, GA

Tortellini Soup:
Heat chicken broth; add meat or cheese tortellini. Just before tortellini is cooked, add scallions and fresh baby spinach. Top with Parmesan cheese.
—SUE-DOUG NIELSEN
HOWELL, NJ

Shrimp Scampi Over Linguine:
I keep frozen shrimp in my freezer because it defrosts quickly, cooks up fast and is a low-cal food. Win, win, win!
—KATHLEEN HARVEY STONE
SALT LAKE CITY, UT

PIZZERIA BURGERS
SEASONED FRIES

MAKEOVER NUTTY MONKEY MALTS
BACON CHEESEBURGER PIZZA

BAKED HORSERADISH SALMON
MUSHROOM BEAN MEDLEY

EAT SMART (5)**INGREDIENTS**
Baked Horseradish Salmon

Just a few pantry staples turn salmon into a mid-week treat. My wife never liked salmon until I came up with this healthy and delicious recipe. Now she's thrilled whenever I serve it!

—JAMES OCKERMAN FLORAL CITY, FL

START TO FINISH: 30 MIN.
MAKES: 4 SERVINGS

- 1 **salmon fillet (1 pound)**
- 1 **tablespoon butter, melted**
- 1 **tablespoon prepared horseradish, drained**
- 2 **teaspoons lemon juice**
- ¼ **teaspoon garlic powder**
- ⅛ **teaspoon pepper**

1. Place salmon skin side down in an 11-in. x 7-in. baking dish coated with cooking spray. In a small bowl, combine the butter, horseradish, lemon juice, garlic powder and pepper; spread over salmon.

2. Bake, uncovered, at 375° for 20-25 minutes or until fish flakes easily with a fork.

PER SERVING *236 cal., 15 g fat (4 g sat. fat), 75 mg chol., 108 mg sodium, 1 g carb., trace fiber, 23 g pro.* **Diabetic Exchanges:** *3 lean meat, 1½ fat.*

EAT SMART (5)**INGREDIENTS**
Mushroom Bean Medley

Fresh mushrooms, onion and a splash of white wine can really dress up frozen veggies. This blend is a tasty accompaniment to fish or chicken.

—TASTE OF HOME TEST KITCHEN

START TO FINISH: 15 MIN.
MAKES: 4 SERVINGS

- ½ **pound sliced fresh mushrooms**
- 1 **small onion, halved and sliced**
- 2 **tablespoons butter**
- 1 **package (16 ounces) frozen waxed beans, green beans and carrots**
- ½ **cup white wine or chicken broth**
- ¼ **teaspoon salt**
- ¼ **teaspoon pepper**

Saute mushrooms and onion in butter in a large skillet until tender. Add vegetables and wine. Bring to a boil. Reduce heat; cover and simmer for 5 minutes or until vegetables are tender. Drain; sprinkle with salt and pepper.

PER SERVING *104 cal., 3 g fat (2 g sat. fat), 10 mg chol., 190 mg sodium, 13 g carb., 4 g fiber, 4 g pro.* **Diabetic Exchanges:** *2 vegetable, 1 fat.*

Beef Tenderloin Stroganoff

Here's a delightful main course that's meant for weeknight celebrations. The creamy sauce drenches the beef tenderloin and noodles. Although it comes together quickly, your family will think you toiled for hours.

—ELIZABETH DEGUIT RICHMOND HILL, GA

START TO FINISH: 30 MIN.
MAKES: 6 SERVINGS

- 2 tablespoons all-purpose flour
- 1½ pounds beef tenderloin, cut into thin strips
- 2 tablespoons olive oil
- 2 tablespoons butter
- 1½ cups beef broth
- ¼ cup sour cream
- 2 tablespoons tomato paste
- ½ teaspoon paprika
  Salt to taste
  Hot cooked noodles

1. Place flour in a large resealable plastic bag; add beef, a few pieces at a time, and shake to coat. In a large skillet, brown beef in oil and butter over medium heat.

2. Gradually stir in broth; bring to a boil. Reduce heat to low. In a small bowl, combine the sour cream, tomato paste, paprika and salt; slowly stir in sour cream mixture (do not boil). Cook, uncovered, over low heat for 15-20 minutes, stirring frequently. Serve with noodles.

(5) INGREDIENTS
Greens with Herb Vinaigrette

Who knew a four-ingredient dressing could pack so much flavor? Dijon mustard adds tanginess to the easy vinaigrette that coats this simple and satisfying salad.

—SALLY HOOK MONTGOMERY, TX

START TO FINISH: 5 MIN.
MAKES: 6 SERVINGS

- 6 cups torn mixed salad greens
- 3 tablespoons olive oil
- 1 tablespoon cider or red wine vinegar
- ½ to 1 teaspoon Dijon mustard
- ½ teaspoon Italian seasoning

Place greens in a salad bowl. Whisk the remaining ingredients in a small bowl; pour over greens and toss to coat.

BEEF TENDERLOIN STROGANOFF
GREENS WITH HERB VINAIGRETTE

BUFFALO SLOPPY JOES
GOLD-MEDAL VEGETABLE DIP

BLACK-EYED PEAS 'N' PASTA
FAST FUDGE SUNDAES

Buffalo Sloppy Joes

Lean ground turkey makes this a lighter sloppy joe than the standard ground beef version. A big splash of hot sauce and optional blue cheese provide that authentic Buffalo-style flavor.

—MARIA REGAKIS SOMERVILLE, MA

START TO FINISH: 30 MIN.
MAKES: 8 SERVINGS

- 2 pounds extra-lean ground turkey
- 2 celery ribs, chopped
- 1 medium onion, chopped
- 1 medium carrot, grated
- 3 garlic cloves, minced
- 1 can (8 ounces) tomato sauce
- ½ cup reduced-sodium chicken broth
- ¼ cup Louisiana-style hot sauce
- 2 tablespoons brown sugar
- 2 tablespoons red wine vinegar
- 1 tablespoon Worcestershire sauce
- ¼ teaspoon pepper
- 8 hamburger buns, split
- 1 cup (4 ounces) crumbled blue cheese, optional

1. Cook the first five ingredients in a Dutch oven over medium heat until turkey is no longer pink. Stir in the tomato sauce, broth, hot sauce, brown sugar, vinegar, Worcestershire sauce and pepper; heat through.
2. Serve on buns; sprinkle with cheese if desired.
PER SERVING *279 cal., 3 g fat (trace sat. fat), 45 mg chol., 475 mg sodium, 30 g carb., 2 g fiber, 33 g pro.* **Diabetic Exchanges:** *4 lean meat, 2 starch.*

Gold-Medal Vegetable Dip

The crowd at our Olympics party gave this tangy dip the gold! With just enough zip from the mustard, it's a great-tasting accompaniment to crisp veggies.

—THERESE JUDGE WESTMINSTER, MD

START TO FINISH: 10 MIN.
MAKES: ABOUT 1¼ CUPS

- 1 carton (8 ounces) spreadable chive and onion cream cheese
- 2 tablespoons mayonnaise
- 1 teaspoon prepared mustard
- ½ teaspoon Worcestershire sauce
- ¼ teaspoon salt

- ⅛ teaspoon pepper
- 1 to 2 tablespoons 2% milk
  Assorted fresh vegetables

Combine the cream cheese, mayonnaise, mustard, Worcestershire sauce, salt and pepper. Add enough milk to achieve desired consistency. Serve with vegetables.

Black-Eyed Peas 'n' Pasta

Tradition has it that if you eat black-eyed peas on New Year's Day, you'll enjoy prosperity all year, but I like to serve this tasty pasta throughout the year.

—MARIE MALSCH BRIDGMAN, MI

START TO FINISH: 30 MIN.
MAKES: 6 SERVINGS

- 1 cup chopped green pepper
- ½ cup chopped onion
- 1 jalapeno pepper, seeded and chopped
- 3 garlic cloves, minced
- 1 tablespoon olive oil
- 1 can (28 ounces) crushed tomatoes
- 1 can (15½ ounces) black-eyed peas, rinsed and drained
- 1 to 3 tablespoons minced fresh cilantro
- 1 teaspoon cider vinegar
- 1 teaspoon sugar
- 1 teaspoon salt
- ⅛ teaspoon pepper
- 5 cups hot cooked bow tie pasta

1. Saute the green pepper, onion, jalapeno and garlic in oil in a large skillet for 5 minutes or until tender. Add tomatoes; bring to a boil. Simmer, uncovered, for 10 minutes.
2. Stir in the peas, cilantro, vinegar, sugar, salt and pepper; simmer 10 minutes longer. Toss with pasta.
NOTE *Wear disposable gloves when cutting hot peppers; the oils can burn skin. Avoid touching your face.*

"Homemade fudge sauce in 10 minutes? You bet! I think this warm, chocolaty topping blows the store-bought kind out of the water."

—SUE GRONHOLZ BEAVER DAM, WI

Fast Fudge Sundaes

START TO FINISH: 10 MIN.
MAKES: 1¼ CUPS

- ½ cup semisweet chocolate chips
- 1 ounce unsweetened chocolate
- 3 tablespoons butter
- 1 cup confectioners' sugar
- 1 can (5 ounces) evaporated milk
- ½ teaspoon vanilla extract
  Ice cream
  Maraschino cherries, optional

Place the chocolate and butter in a microwave-safe dish. Microwave, uncovered, on medium-high for 30-60 seconds. Stir in the sugar, milk and vanilla; beat until smooth. Microwave, uncovered, on medium for 3-4 minutes or until bubbly. Serve over ice cream; top with a cherry if desired.
NOTE *This recipe was tested in a 1,100-watt microwave.*

top tip

Deluxe Fudge Sundaes

Take your sundae over the top with one of these ideas.

- Top a brownie with chocolate or mint chip ice cream; drizzle with fudge sauce; garnish with whipped cream, chopped nuts, and a cherry or chocolate kiss.
- For a s'more sundae, top ice cream with fudge sauce, mini marshmallows, whipped cream and Teddy Grahams or graham cracker crumbs.

Herbed Tuna Sandwiches

Give tuna salad an upgrade in a flash. Herbs and cheese make this simple sandwich stand out. It's perfect for lunch or a no-fuss dinner.
—**MARIE CONNOR** VIRGINIA BEACH, VA

START TO FINISH: 20 MIN.
MAKES: 4 SERVINGS

- 1 can (12 ounces) light water-packed tuna, drained and flaked
- 2 hard-cooked eggs, chopped
- ⅓ cup fat-free mayonnaise
- ¼ cup minced chives
- 2 teaspoons minced fresh parsley
- ½ teaspoon dried basil
- ¼ teaspoon onion powder
- 8 slices whole wheat bread, toasted
- ½ cup shredded reduced-fat cheddar cheese

1. Combine the first seven ingredients. Place four slices of toast on an ungreased baking sheet; top with tuna mixture and sprinkle with cheese.
2. Broil 3-4 in. from the heat for 1-2 minutes or until cheese is melted. Top with remaining toast.
PER SERVING *332 cal., 9 g fat (4 g sat. fat), 144 mg chol., 864 mg sodium, 30 g carb., 4 g fiber, 34 g pro. Diabetic Exchanges: 4 lean meat, 2 starch.*

Cran-Apple Salad

Tart and tasty, this salad is versatile enough to pair with a ton of meals. Best of all, it whips up with just four ingredients!
—**LUCILLE FOSTER** GRANT, NE

START TO FINISH: 5 MIN.
MAKES: 6 SERVINGS

- 1 can (14 ounces) whole-berry cranberry sauce
- 1 medium unpeeled tart apple, diced
- 1 celery rib, thinly sliced
- ½ cup chopped walnuts

Combine the cranberry sauce, apple and celery. Cover and refrigerate until serving. Stir in the chopped walnuts just before serving.
PER SERVING *183 cal., 6 g fat (trace sat. fat), 0 chol., 22 mg sodium, 32 g carb., 2 g fiber, 3 g pro.*

Sweet 'n' Sour Sausage Stir-Fry

Who couldn't use a stir-fry that's low in prep time, yet bursting with flavor? My quick recipe is achievable on even your busiest nights.
—**WENDY WENDLER** INDIAN HARBOUR BEACH, FL

START TO FINISH: 30 MIN.
MAKES: 4 SERVINGS

- 1 package (14 ounces) smoked turkey sausage, cut into ½-inch slices
- 2 small onions, quartered and separated
- 1 cup shredded carrots
- 1 can (8 ounces) unsweetened pineapple chunks, undrained
- 1 tablespoon cornstarch
- ½ to 1 teaspoon ground ginger
- ⅓ cup cold water
- 2 tablespoons reduced-sodium soy sauce
  Hot cooked rice, optional

1. Stir-fry sausage in a large nonstick skillet for 3-4 minutes or until lightly browned. Add onions and carrots; stir-fry until crisp-tender. Drain pineapple, reserving juice. Add pineapple to sausage mixture.
2. Combine cornstarch and ginger. Stir in the water, soy sauce and reserved pineapple juice until smooth. Add to the skillet. Bring to a boil; cook and stir for 1-2 minutes or until thickened. Serve over rice if desired.

Sesame Snow Peas

This side dish is a natural, because I like to use soy sauce and sesame seeds whenever I can. I prefer my recipes simple, using only a few ingredients. These pese are a favorite.
—**KATHLEEN VALLE** PHILADELPHIA, PA

START TO FINISH: 10 MIN.
MAKES: 4 SERVINGS

- 1 pound fresh snow peas
- ½ cup water
- 2 tablespoons sesame seeds
- 2 tablespoons reduced-sodium soy sauce
- 1 tablespoon sesame oil
- ⅛ teaspoon pepper

1. Place the snow peas and water in a microwave-safe bowl. Cover and microwave on high for 6 minutes or until crisp-tender; drain well.
2. Place the remaining ingredients in a jar with a tight-fitting lid; shake well. Drizzle mixture over snow peas and toss to coat.
NOTE *This recipe was tested in a 1,100-watt microwave.*
PER SERVING *111 cal., 6 g fat (1 g sat. fat), 0 chol., 307 mg sodium, 9 g carb., 3 g fiber, 5 g pro. Diabetic Exchanges: 2 vegetable, 1 fat.*

top tip Smart Shopping

I always keep a running list for groceries. When I notice that something is running low, it gets added to the list. I also add items as I plan meals and think of other things that we need. I definitely take advantage of in-season veggies and fruits. I also compare the store ads each week to see who has the best deals.
—**DONNA G.** BLUE SPRINGS, MO

HERBED TUNA SANDWICHES
CRAN-APPLE SALAD

SWEET 'N' SOUR SAUSAGE STIR-FRY
SESAME SNOW PEAS

Tamale Pie

When time is tight on school nights, I can always count on this quick casserole from the microwave . It satisfies my family's cravings for Mexican food and gets me out of the kitchen in no time.

—NANCY ROBERTS CAVE CITY, AR

START TO FINISH: 30 MIN.
MAKES: 6 SERVINGS

- 1 **pound ground beef**
- ¼ **pound bulk pork sausage**
- ¼ **cup chopped onion**
- 1 **garlic clove, minced**
- 1 **can (14½ ounces) stewed tomatoes, drained**
- 1 **can (11 ounces) whole kernel corn, drained**
- 1 **can (6 ounces) tomato paste**
- ¼ **cup sliced ripe olives**
- 1½ **teaspoons chili powder**
- ½ **teaspoon salt**
- 1 **egg**
- ⅓ **cup 2% milk**
- 1 **package (8½ ounces) corn bread/ muffin mix**
  Dash paprika
- ½ **cup shredded cheddar cheese**

1. Combine the beef, sausage, onion and garlic in a 3-qt. microwave-safe dish. Cover and microwave on high for 4-5 minutes, stirring once to crumble meat. Drain.

2. Add the tomatoes, corn, tomato paste, olives, chili powder and salt; mix well. Cover and microwave on high for 4-6 minutes or until heated through.

3. Whisk egg in a large bowl; add milk and corn bread mix. Stir just until moistened. Spoon over meat mixture; sprinkle with paprika.

4. Microwave, uncovered, on high for 14-16 minutes or until a toothpick inserted near the center of the corn bread comes out clean. Sprinkle cheese over the top.

NOTE *This recipe was tested in a 1,100-watt microwave.*

Pantry Salsa

Canned tomatoes make this homemade salsa a snap to prepare. Add a few seasonings, and you have a quick dip that's great with snack chips. Use it in all of your recipes that call for salsa.

—LOIS WYANT MANASSES, VA

START TO FINISH: 5 MIN.
MAKES: 3 CUPS

- 1 **can (14½ ounces) diced tomatoes with onion, drained**
- 1 **can (14½ ounces) diced tomatoes with green chilies, undrained**
- ¾ **teaspoon ground cumin**
- ½ **teaspoon onion powder**
- ½ **teaspoon garlic powder**
- ½ **teaspoon sugar**
- ½ **teaspoon seasoned salt**
- ¼ **teaspoon garlic salt**
  Tortilla chips

Combine the tomatoes, cumin, onion powder, garlic powder, sugar, seasoned salt and garlic salt in a large bowl. Serve with tortilla chips.

Garlic Green Beans

In my house, we like these healthy green beans with baked ham or grilled salmon.

—**MARGARET ALLEN** ABINGDON, VA

START TO FINISH: 15 MIN.
MAKES: 4 SERVINGS

- 1 **pound fresh green beans, trimmed**
- ¼ **cup water**
- 3 **garlic cloves, minced**
- ⅓ **cup minced fresh parsley**
- 1 **tablespoon butter, melted**
- ⅛ **teaspoon salt**
- ⅛ **teaspoon pepper**

Place beans, water and garlic in a 2-qt. microwave-safe dish. Cover and microwave on high for 4-5 minutes or until beans are crisp-tender. Stir in the remaining ingredients.

NOTE *This recipe was tested in a 1,100-watt microwave.*
PER SERVING *66 cal., 3 g fat (2 g sat. fat), 8 mg chol., 113 mg sodium, 9 g carb., 4 g fiber, 2 g pro.*

Artichoke Ravioli

This stress-free entree tastes like you spent hours preparing it. But it's so fast, you can even pick up the ingredients on the way home and enjoy it for dinner that very night!

—**DARLENE BRENDEN** SALEM, OR

START TO FINISH: 30 MIN.
MAKES: 6 SERVINGS

- 2 **packages (9 ounces each) refrigerated cheese ravioli**
- 1 **jar (24 ounces) meatless spaghetti sauce**
- 1 **can (14 ounces) water-packed artichoke hearts, rinsed, drained and chopped**
- 1 **jar (4½ ounces) whole mushrooms, drained**
- 1 **can (2¼ ounces) sliced ripe olives, drained**
- 1½ **cups (6 ounces) shredded part-skim mozzarella cheese**

1. Cook ravioli according to package directions; drain and return to the pan. Add the spaghetti sauce, artichokes, mushrooms and olives; gently toss.
2. Transfer to a greased 13-in. x 9-in. baking dish. Sprinkle with cheese. Bake, uncovered, at 400° for 15-20 minutes or until heated through and cheese is melted.

GARLIC GREEN BEANS
ARTICHOKE RAVIOLI

GINGER BROCCOLI STIR-FRY
GLAZED PORK MEDALLIONS

PEAR PARFAITS
SPAGHETTI SQUASH SUPPER

Ginger Broccoli Stir-Fry

Looking for an appetizing way to serve a nutritious veggie? Try my eye-catching stir-fry. The broccoli keeps its bright color and crisp freshness, while ginger and soy sauce punch it up.

—ZANE ROSSEY CRESTON, OH

START TO FINISH: 15 MIN.
MAKES: 4 SERVINGS

- 4 **cups broccoli florets**
- 2 **tablespoons water**
- 2 **teaspoons canola oil**
- 2 **garlic cloves, minced**
- 1 **teaspoon reduced-sodium soy sauce**
- ½ **teaspoon minced fresh gingerroot**

Place the broccoli and water in a 1½-qt. microwave-safe dish. Cover and microwave on high for 2 minutes; drain. In a nonstick skillet or wok, stir-fry broccoli in oil for 6-7 minutes. Add the garlic, soy sauce and ginger; stir-fry 1-2 minutes longer or until broccoli is crisp-tender.

PER SERVING *41 cal., 3 g fat (trace sat. fat), 0 chol., 70 mg sodium, 4 g carb., 2 g fiber, 2 g pro.* **Diabetic Exchanges:** *1 vegetable, ½ fat.*

Glazed Pork Medallions

When my husband was told to lower his cholesterol, he was worried that trimming the fat would mean losing the flavor. This lean and flavorful entree proves that fish isn't the only option when it comes to keeping dietary fat in line.

—MICHELE FLAGEL SHELLSBURG, IA

START TO FINISH: 30 MIN.
MAKES: 4 SERVINGS

- 1 **pork tenderloin (1¼ pounds)**
- ¼ **teaspoon salt**
- ⅓ **cup reduced-sugar orange marmalade**

- 2 **teaspoons cider vinegar**
- 2 **teaspoons Worcestershire sauce**
- ½ **teaspoon minced fresh gingerroot**
- ⅛ **teaspoon crushed red pepper flakes**

1. Cut pork into 1-in. slices and flatten to ¼-in. thickness; sprinkle with salt. Cook pork in batches over medium-high heat in a large nonstick skillet coated with cooking spray until meat is tender.

2. Reduce heat to low; return all meat to the pan. Combine the remaining ingredients; pour over pork and turn to coat. Heat through.

PER SERVING *200 cal., 5 g fat (2 g sat. fat), 79 mg chol., 231 mg sodium, 9 g carb., trace fiber, 28 g pro.* **Diabetic Exchanges:** *4 lean meat, ½ fruit, ½ fat.*

Pear Parfaits

Although this special dessert requires just four ingredients, the results will have everybody oohing and aahing.

—HEATHER KOBE VANCOUVER, WA

START TO FINISH: 10 MIN.
MAKES: 4 SERVINGS

- 1½ **cups vanilla yogurt**
- ¼ **cup confectioners' sugar**
- 2 **cans (15¼ ounces each) sliced pears, well drained**
- 1¼ **cups cinnamon graham cracker crumbs (about 7 whole crackers)**

Combine yogurt and sugar. Place three to four pear slices in each of four parfait glasses; top each with 2 tablespoons cracker crumbs and 3 tablespoons yogurt mixture. Repeat layers. Sprinkle with remaining crumbs. Refrigerate until serving.

Spaghetti Squash Supper

Hiding vegetables in your kids' supper isn't sneaky; it's smart. Because this dish is loaded with savory Italian flavor, your secret will remain safe.

—JOYCE HUNSBERGER QUAKERTOWN, PA

START TO FINISH: 30 MIN.
MAKES: 6 SERVINGS

- 1 **medium spaghetti squash (3 to 3½ pounds)**
- ½ **cup water**
- 1 **pound bulk Italian sausage**
- 1 **medium onion, chopped**
- 1 **medium green pepper, chopped**
- 1 **small zucchini, chopped**
- 1 **garlic clove, minced**
- 1 **can (15½ ounces) great northern beans, rinsed and drained**
- 1 **can (14½ ounces) Italian stewed tomatoes**
- 1 **teaspoon Italian seasoning**
- ¼ **teaspoon seasoned salt**
    Shredded Parmesan cheese

1. Halve squash lengthwise and discard seeds. Place, cut side down, in a microwave-safe dish. Add the water; cover and microwave on high for 12-15 minutes or until squash is tender. Let stand for 5 minutes.

2. Meanwhile, cook sausage in a large skillet until no longer pink; drain. Add the onion, green pepper, zucchini and garlic. Cook for 10 minutes or until the vegetables are crisp-tender, stirring occasionally; drain. Add the beans, tomatoes, Italian seasoning and salt. Cover and cook for 10 minutes or until heated through.

3. When squash is cool enough to handle, use a fork to separate strands; place in a serving dish. Top with sausage mixture. Sprinkle with Parmesan cheese.

NOTE *This recipe was tested in a 1,100-watt microwave.*

---

top tip
Now That's Smart!

Whenever you're scooping out the insides of produce (whether it's jalapeno peppers or winter squash), use a grapefruit spoon. Its sharp little teeth quickly remove the membranes and seeds.
—LEANDER A. BIRMINGHAM, AL

Italian Garlic Toast

The aroma of garlic and cheese as this speedy toast bakes is truly intoxicating.

—COOKIE CURCI SAN JOSE, CA

START TO FINISH: 10 MIN.
MAKES: 10 SERVINGS

- 1 loaf (1 pound) unsliced French bread
- ½ cup butter, melted
- ¼ cup grated Romano or Parmesan cheese
- 2 garlic cloves, minced or ½ teaspoon garlic powder
- ½ teaspoon dried oregano
  Paprika

1. Split the bread lengthwise; place, cut side up, on a large baking sheet.
2. In a small bowl, combine the butter, cheese, garlic and oregano; brush over cut sides of bread. Sprinkle with paprika.
3. Broil the bread 4 in. from the heat for 2-3 minutes or until lightly toasted. Serve warm.

Turkey Cabbage Stew

Chock-full of ground turkey, cabbage, carrots and tomatoes, this stew delivers down-home comfort food fast.

—SUSAN LASKEN WOODLAND HILLS, CA

START TO FINISH: 25 MIN.
MAKES: 6 SERVINGS

- 1 pound ground turkey
- 1 medium onion, chopped
- 3 garlic cloves, minced
- 4 cups chopped cabbage
- 2 medium carrots, sliced
- 1 can (28 ounces) diced tomatoes, undrained
- ¾ cup water
- 1 tablespoon brown sugar
- 1 tablespoon white vinegar
- 1 teaspoon salt
- 1 teaspoon dried oregano
- ¼ teaspoon dried thyme
- ¼ teaspoon pepper

1. Cook the turkey, onion and garlic in a large saucepan over medium heat until meat is no longer pink; drain.
2. Stir in the remaining ingredients. Bring to a boil; cover and simmer for 12-15 minutes or until the vegetables are tender.

EAT SMART 5 INGREDIENTS
Popeye Corn

The Sailor Man himself would approve of this spinach-rich side dish. It gets a little heat from pepper sauce.

—STACEY CHRISTENSEN WEST VALLEY CITY, UT

START TO FINISH: 15 MIN.
MAKES: 6 SERVINGS

- 1 package (16 ounces) frozen corn
- 1 package (10 ounces) frozen chopped spinach, thawed and squeezed dry
- ¾ cup sour cream
- ¾ teaspoon salt
- ½ teaspoon hot pepper sauce

Combine all ingredients in a 1½ qt. microwave-safe dish. Microwave, uncovered, on high for 5 minutes. Stir; cook 2-3 minutes longer or until heated through.

NOTE *This recipe was tested in a 1,100-watt microwave.*

PER SERVING *138 cal., 6 g fat (4 g sat. fat), 20 mg chol., 345 mg sodium, 19 g carb., 3 g fiber, 5 g pro.* **Diabetic Exchanges:** *1 starch, 1 fat.*

Mustard Tarragon Chicken

I sometimes bread this chicken earlier in the day and refrigerate it in the baking dish until mealtime. Let it stand at room temperature for 30 minutes before popping it in the oven. This makes it a nice option for entertaining.

—BETH BROWN NAPLES, FL

START TO FINISH: 30 MIN.
MAKES: 6 SERVINGS

- ½ cup butter, melted
- ½ teaspoon ground mustard
- ½ teaspoon garlic salt
- ¾ cup dry bread crumbs
- ¼ to ½ teaspoon dried tarragon
- ¼ teaspoon pepper
- 6 boneless skinless chicken breast halves (4 ounces each)

1. Combine the butter, mustard and garlic salt in a shallow bowl. Combine the bread crumbs, tarragon and pepper in another shallow bowl. Dip chicken into butter mixture, then coat with crumb mixture.

2. Place in an ungreased 13-in. x 9-in. baking dish. Bake, uncovered, at 375° for 20-25 minutes or until a thermometer reads 170°.

BUSY COOKS' SECRETS

Stay organized when cooking, and clean as you go.

I KEEP MY MOST-USED ITEMS HANDY, so I don't have to search for them. I also try to get rid of cooking gadgets and tools that I seldom use. The less I have, the easier it is to be organized. I wash utensils, pots, pans and bowls as I dirty them. That's when they're easiest to clean. I also use my sink when mixing batter in a bowl or when things might splatter or spill. Splashes and drips stay there, and the lower height makes it easier to hand-mix or wield an electric mixer.

—TRISHA KRUSE EAGLE, ID

BEFORE I START COOKING, I get out all of the ingredients, as well as all of the bowls, pans and utensils I'll need. I also clean as I go so my workspace isn't cluttered and there is less work at the end.

—NICOLE ROBBINS BURLINGTON, IA

I PREP AS MANY INGREDIENTS AS POSSIBLE the night before. Having a game plan and knowing what's on the menu means there's no rushing around at 5:30 when dinner is at 6:00. I also love to use my slow cooker so that dinner is ready and waiting when I get home from work, especially in the wintertime.

—JULIE KO ROGERS, AR

ITALIAN GARLIC TOAST
TURKEY CABBAGE STEW

POPEYE CORN
MUSTARD TARRAGON CHICKEN

GERMAN-STYLE SPINACH
PORK SCHNITZEL WITH DILL SAUCE

ZUCCHINI 'N' CORN SAUTE
CHICKEN PARMESAN

German-Style Spinach

Grandma's spinach dish is flavored with her Austrian heritage. It's tasty and always looks so pretty on the plate. We children never had to be told to eat our spinach at Grandma's house!

—JOAN HUTTER WARWICK, RI

START TO FINISH: 20 MIN.
MAKES: 8 SERVINGS

- 2 packages (10 ounces each) frozen chopped spinach
- 1 large onion, chopped
- 2 garlic cloves, minced
- 2 tablespoons butter
- 6 bacon strips, cooked and crumbled
- ½ teaspoon ground nutmeg
- ½ teaspoon salt
  Pepper to taste

Cook spinach according to package directions. Drain well and set aside. Saute onion and garlic in butter in a large skillet until tender. Stir in the spinach, bacon, nutmeg, salt and pepper; heat through.

Pork Schnitzel with Dill Sauce

My husband is of German descent, and this is one of his all-time favorites because the flavors take him back to the old country. I like to prepare schnitzel when we have company.

—JOYCE FOLKER PARAOWAN, UT

START TO FINISH: 20 MIN.
MAKES: 6 SERVINGS

- 6 pork sirloin cutlets (½ inch thick and 4 ounces each)
- ½ cup all-purpose flour
- 2 teaspoons seasoned salt
- ½ teaspoon pepper
- 2 eggs
- ¼ cup 2% milk
- 1½ cups dry bread crumbs
- 2 teaspoons paprika
- 6 tablespoons canola oil

DILL SAUCE
- 1½ cups chicken broth, divided
- 2 tablespoons all-purpose flour
- ½ teaspoon dill weed
- 1 cup (8 ounces) sour cream

1. Flatten pork cutlets to ¼-in. thickness. Combine the flour, seasoned salt and pepper in a shallow bowl. In another bowl, beat eggs and milk. Combine bread crumbs and paprika in another bowl. Dip cutlets into flour mixture, then into egg mixture, then coat with crumbs.

2. Cook pork in oil in a large skillet, a few pieces at a time, for 3-4 minutes per side or until tender. Remove to a serving platter; keep warm.

3. Pour 1 cup broth into skillet, scraping bottom of pan to loosen browned bits. Combine flour and remaining broth until smooth; stir into skillet. Bring to a boil; cook and stir for 2 minutes or until thickened. Reduce heat. Stir in dill and sour cream; heat through (do not boil). Serve with pork.

⑤ INGREDIENTS

Zucchini 'n' Corn Saute

This veggie blend tastes fresh and appealing. It complements many entrees and brightens the dinner table.

—VERA REID LARAMIE, WY

START TO FINISH: 15 MIN.
MAKES: 2 SERVINGS

- 1 small zucchini, thinly sliced
- ½ medium sweet red or green pepper, julienned
- 1 tablespoon canola oil
- ½ cup fresh or frozen corn
- ¼ teaspoon garlic salt
- ¼ teaspoon Italian seasoning

Saute zucchini and red pepper in oil in a small skillet for 3-4 minutes or until crisp-tender. Add the corn, garlic salt and Italian seasoning; saute 3-4 minutes longer or until corn is tender.

Chicken Parmesan

Here's an easy version of an Italian classic. Chicken breasts topped with spaghetti sauce and toasty cheese are always delightful.

—MARY DENNIS BRYAN, OH

START TO FINISH: 30 MIN.
MAKES: 2 SERVINGS

- 2 boneless skinless chicken breast halves (8 ounces each)
- 2 teaspoons canola oil
- 1½ cups spaghetti sauce
- 1 can (4 ounces) mushroom stems and pieces, drained
- ½ cup shredded part-skim mozzarella cheese
- 2 tablespoons grated Parmesan cheese
  Hot cooked linguine

1. Brown chicken in oil in a large ovenproof skillet over medium heat. Add spaghetti sauce and mushrooms. Bring to a boil. Reduce heat; cover and simmer for 10-15 minutes or until a thermometer reads 170°.

2. Sprinkle with cheeses. Broil 4-6 in. from the heat for 3-4 minutes or until cheese is melted. Serve with linguine.

AVOCADO SANDWICHES
CREAMY HAM & CORN SOUP

Avocado Sandwiches

Try my sandwiches for an exciting flavor twist on grilled cheese.

—DEB WILLIAMS PEORIA, AZ

START TO FINISH: 15 MIN.
MAKES: 4 SERVINGS

- 8 slices French bread (½ inch thick)
- ⅓ cup apricot preserves
- 8 ounces sliced Havarti cheese
- 2 medium ripe avocados, peeled and sliced
- ⅛ teaspoon salt
- 1 tablespoon butter, softened

1. Spread four bread slices with preserves. Layer with cheese and avocado slices; sprinkle with salt. Top with remaining bread. Butter outsides of sandwiches.

2. Toast sandwiches on a griddle over medium heat for 2-3 minutes on each side or until cheese is melted.

Creamy Ham & Corn Soup

My quick and easy soup really hits the spot on a cold winter night (yes, we do occasionally have those in Arizona). I like to serve it with a green salad and hot homemade bread.

—AUDREY THIBODEAU GILBERT, AZ

START TO FINISH: 30 MIN.
MAKES: 7 SERVINGS

- 2 cans (14½ ounces each) chicken broth
- 2 cups fresh or frozen corn
- 1 cup half-and-half cream
- ⅓ cup chopped onion
- ⅓ cup chopped sweet red pepper
- ¼ cup plus 3 tablespoons all-purpose flour
- ½ cup cold water
- ½ teaspoon salt
- ¼ teaspoon pepper
- 1 cup diced fully cooked ham
  Snipped fresh dill, optional

1. Combine the broth, corn, cream, onion and red pepper in a large saucepan. Bring to a boil. Combine the flour, water, salt and pepper until smooth; gradually stir into pan. Bring to a boil; cook and stir for 2 minutes or until thickened. Stir in ham.

2. Reduce heat; cover and simmer for 10-15 minutes or until vegetables are tender. Garnish servings with dill if desired.

Chicken with Sweet Jalapeno Sauce

This family favorite is not too hot and not too sweet. You can use any type of hot pepper jelly you like.

—JAYE-LYNN BAUBLITZ BRADENTON, FL

START TO FINISH: 30 MIN.
MAKES: 4 SERVINGS

- 4 boneless skinless chicken breast halves (5 ounces each)
- ½ teaspoon salt
- ¼ teaspoon pepper
- 1 tablespoon canola oil
- 1 small onion, thinly sliced
- 1 celery rib, thinly sliced
- ½ cup chicken broth
- 3 tablespoons orange juice
- ¼ teaspoon dried thyme
- ½ cup jalapeno pepper jelly
- 2 tablespoons butter
- 1 tablespoon minced fresh parsley

1. Flatten the chicken to ¼-in. thickness; sprinkle with salt and pepper. Cook chicken in batches in oil in a large skillet over medium heat for 2-3 minutes on each side or until no longer pink. Remove and keep warm.

2. Saute onion and celery in the same pan until crisp-tender. Add the broth, orange juice and thyme.

3. Bring to a boil; cook until liquid is reduced by half. Stir in pepper jelly until melted. Remove from heat; stir in butter and parsley. Serve with chicken.

Sweet Carrots with Bacon

Sweet and smoky carrots are delightful with any meal. I'm often asked to prepare this tasty side.

—BETTY SHARP MECHANICSVILLE, VA

START TO FINISH: 15 MIN.
MAKES: 4 SERVINGS

- 1 package (16 ounces) frozen sliced carrots
- 2 bacon strips
- 1 green onion, thinly sliced
- 1 tablespoon butter
- 1 tablespoon brown sugar
- ¼ teaspoon salt
- ⅛ teaspoon pepper

1. Cook the carrots according to package directions. Cook bacon in a small skillet over medium heat until crisp. Remove to paper towels with a slotted spoon; drain, reserving 1 teaspoon of drippings.

2. Saute onion in butter and reserved drippings. Add brown sugar, salt and pepper; cook and stir until brown sugar is melted.

3. Drain carrots and toss with onion mixture. Crumble bacon; sprinkle over the top.

CHICKEN WITH SWEET JALAPENO SAUCE
SWEET CARROTS WITH BACON

⑤INGREDIENTS

Creamy Italian Pasta with Chicken

I created this recipe one night when I was too tired to wander around the grocery store figuring out what to make. This is even more delicious when topped with Parmesan or mozzarella cheese. To give it some spice, add some red pepper flakes.

—**LAURA KOCH** LINCOLN, NE

START TO FINISH: 20 MIN.
MAKES: 5 SERVINGS

- 3 **cups uncooked bow tie pasta**
- 2 **packages (6 ounces each) ready-to-use grilled chicken breast strips**
- 1 **can (14½ ounces) diced tomatoes with basil, oregano and garlic, undrained**
- 1 **jar (15 ounces) Alfredo sauce**
- 3 **cups fresh baby spinach, coarsely chopped**

1. Cook pasta according to package directions. Meanwhile, in a large skillet, combine the chicken, tomatoes and Alfredo sauce; heat through. Add spinach; cook and stir until wilted.
2. Drain the pasta and toss with chicken mixture.

⑤INGREDIENTS

Parmesan-Basil Breadsticks

What's not to love about fragrant breadsticks hot from the oven? Round out any Italian meal with these beauties.

—**MARY RELYEA** CANASTOTA, NY

START TO FINISH: 15 MIN.
MAKES: 1 DOZEN

- 1 **tube (11 ounces) refrigerated breadsticks**
- 1 **egg**
- 1 **tablespoon 2% milk**
- ⅓ **cup grated Parmesan cheese**
- ½ **teaspoon dried basil**

1. Unroll and separate breadsticks. Twist each breadstick two to three times; place on a greased baking sheet. Whisk egg and milk in a small bowl; brush over breadsticks. Combine cheese and basil; sprinkle over tops.
2. Bake at 375° for 10-12 minutes or until golden brown. Serve warm.

Smoked Sausage Jambalaya

So easy and delicious! You can't go wrong with this New Orleans favorite.

—**MARY MORRIS** LAS ANIMAS, CO

START TO FINISH: 30 MIN.
MAKES: 5 SERVINGS

- 1 package (8 ounces) jambalaya mix
- 1 package (14 ounces) smoked beef sausage, cut into ¼-inch slices
- 1 large onion, chopped
- ⅓ cup each chopped green, sweet red and yellow pepper
- 1 can (14½ ounces) diced tomatoes, drained

Microwave jambalaya mix according to package directions. Meanwhile, lightly brown the sausage in a large nonstick skillet. Add onion and peppers; saute 4-5 minutes longer or until tender. Add tomatoes and heat through. Stir into jambalaya mixture.

NOTE *This recipe was prepared with Zatarain's New Orleans-style Jambalaya Mix.*

⑤ INGREDIENTS
Easy Lemon-Pepper Green Beans

I plant a garden every year, and I always have a lot of green beans to use. My family loves green beans this way.

—**PAULA BROADWAY-JONES** CAMBRIDGE, NE

START TO FINISH: 15 MIN.
MAKES: 4 SERVINGS

- 1 garlic clove, minced
- 1 tablespoon olive oil
- 1 pound fresh or frozen cut green beans
- ½ cup chicken broth
- ¾ teaspoon lemon-pepper seasoning
- ½ teaspoon dried parsley flakes
- ¼ teaspoon salt

Saute garlic in oil in a large skillet for 1 minute. Add the beans, broth, lemon-pepper, parsley and salt. Bring to a boil. Reduce heat; simmer, uncovered, for 4-5 minutes or until beans are tender.

BUSY COOKS' SECRETS

Plan ahead.

I VIEW MY GROCER'S ONLINE AD EVERY WEEK and make a list of the sale items that I use regularly, then stock the pantry and freezer with staples so that they're always on hand. It's a win-win habit: We save money and I don't have to rush out at the last minute to buy groceries.

—**LISA SPEER** PALM BEACH, FL

**Amanda Livesay's
Parmesan Chicken Nuggets**
PAGE 59

Give Me 5 or Fewer

Whether you need a swift party snack, an easy dessert or a quick weeknight meal, it's five or fewer ingredients away with the simple solutions found here. (Recipes may also call for water, salt, pepper, and canola or olive oil.)

**Tricia Richardson's
Pizza Ring**
PAGE 50

**Mabel Nolan's
Ice Cream Cone Treats**
PAGE 60

**Susan Wholley's
Bruschetta-Topped
Chicken & Spaghetti**
PAGE 53

PIZZA RING

Bacon-Swiss Pork Chops

I'm always looking for quick and easy recipes that are impressive enough to serve to company. These pork chops smothered in bacon and Swiss cheese certainly fit the bill.

—**KEITH MILLER** FORT GRATIOT, MI

START TO FINISH: 25 MIN.
MAKES: 4 SERVINGS

- 2 bacon strips, chopped
- 1 medium onion, chopped
- 4 boneless pork loin chops (4 ounces each)
- ½ teaspoon garlic powder
- ¼ teaspoon salt
- 2 slices reduced-fat Swiss cheese, halved

1. In a nonstick skillet coated with cooking spray, cook bacon and onion over medium heat until bacon is crisp, stirring occasionally. Remove with a slotted spoon; drain on paper towels. Discard drippings.

2. Sprinkle pork chops with garlic powder and salt. Add pork chops to same pan; cook over medium heat 3-4 minutes on each side or until a thermometer reads 145°. Top pork with bacon mixture and cheese. Cook, covered, on low 1-2 minutes or until cheese is melted.

PER SERVING *218 cal., 10 g fat (4 g sat. fat), 64 mg chol., 268 mg sodium, 4 g carb., 1 g fiber, 27 g pro.* **Diabetic Exchanges:** *4 lean meat, ½ fat.*

Pizza Ring

Mom made a ring with chicken and broccoli one night. I said I'd rather have pizza. That's how this recipe was born!

—**TRICIA RICHARDSON** SPRINGDALE, AR

START TO FINISH: 30 MIN.
MAKES: 8 SERVINGS

- 1 pound bulk Italian sausage
- 1 can (15 ounces) pizza sauce, divided
- 1½ cups (6 ounces) shredded part-skim mozzarella cheese, divided
- 4 ounces Canadian bacon, chopped
- 2 tubes (8 ounces each) refrigerated crescent rolls

1. Cook sausage in a large skillet over medium heat until no longer pink; drain. Stir in ½ cup pizza sauce, 1 cup cheese and Canadian bacon.

2. Unroll crescent dough and separate into triangles. On an ungreased 14-in. pizza pan, arrange triangles in a ring with points toward the outside and wide ends overlapping at the center, leaving a 4-in. opening. Press overlapping dough to seal.

3. Spoon filling onto wide end of triangles. Fold pointed end of triangles over filling, tucking points under to form a ring (filling will be visible).

4. Bake at 375° for 12-15 minutes or until golden brown and heated through. Sprinkle with remaining cheese. Bake 5 minutes longer or until cheese is melted. Serve with remaining pizza sauce.

BACON-SWISS PORK CHOPS

Cherry-Glazed Chicken with Toasted Pecans

What started out as a way to use up some leftover preserves and cheese turned out to be a winning family dinner that I now make time and again.

—KERI COTTON LAKEVILLE, MN

START TO FINISH: 30 MIN.
MAKES: 4 SERVINGS

- 4 boneless skinless chicken breast halves (4 ounces each)
- ¾ cup cherry preserves
- 1 teaspoon onion powder
- 2 ounces fontina cheese, thinly sliced
- 2 tablespoons chopped pecans, toasted

1. Preheat oven to 375°. Place chicken in an ungreased 11x7-in. baking dish. Top with preserves; sprinkle with onion powder. Bake, uncovered, 18-22 minutes or until a thermometer reads 165°.

2. Top with cheese; bake 5 minutes longer or until cheese is melted. Sprinkle with pecans.

NOTE *To toast nuts, spread in a 15x10x1-in. baking pan. Bake at 350° for 5-10 minutes or until lightly browned, stirring occasionally. Or, spread in a dry nonstick skillet and heat over low heat until lightly browned, stirring occasionally.*

PER SERVING *354 cal., 10 g fat (4 g sat. fat), 79 mg chol., 168 mg sodium, 40 g carb., trace fiber, 27 g pro.*

APPLE-MUSTARD CHICKEN TENDERS

CHERRY-GLAZED CHICKEN WITH TOASTED PECANS

"I'm a big fan of savory meals that have a sweet surprise, like this one. Granny Smith apples offer a bit of tartness. Serve these sassy chicken tenders over rice or small pasta shells if you like." —LINDA CIFUENTES MAHOMET, IL

Apple-Mustard Chicken Tenders

START TO FINISH: 30 MIN.
MAKES: 6 SERVINGS

- 1½ pounds chicken tenderloins
- ½ teaspoon salt
- ¼ teaspoon pepper
- 3 tablespoons butter
- 2 small Granny Smith apples, thinly sliced
- ½ cup packed brown sugar
- ¼ cup stone-ground mustard

1. Sprinkle chicken with salt and pepper. In a large skillet, heat butter over medium heat. Add chicken; cook 4-6 minutes on each side or until no longer pink. Remove from pan.

2. Add apples, brown sugar and mustard to same pan; toss to combine. Cook, covered, over medium heat 3-4 minutes or until apples are tender. Stir in chicken; heat through.

GINGER-CHUTNEY SHRIMP STIR-FRY

Ginger-Chutney Shrimp Stir-Fry

I made this recipe a lot when I was juggling college, work and a growing family. It tastes like you spent a lot of time making it, yet takes less than half an hour to toss together.

—SALLY SIBTHORPE SHELBY TOWNSHIP, MI

START TO FINISH: 25 MIN.
MAKES: 4 SERVINGS

- 2 tablespoons peanut oil
- 1 pound uncooked medium shrimp, peeled and deveined, tails removed
- 1 tablespoon minced fresh gingerroot
- 3 cups frozen pepper and onion stir-fry blend, thawed
- ¾ cup mango chutney
- 2 tablespoons water
- ¾ teaspoon salt

In a large skillet, heat oil over medium-high heat. Add shrimp and ginger; stir-fry 4-5 minutes or until shrimp turn pink. Stir in the remaining ingredients; cook until vegetables are tender, stirring occasionally.

Frozen Sandwich Cookies

With just three ingredients, these cute cookies are a snap to make. Everyone, young and old alike, enjoys these cool, creamy treats.

—MARY ANN IRVINE LOMBARD, IL

PREP: 10 MIN. + FREEZING
MAKES: 8 SANDWICH COOKIES

- ½ cup spreadable strawberry cream cheese
- ¼ cup strawberry yogurt
- 16 chocolate wafers

1. In a small bowl, beat cream cheese and yogurt until blended. Spread on bottoms of half of the chocolate wafers; top with remaining wafers.
2. Place on a baking sheet. Freeze 30 minutes or until firm. Serve or wrap in plastic wrap and return to freezer for serving later.

Bruschetta-Topped Chicken & Spaghetti

This is a healthy version of a classic chicken combination. It's so full of flavor, you'll think you're cheating on your diet.

—SUSAN WHOLLEY FAIRFIELD, CT

START TO FINISH: 30 MIN.
MAKES: 4 SERVINGS

- 8 ounces uncooked whole wheat spaghetti
- 4 boneless skinless chicken breast halves (5 ounces each)
- ½ teaspoon pepper
- 1 cup prepared bruschetta topping
- ⅓ cup shredded Italian cheese blend
- 2 tablespoons grated Parmesan cheese

1. Preheat broiler. Cook spaghetti according to package directions; drain. Pound chicken breasts with a meat mallet to ½-in. thickness. Sprinkle with pepper. In a large nonstick skillet coated with cooking spray, cook chicken over medium heat 5-6 minutes on each side or until no longer pink.
2. Transfer to an 8-in.-square baking pan. Spoon bruschetta topping over chicken; sprinkle with cheeses. Broil 3-4 in. from heat 5-6 minutes or until cheese is golden brown. Serve with spaghetti.
PER SERVING *431 cal., 10 g fat (4 g sat. fat), 87 mg chol., 641 mg sodium, 47 g carb., 8 g fiber, 40 g pro.* **Diabetic Exchanges:** *4 lean meat, 3 starch, ½ fat.*

BRUSCHETTA-TOPPED CHICKEN & SPAGHETTI

FAST FIX

Landmark Hot Chocolate

With or without a nip of rum, my hot chocolate recipe has been a Wisconsin winter warmer for years. When the toboggan hills are calling, I skip the whipped cream and take a thermos to go. It's always a hit and it ensures nobody is left out in the cold!

—MARK PHILLIPS BAYFIELD, WI

START TO FINISH: 15 MIN.
MAKES: 1 SERVING

- ⅓ cup heavy whipping cream
- ¼ cup 2% milk
- 2 ounces dark chocolate candy bar, chopped
- 4½ teaspoons sugar
- 1 cinnamon stick (3 inches)
  Vanilla rum, optional
  Heavy whipping cream, whipped
  Additional cinnamon stick, optional

Heat the first five ingredients over medium heat in a small saucepan just until mixture comes to a simmer, stirring constantly. Remove from heat; stir until smooth. Add rum if desired. Pour into a mug; top with whipped cream. Garnish with cinnamon stick if desired.

LANDMARK HOT CHOCOLATE

PEANUT BUTTER S'MORES BARS

"When I give these as gifts, they're gone in a flash. I sometimes make them ahead because they freeze well. You can use M&M's in different colors for holidays year-round." —JULIE WISCHMEIER BROWNSTOWN, IN

Peanut Butter S'mores Bars

PREP: 10 MIN.
BAKE: 20 MIN. + CHILLING
MAKES: 2 DOZEN

- 1 tube (16½ ounces) refrigerated peanut butter cookie dough
- 3½ cups miniature marshmallows
- ¾ cup milk chocolate chips
- 2 teaspoons shortening
- 1½ cups milk chocolate M&M's

1. Preheat oven to 350°. Let dough stand at room temperature 5-10 minutes to soften. With floured hands, press dough into an ungreased 13x9-in. baking pan. Bake 18-20 minutes or until lightly browned and edges are firm.

2. Sprinkle with marshmallows; bake 2-3 minutes longer or until marshmallows are puffy.

3. In a microwave, melt chocolate chips and shortening; stir until smooth. Sprinkle M&M's over marshmallows; drizzle with chocolate mixture. Refrigerate until set before cutting.

Golden Apricot-Glazed Turkey Breast

Basted with a simple glaze, this tender turkey cooks to a lovely golden brown. Make it the centerpiece of your holiday table; you'll be glad you did.

—**GREG FONTENOT** THE WOODLANDS, TX

PREP: 10 MIN.
BAKE: 1½ HOURS + STANDING
MAKES: 15 SERVINGS

- ½ cup apricot preserves
- ¼ cup balsamic vinegar
- ¼ teaspoon pepper
- Dash salt
- 1 bone-in turkey breast (5 pounds)

1. Preheat oven to 325°. Combine preserves, vinegar, pepper and salt. Place turkey breast on a rack in a large shallow roasting pan.

2. Bake, uncovered, 1½ to 2 hours or until a thermometer reads 170°, basting every 30 minutes with apricot mixture. (Cover loosely with foil if turkey browns too quickly.) Cover and let stand 15 minutes before slicing.

PER SERVING *236 cal., 8 g fat (2 g sat. fat), 81 mg chol., 84 mg sodium, 8 g carb., trace fiber, 32 g pro.* **Diabetic Exchanges:** *4 lean meat, ½ starch.*

GOLDEN APRICOT-GLAZED TURKEY BREAST

Sunday's Corned Beef

Here's an old-fashioned Irish recipe I've been making for decades—and not just on St. Patrick's Day—because it's fast and easy to prepare. The leftovers make a terrific lunch the next day.

—**PAM ALLEN** LEBANON, PA

PREP: 15 MIN. • **COOK:** 2½ HOURS
MAKES: 16 SERVINGS

- 2 corned beef briskets with spice packets (3 pounds each)
- 1 medium head cabbage, cut into 8 wedges
- 1 bottle (2 liters) ginger ale
- ¼ cup mixed pickling spices
- 8 medium potatoes, peeled and quartered

1. Discard spice packets from corned beef or save for another use. Place briskets in a Dutch oven; add cabbage. Pour ginger ale over top. Place pickling spices on a double thickness of cheesecloth; bring up corners of cloth and tie with string to form a bag. Add to the pan.

2. Bring to a boil. Reduce heat; cover and simmer for 2½ to 3 hours or until meat is tender, adding potatoes during the last 20 minutes of cooking. Discard spice bag.

3. Remove meat and vegetables to a serving platter. Thinly slice brisket across the grain; serve with cabbage and potatoes.

Corned Beef for a Crowd

When preparing St. Patrick's Day dinner for a crowd, I cook the corned beef in two large pots. When it's time to start the potatoes and vegetables, I transfer the corned beef to one pot. That way, I have the flavorful broth in my second pot to cook the vegetables.

—**PEGGY A.** PASADENA, CA

PERSONAL MARGHERITA PIZZAS

FAST FIX

Personal Margherita Pizzas

This family-friendly supper is simplicity at its finest. Fresh mozzarella and a sprinkling of basil give these little pies Italian flair.

—**JERRY GULLEY** SAN FRANCISCO, CA

START TO FINISH: 25 MIN.
MAKES: 3 SERVINGS

- 1 package (6½ ounces) pizza crust mix
- ½ teaspoon dried oregano
- ¾ cup pizza sauce
- 6 ounces fresh mozzarella cheese, thinly sliced
- ¼ cup thinly sliced fresh basil leaves

1. Preheat oven to 425°. Prepare pizza dough according to package directions, adding oregano before mixing. Divide into three portions.

2. Pat each portion of dough into an 8-in. circle on greased baking sheets. Bake 8-10 minutes or until edges are lightly browned.

3. Spread each crust with ¼ cup pizza sauce to within ½ in. of edge. Top with cheese. Bake 5-10 minutes longer or until crust is golden and cheese is melted. Sprinkle with basil.

FAST FIX

Caesar Orange Roughy

I'm so thankful that my mother, a fantastic cook, taught me the ropes in the kitchen when I was fairly young. Mom won several cooking contests over the years and this is one of my favorite recipes of hers.

—**MARY LOU BOYCE** WILMINGTON, DE

START TO FINISH: 25 MIN.
MAKES: 8 SERVINGS

- 8 orange roughy fillets (4 ounces each)
- 1 cup creamy Caesar salad dressing
- 2 cups crushed butter-flavored crackers (about 50 crackers)
- 1 cup (4 ounces) shredded cheddar cheese

1. Preheat oven to 400°. Place fillets in an ungreased 13x9-in. baking dish. Drizzle with salad dressing; sprinkle with crushed crackers.

2. Bake, uncovered, 10 minutes. Sprinkle with cheese. Bake 3-5 minutes longer or until fish flakes easily with a fork and cheese is melted.

CAESAR ORANGE ROUGHY

"One of my husband's favorite childhood memories was eating his Grandma Barney's Tater Tot casserole. One day I started preparing it, sure that I had Tots on hand. Instead, I found O'Brien potatoes. Dinner turned out great! Now I always make it this way." —HEATHER MATTHEWS KELLER, TX

CREAMY BEEF & POTATOES

Creamy Beef & Potatoes

START TO FINISH: 20 MIN.
MAKES: 4 SERVINGS

- 4 cups frozen O'Brien potatoes
- 1 tablespoon water
- 1 pound ground beef
- ½ teaspoon salt
- ¼ teaspoon pepper
- 2 cans (10¾ ounces each) condensed cream of mushroom soup, undiluted
- ⅔ cup 2% milk
- 2 cups (8 ounces) shredded Colby-Monterey Jack cheese

1. Place potatoes and water in a microwave-safe bowl. Microwave, covered, on high for 8-10 minutes or until tender, stirring twice.
2. Meanwhile, in a Dutch oven, cook beef over medium heat 6-8 minutes or until no longer pink, breaking into crumbles; drain. Stir in salt and pepper. In a small bowl, whisk soup and milk until blended; add to beef. Stir in potatoes. Sprinkle with cheese. Reduce heat to low; cook, covered, until cheese is melted.
NOTE *This recipe was tested in a 1,100-watt microwave.*

Tex-Mex Pasta

After a recent surgery, I wasn't able to stock up on groceries. One night, I created this out of what I found in my pantry. The results were fabulous!
—MICHELE ORTHNER LETHBRIDGE, AB

START TO FINISH: 30 MIN.
MAKES: 4 SERVINGS

- 2 cups uncooked spiral pasta
- 1 pound ground beef
- 1 jar (16 ounces) salsa
- 1 can (10¾ ounces) condensed cream of chicken soup, undiluted
- 1 cup (4 ounces) shredded Mexican cheese blend, divided

1. Cook pasta according to package directions. Meanwhile, cook beef in a Dutch oven over medium heat until no longer pink; drain.
2. Stir in the salsa, soup and ½ cup cheese; heat through. Drain pasta; stir into meat mixture. Transfer to a greased 11-in. x 7-in. baking dish. Sprinkle with remaining cheese.
3. Cover and bake at 350° for 15-20 minutes or until cheese is melted.

Italian Cheese Popcorn

Perfect for movie night, here's a tasty Italian twist on regular popped popcorn.
—TASTE OF HOME TEST KITCHEN

START TO FINISH: 10 MIN.
MAKES: 3½ QUARTS

- 2¼ teaspoons Italian seasoning
- ¾ teaspoon garlic salt
- 6 tablespoons grated Romano cheese
- ⅓ cup butter
- 3½ quarts popped popcorn

Combine Italian seasoning, garlic salt and cheese. Melt butter; drizzle over popcorn and toss. Sprinkle with cheese mixture; toss.

SIRLOIN WITH MUSHROOM SAUCE

Buffalo Chicken Meatballs

I like to serve these meatballs as appetizers with blue cheese or ranch salad dressing for dipping. If I make them for a meal, I skip the dressing and serve the meatballs with blue cheese polenta on the side.

—AMBER MASSEY ARGYLE, TX

PREP: 15 MIN. • **BAKE:** 20 MIN.
MAKES: 2 DOZEN

- ¾ **cup panko (Japanese) bread crumbs**
- ⅓ **cup plus ½ cup Louisiana-style hot sauce, divided**
- ¼ **cup chopped celery**
- 1 **egg white**
- 1 **pound lean ground chicken**
  Reduced-fat blue cheese or ranch salad dressing, optional

1. Preheat oven to 400°. In a large bowl, combine bread crumbs, ⅓ cup hot sauce, celery and egg white. Add chicken; mix lightly but thoroughly.
2. Shape into twenty-four 1-in. balls. Place on a greased rack in a shallow baking pan. Bake 20-25 minutes or until cooked through.
3. Toss meatballs with remaining hot sauce. If desired, drizzle with salad dressing just before serving.
PER SERVING *35 cal., 1 g fat (trace sat. fat), 14 mg chol., 24 mg sodium, 2 g carb., trace fiber, 4 g pro.*

Sirloin with Mushroom Sauce

A mouthwatering combination of rich mushroom sauce and peppery steak is a welcome way to finish off a busy day. Whenever visitors drop in around dinnertime, I pull out this recipe and it's ready before we know it.

—JOE ELLIOTT WEST BEND, WI

START TO FINISH: 30 MIN.
MAKES: 4 SERVINGS

- 1 **boneless beef sirloin steak (1 pound and ¾ inch thick)**
- 1 **teaspoon coarsely ground pepper**
- 2 **teaspoons canola oil**
- 1½ **cups sliced fresh mushrooms**
- ½ **cup beef broth**
- ½ **cup dry red wine or additional beef broth**

1. Preheat oven to 450°. Rub steak with pepper. In a heavy ovenproof skillet, heat oil over medium-high heat. Brown steak on both sides. Transfer to oven; roast 4 minutes or until meat reaches desired doneness (for medium-rare, a thermometer should read 145°; medium, 160°; well-done, 170°).
2. Remove steak from pan; tent with foil. Let stand 10 minutes before slicing.
3. Add mushrooms to same pan; cook and stir over medium-high heat until golden brown. Add broth and wine, stirring to loosen browned bits from pan. Bring to a boil; cook until liquid is reduced by half. Thinly slice steak; serve with mushroom sauce.
PER SERVING *214 cal., 9 g fat (3 g sat. fat), 77 mg chol., 161 mg sodium, 1 g carb., trace fiber, 27 g pro.* **Diabetic Exchanges:** *3 lean meat, ½ fat.*

BUFFALO CHICKEN MEATBALLS

PARMESAN CHICKEN NUGGETS

Parmesan Chicken Nuggets

My 3-year-old is going through a stage where he'll eat only chicken nuggets and French fries. I like to make these golden nuggets for him so I know what he's eating. They're so good, we like them, too.

—**AMANDA LIVESAY** MOBILE, AL

START TO FINISH: 30 MIN.
MAKES: 8 SERVINGS

- ¼ **cup butter, melted**
- 1 **cup panko (Japanese) bread crumbs**
- ½ **cup grated Parmesan cheese**
- ½ **teaspoon kosher salt**
- 1½ **pounds boneless skinless chicken breasts, cut into 1-inch cubes**
  Marinara sauce, optional

1. Place butter in a shallow bowl. Combine the bread crumbs, cheese and salt in another shallow bowl. Dip chicken in butter, then roll in crumbs.
2. Place in a single layer on two 15-in. x 10-in. x 1-in. baking pans. Bake at 375° for 15-18 minutes until no longer pink, turning once. Serve with marinara sauce if desired.

Lasagna Rolls

Folks can't believe these flavorful rolls have just five ingredients. Using prepared spaghetti sauce saves cooking time. My family is very happy when these appear on the table.

—**MARY LEE THOMAS** LOGANSPORT, IN

PREP: 25 MIN. • **BAKE:** 10 MIN.
MAKES: 6 SERVINGS

- 6 **lasagna noodles**
- 1 **pound ground beef**
- 1 **jar (14 ounces) spaghetti sauce**
- 1 **teaspoon fennel seed, optional**
- 2 **cups (8 ounces) shredded part-skim mozzarella cheese, divided**

1. Cook lasagna noodles according to package directions. Meanwhile, in a large skillet, cook beef over medium heat until no longer pink; drain. Stir in spaghetti sauce and fennel seed if desired; heat through.
2. Drain noodles. Spread ¼ cup meat sauce over each noodle; sprinkle with 2 tablespoons cheese. Carefully roll up noodles and place seam side down in an 8-in.-square baking dish. Top with remaining sauce and cheese.
3. Bake, uncovered, at 400° for 10-15 minutes or until heated through and cheese is melted.

LASAGNA ROLLS

"Flank steak is always a winner in our house, but I like to make it even more special with salsa verde and chopped fresh tomato and avocado."

—LILY JULOW LAWRENCEVILLE, GA

ICE CREAM CONE TREATS

FAST FIX

Flank Steak with Cilantro Salsa Verde

START TO FINISH: 25 MIN.
MAKES: 4 SERVINGS

- 1 beef flank steak or top sirloin steak, 1 inch thick (about 1¼ pounds)
- ¼ teaspoon salt
- ¼ teaspoon pepper
- 1 cup salsa verde
- ½ cup fresh cilantro leaves
- 1 medium ripe avocado, peeled and cubed
- 1 medium tomato, seeded and chopped

1. Sprinkle steak with salt and pepper. Grill steak, covered, over medium heat or broil 4 in. from heat 6-9 minutes on each side or until meat reaches desired doneness (for medium-rare, a thermometer should read 145°; medium, 160°; well-done, 170°). Let stand 5 minutes.

2. Meanwhile, place salsa and cilantro in a food processor; process until blended. Slice steak thinly across the grain; serve with salsa mixture, avocado and tomato.

FLANK STEAK WITH CILANTRO SALSA VERDE

FAST FIX

Ice Cream Cone Treats

I came up with this recipe as a way for my grandkids to enjoy Rice Krispies Treats without getting sticky hands. An alternate version is to pack the cereal mixture into paper cups and insert a freezer pop stick— to form fun suckers.

—MABEL NOLAN VANCOUVER, WA

START TO FINISH: 15 MIN.
MAKES: 12 SERVINGS

- Colored sprinkles
- 4 cups miniature marshmallows
- 3 tablespoons butter
- 6 cups crisp rice cereal
- 12 ice cream cones

1. Place sprinkles in a shallow bowl. In a microwave or in a large saucepan over low heat, melt marshmallows and butter. Remove from the heat; stir in rice cereal.

2. Using greased hands, shape cereal mixture into 12 balls. Pack each ball into an ice cream cone. Dip the tops in sprinkles.

Quick Cherry Turnovers

Refrigerated crescent rolls let you make these fruit-filled pastries in a hurry. My family loves the turnovers for breakfast, although the pastries would be welcome any time of the day. Feel free to experiment with other pie fillings.

—**ELLEEN OBERRUETER** DANBURY, IA

START TO FINISH: 20 MIN.
MAKES: 4 SERVINGS

- 1 tube (8 ounces) refrigerated crescent rolls
- 1 cup cherry pie filling
- ½ cup confectioners' sugar
- 1 to 2 tablespoons milk

1. Preheat oven to 375°. Unroll crescent dough and separate into four rectangles; place on an ungreased baking sheet. Press perforations to seal. Place ¼ cup pie filling on one half of each rectangle. Fold dough over filling; pinch edges to seal. Bake 10-12 minutes or until golden.

2. Place confectioners' sugar in a small bowl; stir in enough milk to achieve a drizzling consistency. Drizzle over turnovers. Serve warm.

QUICK CHERRY TURNOVERS

CHILI-CHEESE BURGERS

Chili-Cheese Burgers

Instead of putting cheese on the top of burgers, I like to shred and mix it into the meat when shaping the patties. This way, you'll be sure to get a little cheesy goodness in every bite.

—**DEB WILLIAMS** PEORIA, AZ

START TO FINISH: 25 MIN.
MAKES: 4 SERVINGS

- ½ cup shredded cheddar cheese
- 6 tablespoons chili sauce, divided
- 1 tablespoon chili powder
- 1 pound ground beef
- 4 hamburger buns, split
  Lettuce leaves, tomato slices and mayonnaise, optional

1. In a large bowl, combine cheese, 2 tablespoons chili sauce and chili powder. Add beef; mix lightly but thoroughly. Shape into four ½-in. thick patties.

2. Grill burgers, covered, over medium heat or broil 4 in. from heat 4-5 minutes on each side or until a thermometer reads 160°.

3. Serve on buns with remaining chili sauce and, if desired, lettuce, tomato and mayonnaise.

RAVIOLI LASAGNA

Ravioli Lasagna

When people sample this, they think it's a from-scratch recipe. But the lasagna actually starts with frozen ravioli and requires just three other ingredients.

—**PATRICIA SMITH** ASHEBORO, NC

PREP: 25 MIN. • **BAKE:** 40 MIN.
MAKES: 6-8 SERVINGS

- 1 **pound ground beef**
- 1 **jar (28 ounces) spaghetti sauce**
- 1 **package (25 ounces) frozen sausage or cheese ravioli**
- 1½ **cups (6 ounces) shredded part-skim mozzarella cheese**

1. In a large skillet, cook beef over medium heat until no longer pink; drain. In a greased 2½-qt. baking dish, layer a third of the spaghetti sauce, half of the ravioli and beef and ½ cup cheese; repeat layers. Top with remaining sauce and cheese.
2. Cover and bake at 400° for 40-45 minutes or until heated through.

Crumb-Topped Haddock

My delightful fish with a creamy sauce and crispy topping is a breeze to make.

—**DEBBIE SOLT** LEWISTOWN, PA

PREP: 5 MIN. • **BAKE:** 35 MIN.
MAKES: 6 SERVINGS

- 2 **pounds haddock or cod fillets**
- 1 **can (10¾ ounces) condensed cream of shrimp soup, undiluted**
- 1 **teaspoon grated onion**
- 1 **teaspoon Worcestershire sauce**
- 1 **cup crushed butter-flavored crackers (about 25 crackers)**

1. Arrange fillets in a greased 13-in. x 9-in. baking dish. Combine the soup, onion and Worcestershire sauce; pour over fish.
2. Bake, uncovered, at 375° for 20 minutes. Sprinkle with cracker crumbs. Bake 15 minutes longer or until fish flakes easily with a fork.
PER SERVING *248 cal., 7 g fat (2 g sat. fat), 94 mg chol., 631 mg sodium, 14 g carb., trace fiber, 31 g pro.* **Diabetic Exchanges:** *4 lean meat, 1 starch, 1 fat.*

VEGETABLE BEEF PIE

Vegetable Beef Pie

On my busiest days, I rely on easy recipes that also taste great. My potpie recipe originally called for a homemade crust, but I use refrigerated crust to save time.

—**VALORIE HALL WALKER** BRADLEY, SC

PREP: 15 MIN. • **BAKE:** 30 MIN.
MAKES: 4-6 SERVINGS

- **Pastry for double-crust pie (9 inches)**
- 1 **pound ground beef, cooked and drained**
- 1 **can (15 ounces) mixed vegetables, drained or 1½ cups frozen mixed vegetables**
- 1 **can (10¾ ounces) condensed cream of onion soup, undiluted**
- ½ **teaspoon pepper**

1. Line a 9-in. pie plate with bottom pastry; trim pastry even with edge. In a large bowl, combine beef, vegetables, soup and pepper. Spoon into crust.
2. Roll out the remaining pastry to fit top of pie. Place over filling; trim, seal and flute edges. Cut slits in top. Bake at 400° for 30-35 minutes or until crust is golden brown.

Breaded Pork Chops

I think this favorite came from my maternal grandmother. We kids had a birthday tradition in our family where we got to choose the dinner and Mom would prepare it. I always chose these pork chops as part of my dinner.

—**DEBORAH AMRINE** FORT MYERS, FL

START TO FINISH: 20 MIN.
MAKES: 6 SERVINGS

- 1 **egg, lightly beaten**
- ½ **cup 2% milk**
- 1½ **cups crushed saltine crackers**
- 6 **boneless pork loin chops (1-inch thick and 4 ounces each)**
- ¼ **cup canola oil**

1. In a shallow bowl, combine the egg and milk. Place cracker crumbs in another shallow bowl. Dip each pork chop in egg mixture, then coat with cracker crumbs, patting to make a thick coating.
2. In a large skillet, cook chops in oil for 4-5 minutes on each side or until a thermometer reads 145°. Let meat stand for 5 minutes before serving.

BREADED PORK CHOPS

Bacon-Topped
Mini Meat Loaves
PAGE 69

Shop Once... Eat All Week

Our Test Kitchen pros take the work out of meal planning with three weeks' worth of tasty dinners and handy shopping lists. You'll be out of the grocery store (and the kitchen) fast, and your family will love the variety.

**Meatball Hoagies
with Seasoned Fries**
PAGE 75

Chicken Salad Pizzas
PAGE 68

**Sweet & Spicy
Glazed Salmon**
PAGE 70

WEEK ONE

Shopping List
Choose recipes from pp. 66-69, then check to see which staples you already have. Shop for what you need with this handy list.

PRODUCE
☐ **arugula** _____ (amount you need)
☐ **garlic** _____
☐ **medium carrots** _____
☐ **medium green peppers** _____
☐ **medium red onions** _____
☐ **medium yellow pepper** _____

MEAT & SEAFOOD
☐ **bacon** _____
☐ **bone-in pork loin chops** _____
☐ **boneless skinless chicken breasts** _____
☐ **ground beef** _____
☐ **orange roughy fillets** _____

DAIRY & REFRIGERATED
☐ **butter** _____
☐ **cream cheese** _____
☐ **Dijon mustard** _____
☐ **eggs** _____
☐ **ketchup** _____
☐ **mayonnaise** _____
☐ **milk** _____
☐ **Parmesan cheese** _____
☐ **shredded cheddar cheese** _____
☐ **Worcestershire sauce** _____

FROZEN
☐ **frozen broccoli-cauliflower blend** _____

PACKAGED
☐ **butter-flavored crackers** _____
☐ **chicken broth** _____
☐ **dry red wine** _____
☐ **finely chopped walnuts** _____
☐ **fire-roasted diced tomatoes** _____
☐ **honey** _____
☐ **instant rice** _____
☐ **Italian salad dressing mix** _____
☐ **Lipton savory herb with garlic soup mix** _____
☐ **mandarin oranges** _____
☐ **olive oil** _____
☐ **penne pasta** _____
☐ **pinto beans** _____
☐ **whole pita bread** _____

SPICES/SEASONINGS
☐ **all-purpose flour** _____
☐ **cayenne pepper** _____
☐ **chili powder** _____
☐ **dill weed** _____
☐ **garlic powder** _____
☐ **ground cumin** _____
☐ **Italian seasoning** _____
☐ **lemon-pepper seasoning** _____
☐ **pepper** _____
☐ **salt** _____
☐ **seasoned salt** _____

BAKED ORANGE ROUGHY AND RICE

Baked Orange Roughy and Rice
It might sound too good to be true, but we promise you this delectable fish dinner will dirty just one dish. Your family will line up to dig in once they see the results.
—**TASTE OF HOME TEST KITCHEN**

PREP: 10 MIN. • **BAKE:** 30 MIN. • **MAKES:** 4 SERVINGS

- 2 cups uncooked instant rice
- 1 package (16 ounces) frozen broccoli-cauliflower blend, thawed
- 4 orange roughy fillets (6 ounces each)
- 1 can (14½ ounces) chicken broth
- 1 can (14½ ounces) fire-roasted diced tomatoes, undrained
- 1 teaspoon garlic powder
- 1 teaspoon lemon-pepper seasoning
- ¼ to ½ teaspoon cayenne pepper
- ½ cup shredded cheddar cheese

1. Place rice in a greased 13-in. x 9-in. baking dish. Layer with the vegetables and fish. Pour the broth and tomatoes over the top; sprinkle with seasonings.

2. Cover and bake at 375° for 25-30 minutes or until fish flakes easily with a fork and rice is tender. Sprinkle with cheese; bake 5 minutes longer or until cheese is melted.

Walnut-Breaded Chops with Honey Mustard Sauce

A crispy, golden brown coating keeps these pork chops tender and juicy.

—TASTE OF HOME TEST KITCHEN

PREP: 20 MIN. • **COOK:** 15 MIN.
MAKES: 4 SERVINGS

- ¼ cup all-purpose flour
- 2 eggs, beaten
- ½ cup crushed butter-flavored crackers (about 12 crackers)
- ½ cup finely chopped walnuts
- 1 envelope Lipton savory herb with garlic soup mix
- 4 bone-in pork loin chops (8 ounces each)
- 1 tablespoon plus 1 teaspoon butter, divided
- 1 pound medium carrots, sliced
- ¼ teaspoon dill weed
  Dash salt
- 1 teaspoon plus 2 tablespoons Dijon mustard, divided
- 1 teaspoon plus 1 tablespoon honey, divided
- ½ cup mayonnaise

1. Place flour and eggs in separate shallow bowls. Combine the crackers, walnuts and soup mix in another shallow bowl. Dip pork chops in the flour, eggs, then cracker mixture.

2. Cook chops in 1 tablespoon butter in a large skillet over medium heat for 5-7 minutes on each side or until a thermometer reads 145°.

3. Meanwhile, place 1 in. of water and carrots in a small saucepan. Bring to a boil. Reduce heat; cover and simmer for 5-8 minutes or until tender. Drain. Add the dill, salt, 1 teaspoon mustard, 1 teaspoon honey and remaining butter. Cook and stir over low heat until well coated.

4. Combine mayonnaise and the remaining mustard and honey; serve with pork chops and carrots.

WALNUT-BREADED CHOPS WITH HONEY MUSTARD SAUCE

CHICKEN PENNE ALFREDO

FAST FIX >

Chicken Penne Alfredo

Cream cheese and cheddar create a rich and silky sauce for chicken and penne pasta with veggies.

—TASTE OF HOME TEST KITCHEN

START TO FINISH: 30 MIN.
MAKES: 5 SERVINGS

- 2 cups uncooked penne pasta
- 1 package (16 ounces) frozen broccoli-cauliflower blend
- 1 pound boneless skinless chicken breasts, cut into 1-inch cubes
- 1 tablespoon butter
- 1 package (8 ounces) cream cheese, cubed
- 1 cup (4 ounces) shredded cheddar cheese
- 1 cup chicken broth
- 1 envelope Lipton savory herb with garlic soup mix

1. Cook pasta according to the package directions in a Dutch oven, adding the vegetables during the last 6 minutes of cooking.

2. Meanwhile, cook chicken in butter in a large skillet until no longer pink. Add the cheeses, broth and soup mix; cook and stir until cheeses are melted. Drain pasta and vegetables; add to chicken mixture and toss to coat.

SOUTHWEST GYROS

FAST FIX

Southwest Gyros

These fun, easy sandwiches with bold Southwestern flavors are perfect for a casual dinner with friends.
—**TASTE OF HOME TEST KITCHEN**

START TO FINISH: 25 MIN.
MAKES: 5 SERVINGS

- 1 **pound ground beef**
- 1 **medium green pepper, chopped**
- 1 **can (15 ounces) pinto beans, rinsed and drained**
- 1 **can (14½ ounces) fire-roasted diced tomatoes, undrained**
- ¼ **cup water**
- 1 **tablespoon chili powder**
- 2 **teaspoons ground cumin**
- ½ **to 1 teaspoon garlic powder**
- ½ **cup mayonnaise**
- ¾ **teaspoon Italian salad dressing mix**
- 5 **whole pita breads, warmed**
- 1 **cup fresh arugula or baby spinach**
- ⅔ **cup shredded cheddar cheese**

1. Cook beef and pepper in a large skillet over medium heat until meat is no longer pink; drain. Stir in the beans, tomatoes, water, chili powder, cumin and garlic powder. Bring to a boil. Reduce heat; simmer, uncovered, for 2-3 minutes or until thickened.

2. Combine mayonnaise and salad dressing mix in a small bowl. Spoon beef mixture over pita breads; top with arugula, cheddar cheese and the mayonnaise mixture.

FAST FIX

Chicken Salad Pizzas

Sometimes it just takes a little creative spin to get the kids to gobble up an otherwise grown-up dish. Call this goorgeous piled-high salad by a pizza name, and you won't have to worry about having leftovers.
—**TASTE OF HOME TEST KITCHEN**

START TO FINISH: 30 MIN.
MAKES: 5 SERVINGS

- 5 **ounces cream cheese, softened**
- ⅓ **cup mayonnaise**
- ½ **teaspoon plus ⅛ teaspoon garlic powder, divided**
- 1 **pound boneless skinless chicken breasts, cubed**
- 1 **medium sweet yellow pepper, chopped**
- 1 **medium green pepper, chopped**
- 1 **medium red onion, halved and sliced**
- ¼ **teaspoon salt**
- 2 **teaspoons olive oil**
- 5 **whole pita breads, warmed**
- 1⅔ **cups fresh arugula or baby spinach**
- 1 **can (11 ounces) mandarin oranges, drained**
- 4 **bacon strips, cooked and crumbled**
- ⅔ **cup shredded cheddar cheese**

1. Combine the cream cheese, mayonnaise and ½ teaspoon garlic powder in a small bowl; set aside.

2. Cook chicken, peppers, onion, salt and remaining garlic powder in oil in a large skillet over medium heat until chicken is no longer pink. Spread cream cheese mixture over pita breads; top with arugula, chicken mixture and oranges. Sprinkle with bacon and cheddar cheese.

CHICKEN SALAD PIZZA

BACON-TOPPED MINI MEAT LOAVES

FAST FIX ▸

Bacon-Topped Mini Meat Loaves

Here's all the delicious savory taste of Mom's meat loaf in a single-serving size.

—TASTE OF HOME TEST KITCHEN

START TO FINISH: 30 MIN.
MAKES: 5 SERVINGS

- 5 bacon strips
- 1 egg, lightly beaten
- ⅓ cup 2% milk
- 2 tablespoons Worcestershire sauce
- 1 cup shredded carrots
- 1 medium green pepper, chopped
- ¾ cup crushed butter-flavored crackers
- ¾ cup shredded cheddar cheese, divided
- 1 medium red onion, chopped
- ½ teaspoon seasoned salt
- ¼ teaspoon pepper
- ⅛ teaspoon cayenne pepper
- 1½ pounds ground beef
- ¼ cup ketchup

1. Cook bacon in a large skillet over medium heat until partially cooked but not crisp. Drain on a paper towel; set aside.
2. Combine egg, milk, Worcestershire sauce, carrots, green pepper, crackers, ½ cup cheese, onion and seasonings in a large bowl. Crumble beef over mixture and mix well.
3. Shape into five loaves. Arrange around the edge of a microwave-safe deep-dish pie plate; top each with a strip of bacon.
4. Cover and microwave on high for 8-10 minutes or until meat is no longer pink and a meat thermometer reads 160°. Spread ketchup over tops and sprinkle with remaining cheese. Let stand for 5 minutes.
NOTE *This recipe was tested in a 1,100-watt microwave.*

FAST FIX ▸

Italian Chops With Pasta

Thanks to an Italian makeover, this pork is perfection in a pan. Tender chops, red wine, fire-roasted tomatoes and penne pasta combine to create a luscious meal in mere minutes.

—TASTE OF HOME TEST KITCHEN

START TO FINISH: 30 MIN.
MAKES: 4 SERVINGS

- 4 bone-in pork loin chops (8 ounces each)
- ½ teaspoon salt
- ½ teaspoon pepper
- 1 tablespoon olive oil
- 1 medium green pepper, chopped
- 1 medium red onion, chopped
- 3 garlic cloves, minced
- ⅓ cup dry red wine or chicken broth
- 2 cans (14½ ounces each) fire-roasted diced tomatoes, undrained
- 1½ teaspoons Italian seasoning
   Hot cooked penne pasta
   Shredded Parmesan cheese, optional

1. Sprinkle pork chops with salt and pepper. Brown chops in oil in a large skillet. Remove and keep warm. Saute green pepper and onion in the same skillet until crisp-tender. Add garlic; cook 1 minute longer.
2. Add wine, stirring to loosen browned bits from pan. Bring to a boil; cook until liquid is almost evaporated. Add tomatoes and Italian seasoning. Cook and stir for 2-3 minutes or until sauce is slightly thickened.
3. Return chops to the skillet. Cover and simmer for 3-5 minutes or until a thermometer reads 145°. Let stand for 5 minutes before serving. Serve with pasta. Sprinkle with cheese if desired.

ITALIAN CHOPS WITH PASTA

WEEK **TWO**

Pantry List

Choose recipes from pp. 70–73, then check to see which staples you already have. Shop for what you need with this handy list.

PRODUCE
- ☐ **fresh baby spinach** _____ (amount you need)
- ☐ **garlic cloves** _____
- ☐ **medium onion** _____
- ☐ **medium sweet red pepper** _____
- ☐ **medium sweet yellow pepper** _____
- ☐ **sliced fresh mushrooms** _____
- ☐ **small red potatoes** _____

MEAT & SEAFOOD
- ☐ **Italian turkey sausage links** _____
- ☐ **pork tenderloins** _____
- ☐ **salmon fillets** _____

DAIRY & REFRIGERATED
- ☐ **butter** _____
- ☐ **heavy whipping cream** _____
- ☐ **shredded Mexican cheese blend** _____

FROZEN
- ☐ **frozen broccoli, carrots and water chestnuts** _____
- ☐ **frozen Italian vegetables** _____
- ☐ **frozen peas** _____

PACKAGED
- ☐ **all-purpose flour** _____
- ☐ **brown sugar** _____
- ☐ **chicken broth** _____
- ☐ **chipotle peppers in adobo sauce** _____
- ☐ **cornstarch** _____
- ☐ **diced tomatoes with mild green chilies** _____
- ☐ **Dijon mustard** _____
- ☐ **garden-style spaghetti sauce** _____
- ☐ **instant rice** _____
- ☐ **olive oil** _____
- ☐ **orzo pasta** _____
- ☐ **reduced-sodium soy sauce** _____
- ☐ **salsa** _____
- ☐ **sesame oil** _____
- ☐ **thin spaghetti** _____
- ☐ **tomato sauce** _____
- ☐ **white kidney or cannellini beans** _____

SPICES/SEASONINGS
- ☐ **chili powder** _____
- ☐ **crushed red pepper flakes** _____
- ☐ **dried marjoram** _____
- ☐ **dried oregano** _____
- ☐ **dried thyme** _____
- ☐ **garlic salt** _____
- ☐ **ground cumin** _____
- ☐ **ground ginger** _____
- ☐ **paprika** _____
- ☐ **pepper** _____
- ☐ **salt** _____

FAST FIX ▸

Sweet & Spicy Glazed Salmon

There's a bit of magic going on here: Salmon baked with a glaze of brown sugar, mustard, soy sauce and ginger creates a sweet and zesty entree. This recipe rewards your family with a little something special.

—TASTE OF HOME TEST KITCHEN

START TO FINISH: 30 MIN. • **MAKES:** 4 SERVINGS

- ¼ cup brown sugar
- 3 tablespoons Dijon mustard
- 2 tablespoons reduced-sodium soy sauce
- 1 teaspoon paprika
- ¼ teaspoon ground ginger
- ¼ teaspoon sesame oil
- 4 salmon fillets (6 ounces each)
- ½ teaspoon pepper
- ¼ teaspoon salt

1. Combine the brown sugar, mustard, soy sauce, paprika, ginger and oil in a small saucepan. Bring to a boil. Cook and stir until brown sugar is dissolved.

2. Place salmon skin side down on a greased broiler pan. Sprinkle with pepper and salt.

3. Broil 6 in. from the heat for 10-15 minutes or until fish flakes easily with a fork, brushing glaze over salmon during the last 1-2 minutes of cooking.

SWEET & SPICY GLAZED SALMON

SALMON SKILLET

Salmon Skillet

Is there anything salmon can't do? It is high in heart-healthy omega-3 and it lends itself to simple preparation techniques. It also looks beautiful on the dinner table.
—TASTE OF HOME TEST KITCHEN

PREP: 15 MIN. • **COOK:** 20 MIN.
MAKES: 4 SERVINGS

- 1   pound small red potatoes, quartered
- 2   packages (6 ounces each) fresh baby spinach
- ½ cup all-purpose flour
- 2   teaspoons garlic salt, divided
- 2   teaspoons paprika
- ½ teaspoon pepper
- 4   salmon fillets (6 ounces each)
- 3   tablespoons butter, divided
- 1   medium onion, halved and thinly sliced
- 1   can (15 ounces) white kidney or cannellini beans, rinsed and drained
- ¾ cup heavy whipping cream
- ½ teaspoon dried thyme

1. Place potatoes in a Dutch oven and cover with water. Bring to a boil. Reduce heat; cover and cook for 10 minutes or until tender, adding spinach during the last 2 minutes of cooking.
2. Meanwhile, combine the flour, 1 teaspoon garlic salt, paprika, and pepper in a shallow bowl. Coat salmon with flour mixture.

3. Cook salmon in 2 tablespoons butter in a large skillet over medium heat for 3-5 minutes on each side or until fish flakes easily with a fork. Remove and keep warm.
4. Saute onion in remaining butter in the same pan until tender. Add the beans, cream, thyme and remaining garlic salt. Bring to a boil; cook and stir for 2 minutes or until thickened. Drain potatoes and spinach; add to skillet. Serve with salmon.

FAST FIX ▶

Creamy Chipotle Pasta with Sausage

After one taste of the rich and spicy sauce, you'll have this satisfying recipe on your short list.
—TASTE OF HOME TEST KITCHEN

START TO FINISH: 30 MIN.
MAKES: 6 SERVINGS

- 1   pound Italian turkey sausage links, cut into ¾-inch slices
- ½ pound sliced fresh mushrooms
- 1   medium sweet red pepper, chopped
- 2   teaspoons olive oil
- 1   tablespoon brown sugar
- 1   tablespoon minced chipotle pepper in adobo sauce
- 2   teaspoons chili powder
- ¾ teaspoon salt
- ½ teaspoon dried marjoram
- 1½ cups heavy whipping cream
- 1½ cups (6 ounces) shredded Mexican cheese blend, divided
- 2   cups frozen peas
      Hot cooked thin spaghetti

1. Cook sausage in a large skillet over medium heat until no longer pink; drain. Remove and keep warm.
2. Saute mushrooms and red pepper in oil in the same pan until tender. Stir in the brown sugar, chipotle pepper, chili powder, salt and marjoram; cook 1 minute longer.
3. Add cream, stirring to loosen browned bits from pan. Bring to a boil; cook and stir for 2-3 minutes or until slightly thickened. Reduce heat.
4. Add 1 cup cheese; cook and stir until melted. Stir in sausage and peas; heat through. Serve with spaghetti. Sprinkle with remaining cheese.

CREAMY CHIPOTLE PASTA WITH SAUSAGE

PORK AND VEGETABLE LO MEIN

FAST FIX >

Hearty Sausage and Rice Skillet

At the end of the day, who wants a stack of dishes to wash? That's why we love this entree: It cooks in one skillet and all clean their plates!

—TASTE OF HOME TEST KITCHEN

START TO FINISH: 30 MIN.
MAKES: 5 SERVINGS

- 1 pound Italian turkey sausage links, cut into ½-inch slices
- ½ pound sliced fresh mushrooms
- 1 medium sweet yellow pepper, chopped
- 1 medium onion, chopped
- 2 teaspoons olive oil
- 1 can (14½ ounces) diced tomatoes with mild green chilies, undrained
- 2 cups fresh baby spinach, coarsely chopped
- 1½ cups water
- 1 can (8 ounces) tomato sauce
- 1 teaspoon dried oregano
- 1 teaspoon chili powder
- ½ teaspoon garlic salt
- 2 cups uncooked instant rice

1. Cook sausage in a Dutch oven over medium heat until no longer pink; drain. Remove and keep warm. Saute the mushrooms, pepper and onion in oil in the same pan until tender.
2. Return sausage to pan. Stir in the tomatoes, spinach, water, tomato sauce and seasonings.
3. Bring to a boil; cook for 2 minutes. Stir in rice. Remove from the heat; cover and let stand for 5-7 minutes or until rice is tender. Fluff with a fork.

HEARTY SAUSAGE AND RICE SKILLET

Pork and Vegetable Lo Mein

Traditional Asian flavors blend well together in this quick dinner the whole family will enjoy. The homemade sauce is simple to make.

—TASTE OF HOME TEST KITCHEN

PREP: 20 MIN. • **COOK:** 15 MIN.
MAKES: 5 SERVINGS

- 6 ounces uncooked thin spaghetti
- 1 tablespoon cornstarch
- 1¾ cups chicken broth
- ⅓ cup reduced-sodium soy sauce
- 2 tablespoons brown sugar
- 1 teaspoon ground ginger
- ¼ teaspoon salt
- ¼ teaspoon crushed red pepper flakes, optional
- 1 pork tenderloin (1 pound), halved lengthwise and thinly sliced
- 2 teaspoons sesame oil
- 1 medium onion, chopped
- 1 package (16 ounces) frozen broccoli, carrots and water chestnuts
- 1 cup frozen peas

1. Cook spaghetti according to package directions. Meanwhile, combine the cornstarch, broth, soy sauce, brown sugar, ginger and salt in a small bowl until smooth. Add pepper flakes if desired; set aside.
2. Stir-fry pork in oil in a large skillet or wok for 4-6 minutes or until browned. Remove with a slotted spoon; keep warm. Stir-fry onion for 2 minutes. Add broccoli mixture; stir-fry 4-5 minutes longer or until vegetables are crisp-tender.
3. Stir cornstarch mixture and add to the pan. Stir in peas. Bring to a boil; cook and stir for 3-4 minutes or until thickened. Drain spaghetti. Add pork and spaghetti to the pan; heat through.

VEGETABLE ORZO SOUP

2 garlic cloves, minced
2 cups fresh baby spinach, coarsely chopped
1 tablespoon minced chipotle pepper in adobo sauce
1 teaspoon ground cumin
2 pork tenderloins (1 pound each)
1 teaspoon salt
½ teaspoon pepper
2 cups (8 ounces) shredded Mexican cheese blend
Hot cooked rice and salsa

1. Saute red pepper in oil in a large skillet until tender. Add garlic and cook 1 minute longer. Add the spinach, chipotle pepper and cumin; cook until spinach is wilted.
2. Make a lengthwise slit down center of each tenderloin to within ½ in. of bottom. Open tenderloins so they lie flat; cover with plastic wrap. Flatten to ¼-in. thickness; remove plastic.
3. Sprinkle salt and pepper over pork; top with spinach mixture and cheese.
4. Close tenderloins; tie with kitchen string and secure ends with toothpicks. Place in a shallow baking pan.
5. Bake, uncovered, at 425° for 20-25 minutes or until a thermometer inserted in pork reads 145°. Let stand for 5 minutes before slicing. Discard string and toothpicks. Serve with rice and salsa.

Vegetable Orzo Soup

This hearty soup is a perfect way to straddle winter and spring. Beans, red potatoes and orzo fortify against the cold, while fresh and frozen vegetables hint at the warmer, sunnier days to come.
—TASTE OF HOME TEST KITCHEN

PREP: 15 MIN. • **COOK:** 25 MIN.
MAKES: 6 SERVINGS (2 QUARTS)

1 medium sweet yellow pepper, chopped
1 medium onion, chopped
2 teaspoons olive oil
3 garlic cloves, minced
1 jar (24 ounces) garden-style spaghetti sauce
1 package (16 ounces) frozen Italian vegetables
1 can (15 ounces) white kidney or cannellini beans, rinsed and drained
1 can (14½ ounces) chicken broth
½ pound small red potatoes, quartered
1 cup water
⅓ cup uncooked orzo pasta
½ teaspoon dried marjoram
½ teaspoon dried thyme

Saute pepper and onion in oil in a Dutch oven until tender. Add garlic; cook 1 minute longer. Stir in the remaining ingredients. Bring to a boil. Reduce heat; cover and simmer for 15-20 minutes or until potatoes and pasta are tender.

Southwest Stuffed Pork Tenderloin

Sight, smell, taste—your senses will thank you for going Southwestern with this festive entree.
—TASTE OF HOME TEST KITCHEN

PREP: 30 MIN. • **BAKE:** 20 MIN.
MAKES: 6 SERVINGS

1 medium sweet red pepper, chopped
2 teaspoons olive oil

SOUTHWEST STUFFED PORK TENDERLOIN

WEEK **THREE**

||||||||||||||||||||||||||||||||||||||||||||||||||||||||||||||||||||||||

Pantry List

Choose recipes from pages 74-77, then check to see which staples you already have. Shop for what you need with this handy list.

PRODUCE
- ☐ asparagus _____ (amount you need)
- ☐ carrots _____
- ☐ garlic _____
- ☐ green onions _____
- ☐ lettuce leaves _____
- ☐ limes _____
- ☐ onions _____
- ☐ plum tomatoes _____
- ☐ sliced fresh mushrooms _____
- ☐ sweet red pepper _____

MEAT & SEAFOOD
- ☐ bacon _____
- ☐ pork tenderloins _____
- ☐ sliced deli ham _____
- ☐ turkey breast cutlets _____
- ☐ uncooked medium shrimp _____

DAIRY & REFRIGERATED
- ☐ butter _____
- ☐ Dijon-mayonnaise blend _____
- ☐ grated Romano cheese _____
- ☐ milk _____
- ☐ sliced provolone cheese _____

FROZEN
- ☐ frozen fully cooked Italian meatballs _____
- ☐ frozen steak fries _____

PACKAGED
- ☐ angel hair pasta _____
- ☐ apricot preserves _____
- ☐ barbecue sauce _____
- ☐ chicken broth _____
- ☐ chopped pecans _____
- ☐ cornstarch _____
- ☐ hoagie buns _____
- ☐ unsweetened pineapple chunks _____

SPICES/SEASONINGS
- ☐ celery salt _____
- ☐ dill weed _____
- ☐ dried oregano _____
- ☐ ground cumin _____
- ☐ Italian seasoning _____
- ☐ olive oil _____
- ☐ pepper _____
- ☐ poultry seasoning _____
- ☐ salt _____
- ☐ seasoned salt _____

Turkey Club Roulades

Weeknights turn elegant when these short-prep roulades are on the menu. Not a fan of turkey? Substitute lightly pounded chicken breasts.
—TASTE OF HOME TEST KITCHEN

PREP: 20 MIN. • **COOK:** 15 MIN. • **MAKES:** 8 SERVINGS

- ¾ pound fresh asparagus, trimmed
- 8 turkey breast cutlets (about 1 pound)
- 1 tablespoon Dijon-mayonnaise blend
- 8 slices deli ham
- 8 slices provolone cheese
- ½ teaspoon poultry seasoning
- ½ teaspoon pepper
- 8 bacon strips

SAUCE
- ⅔ cup Dijon-mayonnaise blend
- 4 teaspoons 2% milk
- ¼ teaspoon poultry seasoning

1. Bring 4 cups water to a boil in a large saucepan. Add asparagus; cook, uncovered, for 3 minutes or until crisp-tender. Drain and immediately place asparagus in ice water. Drain and pat dry. Set aside.

2. Spread turkey with Dijon-mayonnaise. Layer with ham, cheese and asparagus. Sprinkle with poultry seasoning and pepper. Roll up tightly and wrap with bacon.

3. Cook roulades in a large skillet over medium-high heat for 12-15 minutes, turning occasionally, or until bacon is crisp and turkey is no longer pink. Combine sauce ingredients; serve with roulades.

TURKEY CLUB ROULADES

PECAN TURKEY CUTLETS WITH DILLED CARROTS

Meatball Hoagies with Seasoned Fries

Try this fresh take on a classic combo, and you'll never stop by a delicatessen again! Apricot barbecue sauce and bacon give the sandwich a sweet-savory twist.

—TASTE OF HOME TEST KITCHEN

START TO FINISH: 30 MIN.
MAKES: 4 SERVINGS

- 4 cups frozen steak fries
- 1 tablespoon olive oil
- ½ teaspoon seasoned salt
- ¼ teaspoon celery salt
- 1 package (12 ounces) frozen fully cooked Italian meatballs, thawed
- 2 cups barbecue sauce
- ¼ cup apricot preserves
- 4 hoagie buns, split and toasted
- 4 large lettuce leaves
- 3 plum tomatoes, sliced
- 8 ready-to-serve fully cooked bacon strips, warmed
- 8 slices provolone cheese

1. Place steak fries in a single layer in a 15-in. x 10-in. x 1-in. baking pan. Drizzle with oil; sprinkle with seasonings. Toss to coat. Bake according to package directions.
2. Meanwhile, place the meatballs, barbecue sauce and preserves in a large saucepan. Bring to a boil over medium heat; cook and stir for 6-8 minutes or until heated through.
3. Layer the bun bottoms with lettuce, tomatoes, bacon, meatball mixture and cheese; replace bun tops. Serve with fries.

MEATBALL HOAGIES WITH SEASONED FRIES

Pecan Turkey Cutlets with Dilled Carrots

The recipe may look long, but don't let it fool you. It is easier than it appears and it uses everyday ingredients and staples you have on hand.

—TASTE OF HOME TEST KITCHEN

START TO FINISH: 30 MIN.
MAKES: 4 SERVINGS

- ¾ cup chopped pecans
- ½ cup grated Romano cheese
- ½ teaspoon seasoned salt
- ½ teaspoon dill weed
- 1 package (17.6 ounces) turkey breast cutlets
- 3 tablespoons butter, divided
- 2 garlic cloves, minced
- 1 teaspoon cornstarch
- ½ cup chicken broth
- 2 tablespoons lime juice
- ½ teaspoon grated lime peel

CARROTS
- 1½ pounds sliced fresh carrots
- 1½ teaspoons butter
- ¾ teaspoon grated lime peel
- ½ teaspoon dill weed
- ¼ teaspoon seasoned salt

1. Place pecans in a food processor; cover and process until ground. Combine the pecans, cheese, seasoned salt and dill in a shallow bowl. Coat turkey with pecan mixture.
2. In a large skillet over medium heat, cook turkey in batches in 1 tablespoon butter for 3-4 minutes on each side or until no longer pink; remove and keep warm. Cook garlic in remaining butter in the same pan.
3. Combine cornstarch, broth and lime juice until blended; gradually add to pan, stirring to loosen browned bits. Bring to a boil; cook and stir 2 minutes or until thickened. Stir in lime peel. Remove from the heat; keep warm.
4. Meanwhile, place 1 in. of water in a small saucepan; add carrots. Bring to a boil. Reduce heat; cover and simmer for 7-9 minutes or until crisp-tender. Drain. Stir in the butter, lime peel, dill and seasoned salt. Serve with turkey and sauce.

GARLIC SHRIMP & MUSHROOM PASTA

FAST FIX

Garlic Shrimp & Mushroom Pasta

Effortless and delicious. These are the qualities we look for in Monday-to-Friday meals—such as this great dish. The lightly coated pasta and veggie mixture tastes like it came from a restaurant, but costs just a few dollars per serving.

—TASTE OF HOME TEST KITCHEN

START TO FINISH: 30 MIN.
MAKES: 5 SERVINGS

- 8 ounces uncooked angel hair pasta
- ½ pound sliced fresh mushrooms
- 1 medium onion, chopped
- ⅓ cup olive oil
- 4 garlic cloves, minced
- 1 pound uncooked medium shrimp, peeled and deveined
- ½ cup chicken broth
- 1 tablespoon Italian seasoning
- ½ teaspoon salt
- ¼ teaspoon pepper
- 2 plum tomatoes, chopped
- ½ cup grated Romano cheese, divided
- 1 tablespoon butter

1. Cook pasta according to package directions. Meanwhile, saute mushrooms and onion in oil in a large skillet until tender. Add the garlic; cook 1 minute longer.

2. Add the shrimp, broth and seasonings. Bring to a boil. Reduce heat; cook and stir for 4-5 minutes or until sauce is slightly thickened and shrimp turn pink.

3. Stir in the tomatoes, ¼ cup cheese and butter. Drain pasta; toss with shrimp mixture. Sprinkle with remaining cheese.

Grilled Pineapple Pork & Vegetables

Celebrate spring with a tasty grilled dinner. The pork takes just an hour to marinate, so you'll enjoy a little hands-free time with this carefree meal.

—TASTE OF HOME TEST KITCHEN

PREP: 25 MIN. + MARINATING
GRILL: 15 MIN. • **MAKES:** 5 SERVINGS

- 1 can (8 ounces) unsweetened pineapple chunks, undrained
- ¼ cup olive oil, divided
- 2 garlic cloves, peeled and halved
- 2 teaspoons ground cumin
- 2 teaspoons dried oregano
- ¾ teaspoon pepper, divided
- ¾ teaspoon salt, divided
- 2 pounds pork tenderloin, cut into ¾-inch slices
- 1 pound fresh asparagus, trimmed
- 4 medium carrots, halved lengthwise
- 1 large sweet red pepper, halved
- 1 bunch green onions, trimmed

1. Place the pineapple, 2 tablespoons oil, garlic, cumin, oregano, ½ teaspoon pepper and ¼ teaspoon salt in a blender; cover and process until blended. Place in a large resealable plastic bag; add pork. Seal bag and turn to coat; refrigerate 1 hour.

2. Drain pork and discard the marinade. Moisten a paper towel with cooking oil; using long-handled tongs, lightly coat the grill rack. Grill, uncovered, over medium heat for 3-4 minutes on each side or until a thermometer reads 145°. Let stand for 5 minutes before serving.

3. Place vegetables in a grill wok or basket. Brush with remaining oil; sprinkle with remaining salt and pepper.

4. Grill, uncovered, over medium heat for 6-8 minutes or until tender, stirring frequently. Cut vegetables into 2-in. pieces. Serve with pork.

NOTE *If you do not have a grill wok or basket, use a disposable foil pan. Poke holes in the bottom of the pan with a meat fork to allow liquid to drain.*

GRILLED PINEAPPLE PORK & VEGETABLES

**Richard Devore's
Cinnamon Applesauce Pancakes**
PAGE 81

Breakfast & Brunch Favorites

Rise and shine with the eye-opening specialties in this chapter. From hearty entrees to tempting treats and refreshing beverages, you'll find the fixings to make any day bright.

Lynne Dieterle's Goat Cheese Omelet
PAGE 82

Sonya Labbe's Creamy Berry Smoothies
PAGE 88

Marlene Neideigh's Sausage Cheese Biscuits
PAGE 91

STEAK & MUSHROOM
BREAKFAST HASH

FAST FIX

Steak & Mushroom Breakfast Hash

We call this savory dish a breakfast hash. But it's so loaded with delectable veggies and cheese, it's a meal we bet your family will love at any time of the day.

—TASTE OF HOME TEST KITCHEN

START TO FINISH: 30 MIN.
MAKES: 4 SERVINGS

- 4 **medium potatoes, cubed**
- ½ **cup water**
- ½ **pound sliced fresh mushrooms**
- 1 **medium zucchini, quartered and sliced**
- 2 **tablespoons butter, divided**
- ⅔ **cup beef broth**
- 1 **tablespoon Dijon mustard**
- ¾ **teaspoon dried rosemary, crushed**
- 6 **ounces cooked sirloin steak, thinly sliced and cut into 1-inch pieces**
- 4 **eggs**
- ½ **cup shredded cheddar cheese**
  Coarsely ground pepper

1. Place potatoes and water in a microwave-safe dish. Cover and microwave on high for 9 minutes or until tender. Meanwhile, saute mushrooms and zucchini in 1 tablespoon butter in a large skillet until crisp-tender. Drain potatoes and add to the skillet. Stir in broth, mustard and rosemary. Bring to a boil. Reduce heat; simmer, uncovered, for 3 minutes. Add steak; heat through.
2. Fry eggs in remaining butter in another skillet as desired. Serve with hash; sprinkle with cheese and pepper.

EAT SMART **5 INGREDIENTS**

Chunky Peach Spread

Here's a fruit spread that captures the taste of late summer. It's low in sugar and not overly sweet, allowing the fresh peach flavor to shine through.

—REBECCA BAIRD SALT LAKE CITY, UT

PREP: 20 MIN. • **COOK:** 10 MIN. + COOLING
MAKES: ABOUT 3½ CUPS

- 7 **medium peaches (2 to 2½ pounds)**
- 1 **envelope unflavored gelatin**
- ¼ **cup cold water**
- ⅓ **cup sugar**
- 1 **tablespoon lemon juice**

1. Fill a large saucepan two-thirds full with water; bring to a boil. Cut a shallow "X" on the bottom of each peach. Using tongs, place peaches, a few at a time, in boiling water for 30-60 seconds or just until skin at the "X" begins to loosen. Remove peaches and immediately drop into ice water. Pull off skins with tip of a knife; discard skins. Chop peaches.
2. In a small bowl, sprinkle gelatin over cold water; let stand 1 minute. Meanwhile, in a large saucepan, combine peaches, sugar and lemon juice; bring to a boil. Mash peaches. Reduce heat; simmer, uncovered, 5 minutes. Add gelatin mixture; cook 1 minute longer, stirring until gelatin is completely dissolved. Cool 10 minutes.
3. Pour into jars. Refrigerate, covered, up to 3 weeks.

PER (2-TABLESPOON) SERVING *21 cal., trace fat (0 sat. fat), 0 chol., 1 mg sodium, 5 g carb., trace fiber, trace pro.* **Diabetic Exchange:** *Free food.*

Quick Blueberry French Toast

Sit down to hot-off-the-griddle stuffed French toast and fresh blueberry sauce in just 30 minutes. The delicious filling features rich cream cheese, blueberry preserves and maple syrup. It's out of this world!

—TASTE OF HOME TEST KITCHEN

START TO FINISH: 30 MIN.
MAKES: 8 SERVINGS (1¾ CUPS SAUCE)

- 1 package (8 ounces) cream cheese, softened
- ¼ cup maple syrup, divided
- 2 tablespoons blueberry preserves
- 16 slices French bread (½ inch thick)
- 2 eggs
- 1 cup 2% milk
- 2 tablespoons all-purpose flour
- 2 teaspoons vanilla extract
- ¼ teaspoon salt

SAUCE
- 1 cup sugar
- 1 cup water
- 2 tablespoons cornstarch
- 1 cup fresh or frozen blueberries
- 1 tablespoon butter

1. Beat cream cheese, 2 tablespoons syrup and preserves in a small bowl. Spread over eight slices of bread; top with remaining bread.
2. Whisk the eggs, milk, flour, vanilla, salt and remaining syrup in a shallow bowl. Dip both sides of sandwiches into egg mixture. Cook on a greased hot griddle until golden brown on both sides.
3. Combine the sugar, water and cornstarch until smooth in a small saucepan. Bring to a boil over medium heat; cook and stir for 3 minutes or until thickened. Stir in blueberries; bring to a boil. Reduce heat and simmer for 8-10 minutes or until berries burst. Remove from heat; stir in butter. Serve with French toast.

CINNAMON APPLESAUCE PANCAKES

QUICK BLUEBERRY FRENCH TOAST

Cinnamon Applesauce Pancakes

These fluffy, tender pancakes are so good, you just might skip the syrup. They were created for Christmas morning but have since wowed folks at church breakfasts as well as family and friends. The cinnamon is a delightful touch.

—RICHARD DEVORE GIBSONBURG, OH

START TO FINISH: 20 MIN.
MAKES: 3 SERVINGS

- 1 cup complete buttermilk pancake mix
- 1 teaspoon ground cinnamon
- 1 cup chunky cinnamon applesauce
- ¼ cup water
  Maple syrup and butter

1. Combine pancake mix and cinnamon. Add applesauce and water; stir just until moistened.
2. Pour batter by ¼ cupfuls onto a greased hot griddle; turn when bubbles form on top. Cook until the second side is golden brown. Serve with syrup and butter.
PER SERVING *218 cal., 2 g fat (trace sat. fat), 0 chol., 649 mg sodium, 50 g carb., 2 g fiber, 3 g pro.*

EAT SMART FAST FIX

Goat Cheese Omelet

START TO FINISH: 20 MIN.
MAKES: 1 SERVING

- 4 **egg whites**
- 2 **teaspoons water**
- ⅛ **teaspoon pepper**
- 1 **slice deli ham, finely chopped**
- 2 **tablespoons finely chopped green pepper**
- 2 **tablespoons finely chopped onion**
- 2 **tablespoons crumbled goat cheese**
  Minced fresh parsley, optional

1. In a small bowl, whisk egg whites, water and pepper until blended; stir in ham, green pepper and onion. Heat a large nonstick skillet coated with cooking spray over medium-high heat. Pour in egg white mixture. Mixture should set immediately at edges. As egg whites set, push cooked portions toward the center, letting uncooked egg flow underneath.

2. When no liquid egg remains, sprinkle goat cheese on one side. Fold omelet in half; slide onto a plate. If desired, sprinkle with parsley.

PER SERVING *143 cal., 4 g fat (2 g sat. fat), 27 mg chol., 489 mg sodium, 5 g carb., 1 g fiber, 21 g pro.* **Diabetic Exchanges:** *3 lean meat, ½ fat.*

"As a busy working mom, I need a breakfast that requires minimal prep. I often whip up the egg mixture the night before and refrigerate it overnight. Then all I have to do in the morning is heat up the skillet." **—LYNNE DIETERLE** ROCHESTER HILLS, MI

GOAT CHEESE OMELET

ISLAND BREEZES COFFEE CAKE

Island Breezes Coffee Cake

Invite sunshine to brunch with this beautiful pull-apart bread. You won't believe how simple it is.
—DEBRA GOFORTH NEWPORT, TN

PREP: 20 MIN. + CHILLING
BAKE: 35 MIN. + COOLING
MAKES: 12 SERVINGS

- ⅔ **cup packed brown sugar**
- ½ **cup flaked coconut, toasted**
- 1 **package (3.4 ounces) cook-and-serve coconut cream pudding mix**
- 20 **frozen bread dough dinner rolls**
- 1 **can (20 ounces) pineapple tidbits, drained**
- 1 **jar (3 ounces) macadamia nuts, coarsely chopped**
- ½ **cup butter, cubed**

1. In a small bowl, mix brown sugar, coconut and pudding mix. Place 10 rolls in a greased 10-in. fluted tube pan; layer with half of the sugar mixture, 1 cup pineapple tidbits, ⅓ cup macadamia nuts and ¼ cup butter. Repeat layers. Cover with plastic wrap and refrigerate overnight.

2. Remove pan from refrigerator about 1¾ hours before serving; let rise in a warm place until dough reaches top of pan, about 1 hour. Preheat oven to 350°.

3. Remove plastic wrap. Bake coffee cake 35-40 minutes or until golden brown. (Cover loosely with foil if top browns too quickly.) Cool 10 minutes before inverting onto a serving plate; serve warm.

NOTE *To toast coconut, spread in a 15x10x1-in. baking pan. Bake at 350° for 5-10 minutes or until golden brown, stirring frequently.*

Waffle Sandwich

Keep 'em going right through to lunchtime with this quick breakfast idea. I like to serve it with crisp apples on the side.

—**MICHELE MCHENRY** BELLINGHAM, WA

START TO FINISH: 20 MIN.
MAKES: 1 SERVING

- 1 slice Canadian bacon
- 1 egg
- 1 green onion, chopped
- 2 frozen low-fat multigrain waffles
- 1 tablespoon shredded reduced-fat cheddar cheese
  Sliced tomato, optional

1. In a nonstick skillet coated with cooking spray, cook Canadian bacon over medium-high heat 1-2 minutes on each side or until lightly browned. Remove and keep warm.
2. In a small bowl, whisk egg and green onion; add to the same pan. Cook and stir until egg is thickened and no liquid egg remains.
3. Meanwhile, prepare waffles according to package directions.

Place one waffle on a plate. Top with Canadian bacon, scrambled egg, cheese and, if desired, tomato. Top with remaining waffle.

PER SERVING *261 cal., 10 g fat (3 g sat. fat), 223 mg chol., 733 mg sodium, 30 g carb., 3 g fiber, 16 g pro.* **Diabetic Exchanges:** *2 starch, 2 medium-fat meat.*

Doughnut Muffins

After many tries, I finally created my own version of a doughnut muffin. It has the taste of a cake doughnut and it's a lot simpler to make.

—**MORGAN BOTWINICK** RICHMOND, VA

PREP: 30 MIN. • **BAKE:** 20 MIN.
MAKES: 1 DOZEN

- ¾ cup butter, softened
- ⅔ cup packed brown sugar
- ¼ cup sugar
- 2 eggs
- 1¼ cups 2% milk
- 1 teaspoon vanilla extract
- 3 cups all-purpose flour
- 2½ teaspoons baking powder
- ¾ teaspoon salt
- ½ teaspoon ground nutmeg
- ½ teaspoon ground cinnamon
- ¼ teaspoon baking soda

COATING
- 1 cup coarse sugar
- 1 tablespoon ground cinnamon
- ⅓ cup butter, melted

1. Preheat oven to 350°. In a large bowl, cream butter and sugars until light and fluffy. Add eggs, one at a time, beating well after each addition. Gradually beat in milk and vanilla. In another bowl, whisk flour, baking powder, salt, nutmeg, cinnamon and baking soda. Add to creamed mixture; stir just until moistened.
2. Fill greased or paper-lined muffin cups. Bake 18-20 minutes or until a toothpick inserted in center comes out clean. Cool 5 minutes before removing from pan to a wire rack.
3. Meanwhile, for coating, combine coarse sugar and cinnamon. Dip tops of warm muffins in butter, then coat in cinnamon-sugar.

DOUGHNUT MUFFINS

Lemon-Blueberry Muffins

Bursting with berries and drizzled with a lemony glaze, these muffins are moist, tender and truly something special. This is one recipe you simply must try for family and friends.

—**KATHY HARDING** RICHMOND, MO

PREP: 30 MIN. • **BAKE:** 25 MIN.
MAKES: 11 MUFFINS

- ½ **cup butter, softened**
- 1 **cup sugar**
- 2 **eggs**
- ½ **cup 2% milk**
- 2 **tablespoons lemon juice**
- 2 **teaspoons grated lemon peel**
- 2 **cups all-purpose flour**
- 2 **teaspoons baking powder**
  Dash salt
- 2 **cups fresh or frozen blueberries**

GLAZE

- 1½ **cups confectioners' sugar**
- 2 **tablespoons lemon juice**
- 1 **teaspoon butter, melted**
- ¼ **teaspoon vanilla extract**

1. In a large bowl, cream butter and sugar until light and fluffy. Add eggs, one at a time, beating well after each addition. Beat in the milk, lemon juice and peel. Combine the flour, baking powder and salt; add to creamed mixture just until moistened. Fold in the blueberries.

2. Fill paper-lined muffin cups three-fourths full. Bake at 400° for 25-30 minutes or until a toothpick inserted in muffin comes out clean. Cool for 5 minutes before removing from pan to a wire rack.

3. In a small bowl, combine the confectioners' sugar, lemon juice, butter and vanilla; drizzle over the warm muffins.

NOTE *If using frozen blueberries, use without thawing to avoid discoloring the batter.*

LEMON-BLUEBERRY MUFFINS

Get-Up-and-Go Granola

My family loves to have this granola before hiking or biking or even when we're camping. It smells delicious while baking, and you can easily make it in large batches for special occasions or to send in gift packages to family and friends.

—**SABRINA OLSON** OTSEGO, MN

PREP: 15 MIN. • **BAKE:** 30 MIN. + COOLING
MAKES: 7½ CUPS

- 6 **cups old-fashioned oats**
- ½ **cup unblanched almonds, coarsely chopped**
- ¼ **cup packed brown sugar**
- ¼ **cup flaxseed**
- ¼ **cup canola oil**

GET-UP-AND-GO GRANOLA

- ¼ **cup honey**
- 1 **tablespoon maple syrup**
- 1 **teaspoon apple pie spice**
- ½ **teaspoon salt**
- ½ **teaspoon vanilla extract**
- ½ **cup dried cranberries**
- ½ **cup raisins**

1. Preheat oven to 300°. In a large bowl, combine oats, almonds, brown sugar and flax. In a microwave-safe dish, whisk oil, honey, maple syrup, pie spice and salt. Microwave on high for 30-45 seconds or until heated through, stirring once. Stir in vanilla. Pour over oat mixture; toss to coat.

2. Spread evenly in a 15-in.x10-in. x1-in. baking pan coated with cooking spray. Bake 30-40 minutes or until golden brown, stirring every 10 minutes. Cool completely on a wire rack. Stir in cranberries and raisins. Store in an airtight container.

NOTE *This recipe was tested in a 1,100-watt microwave.*

PER (½ -CUP) SERVING *255 cal., 10 g fat (1 g sat. fat), 0 chol., 84 mg sodium, 40 g carb., 5 g fiber, 7 g pro.*

JAVA MUFFINS

Java Muffins

These muffins get me going in the morning, and they're especially delicious with a good cup of coffee.

—**ZAINAB AHMED** MOUNTLAKE TERRACE, WA

START TO FINISH: 30 MIN.
MAKES: 1 DOZEN

- ¼ cup butter, softened
- 1 cup packed brown sugar
- 2 eggs
- ¼ cup unsweetened applesauce
- ½ cup buttermilk
- ½ cup strong brewed coffee
- 1 tablespoon instant coffee granules
- ½ teaspoon vanilla extract
- 1 cup all-purpose flour
- ¾ cup whole wheat flour
- 1½ teaspoons baking powder
- ½ teaspoon baking soda
- ½ teaspoon ground cinnamon
- ¼ teaspoon salt
- ½ cup finely chopped pecans, divided

1. Preheat oven to 375°. In a large bowl, beat butter and brown sugar until crumbly, about 2 minutes. Add eggs; mix well. Beat in applesauce. In a small bowl, whisk buttermilk, coffee, coffee granules and vanilla until granules are dissolved; gradually add to butter mixture.
2. In another bowl, whisk flours, baking powder, baking soda, cinnamon and salt. Add to butter mixture; stir just until moistened. Fold in ¼ cup pecans.
3. Coat muffin cups with cooking spray or use paper liners; fill three-fourths full. Sprinkle with remaining pecans. Bake 15-20 minutes or until a toothpick inserted in center comes out clean. Cool 5 minutes before removing from pan to a wire rack. Serve warm.
PER SERVING *220 cal., 9 g fat (3 g sat. fat), 46 mg chol., 209 mg sodium, 33 g carb., 2 g fiber, 4 g pro.* **Diabetic Exchanges:** *2 starch, 1½ fat.*

Broccoli-Mushroom Bubble Bake

PREP: 20 MIN. • **BAKE:** 25 MIN.
MAKES: 12 SERVINGS

- 1 teaspoon canola oil
- ½ pound sliced fresh mushrooms, finely chopped
- 1 medium onion, finely chopped
- 1 tube (16.3 ounces) large refrigerated flaky biscuits
- 1 package (10 ounces) frozen broccoli and cheese sauce
- 3 eggs
- 1 can (5 ounces) evaporated milk
- 1 teaspoon Italian seasoning
- ½ teaspoon garlic powder
- ½ teaspoon salt
- ¼ teaspoon pepper
- 1½ cups (6 ounces) shredded Colby-Monterey Jack cheese

1. Preheat oven to 350°. In a large skillet, heat oil over medium-high heat. Add mushrooms and onion; cook and stir 4-6 minutes or until tender.
2. Cut each biscuit into eight pieces; place in a greased 13-in.x9-in. baking dish. Top with mushroom mixture.
3. Cook broccoli and cheese sauce according to package directions. Spoon over mushroom mixture.
4. In a large bowl, whisk eggs, milk and seasonings; pour over top. Sprinkle with cheese. Bake 25-30 minutes or until golden brown.

"I got bored with the same old breakfast casseroles served at our monthly moms' meetings, so I created something new. Judging by the reactions of the other moms, this one's a keeper."—SHANNON KOENE BLACKSBURG, VA

BROCCOLI-MUSHROOM BUBBLE BAKE

SPANISH OMELET

Spanish Omelet

Wake up your taste buds with this Mexican-flavored omelet featuring warm refried beans, salsa and shredded cheese. Whip up a satisfying hot breakfast in 15 minutes; spice it up with a hot salsa or add sizzling cooked bacon for a smoky twist.

—**TERESA GUNNELL** LOVETTSVILLE, VA

START TO FINISH: 15 MIN.
MAKES: 2 SERVINGS

- 6 **eggs**
- ¼ **cup water**
- 1 **cup refried beans, warmed**
- ¼ **cup chopped red onion**
- ½ **cup shredded Mexican cheese blend, divided**
- ¼ **cup salsa**

1. Heat a 10-in. nonstick skillet coated with cooking spray over medium heat. Whisk eggs and water. Add half of the egg mixture to skillet (mixture should set immediately at edges).

2. As eggs set, push cooked edges toward the center, letting uncooked portion flow underneath. When the eggs are set, spoon half of the beans and half of the onion on one side and sprinkle with 2 tablespoons cheese; fold other side over filling. Slide omelet onto a plate. Repeat. Garnish with salsa and remaining cheese.

Maple Nut Bagel Spread

You won't believe how easy it is to make this creamy bagel spread. It's also delicious on toast or muffins.

—**TASTE OF HOME TEST KITCHEN**

START TO FINISH: 10 MIN.
MAKES: 1¼ CUPS

- 1 **carton (8 ounces) reduced-fat spreadable cream cheese**
- 3 **tablespoons maple syrup**
- ⅛ **teaspoon ground cinnamon**
- ¼ **cup finely chopped walnuts, toasted**
  Bagels, split

In a large bowl, beat the cream cheese, syrup and cinnamon until smooth; stir in walnuts. Chill until serving. Serve with bagels.

Brunch-Style Portobello Mushrooms

I've always loved portobellos because you can stuff them. I combined my favorite ingredients for this rich, savory main dish. It's wonderful for breakfast, brunch or even dinner.

—**SYLVIA WALDSMITH** ROCKTON, IL

START TO FINISH: 30 MIN.
MAKES: 4 SERVINGS

- 4 **large portobello mushrooms, stems removed**
- 2 **packages (10 ounces each) frozen creamed spinach, thawed**
- 4 **eggs**
- ¼ **cup shredded Gouda cheese**
- ½ **cup crumbled cooked bacon**
  Salt and pepper, optional

1. Place mushrooms, stem side up, in an ungreased 15-in.x10-in.x1-in. baking pan. Spoon spinach onto mushrooms, building up the sides. Carefully crack an egg into the center of each mushroom; sprinkle with cheese and bacon.

2. Bake at 375° for 18-20 minutes or until eggs are set. Sprinkle with salt and pepper if desired.

Walnut Cranberry Butter

This cranberry butter is delicious on warm bread or biscuits. Be sure to use real butter—the lower-fat products have a higher water content and don't give the same results.

—**CORKY HUFFSMITH** INDIO, CA

PREP: 20 MIN. + CHILLING
MAKES: 1⅓ CUPS

- ¾ **cup butter, softened**
- 2 **tablespoons brown sugar**
- 2 **tablespoons honey**
- 1 **cup chopped fresh cranberries**
- 2 **tablespoons chopped walnuts, toasted**

1. In a small bowl, beat the butter, brown sugar and honey until fluffy, about 5 minutes. Add cranberries and walnuts; beat 5 minutes longer or until butter turns pink.

2. Transfer to a sheet of plastic wrap; roll into a log. Refrigerate until chilled. Unwrap and slice or place on a butter dish.

BRUNCH-STYLE PORTOBELLO MUSHROOMS

CREAMY BERRY SMOOTHIES

FAST FIX ▸

Pear, Ham & Cheese Pastry Pockets

I came up with this recipe on the fly once. The sweet-savory flavor combo also makes it a good dinner choice. Just add a cup of soup and supper's ready!

—TERRI CRANDALL GARDNERVILLE, NV

START TO FINISH: 30 MIN.
MAKES: 8 SERVINGS

- 1 package (17.3 ounces) frozen puff pastry, thawed
- ¼ cup honey Dijon mustard
- 1 egg, lightly beaten
- 8 slices deli ham
- 4 slices Muenster cheese, halved diagonally
- 1 medium red pear, very thinly sliced
- 1 small red onion, thinly sliced

1. Preheat oven to 400°. Unfold each sheet of puff pastry. Cut each into four squares. Spread 1½ teaspoons mustard over each square to within ½ in. of edges. Brush egg over edges of pastry.
2. On one corner of each square, layer ham, cheese, pear and onion. Fold opposite corner over filling, forming a triangle; press edges with a fork to seal. Transfer to ungreased baking sheets. Brush tops with remaining egg.
3. Bake 10-14 minutes or until golden brown. Serve warm.

PEAR, HAM & CHEESE PASTRY POCKETS

"No one will guess this smoothie is made with tofu! The blend of berries and pomegranate makes it a refreshing delight!"
—SONYA LABBE WEST HOLLYWOOD, CA

EAT SMART ⑤INGREDIENTS FAST FIX ▸

Creamy Berry Smoothies

START TO FINISH: 10 MIN.
MAKES: 2 SERVINGS

- ½ cup pomegranate juice
- 1 tablespoon agave syrup or honey
- 3 ounces silken firm tofu (about ½ cup)
- 1 cup frozen unsweetened mixed berries
- 1 cup frozen unsweetened strawberries

Place all ingredients in a blender; cover and process until blended. Serve immediately.
PER SERVING *157 cal., 1 g fat (trace sat. fat), 0 chol., 24 mg sodium, 35 g carb., 3 g fiber, 4 g pro.*

Easy Espresso

Capture the classic taste of espresso without the hassle of expensive brewing equipment. For best flavor, serve espresso immediately. Pour leftover espresso into ice cube trays and freeze to use later in cold drinks.

—TASTE OF HOME TEST KITCHEN

START TO FINISH: 10 MIN.
MAKES: 4 SERVINGS

½ cup ground coffee
    (French or other dark roast)
1½ cups cold water
    Lemon twists, optional

Place ground coffee in the filter of a drip coffeemaker. Add water; brew according to manufacturer's instructions. Serve immediately in espresso cups; garnish with lemon twists if desired.

NOTE *This recipe was tested with Starbucks French Roast ground coffee.*

Ham & Egg Pita Pockets

I made these pitas one day when the kids were running late for school and I needed a fast, healthy and portable breakfast. The eggs always cook quickly in the microwave, and the sandwiches are ready to eat in just 10 minutes.

—SUE OLSEN FREMONT, CA

START TO FINISH: 10 MIN.
MAKES: 1 SERVING

2 egg whites
1 egg
⅛ teaspoon smoked or plain paprika
⅛ teaspoon freshly ground pepper
1 slice deli ham, chopped
1 green onion, sliced
2 tablespoons shredded reduced-fat cheddar cheese
2 whole wheat pita pocket halves

In a microwave-safe bowl, whisk egg whites, egg, paprika and pepper until blended; stir in ham, green onion and cheese. Microwave, covered, on high for 1 minute. Stir; cook on high 30-60 seconds longer or until almost set. Serve in pitas.

NOTE *This recipe was tested in a 1,100-watt microwave.*

PER SERVING *323 cal., 10 g fat (4 g sat. fat), 231 mg chol., 769 mg sodium, 34 g carb., 5 g fiber, 27 g pro.* **Diabetic Exchanges:** *3 lean meat, 2 starch.*

HAM & EGG PITA POCKETS

BACON & CHEDDAR STRATA

(5) INGREDIENTS FAST FIX
Cuban Breakfast Sandwiches

Take charge of breakfast time by serving these warm energy-boosting sandwiches. They travel well for hectic mornings, and the hearty helping of protein will keep hunger at bay.
—**LACIE GRIFFIN** AUSTIN, TX

START TO FINISH: 20 MIN.
MAKES: 4 SERVINGS

- 1 loaf (1 pound) Cuban or French bread
- 4 eggs
- 16 pieces thinly sliced hard salami
- 8 slices deli ham
- 8 slices Swiss cheese

1. Split bread in half lengthwise; cut into four pieces. Fry eggs in a large non-stick skillet coated with cooking spray until yolks are set. Layer bread bottoms with salami, ham, egg and cheese; replace tops.
2. Cook on a panini maker or indoor grill for 2 minutes or until bread is browned and cheese is melted.

CUBAN BREAKFAST SANDWICHES

Bacon & Cheddar Strata

We love to have this sunrise specialty on Christmas morning, but I prepare it whenever we want a hot and hearty weekend meal. The no-fuss breakfast casserole is ready to pop into the oven when you wake up.
—**DEB HEALEY** COLD LAKE, AB

PREP: 20 MIN. + CHILLING • **BAKE:** 45 MIN.
MAKES: 10 SERVINGS

- 1 pound bacon strips
- 1 medium sweet red pepper, finely chopped
- 8 green onions, thinly sliced
- ½ cup chopped oil-packed sun-dried tomatoes
- 8 slices white bread, cubed
- 2 cups (8 ounces) shredded cheddar cheese
- 6 eggs, lightly beaten
- 1½ cups 2% milk
- ¼ cup mayonnaise
- ½ teaspoon salt
- ¼ teaspoon ground mustard
- ⅛ teaspoon pepper

1. In a large skillet, cook bacon in batches until crisp; drain on paper towels. Crumble into a small bowl. Add red pepper, onions and tomatoes. In a greased 13-in.x9-in. baking dish, layer half of the bread, bacon mixture and cheese. Top with remaining bread and bacon mixture.
2. In another bowl, combine eggs, milk, mayonnaise and seasonings. Pour over top. Sprinkle with remaining cheese. Cover and refrigerate overnight.
3. Remove from the refrigerator 30 minutes before baking. Preheat oven to 350°. Bake, covered, 40 minutes. Uncover and bake 5-10 minutes or until a knife inserted near center comes out clean. Let stand 5 minutes before cutting.

(5) INGREDIENTS FAST FIX
Cream Cheese 'n' Ham Bagels

Here's a good quick breakfast. Served with a salad and cold drink, it doubles nicely as a light lunch or a late-night snack.
—**BILL HILBRICH** ST. CLOUD, MN

START TO FINISH: 15 MIN.
MAKES: 2 SERVINGS

- 2 plain bagels, split and toasted
- 2 garlic cloves, halved
- 2 ounces cream cheese, softened
- 1 cup finely chopped fully cooked ham
- 2 tablespoons shredded Parmesan cheese

1. Place bagels cut side up on an ungreased baking sheet; rub with cut sides of garlic. Spread with cream cheese. Top with ham.
2. Broil 4 in. from the heat for 2-3 minutes or until heated through. Sprinkle with Parmesan cheese. Broil 1 minute longer or until cheese is slightly melted.

(5) INGREDIENTS FAST FIX >

Sausage Cheese Biscuits

These delectable biscuits are a brunch-time favorite. I love that they don't require any special ingredients.

—**MARLENE NEIDEIGH** MYRTLE POINT, OR

START TO FINISH: 30 MIN.
MAKES: 10 SERVINGS

- 1 tube (12 ounces) refrigerated buttermilk biscuits
- 1 package (8 ounces) brown-and-serve sausage links
- 2 eggs
- ½ cup shredded cheddar cheese
- 3 tablespoons chopped green onions

1. Roll out each biscuit into a 5-in. circle; place each in an ungreased muffin cup. Cut sausages into fourths; brown in a skillet. Drain. Divide sausages among cups.

2. In a small bowl, combine eggs, cheese and onions; spoon mixture into cups. Bake at 400° for 13-15 minutes or until browned.

SAUSAGE CHEESE BISCUITS

BREAKFAST SKEWERS

(5) INGREDIENTS

Breakfast Skewers

Kabobs make for a fun and different breakfast, plus they're delicious with any egg main dish.

—**BOBI RAAB** SAINT PAUL, MN

START TO FINISH: 20 MIN.
MAKES: 5 SERVINGS

- 1 package (7 ounces) brown-and-serve sausage links
- 1 can (20 ounces) pineapple chunks, drained
- 10 medium fresh mushrooms
- 2 tablespoons butter, melted
  Maple syrup

1. Cut sausages in half; on 5 metal or soaked wooden skewers, alternately thread sausages, pineapple and mushrooms. Brush with butter and syrup.

2. Grill, uncovered, over medium-hot heat, turning and basting with syrup, for 8 minutes or until sausages are lightly browned and fruit is heated through.

(5) INGREDIENTS FAST FIX >

Chipotle Cheese Sauce

Fans of Mexican flavor are sure to enjoy this rich and smoky cheese sauce with a touch of heat from chipotle peppers.

—**MELISSA JELINEK** MENOMONEE FALLS, WI

START TO FINISH: 15 MIN.
MAKES: 2¾ CUPS

- ¼ cup butter, cubed
- 2 tablespoons chopped chipotle peppers in adobo sauce
- ¼ cup all-purpose flour
- ⅛ teaspoon pepper
- 2½ cups 2% milk
- 1½ cups (6 ounces) shredded Colby-Monterey Jack cheese
  Breakfast potatoes or eggs

In a small saucepan, melt butter over medium heat. Add chipotle peppers; cook and stir for 2 minutes. Stir in flour and pepper until blended; gradually add milk. Bring to a boil; cook and stir for 1-2 minutes or until thickened. Stir in cheese until melted. Serve over potatoes.

ORANGE PECAN WAFFLES

FAST FIX

Orange Pecan Waffles

Served with butter and maple syrup, these waffles are irresistible. Sometimes I make them into sandwiches with scrambled eggs and bacon.

—RUTH HARROW ALEXANDRIA, NH

START TO FINISH: 20 MIN.
MAKES: 3 WAFFLES

- 1 **cup biscuit/baking mix**
- 1 **egg, lightly beaten**
- 3 **tablespoons canola oil**
- 1 **tablespoon sugar**
- ½ **teaspoon vanilla extract**
- ¼ **teaspoon grated orange peel**
- ½ **cup club soda**
- 3 **tablespoons finely chopped pecans, toasted**
  Maple syrup, optional

1. In a small bowl, combine the first six ingredients. Stir in club soda until smooth. Gently fold in pecans.

2. Bake in a preheated waffle iron according to manufacturer's directions until golden brown. Serve with syrup if desired.

Chili 'n' Cheese Grits

Although I live in the city, I'm really a country cook at heart. Most of our friends laugh at the idea of eating grits, but they're pleasantly surprised when they try these.

—ROSEMARY WEST LAS VEGAS, NV

PREP: 20 MIN. • **BAKE:** 30 MIN.
MAKES: 6-8 SERVINGS

- 2 **cups water**
- 2 **cups milk**
- 1 **cup grits**
- 2 **egg yolks**
- 1 **cup (4 ounces) shredded cheddar cheese, divided**
- ¼ **cup butter, cubed**
- 1 **can (4 ounces) chopped green chilies, drained**
- 1 **teaspoon salt**

1. In a large saucepan, bring water and milk to a boil. Add grits; cook and stir over medium heat for 5 minutes or until thickened.

2. In a small bowl, beat the egg yolks. Stir a small amount of hot grits into yolks; return all to the pan, stirring constantly.

3. Add ¾ cup of cheese, butter, chilies and salt; stir until butter is melted.

4. Pour into a greased 1½-qt. baking dish and sprinkle remaining cheese over the top.

5. Bake, uncovered, at 350° for 30-35 minutes or until a thermometer inserted in the center reads 160°.

CHILI 'N' CHEESE GRITS

"I always thought eating healthy wouldn't be as enjoyable as eating whatever I wanted. This recipe proved me wrong. Healthy ingredients taste wonderful and are just as mouthwatering without the extra calories." —**NICOLE HACKLEY** CULBERTSON, MT

SOUTHWEST BREAKFAST WRAPS

EAT SMART FAST FIX
Southwest Breakfast Wraps

START TO FINISH: 30 MIN.
MAKES: 4 SERVINGS

- 1 **tablespoon olive oil**
- 1 **medium red onion, chopped**
- ½ **cup sliced fresh mushrooms**
- 1 **small green pepper, finely chopped**
- 1 **small sweet red pepper, finely chopped**
- 1 **jalapeno pepper, seeded and finely chopped**
- 1 **can (4 ounces) chopped green chilies**
- 1 **garlic clove, minced**
- 8 **egg whites**
- ¼ **cup shredded reduced-fat Mexican cheese blend**
- 4 **whole wheat tortillas (8 inches), warmed**

1. In a large nonstick skillet, heat oil over medium-high heat. Add onion, mushrooms, peppers, chilies and garlic; cook and stir until peppers are crisp-tender. Remove from pan and keep warm.
2. In a small bowl, whisk egg whites and cheese until blended. Add egg white mixture to pan; cook and stir over medium heat until egg whites begin to set and no liquid egg remains.
3. Spoon egg white mixture across center of each tortilla; top with vegetable mixture. Fold bottom and sides of tortilla over filling and roll up.
NOTE *Wear disposable gloves when cutting hot peppers; the oils can burn skin. Avoid touching your face.*
PER SERVING *254 cal., 8 g fat (1 g sat. fat), 5 mg chol., 446 mg sodium, 29 g carb., 4 g fiber, 14 g pro.* **Diabetic Exchanges:** *1½ starch, 1 lean meat, 1 vegetable, 1 fat.*

⑤ INGREDIENTS FAST FIX
Breakfast Potatoes

These cheesy potatoes are a nice morning side dish. I prepare them often for my husband and me. They go with just about any breakfast main dish.
—**JUDY DUPREE** THIEF RIVER FALLS, MN

START TO FINISH: 15 MIN.
MAKES: 2 SERVINGS

- 2 **medium potatoes, peeled and sliced**
- ¼ **cup sliced onion**
- ¼ **teaspoon salt**
- ⅛ **teaspoon pepper**
- ¼ **teaspoon garlic salt**
- ¼ **cup shredded cheddar cheese**

1. Coat a 9-in. microwave-safe plate with cooking spray. Arrange potato and onion slices on plate; sprinkle with seasonings.
2. Cover and microwave on high for 9-10 minutes or until potatoes are tender, adding cheese in the last 30 seconds of cooking.

⑤ INGREDIENTS FAST FIX
Cherry Syrup

My mom and grandma have been making this fruity syrup to serve with waffles and pancakes ever since I was a little girl. Now I make it for my sons, who love it as much as I do.
—**SANDRA HARRINGTON** NIPOMO, CA

START TO FINISH: 30 MIN.
MAKES: 3 CUPS

- 1 **package (12 ounces) frozen pitted dark sweet cherries, thawed**
- 1 **cup water**
- 2½ **cups sugar**
- 2 **tablespoons butter**
- ½ **teaspoon almond extract**
  Dash ground cinnamon

1. Bring cherries and water to a boil in a small saucepan. Reduce heat; simmer, uncovered, for 20 minutes.
2. Add sugar and butter; cook and stir until sugar is dissolved. Remove from the heat; stir in extract and cinnamon.
3. Cool leftovers; transfer to airtight containers. Store in the refrigerator for up to 2 weeks.

**Jacyn Siebert's
Pea Soup Shooters**
PAGE 103

Swift Snacks & Appetizers

Whether the gathering is small and casual or grand and formal, we have the perfect batch of appetizers that will get the party started. These quick munchies take little effort so you can enjoy yourself.

Janet Telleen's
BBQ Chicken Waffle Fries
PAGE 102

Joni Hilton's
Bacon-Wrapped Tater Tots
PAGE 97

Deborah Peirce's
Creamy Jalapeno Popper Dip
PAGE 109

EAT SMART
Mandarin Turkey Pinwheels

Curry, smoked turkey and mandarin oranges give these pinwheels their flavor twist. My cousin and I made these for an open house and people came back for seconds...and thirds.

—**LORIE MINER** KAMAS, UT

PREP: 15 MIN. + CHILLING
MAKES: 2½ DOZEN

- 1 package (8 ounces) reduced-fat cream cheese
- ½ teaspoon curry powder
- ½ cup mandarin oranges, drained and chopped
- 3 flour tortillas (12 inches), room temperature
- ½ pound sliced deli smoked turkey
- 3 cups fresh baby spinach
- 2 green onions, chopped

1. In a small bowl, beat cream cheese and curry powder until blended. Stir in oranges. Spread ½ cup mixture over each tortilla. Layer with turkey, spinach and green onions; roll up tightly. Wrap in plastic wrap and refrigerate for 2 hours or until firm enough to cut.

2. Unwrap and cut each roll-up into 10 slices.

PER SERVING *50 cal., 2 g fat (1 g sat. fat), 8 mg chol., 149 mg sodium, 4 g carb., 1 g fiber, 3 g pro.*

Nacho Scoops

Serve your group a big platter of these fun and crazy-tasty nacho bites as you cheer for your team. You'll score big with these cute tortilla cups.

—**RAINE GOTTESS** POMPANO BEACH, FL

PREP: 40 MIN. • **BAKE:** 5 MIN./BATCH
MAKES: 12 DOZEN

- ¾ pound ground beef
- 1 medium onion, finely chopped
- 1 medium sweet red pepper, finely chopped
- 1 envelope taco seasoning
- 1 can (14½ ounces) diced tomatoes and green chilies, undrained
- 1 can (4 ounces) chopped green chilies
- 8 ounces pepper jack cheese, cubed
- 4 ounces process cheese (Velveeta), cubed
- 4 ounces cream cheese, softened, cubed
- 1 package (12 ounces) tortilla chip scoops
- 2 cups (8 ounces) shredded Mexican cheese blend
  Sour cream and pickled jalapeno slices

1. In a large skillet, cook the beef, onion and red pepper over medium heat until meat is no longer pink; drain. Stir in the taco seasoning, tomatoes and green chilies. Cook and stir for 5-7 minutes or until thickened.

2. Reduce heat to low. Stir in the pepper jack, process cheese and cream cheese until melted.

3. Place 4 dozen scoops on an ungreased baking sheet. Add a rounded teaspoon of beef mixture to each. Sprinkle with the Mexican cheese blend.

4. Bake at 375° for about 5 minutes or until heated through. Garnish each appetizer with sour cream and a jalapeno pepper slice. Repeat with remaining tortilla chip scoops.

NACHO SCOOPS

BACON-WRAPPED TATER TOTS

Gingered Sweet & Spicy Hot Wings

These hot wings are a zesty appetizer or snack. Thanks to sweet (orange marmalade) and hot (Sriracha) flavors bursting through with every bite, these wings are a winner on game day or any day of the week.

—JENNIFER LOCKLIN CYPRESS, TX

PREP: 15 MIN. + MARINATING
BAKE: 35 MIN.
MAKES: ABOUT 3 DOZEN

- 1 cup orange marmalade
- ½ cup minced fresh cilantro
- ½ cup Sriracha Asian hot chili sauce
- ½ cup reduced-sodium soy sauce
- ¼ cup lime juice
- ¼ cup rice vinegar
- ¼ cup ketchup
- ¼ cup honey
- 4 garlic cloves, minced
- 1 tablespoon minced fresh gingerroot
- 1 tablespoon grated lime peel
- 1 tablespoon sesame oil
- 1 teaspoon salt
- 1 teaspoon pepper
- 4 pounds chicken wingettes and drumettes

1. In a large resealable plastic bag, combine the first 14 ingredients. Add chicken; seal bag and turn to coat. Refrigerate 8 hours or overnight.
2. Preheat oven to 375°. Drain chicken, discarding marinade. Transfer chicken to two greased 15x10x1-in. baking pans. Bake 35-45 minutes or until juices run clear.

"Indulge in just one of these scrumptious bacon-wrapped goodies and you'll taste why they're a hit with kids of all ages. They'll go fast, so you may want to double the recipe."
—JONI HILTON ROCKLIN, CA

FAST FIX
Bacon-Wrapped Tater Tots

START TO FINISH: 25 MIN.
MAKES: 32 APPETIZERS

- 16 bacon strips, cut in half
- ½ cup maple syrup
- 1 teaspoon crushed red pepper flakes
- 32 frozen Tater Tots

1. Cook bacon in a large skillet over medium heat until partially cooked but not crisp. Remove to paper towels to drain; keep warm.
2. Combine syrup and pepper flakes. Dip each bacon piece in syrup mixture, then wrap around a Tater Tot. Secure with toothpicks.
3. Place on a greased rack in a 15-in. x 10-in. x 1-in. baking pan. Bake appetizers at 400° for 12-15 minutes or until bacon is crisp.

Last-Minute Appetizers

To make quick appetizer kabobs, thread cubed salami or deli ham, cherry tomatoes, fresh mozzarella cheese pearls, and pitted olives onto skewers. Drizzle kabobs with Italian salad dressing for an attractive and easy-to-eat antipasto plate.

MINI CRAB TARTS

Shrimp and Goat Cheese Stuffed Mushrooms

Here's an easy but special recipe that makes a delicious appetizer for all your holiday parties.

—MARY ANN LEE CLIFTON PARK, NY

START TO FINISH: 30 MIN.
MAKES: ABOUT 2 DOZEN

- ½ **pound uncooked shrimp, peeled, deveined and finely chopped**
- 1 **log (4 ounces) herbed fresh goat cheese, crumbled**
- ⅓ **cup chopped green onions**
- ¼ **cup panko (Japanese) bread crumbs**
- 1 **teaspoon minced fresh gingerroot**
- ½ **teaspoon crushed red pepper flakes**
- ½ **teaspoon salt**
- ¼ **teaspoon pepper**
- ½ **pound whole baby portobello mushrooms, stems removed**
- 2 **tablespoons sesame oil**
   Thinly sliced green onions, optional

1. Combine the shrimp, goat cheese, onions, bread crumbs, ginger, pepper flakes, salt and pepper in a small bowl. Mound shrimp mixture into mushroom caps and place on an ungreased baking sheet. Drizzle with sesame oil.
2. Bake at 350° for 10-15 minutes or until shrimp turn pink. Garnish with green onions if desired. Serve warm.

SHRIMP AND GOAT CHEESE STUFFED MUSHROOMS

Mini Crab Tarts

Crisp phyllo tart shells are heavenly with this warm, rich, creamy crab filling. They're always a hit at get-togethers.

—LINDA STEMEN MONROEVILLE, IN

START TO FINISH: 25 MIN.
MAKES: 30 APPETIZERS

- 2 **packages (1.9 ounces each) frozen miniature phyllo tart shells**
- 1 **egg**
- ¼ **cup 2% milk**
- ¼ **cup mayonnaise**
- 1 **tablespoon all-purpose flour**
- ⅛ **teaspoon salt**
- 1 **can (6 ounces) lump crabmeat, drained**
- 2 **tablespoons shredded Monterey Jack cheese**
- 1 **tablespoon chopped green onion**
   Thinly sliced green onions, optional

1. Place tart shells on an ungreased baking sheet. In a small bowl, whisk the egg, milk, mayonnaise, flour and salt until smooth. Stir in crab, cheese and chopped onion. Spoon into shells.
2. Bake at 375° for 9-11 minutes or until set. Sprinkle with sliced green onions if desired.

Apple-Mustard Glazed Meatballs

Convenient frozen meatballs simplify the prep; then they're glazed with a sweet-and-savory sauce that features apple jelly and spicy brown mustard.

—PAM CORDER MONROE, LA

PREP: 10 MIN. • **BAKE:** 30 MIN.
MAKES: 32 MEATBALLS

- 32 **frozen fully cooked homestyle meatballs (½ ounce each)**
- ⅓ **cup apple jelly**
- 3 **tablespoons unsweetened apple juice**
- 3 **tablespoons spicy brown mustard**
- ½ **teaspoon Worcestershire sauce**
- ¼ **teaspoon hot pepper sauce**

1. Place meatballs in a single layer in a greased 15-in. x 10-in. baking pan. Bake according to package directions.
2. Meanwhile, combine the remaining ingredients in a large saucepan. Bring to a boil over medium heat.
3. Transfer meatballs to sauce; stir gently to coat. Return to a boil. Reduce heat; simmer, uncovered, for 3-5 minutes or until sauce is thickened, stirring occasionally.

Holiday Salsa

You know the recipe is a success when guests hover around the serving dish till it's scraped clean. The longer this salsa marinates in the refrigerator, the better it tastes.

—**SHELLY PATTISON** LUBBOCK, TX

PREP: 20 MIN. + CHILLING
MAKES: 12 SERVINGS

- 1 **package (12 ounces) fresh or frozen cranberries**
- 1 **cup sugar**
- 6 **green onions, chopped**
- ½ **cup fresh cilantro leaves, chopped**
- 1 **jalapeno pepper, seeded and finely chopped**
- 1 **package (8 ounces) cream cheese, softened**
  Assorted crackers or tortilla chips

1. Place cranberries and sugar in a food processor; cover and pulse until coarsely chopped. Transfer to a small bowl. Stir in the onions, cilantro and pepper. Cover and refrigerate for several hours or overnight.
2. To serve, place cream cheese on a serving plate. Drain salsa and spoon over cream cheese. Serve with crackers or chips.
NOTE *Wear disposable gloves when cutting hot peppers; the oils can burn skin. Avoid touching your face.*

Greek Breadsticks

PREP: 20 MIN. • **BAKE:** 15 MIN.
MAKES: 32 BREADSTICKS

- ¼ **cup marinated quartered artichoke hearts, drained**
- 2 **tablespoons pitted Greek olives**
- 1 **package (17.3 ounces) frozen puff pastry, thawed**
- 1 **carton (6½ ounces) spreadable spinach and artichoke cream cheese**
- 2 **tablespoons grated Parmesan cheese**
- 1 **egg**
- 1 **tablespoon water**
- 2 **teaspoons sesame seeds**
  Refrigerated tzatziki sauce, optional

1. Place artichokes and olives in a food processor; cover and pulse until finely chopped. Unfold one pastry sheet on a lightly floured surface; spread half of the cream cheese over half of pastry. Top with half of the artichoke mixture. Sprinkle with half of the Parmesan cheese. Fold plain half over filling; press gently to seal.
2. Repeat with remaining pastry, cream cheese, artichoke mixture and Parmesan cheese. Whisk egg and water; brush over tops. Sprinkle with sesame seeds. Cut each rectangle into sixteen ¾-in.-wide strips. Twist strips several times; place 2 in. apart on greased baking sheets.
3. Bake at 400° for 12-14 minutes or until golden brown. Serve warm with tzatziki sauce if desired.

"Get ready for rave reviews with these crispy Greek-inspired appetizers. They're best served hot and fresh from the oven with your favorite tzatziki sauce."
—**JANE MCMILLAN** DANIA BEACH, FL

GREEK BREADSTICKS

QUESO FUNDIDO

Queso Fundido

Dig into this hot one-skillet dip and enjoy the spicy kick from chorizo and pepper jack cheese.

—JULIE MERRIMAN COLD BROOK, NY

PREP: 20 MIN. • **BAKE:** 15 MIN.
MAKES: 6 CUPS

- 1 **pound uncooked chorizo**
- 2 **cups fresh or frozen corn, thawed**
- 1 **large red onion, chopped**
- 1 **poblano pepper, chopped**
- 8 **ounces fresh goat cheese, crumbled**
- 2 **cups cubed Monterey Jack cheese**
- 1 **cup cubed pepper jack cheese**
- 1 **large tomato, seeded and chopped**
- 3 **green onions, thinly sliced**
  Blue corn tortilla chips

1. Crumble chorizo into a 10-in. ovenproof skillet; add the corn, red onion and pepper. Cook over medium heat for 6-8 minutes or until meat is fully cooked; drain. Stir in the cheeses.
2. Bake at 350° for 14-16 minutes or until bubbly. Sprinkle with tomato and green onions. Serve with chips.

⑤INGREDIENTS

Savory Party Bread

It's impossible to stop nibbling on warm pieces of this cheesy, oniony loaf. The bread fans out for a fun presentation.

—KAY DALY RALEIGH, NC

PREP: 10 MIN. • **BAKE:** 25 MIN.
MAKES: 8 SERVINGS

- 1 **unsliced round loaf sourdough bread (1 pound)**
- 1 **pound Monterey Jack cheese**
- ½ **cup butter, melted**
- ½ **cup chopped green onions**
- 2 **to 3 teaspoons poppy seeds**

1. Preheat oven to 350°. Cut bread widthwise into 1-in. slices to within ½ in. of bottom of loaf. Repeat cuts in opposite direction. Cut cheese into ¼-in. slices; cut slices into small pieces. Place cheese in cuts.
2. In a small bowl, mix butter, green onions and poppy seeds; drizzle over bread. Wrap in foil; place on a baking sheet. Bake 15 minutes. Unwrap; bake 10 minutes longer or until cheese is melted.

ANTIPASTO BRAID

"We're fans of Mediterranean food, so this play on antipasto is a favorite in my family. Meat and cheese make it a nice, hearty appetizer." —PATRICIA HARMON BADEN, PA

Antipasto Braid

PREP: 25 MIN. • **BAKE:** 30 MIN. + STANDING
MAKES: 12 SERVINGS

- ⅓ **cup pitted Greek olives, chopped**
- ¼ **cup marinated quartered artichoke hearts, drained and chopped**
- ¼ **cup julienned oil-packed sun-dried tomatoes**
- 2 **tablespoons plus 2 teaspoons grated Parmesan cheese, divided**
- 3 **tablespoons olive oil, divided**
- 1 **tablespoon chopped fresh basil or 1 teaspoon dried basil**
- 1 **tube (11 ounces) refrigerated crusty French loaf**
- 6 **thin slices prosciutto or deli ham**
- 4 **slices provolone cheese**
- ¾ **cup julienned roasted sweet red peppers**

1. Preheat oven to 350°. In a small bowl, toss olives, artichokes, tomatoes, 2 tablespoons Parmesan cheese, 2 tablespoons oil and basil until combined.
2. On a lightly floured surface, carefully unroll French loaf dough; roll into a 15x10-in. rectangle. Transfer to a greased 15x10x1-in. baking pan. Layer prosciutto, provolone cheese and red peppers lengthwise down center third of rectangle. Top with olive mixture.
3. On each long side, cut 10 strips about 3½ in. into the center. Starting at one end, fold alternating strips at an angle across filling, pinching ends to seal. Brush dough with remaining oil and sprinkle with remaining Parmesan cheese.
4. Bake 30-35 minutes or until golden brown. Let stand 10 minutes before cutting. Serve warm.

BBQ CHICKEN WAFFLE FRIES

FAST FIX

Leah's Party Popcorn

Popcorn is good just about any way, but spicing it up makes it all the more special. I love this recipe because so many people enjoy it! Pile it in bowls for parties or spoon individual portions into sealed bags for take-home treats.

—**LEAH STEENBERG** CIRCLE PINES, MN

START TO FINISH: 30 MIN.
MAKES: ABOUT 4 QUARTS

- 4 **quarts popped popcorn**
- 2 **cups miniature sesame breadsticks or sesame sticks**
- 2 **cups mixed nuts**
- 1 **cup sunflower kernels**
- 1 **cup salted pumpkin seeds or pepitas**
- 1 **cup potato sticks, optional**
- ¼ **cup olive oil**
- 2 **tablespoons lemon juice**
- 1 **tablespoon Worcestershire sauce**
- 1 **teaspoon salt**
- 1 **teaspoon dill weed**
- 1 **teaspoon coarsely ground pepper**
- ½ **teaspoon onion powder**
- ½ **teaspoon garlic powder**
- ½ **teaspoon hot pepper sauce**

1. Preheat oven to 325°. In a large bowl, combine the first five ingredients. If desired, stir in potato sticks. In a small bowl, whisk remaining ingredients. Drizzle over popcorn mixture; toss to coat.
2. Transfer to two greased 15x10x1-in. baking pans. Bake 10-15 minutes or until toasted, stirring every 5 minutes. Cool completely on wire racks. Store in airtight containers.

"This is one of those dishes that sounds so wrong but tastes so right. Trust me... barbecue chicken leftovers are fantastic with the fries. We like it with lettuce, tomato and pickle, but you can add almost any toppings you like." —**JANET TELLEEN** RUSSELL, IA

Pretty Presentation

When serving healthy appetizers such as fresh veggies with low-fat dip, I like to dress up the serving platter. So I cut the tops off of red or green peppers and remove the seeds and membranes. Then I fill the pepper cups with the dip.

—**EMMA K.** CLAXTON, GA

BBQ Chicken Waffle Fries

PREP: 10 MIN. • **BAKE:** 25 MIN.
MAKES: 8 SERVINGS

- 1 **package (22 ounces) frozen waffle-cut fries**
- 12 **ounces refrigerated shredded barbecued chicken (1½ cups)**
- 1 **cup (4 ounces) shredded Colby-Monterey Jack cheese**
- ¼ **cup chopped red onion**
- ½ **cup shredded lettuce**
- 1 **medium tomato, chopped**
- ¼ **cup chopped dill pickle**
  Pickled banana peppers

Bake fries according to package directions. Transfer to a 10-in. ovenproof skillet. Top with chicken, cheese and onion. Bake 5 minutes longer or until cheese is melted. Top with lettuce, tomato and pickle; serve with peppers.

Smoked Salmon Bites with Shallot Sauce

Tangy Dijon-mayo sauce adds zip to puff pastry and layers of crisp arugula, smoked salmon and shaved Asiago cheese. I make these a couple of times a year.

—JAMIE BROWN-MILLER NAPA, CA

START TO FINISH: 30 MIN.
MAKES: 25 APPETIZERS

- 1 **sheet frozen puff pastry, thawed**

SAUCE
- 2 **shallots**
- 2 **tablespoons Dijon mustard**
- 1 **tablespoon mayonnaise**
- 1 **tablespoon red wine vinegar**
- ¼ **cup olive oil**

FINISHING
- 1 **cup fresh arugula or baby spinach, coarsely chopped**
- 4½ **ounces smoked salmon or lox, thinly sliced**
- ½ **cup shaved Asiago cheese**

1. Unfold puff pastry; cut into 25 squares. Transfer to greased baking sheets. Bake at 400° for 11-13 minutes or until golden brown.
2. Meanwhile, grate one shallot and finely chop the other. In a small bowl, combine the shallots, mustard, mayonnaise and vinegar. While whisking, gradually add oil in a slow, steady stream.
3. Spoon a small amount of sauce onto each pastry; layer with arugula and salmon. Drizzle with remaining sauce and sprinkle with cheese.

Pea Soup Shooters

Appetizers really don't get any easier than this. These shooters can be made ahead, they're colorful, and they won't weigh you down. Top with a dollop of yogurt for a little more tang.

—JACYN SIEBERT WALNUT CREEK, CA

PREP: 20 MIN. + CHILLING
MAKES: 2 DOZEN

- 1 **package (16 ounces) frozen peas, thawed**
- 1 **cup reduced-sodium chicken broth**
- ¼ **cup minced fresh mint**
- 1 **tablespoon lime juice**
- 1 **teaspoon ground cumin**
- ¼ **teaspoon salt**
- 1½ **cups plain yogurt**
  Fresh mint leaves

1. Place the first six ingredients in a blender; cover and process until smooth. Add yogurt; process until blended. Transfer to a pitcher; refrigerate 1 hour to allow flavors to blend.
2. To serve, pour soup into shot glasses; top with mint leaves.
PER SERVING 30 cal., 1 g fat (trace sat. fat), 2 mg chol., 92 mg sodium, 4 g carb., 1 g fiber, 2 g pro.

SMOKED SALMON BITES WITH SHALLOT SAUCE

Savory Pear Tarts

Tiny pear tarts are a quick, easy and elegant addition to the party. Sprinkle the tops with a bit of candied pecans or walnuts for a slight crunch that compliments the tender pears and flaky pastry.

—LEE BELL HOUSTON, TX

PREP: 30 MIN. • **BAKE:** 10 MIN./BATCH
MAKES: 50 APPETIZERS

- 2 shallots, thinly sliced
- ¼ cup orange juice
- ¼ cup balsamic vinegar
- ¼ cup honey
- 2 tablespoons sugar
- 1 tablespoon lemon juice
- 1 garlic clove, minced
- ⅛ teaspoon salt
- ⅛ teaspoon pepper
- 2 Bosc pears, halved and sliced
- 1 package (17.3 ounces) frozen puff pastry, thawed
- ⅓ cup crumbled blue cheese
  Chopped glazed pecans, optional

1. Combine the first nine ingredients in a small saucepan. Bring to a boil over medium heat; cook until liquid is reduced by half. Add the pears; cook and stir for 6-8 minutes or until pears are tender.

2. Meanwhile, unfold puff pastry. Roll each pastry into a 10-in. square. Using a 2-in. round cookie cutter, cut out 25 circles from each square. Transfer to a greased baking sheet. Bake at 400° for 7-9 minutes or until golden brown.

3. Spoon pear mixture over pastries; sprinkle with cheese and pecans if desired.

GARBANZO-STUFFED MINI PEPPERS

EAT SMART FAST FIX

Garbanzo-Stuffed Mini Peppers

Pretty mini peppers are the right size for a two-bite snack. They have all the crunch of a pita chip, but without the extra carbs and calories.

—CHRISTINE HANOVER LEWISTON, CA

START TO FINISH: 20 MIN.
MAKES: 32 APPETIZERS

- 1 teaspoon cumin seeds
- 1 can (15 ounces) garbanzo beans or chickpeas, rinsed and drained
- ¼ cup fresh cilantro leaves
- 3 tablespoons water
- 3 tablespoons cider vinegar
- ¼ teaspoon salt
- 16 miniature sweet peppers, halved lengthwise
  Additional fresh cilantro leaves

1. In a dry small skillet, toast cumin seeds over medium heat 1-2 minutes or until aromatic, stirring frequently. Transfer to a food processor. Add garbanzo beans, cilantro, water, vinegar and salt; pulse until blended.

2. Spoon into pepper halves. Top with additional cilantro. Refrigerate until serving.

PER SERVING *15 cal., trace fat (trace sat. fat), 0 chol., 36 mg sodium, 3 g carb., 1 g fiber, 1 g pro.*

SAVORY PEAR TARTS

Chicken Wing Dings

PREP: 30 MIN. ● **COOK:** 10 MIN./BATCH
MAKES: 2½ DOZEN MEATBALLS (1½ CUPS DIP)

- ¼ cup finely chopped celery
- ¼ cup finely chopped onion
- ¼ cup finely chopped carrot
- 1 envelope ranch salad dressing mix
- 1 egg, lightly beaten
- 1 pound ground chicken
- 2 cups crushed potato chips
- 2 tablespoons canola oil
- 1 container (10 ounces) Philadelphia original cooking creme
- ¾ cup crumbled blue cheese
- 2 garlic cloves, minced
- ½ cup buffalo wing sauce

1. Combine the first five ingredients in a large bowl. Crumble chicken over mixture and mix well. Shape into 1-in. balls and roll in potato chips.

2. Cook meatballs in oil in batches in a large skillet until no longer pink; drain.

3. For dip, combine the cooking creme, blue cheese and garlic in a small bowl. Drizzle meatballs with wing sauce and serve with dip.

"Your guests will have a ball sampling this appetizer that has all the flavor and saucy goodness of traditional Buffalo chicken wings, but without the bones."
—**SUZANNE CLARK** PHOENIX, AZ

CHICKEN WING DINGS

FAST FIX ▶
Asian Delight Popcorn

Here's a fun twist on popcorn that's perfect for movie night.
—**TASTE OF HOME TEST KITCHEN**

START TO FINISH: 10 MIN.
MAKES: 3½ QUARTS

- ¼ cup butter
- ½ teaspoon sesame oil
  Splash of soy sauce
  Sprinkle of ground ginger
- 3½ quarts popped popcorn
  Rice cracker mix (with wasabi peas)
  Honey-roasted peanuts

Melt butter; stir in sesame oil, soy sauce and ginger. Drizzle over popcorn; toss. Add the rice cracker mix and honey-roasted peanuts; toss to combine.

Sweet 'n' Salty Party Mix

These crunchy munchies are sure to rank high with your family and friends. The combination of sweet and salty flavors is just right.
—**CANDICE LUMLEY** CHARLES CITY, IA

PREP: 10 MIN. ● **BAKE:** 1¼ HOURS +COOLING
MAKES: ABOUT 10 QUARTS

- 1 package (12 ounces) Corn Chex
- 1 package (10 ounces) Cheerios
- 1 package (10 ounces) Honeycomb cereal
- 1 package (10 ounces) pretzel sticks
- 1¾ cups sugar
- 1½ cups canola oil
- 1¼ cups butter, melted
- 3 tablespoons soy sauce
- 2 tablespoons garlic salt

1. Preheat oven to 275°. In a very large bowl, combine cereals and pretzels. In another bowl, mix the remaining ingredients until sugar is dissolved. Pour over cereal mixture; toss to coat.

2. Transfer to a large roasting pan. Bake, uncovered, 1¼ hours or until cereal is crisp, stirring every 15 minutes. Cool completely. Store in an airtight container.

FAST FIX ▶

Cherry-Brandy Baked Brie

You won't believe how fast and easy this is to prepare: It's just that delicious! If you like, you can substitute dried cranberries or apricots for the cherries.

—**KEVIN PHEBUS** KATY, TX

START TO FINISH: 20 MIN.
MAKES: 8 SERVINGS

- 1 round (8 ounces) Brie cheese
- ½ cup dried cherries
- ½ cup chopped walnuts
- ¼ cup packed brown sugar
- ¼ cup brandy or unsweetened apple juice
  French bread baguette, sliced and toasted or assorted crackers

1. Place Brie cheese in a 9-in. pie plate. Combine the dried cherries, walnuts, brown sugar and brandy; spoon over the cheese.
2. Bake at 350° for 15-20 minutes or until cheese is softened. Serve with baguette.

EAT SMART

Party Shrimp

An herby marinade makes the shrimp so flavorful, you won't even need to fuss with making a dipping sauce.

—**KENDRA DOSS** COLORADO SPRINGS, CO

PREP: 15 MIN. + MARINATING
BROIL: 10 MIN.
MAKES: ABOUT 2½ DOZEN

- 1 tablespoon olive oil
- 1½ teaspoons brown sugar
- 1½ teaspoons lemon juice
- 1 garlic clove, thinly sliced
- ½ teaspoon paprika
- ½ teaspoon Italian seasoning
- ½ teaspoon dried basil
- ¼ teaspoon pepper
- 1 pound uncooked large shrimp, peeled and deveined

1. In a large resealable plastic bag, combine the first eight ingredients. Add shrimp; seal bag and turn to coat. Refrigerate 2 hours.
2. Drain shrimp, discarding marinade. Place shrimp on an ungreased baking sheet. Broil 4 in. from heat 3-4 minutes on each side or until shrimp turn pink.
PER SERVING *14 cal., trace fat (trace sat. fat), 18 mg chol., 18 mg sodium, trace carb., trace fiber, 2 g pro.* **Diabetic Exchange:** *Free food.*

⑤ INGREDIENTS

Bacon-Wrapped Cajun Jalapenos

These peppers are so addictive that if I want any for myself, I either need to make a double batch or hide some. They have a wonderful flavor.

—**LINDA FOREMAN** LOCUST GROVE, OK

PREP: 20 MIN. • **BAKE:** 25 MIN.
MAKES: 16 APPETIZERS

- 8 large jalapeno peppers
- 1 package (3 ounces) cream cheese, softened
- ½ cup finely shredded cheddar cheese
- 1 teaspoon Cajun seasoning
- 8 thick-sliced peppered bacon strips

1. Cut jalapenos in half lengthwise; remove seeds and membranes. In a small bowl, combine the cream cheese, cheddar cheese and Cajun seasoning. Stuff about 1½ teaspoons into each pepper half.
2. Cut bacon strips in half widthwise. In a large skillet, cook bacon until partially cooked but not crisp. Wrap a bacon piece around each pepper; secure with a toothpick.
3. Place the peppers on a wire rack in a shallow baking pan. Bake, uncovered, at 350° for 25-30 minutes or until bacon is crisp. Discard toothpicks. Serve immediately.
NOTE *Wear disposable gloves when cutting hot peppers; the oils can burn skin. Avoid touching your face.*

PARTY SHRIMP

THAI VEGGIE DIP

Thai Veggie Dip

This delicious dip is full of flavor, color and crunch, but not calories. There's mild sweetness from the honey with a bit of heat at the end from the pepper flakes. If spicy food is your thing, feel free to add an extra dash of crushed red pepper.

—**JEANNE HOLT** MENDOTA HEIGHTS, MN

PREP: 15 MIN. + CHILLING
MAKES: 3 CUPS

- 3 **tablespoons reduced-fat creamy peanut butter**
- 1 **tablespoon reduced-sodium soy sauce**
- 1 **tablespoon honey**
- 1 **cup (8 ounces) reduced-fat sour cream**
- 1 **cup fat-free plain Greek yogurt**
- 1 **cup fresh baby spinach, chopped**
- ½ **cup sliced water chestnuts, chopped**
- 1 **small sweet red pepper, finely chopped**
- 3 **tablespoons finely chopped green onions**
- 3 **tablespoons minced fresh cilantro**
- 1 **tablespoon minced fresh mint**
- 1 **teaspoon crushed red pepper flakes**
  Assorted fresh vegetables

In a large bowl, mix peanut butter, soy sauce and honey until blended. Stir in sour cream, yogurt, spinach, water chestnuts, pepper, green onions, cilantro, mint and pepper flakes. Refrigerate, covered, 1-2 hours. Serve with assorted vegetables.

PER (¼-CUP) SERVING *73 cal., 3 g fat (1 g sat. fat), 7 mg chol., 99 mg sodium, 7 g carb., 1 g fiber, 5 g pro.* **Diabetic Exchanges:** *½ starch, ½ fat.*

Buffalo Wing Bites

PREP: 25 MIN. • **BAKE:** 15 MIN.
MAKES: 2 DOZEN (2 CUPS DRESSING)

- 2 **tablespoons grated Parmesan cheese**
- 1 **envelope ranch salad dressing mix, divided**
- 1 **cup mayonnaise**
- 1 **cup 2% milk**
- ¼ **cup crumbled blue cheese, optional**
- 1¼ **cups finely chopped cooked chicken breast**
- 1¼ **cups (5 ounces) shredded cheddar-Monterey Jack cheese**
- ¼ **cup Buffalo wing sauce**
- 1 **tube (13.8 ounces) refrigerated pizza crust**
- 2 **tablespoons butter, melted**

1. Preheat oven to 400°. In a small bowl, combine Parmesan cheese and 1 teaspoon dressing mix. In another bowl, mix mayonnaise, milk and remaining dressing mix. If desired, stir in blue cheese. Refrigerate until serving.
2. In a large bowl, mix chicken, cheddar-Monterey Jack cheese and wing sauce. On a lightly floured surface, unroll pizza crust dough and pat into a 14x12-in. rectangle. Cut into 24 squares.
3. Place 1 rounded tablespoon chicken mixture on the center of each square. Pull corners together to enclose filling; pinch to seal. Place 1 in. apart on greased baking sheets, seam side down. Brush tops with butter; sprinkle with Parmesan cheese mixture.
4. Bake 15-17 minutes or until golden brown. Serve with dressing.

"The Buffalo wing fans in my family were happy to taste test when I invented these snacks. We love them anytime."
—**JASEY MCBURNETT** ROCK SPRINGS, WY

BUFFALO WING BITES

SIMPLE SWISS CHEESE FONDUE

Simple Swiss Cheese Fondue

When I was growing up, my friend's mother would make this rich fondue when I spent the night. Every time I prepare it, it brings back fond memories.
—**TRACY LAWSON** FARR WEST, UT

START TO FINISH: 20 MIN.
MAKES: ⅔ CUP

- 1 cup (4 ounces) shredded Swiss cheese
- 1 tablespoon all-purpose flour
- ⅛ teaspoon ground mustard
  Dash ground nutmeg
- ¼ cup half-and-half cream
- ¼ cup beer or nonalcoholic beer
- 4 slices French bread (1 inch thick), cut into 1-inch cubes

1. In a small bowl, combine the cheese, flour, mustard and nutmeg. In a small saucepan, heat cream and beer over medium heat until bubbles form around sides of saucepan. Stir in cheese mixture. Bring just to a gentle boil; cook and stir for 1-2 minutes or until smooth.
2. Transfer to a small fondue pot and keep warm. Serve with bread cubes.

Crisp Finger Sandwich

I love snacking on this delicious sandwich with its crisp English cucumber. I have also made batches of these for parties and showers, using a small party loaf of whole wheat or sourdough bread.
—**MISSI SELIN** BOTHELL, WA

START TO FINISH: 10 MIN.
MAKES: 1 SERVING

- 1 slice whole wheat bread, toasted
- 2 tablespoons reduced-fat spreadable garden vegetable cream cheese
- ⅓ cup thinly sliced English cucumber
- 3 tablespoons alfalfa sprouts
  Dash coarsely ground pepper

Spread toast with cream cheese. Top with cucumber, sprouts and pepper.
PER SERVING *136 cal., 6 g fat (3 g sat. fat), 15 mg chol., 323 mg sodium, 13 g carb., 2 g fiber, 7 g pro.* **Diabetic Exchanges:** *1 starch, 1 fat.*

"This irresistible recipe will remind you of a jalapeno popper without all the mess. If my husband had his way, I would make this for him every weekend. The versatile dip also goes great with whole wheat crackers or pita chips." —**DEBORAH PEIRCE** VIRGINIA BEACH, VA

CREAMY JALAPENO POPPER DIP

Creamy Jalapeno Popper Dip

PREP: 15 MIN. • **BAKE:** 30 MIN.
MAKES: 2 CUPS

- 4 bacon strips, chopped
- 1 package (8 ounces) cream cheese, softened
- 2 cups (8 ounces) shredded cheddar cheese
- ½ cup sour cream
- ¼ cup 2% milk
- 3 jalapeno peppers, seeded and chopped
- 1 teaspoon white wine vinegar
- ⅓ cup panko (Japanese) bread crumbs
- 2 tablespoons butter
  Tortilla chips

1. Preheat oven to 350°. In a small skillet, cook bacon over medium heat until crisp, stirring occasionally. Remove with a slotted spoon; drain on paper towels. Discard drippings, reserving 1 tablespoon.
2. In a large bowl, mix cream cheese, cheddar cheese, sour cream, milk, jalapenos, vinegar, cooked bacon and reserved drippings. Transfer to a greased 8-in.-square baking dish. Sprinkle with bread crumbs and dot with butter.
3. Bake 30-35 minutes or until bubbly and topping is golden brown. Serve with chips.
NOTE *Wear disposable gloves when cutting hot peppers; the oils can burn skin. Avoid touching your face.*

Judy Wilson's
Turkey Focaccia Club
PAGE 115

Snappy Soups, Salads & Sandwiches

For an easygoing meal at home or out of the lunch box, nothing beats a piled-high sandwich, crispy main dish salad or hot bowlful of comforting soup. Here you'll find fresh, fast choices for any time of year.

Jenna Rempe's
Chicken Chili Chowder
PAGE 119

Daniel Anderson's
Italian Chopped Salad with Chicken
PAGE 115

Lisa Renshaw's
Fruited Turkey Wraps
PAGE 129

LEMONY TORTELLINI BACON SALAD

FAST FIX

BLT with Peppered Balsamic Mayo

START TO FINISH: 25 MIN.
MAKES: 4 SERVINGS

- 8 bacon strips, halved
- ½ cup mayonnaise
- 1 tablespoon balsamic vinegar
- ½ teaspoon pepper
- ⅛ teaspoon salt
- 8 slices bread, toasted
- 2 cups spring mix salad greens
- 8 cherry tomatoes, sliced
- 1 medium ripe avocado, peeled and sliced

1. In a large skillet, cook bacon over medium heat until crisp. Remove to paper towels to drain.
2. In a small bowl, mix mayonnaise, vinegar, pepper and salt. Spread half of the mixture over four toast slices. Layer with bacon, salad greens, tomatoes and avocado. Spread remaining mayonnaise over remaining toast; place over top.

"Here's my twist on a classic. Creamy avocado, balsamic mayo and crisp salad greens make this version memorable in my book. For a lighter take, I often use turkey bacon." —**AMI BOYER** SAN FRANSISCO, CA

BLT WITH PEPPERED BALSAMIC MAYO

FAST FIX

Lemony Tortellini Bacon Salad

Summer meals shouldn't be complicated. We love this simple and tasty salad on warm nights. Add a glass of iced tea or lemonade and dinner couldn't be easier.

—**SAMANTHA VICARS** KENOSHA, WI

START TO FINISH: 20 MIN.
MAKES: 4 SERVINGS

- 2 cups frozen cheese tortellini (about 8 ounces)
- 4 cups fresh broccoli florets
- ¾ cup mayonnaise
- 1 tablespoon balsamic vinegar
- 2 teaspoons lemon juice
- ¾ teaspoon dried oregano
- ¼ teaspoon salt
- 1 package (5 ounces) spring mix salad greens
- 4 bacon strips, cooked and crumbled

1. In a large saucepan, cook tortellini according to package directions, adding broccoli during the last 5 minutes of cooking. Meanwhile, in a small bowl, mix mayonnaise, vinegar, lemon juice, oregano and salt.
2. Drain tortellini and broccoli; gently rinse with cold water. Transfer to a large bowl. Add dressing and toss to coat. Serve over salad greens; sprinkle with bacon.

Orzo Shrimp Stew

My husband and I really enjoy seafood, so I don't skimp on shrimp in this mildly seasoned stew. It has plenty of broccoli and pasta, which makes it satisfying.

—LISA STINGER HAMILTON, NJ

START TO FINISH: 20 MIN.
MAKES: 4 SERVINGS

- 2½ cups reduced-sodium chicken broth
- 5 cups fresh broccoli florets
- 1 can (14½ ounces) diced tomatoes, undrained
- 1 cup uncooked orzo
- 1 pound uncooked medium shrimp, peeled and deveined
- ¾ teaspoon salt
- ¼ teaspoon pepper
- 2 teaspoons dried basil
- 2 tablespoons butter

1. Bring broth to a boil in a Dutch oven. Add the broccoli, tomatoes and orzo. Reduce heat; simmer, uncovered, for 5 minutes, stirring occasionally.
2. Add the shrimp, salt and pepper. Cover and cook for 4-5 minutes or until shrimp turn pink and orzo is tender. Stir in basil and butter.

PER SERVING *401 cal., 10 g fat (5 g sat. fat), 190 mg chol., 919 mg sodium, 45 g carb., 4 g fiber, 35 g pro.* **Diabetic Exchanges:** *3 lean meat, 2½ starch, 1 vegetable.*

VEGETARIAN SLOPPY JOES

ORZO SHRIMP STEW

Vegetarian Sloppy Joes

You won't miss the meat in my version of sloppy joes. These taste like the classic recipe, but are lower in fat. The dish is an easy option for a meatless lunch or supper.

—LINDA WINTER OAK HARBOR, WA

START TO FINISH: 25 MIN.
MAKES: 6 SERVINGS

- 2 teaspoons butter
- 1 small onion, finely chopped
- 1 package (12 ounces) frozen vegetarian meat crumbles
- ½ teaspoon pepper
- 2 tablespoons all-purpose flour
- ⅔ cup ketchup
- 1 can (8 ounces) no-salt-added tomato sauce
- 6 hamburger buns, split and toasted

1. In a large nonstick skillet coated with cooking spray, melt butter over medium-high heat. Add onion; cook and stir until tender. Stir in meat crumbles and pepper; heat through.
2. Sprinkle flour over mixture and stir until blended. Stir in ketchup and tomato sauce. Bring to a boil; cook and stir 1-2 minutes or until thickened. Serve on buns.

NOTE *Vegetarian meat crumbles are a nutritious protein source made from soy. Look for them in the natural foods freezer section.*

PER SERVING *273 cal., 6 g fat (2 g sat. fat), 4 mg chol., 815 mg sodium, 39 g carb., 5 g fiber, 15 g pro.* **Diabetic Exchanges:** *2½ starch, 2 lean meat.*

MINESTRONE WITH TURKEY

1. Saute onion in 1 teaspoon butter in a small skillet until tender and lightly browned. Add olives; cook 1 minute longer. Spread mustard over bread slices. Layer one slice with onion mixture and cheeses. Top with remaining bread. Spread outside of sandwich with remaining butter.
2. Toast sandwich in a small skillet over medium heat for 2-4 minutes on each side or until cheese is melted.

FAST FIX

Corned Beef and Coleslaw Sandwiches

These open-faced sandwiches with layers of savory beef, creamy slaw and Swiss take only 15 minutes to put together.

—MARILOU ROBINSON PORTLAND, OR

START TO FINISH: 15 MIN.
MAKES: 4 SERVINGS

- 2 cups coleslaw mix
- 3 tablespoons sour cream
- 4 teaspoons mayonnaise
- 1 tablespoon horseradish sauce
- 1 teaspoon prepared mustard
- ⅛ teaspoon salt
- 4 slices rye bread
- ½ pound thinly sliced corned beef
- 8 slices Swiss cheese

1. Place coleslaw mix in a small bowl. Combine the sour cream, mayonnaise, horseradish sauce, mustard and salt. Pour over coleslaw mix and toss to coat.
2. Place bread slices on an ungreased baking sheet. Broil 4 in. from the heat for 2-3 minutes on each side or until toasted. Layer with corned beef, coleslaw mixture and cheese. Broil for 2-3 minutes or until cheese is melted.

CORNED BEEF AND COLESLAW SANDWICHES

FAST FIX

Minestrone with Turkey

I have fond memories of my mom making this soup for me when I was a little girl. I loved it then, and I still love it today.

—ANGELA GOODMAN KANEOHE, HI

START TO FINISH: 30 MIN.
MAKES: 6 SERVINGS (2 QUARTS)

- 1 tablespoon olive oil
- 1 medium onion, chopped
- 1 medium carrot, sliced
- 1 celery rib, sliced
- 1 garlic clove, minced
- 4 cups chicken broth or homemade turkey stock
- 1 can (14½ ounces) diced tomatoes, undrained
- ⅔ cup each frozen peas, corn and cut green beans, thawed
- ½ cup uncooked elbow macaroni
- 1 teaspoon salt
- ¼ teaspoon dried basil
- ¼ teaspoon dried oregano
- ¼ teaspoon pepper
- 1 bay leaf
- 1 cup cubed cooked turkey
- 1 small zucchini, halved lengthwise and cut into ¼-inch slices
- ¼ cup grated Parmesan cheese, optional

1. In a Dutch oven, heat oil over medium-high heat. Add onion, carrot and celery; cook and stir until tender. Add garlic; cook 1 minute longer.
2. Stir in broth, vegetables, macaroni and seasonings. Bring to a boil. Reduce heat; simmer, uncovered, 5 minutes or until macaroni is al dente.
3. Stir in turkey and zucchini; cook until zucchini is crisp-tender. Discard bay leaf. If desired, sprinkle servings with cheese.

FAST FIX

Gourmet Grilled Cheese Sandwich

This is a mouthwatering twist on grilled cheese that's a cheese-lover's dream come true. Feel free to skip the olives or swap breads to suit your taste.

—BETH DUNAHAY LIMA, OH

START TO FINISH: 15 MIN.
MAKES: 1 SERVING

- 2 slices sweet onion
- 1 teaspoon plus 1 tablespoon butter, divided
- 5 Greek olives, sliced
- 2 teaspoons spicy brown mustard
- 2 slices rye or pumpernickel bread
- 3 tablespoons crumbled feta cheese
- 2 slices Swiss cheese

SNAPPY SOUPS, SALADS & SANDWICHES

"Don't let the ingredient list fool you. This summery chicken salad is simple. Prepare it in the morning and let it chill all day. Then, toss in the dressing right before serving. For another spin, I sometimes add grilled fresh corn." —DANIEL ANDERSON PLEASANT PRAIRIE, WI

ITALIAN CHOPPED SALAD WITH CHICKEN

FAST FIX ▶

Italian Chopped Salad with Chicken

START TO FINISH: 30 MIN.
MAKES: 8 SERVINGS

- ¼ pound sliced pancetta or bacon strips, chopped

DRESSING
- 3 tablespoons prepared pesto
- 2 tablespoons olive oil
- 1 tablespoon lemon juice
- ¼ teaspoon salt
- ¼ teaspoon pepper

SALAD
- 10 cups torn iceberg and romaine lettuce blend
- 1 cup cubed rotisserie chicken
- 1 cup sliced fresh mushrooms
- 1 small red onion, chopped
- 1 small cucumber, peeled and chopped
- ½ cup grape tomatoes, halved
- ½ cup canned black-eyed peas, rinsed and drained
- ½ cup cubed pepper Jack cheese
- ½ cup cubed part-skim mozzarella cheese
- ¼ cup chopped fresh basil

1. In a large skillet, cook pancetta over medium heat until crisp, stirring occasionally. Remove with a slotted spoon; drain on paper towels.
2. In a small bowl, whisk dressing ingredients. In a large bowl, combine salad ingredients; sprinkle with pancetta. Drizzle with dressing; toss to coat.

FAST FIX ▶

Turkey Focaccia Club

My family thinks this sandwich is pure heaven, thanks to the cranberry-pecan mayo. It's so good, I'm asked to make it many times throughout the year.
—**JUDY WILSON** SUN CITY WEST, AZ

START TO FINISH: 20 MIN.
MAKES: 4 SERVINGS

- ½ cup mayonnaise
- ½ cup whole-berry cranberry sauce
- 2 tablespoons chopped pecans, toasted
- 2 tablespoons Dijon mustard
- 1 tablespoon honey
- 1 loaf (8 ounces) focaccia bread
- 3 lettuce leaves
- ½ pound thinly sliced cooked turkey
- ¼ pound sliced Gouda cheese
- 8 slices tomato
- 6 bacon strips, cooked

In a small bowl, mix the first five ingredients until blended. Using a long serrated knife, cut focaccia horizontally in half. Spread cut sides with mayonnaise mixture. Layer bottom half with lettuce, turkey, cheese, tomato and bacon; replace bread top. Cut into wedges.
NOTE *To toast nuts, spread in a 15x10x1-in. baking pan. Bake at 350° for 5-10 minutes or until lightly browned, stirring occasionally. Or, spread in a dry nonstick skillet and heat over low heat until lightly browned, stirring occasionally.*

TURKEY FOCACCIA CLUB

CURRIED BEEF PITAS WITH CUCUMBER SAUCE

EAT SMART FAST FIX

Turkey Gyros

Greek seasoning, feta cheese and cool cucumber sauce give my lightened-up gyros an authentic taste. Instead of feta cheese, we sometimes use cheddar or Monterey Jack.

—**DONNA GARVIN** GLENS FALLS, NY

START TO FINISH: 25 MIN.
MAKES: 4 SERVINGS

- 1 medium cucumber, peeled
- ⅔ cup reduced-fat sour cream
- ¼ cup finely chopped onion
- 2 teaspoons dill weed
- 2 teaspoons lemon juice
- 1 teaspoon olive oil
- ½ pound turkey breast tenderloin, cut into ¼-inch slices
- 1½ teaspoons salt-free Greek seasoning
- 8 thin tomato slices
- 4 pita breads (6 inches), warmed
- 1½ cups shredded lettuce
- 2 tablespoons crumbled feta cheese

1. Finely chop one-third of the cucumber; place in a small bowl. Toss with sour cream, onion, dill and lemon juice. Thinly slice the remaining cucumber; set aside.
2. In a nonstick skillet, heat oil over medium-high heat. Add turkey; cook and stir 5-7 minutes or until no longer pink. Sprinkle with Greek seasoning.
3. Serve turkey, tomato and sliced cucumber on pita breads. Top with lettuce, cheese and sauce.
TO MAKE YOUR OWN SALT-FREE GREEK SEASONING *In a small bowl, combine 1½ tsp. dried oregano, 1 tsp. each dried mint and dried thyme and ½ tsp. each dried basil, dried marjoram and dried minced onion and ¼ tsp. dried minced garlic. Store airtight in a cool dry place for up to 6 months. Yield: 2 Tbsp.*
PER SERVING *328 cal., 7 g fat (4 g sat. fat), 53 mg chol., 446 mg sodium, 42 g carb., 3 g fiber, 24 g pro.* **Diabetic Exchanges:** *2½ starch, 2 lean meat, 1 vegetable, 1 fat.*

EAT SMART FAST FIX

Curried Beef Pitas with Cucumber Sauce

A good friend gave me this recipe when I first got married. Since some of the ingredients weren't very familiar to me, I was apprehensive about trying it. But it's now a family favorite.

—**SHANNON KOENE** BLACKSBURG, VA

START TO FINISH: 25 MIN.
MAKES: 4 SERVINGS (1½ CUPS SAUCE)

- 1 cup fat-free plain Greek yogurt
- 1 cup finely chopped peeled cucumber
- 1 tablespoon minced fresh mint
- 2 garlic cloves, minced
- 2 teaspoons snipped fresh dill
- 2 teaspoons lemon juice
- ¼ teaspoon salt

PITAS
- 1 pound lean ground beef (90% lean)
- 1 small onion, chopped
- 1 medium Golden Delicious apple, finely chopped
- ¼ cup raisins
- 2 teaspoons curry powder
- ¼ teaspoon salt
- 8 whole wheat pita pocket halves

1. In a small bowl, mix the first seven ingredients. Refrigerate until serving.
2. In a large skillet, cook beef and onion over medium heat 6-8 minutes or until beef is no longer pink, breaking up beef into crumbles; drain. Add apple, raisins, curry powder and salt; cook until apple is tender, stirring occasionally. Serve in pita halves with cucumber sauce.
PER SERVING *429 cal., 11 g fat (4 g sat. fat), 71 mg chol., 686 mg sodium, 50 g carb., 6 g fiber, 36 g pro.*

TURKEY GYROS

Bazaar Soup Mix

This soup mix makes a nice-looking gift layered into a jar. Be sure to list the additional ingredients needed and the cooking instructions on the gift tag.
—**PEARL BROCK** COUDERSPORT, PA

PREP: 15 MIN. • **COOK:** 1¼ HOURS
MAKES: 8 SERVINGS (2 QUARTS)

- ¼ cup dried lentils, sorted
- ¼ cup dried green split peas, sorted
- ¼ cup uncooked long grain rice
- 2 tablespoons medium pearl barley
- 4 teaspoons beef or chicken bouillon granules
- 2 tablespoons dried minced onion
- 1 teaspoon celery salt
- ½ teaspoon Italian seasoning
- 3 tablespoons dried parsley flakes
- ½ cup uncooked small pasta shells

ADDITIONAL INGREDIENTS

- ½ pound ground beef
- 8 cups water
- 1 can (14½ ounces) diced tomatoes, undrained

In a 1-pint jar or container with a tight-fitting lid, layer the first nine ingredients in the order listed. Wrap pasta in a small piece of plastic wrap; add to jar. Seal tightly. Store in a cool dry place for up to 3 months.
TO PREPARE SOUP *Remove pasta from top of jar and set aside. In a Dutch oven, cook beef over medium heat until no longer pink; drain. Add the water, tomatoes and soup mix; bring to a boil. Reduce heat; cover and simmer for 45 minutes. Stir in reserved pasta; cover and simmer 15-20 minutes longer or until pasta, lentils, peas and barley are tender.*

BAZAAR SOUP MIX

VEGGIE-SESAME CHICKEN SALAD

FAST FIX
Veggie-Sesame Chicken Salad

Sweet, crisp, sunshine-packed and fun, this delightful salad has it all. It's perfect for those nights when you don't want to cook.
—**BETTY SLIVON** SUN CITY, AZ

START TO FINISH: 10 MIN.
MAKES: 4 SERVINGS

- 1 package (5 ounces) spring mix salad greens
- 2½ cups shredded rotisserie chicken
- 1 can (8 ounces) unsweetened pineapple chunks, drained
- ½ cup shredded carrots
- ½ cup frozen shelled edamame, thawed
- ½ cup chopped sweet red pepper
- 2 green onions, chopped
- ½ cup sesame ginger salad dressing
- ½ cup wonton strips

Combine the first seven ingredients in a large bowl. Drizzle with dressing and toss to coat. Sprinkle with wonton strips. Serve immediately.

top tip
Dressed-Up Chicken Salad

Chicken salad is anything but ordinary when I add a dash of curry powder, a handful of grapes and a small can of drained mandarin oranges to the mayonnaise dressing. I serve a generous scoop of the salad on a bed of lettuce with hard rolls.
—**SUSIE B.** BONHAM, TX

Chicken Chili Chowder

One chilly April afternoon, I craved a hearty soup but had less than an hour to prepare a meal. I came up with this chowder that uses pantry ingredients, and everyone thought it hit the spot.

—JENNA REMPE LINCOLN, NE

PREP: 15 MIN. • **COOK:** 25 MIN.
MAKES: 6 SERVINGS (2 QUARTS)

- 1 medium onion, chopped
- 2 teaspoons canola oil
- 5 medium red potatoes, cubed
- 1 can (14½ ounces) chicken broth
- 1 can (10¾ ounces) condensed cream of chicken soup, undiluted
- ½ cup salsa verde
- 1 teaspoon chili powder
- ½ teaspoon garlic powder
- ½ teaspoon ground cumin
- ½ teaspoon pepper
- ¼ teaspoon salt
- 2 cups cubed cooked chicken breast
- 1 can (15½ ounces) great northern beans, rinsed and drained
- 1 can (14¾ ounces) cream-style corn
  Shredded cheddar cheese and sour cream, optional

Saute onion in oil in a large saucepan until tender. Add potatoes, broth, soup, salsa and seasonings. Bring to a boil. Reduce heat; cover and simmer for 15-20 minutes or until potatoes are tender. Stir in the chicken, beans and corn; heat through. Serve with cheese and sour cream if desired.

TURKEY SLOPPY JOES WITH AVOCADO SLAW

Turkey Sloppy Joes with Avocado Slaw

Sloppy Joes are a suppertime staple, but my friends say this avocado slaw makes them seem brand new. The creamy slaw tastes perfect with the tangy sandwich filling. Try them—you'll agree!

—JACYN SIEBERT WALNUT CREEK, CA

PREP: 15 MIN. • **COOK:** 20 MIN.
MAKES: 6 SERVINGS

- 1 pound ground turkey
- 1 medium onion, chopped
- 1 envelope sloppy joe mix
- 1 can (6 ounces) tomato paste
- 1¼ cups water

SLAW

- 1 medium ripe avocado, peeled and cubed
- 1 tablespoon olive oil
- 2 teaspoons lemon juice
- ½ teaspoon ground cumin
- ¼ teaspoon salt
- ¼ teaspoon pepper
- 2½ cups coleslaw mix
- 6 hamburger buns, split

1. In a large skillet, cook turkey and onion over medium heat 7-8 minutes or until turkey is no longer pink and onion is tender, breaking up turkey into crumbles; drain.

2. Stir in sloppy joe mix, tomato paste and water. Bring to a boil. Reduce heat; simmer, uncovered, 8-10 minutes or until thickened, stirring occasionally.

3. Meanwhile, place avocado, oil, lemon juice, cumin, salt and pepper in a blender; cover and process until smooth. Transfer to a small bowl; stir in coleslaw mix. Spoon meat mixture onto bun bottoms and top with slaw. Replace tops.

CHICKEN CHILI CHOWDER

FAST FIX ▶
Chicken & Apple Salad with Greens

My favorite memory of eating this dish was when my mom made it on weekends when we could have something other than brown-bag school lunches. Happy memories of childhood days make this salad extra special for me.

—TRISHA KRUSE EAGLE, ID

START TO FINISH: 30 MIN.
MAKES: 6 SERVINGS

VINAIGRETTE
- ¼ cup balsamic vinegar
- ¼ cup orange juice
- ¼ cup olive oil
- 2 tablespoons lemon juice
- 2 tablespoons reduced-sodium soy sauce
- 1 tablespoon brown sugar
- 1 tablespoon Dijon mustard
- ½ teaspoon curry powder, optional
- ½ teaspoon salt
- ¼ teaspoon pepper
- ¼ teaspoon ground ginger

SALAD
- 2 cups shredded cooked chicken
- 2 medium apples, chopped
- ½ cup thinly sliced red onion
- 10 cups torn mixed salad greens
- ½ cup chopped walnuts, toasted

In a large bowl, whisk the vinaigrette ingredients until blended. Add chicken, apples and onion; toss to coat. Just before serving, place greens on a large serving plate; top with chicken mixture. Sprinkle with walnuts.

NOTE *To toast nuts, spread in a 15x10x1-in. baking pan. Bake at 350° for 5-10 minutes or until lightly browned, stirring occasionally. Or, spread in a dry nonstick skillet and heat over low heat until lightly browned, stirring occasionally.*

CHICKEN & APPLE SALAD WITH GREENS

FAST FIX ▶
Margie's Chili

I spice up canned tomato soup to create a flavorful and easy chili.

—MARGARET GANZEL MANKATO, MN

START TO FINISH: 25 MIN.
MAKES: 4 SERVINGS

- 1 pound ground beef
- 2 small onions, chopped
- 1 can (10¾ ounces) condensed tomato soup, undiluted
- 1 can (15½ ounces) kidney beans, rinsed and drained
- ¾ cup chili sauce
- 2 teaspoons chili powder or prepared horseradish
- ¼ teaspoon salt
- ¼ teaspoon pepper

In a large saucepan, brown beef and onions; drain. Add remaining ingredients; bring to a boil. Reduce heat; simmer, uncovered, for 5-10 minutes or until thickened.

FAST FIX ▶
Hearty Italian Salad

Meat lovers won't be able to resist my antipasto-inspired salad that eats like a meal. Just add bread and dipping oil.

—MELISSA JELINEK MENOMONEE FALLS, WI

START TO FINISH: 20 MIN.
MAKES: 4 SERVINGS

- 8 cups ready-to-serve salad greens
- 8 slices deli pastrami, cut into strips
- 2 cups cubed fully cooked ham
- 1 cup shredded Italian cheese blend
- 4 plum tomatoes, chopped
- ½ cup Italian salad dressing
  Seasoned salad croutons, sliced ripe olives and sliced pepperoncini

Divide salad greens among four plates; layer with pastrami, ham, cheese and tomatoes. Drizzle with dressing. Top salads with croutons, olives and pepperoncini. Serve immediately.

MEDITERRANEAN TORTELLINI SALAD

"A childhood friend moved to Italy 20 years ago. During a recent visit to see her, I enjoyed a scrumptious salad made with tortellini and fresh vegetables. Here's my version."

—**KELLY MAPES** FORT COLLINS, CO

FAST FIX
Mediterranean Tortellini Salad

START TO FINISH: 30 MIN.
MAKES: 6 SERVINGS

- 1 package (19 ounces) frozen cheese tortellini
- 1 package (14 ounces) smoked turkey sausage, sliced
- ¾ cup prepared pesto
- 2 cups fresh baby spinach, chopped
- 2 cups sliced baby portobello mushrooms
- 1 can (15 ounces) white kidney or cannellini beans, rinsed and drained
- 1 cup roasted sweet red peppers, chopped
- 1 cup (4 ounces) crumbled feta cheese
- ¼ cup pitted Greek olives, sliced

1. Cook tortellini according to package directions.
2. Meanwhile, in a large nonstick skillet coated with cooking spray, cook and stir sausage over medium heat 6-7 minutes or until lightly browned. Transfer to a large bowl.
3. Drain tortellini; add to sausage. Stir in pesto. Add remaining ingredients; toss to combine. Serve warm or refrigerate until chilled.

Sausage & Cannellini Bean Soup

Here's my reproduction of a dish from a famous Chicago eatery. We think it rivals the original. I usually cook this at least once a week. It's a tasty way to keep my lunch box full of healthy options.
—**MARILYN MCGINNIS** PEORIA, AZ

START TO FINISH: 30 MIN.
MAKES: 4 SERVINGS

- 3 Italian turkey sausage links (4 ounces each), casings removed
- 1 medium onion, chopped
- 2 garlic cloves, minced
- 1 can (15 ounces) cannellini or white kidney beans, rinsed and drained
- 1 can (14½ ounces) reduced-sodium chicken broth
- 1 cup water
- ¼ cup white wine or additional reduced-sodium chicken broth
- ¼ teaspoon pepper
- 1 bunch escarole or spinach, chopped
- 4 teaspoons shredded Parmesan cheese

1. Cook the sausage and onion in a large saucepan over medium heat until meat is no longer pink; drain. Add garlic; cook 1 minute longer.
2. Stir in the beans, broth, water, wine and pepper. Bring to a boil. Add escarole; heat through. Sprinkle with cheese.
PER SERVING *232 cal., 6 g fat (2 g sat. fat), 33 mg chol., 837 mg sodium, 24 g carb., 9 g fiber, 17 g pro.*

SAUSAGE & CANNELLINI BEAN SOUP

GRILLED GOAT CHEESE & ARUGULA SANDWICHES

Grilled Goat Cheese & Arugula Sandwiches

To create a more grown-up grilled cheese sandwich, I threw in tangy goat cheese and peppery arugula. I enjoy a similar combination on pizza, and it works here, too.

—JESS APFE BERKELEY, CA

START TO FINISH: 30 MIN.
MAKES: 4 SERVINGS

- ½ cup sun-dried tomato pesto
- 8 slices sourdough bread
- 1½ cups roasted sweet red peppers, drained and patted dry
- 8 slices part-skim mozzarella cheese
- ½ cup crumbled goat cheese
- 1 cup fresh arugula
- ¼ cup butter, softened

1. Spread pesto over four slices of bread. Layer with peppers, mozzarella cheese, goat cheese and arugula; top with remaining bread. Spread outsides of sandwiches with butter.

2. In a large skillet, toast sandwiches over medium heat 3-4 minutes on each side or until golden brown and cheese is melted.

FAST FIX ▶
Hearty Wild Rice Soup

When I was a judge at a local fair, this soup recipe received my highest score. Of all the soups I tasted that day, it was the only recipe that I took home. It's always a winner at my house.

—KATHY HERINK GLADBROOK, IA

START TO FINISH: 20 MIN.
MAKES: 8 SERVINGS (ABOUT 2 QUARTS)

- 1 pound ground beef
- 4 celery ribs, chopped
- 2 large onions, chopped
- 3 cups water
- 1 can (14½ ounces) chicken broth
- 1 can (10¾ ounces) condensed cream of mushroom soup, undiluted
- 1 package (6¾ ounces) quick-cooking long grain and wild rice mix
- 5 bacon strips, cooked and crumbled

1. In a Dutch oven, cook beef, celery and onions over medium heat until beef is no longer pink and vegetables are tender, breaking up beef into crumbles; drain.

2. Stir in water, broth, soup, rice mix and contents of the seasoning packet. Bring to a boil. Reduce heat; simmer, covered, 5 minutes or until heated through. Top servings with bacon.

HEARTY WILD RICE SOUP

FAST FIX ▶
Asian Sesame Chicken Salad

START TO FINISH: 30 MIN.
MAKES: 6 SERVINGS

- 6 **cups torn romaine (about 1 small bunch)**
- 2 **cups shredded cooked chicken**
- 1 **can (15 ounces) mandarin oranges, drained**
- 1 **large cucumber, peeled and finely chopped**
- ½ **cup chopped salted peanuts**
- ½ **cup shredded carrots**
- ¼ **cup minced fresh cilantro**
- 1 **jalapeno pepper, seeded and minced**
- 1 **green onion, thinly sliced**
- 1 **cup wonton strips**
- ¾ **cup Asian toasted sesame salad dressing, divided**

In a large bowl, combine the first nine ingredients. Just before serving, add wonton strips and drizzle with ¼ cup dressing; toss to combine. Serve with remaining dressing.

NOTE *Wear disposable gloves when cutting hot peppers; the oils can burn skin. Avoid touching your face.*

"When my friends and I meet for Sunday get-togethers, this is one dish they always ask me to bring. I don't mind because it travels well, is very easy to make, and is absolutely delicious." —**STACY REED** GRESHAM, OR

ASIAN SESAME CHICKEN SALAD

TACO TWIST SOUP

EAT SMART | FAST FIX ▶
Taco Twist Soup

Warm and comforting, this meatless soup comes together in minutes from pantry staples. To keep it lighter, I top bowlfuls with reduced-fat sour cream and cheese.
—**COLLEEN ZERTLER** MENOMONIE, WI

START TO FINISH: 30 MIN.
MAKES: 6 SERVINGS

- 1 **medium onion, chopped**
- 2 **garlic cloves, minced**
- 2 **teaspoons olive oil**
- 3 **cups vegetable broth or reduced-sodium beef broth**
- 1 **can (15 ounces) black beans, rinsed and drained**
- 1 **can (14½ ounces) diced tomatoes, undrained**
- 1½ **cups picante sauce**
- 1 **cup uncooked spiral pasta**
- 1 **small green pepper, chopped**
- 2 **teaspoons chili powder**
- 1 **teaspoon ground cumin**
- ½ **cup shredded reduced-fat cheddar cheese**
- 3 **tablespoons reduced-fat sour cream**

1. Saute onion and garlic in oil in a large saucepan until tender.
2. Add the broth, beans, tomatoes, picante sauce, pasta, green pepper and seasonings. Bring to a boil, stirring frequently. Reduce heat; cover and simmer for 10-12 minutes or until pasta is tender, stirring occasionally. Serve with cheese and sour cream.

PER SERVING *216 cal., 5 g fat (2 g sat. fat), 12 mg chol., 1,052 mg sodium, 33 g carb., 6 g fiber, 10 g pro.* **Diabetic Exchanges:** *2 vegetable, 1½ starch, 1 lean meat, ½ fat.*

FAST FIX
Chicken Croissant Sandwiches

These sandwiches are easy to pull together when you need a company-worthy meal in a flash. I make them often for family brunches, church youth meetings and impromptu gatherings with friends.

—**CHERYL SIGLER** LOUISVILLE, OH

START TO FINISH: 15 MIN.
MAKES: 4 SERVINGS

- ⅓ **cup mayonnaise**
- ¼ **teaspoon ground ginger**
- ¼ **teaspoon ground mustard**
  Dash salt
- 1½ **cups diced cooked chicken**
- ⅓ **cup diced apple**
- ⅓ **cup sunflower kernels**
- 2 **green onions, finely chopped**
- ⅓ **cup mandarin oranges**
- 4 **croissants, split**
  Lettuce leaves, optional

In a small bowl, mix mayonnaise, ginger, mustard and salt. Stir in chicken, apple, sunflower kernels and green onions. Gently fold in mandarin oranges. Serve on croissants with lettuce if desired.

Broth Cubes

I recently boiled a hen to make chicken salad sandwiches for a potluck. I didn't want to waste the broth, so I strained and froze it in ice cube trays. Once the cubes were frozen, I transferred them to freezer bags. When a recipe calls for broth, I simply toss in my broth cubes. You can stretch the broth with a little water and bouillon if needed.

—**GARY S.** GROVE CITY, OH

CHICKEN CROISSANT SANDWICHES

BLT BOW TIE PASTA SALAD

Watermelon Gazpacho

Nothing cools off the dog days of summer like a bowl of this refreshing watermelon soup. Its subtle sweetness, touch of mint and pretty pink color make it so appealing.

—**JILL SPARROW** INDIANAPOLIS, IN

PREP: 20 MIN. + CHILLING
MAKES: 9 SERVINGS (2¼ QUARTS)

- ½ cup sugar
- ½ cup water
- 12 cups seeded chopped watermelon
- 2 cups chopped honeydew
- ½ cup fresh mint leaves
- ¼ cup lime juice
- 1 teaspoon salt

TOPPING

- ½ cup sour cream
- 2 tablespoons sugar

1. In a small saucepan, combine sugar and water. Bring to a boil over medium heat. Reduce heat; simmer, uncovered, for 2-3 minutes or until sugar is dissolved, stirring occasionally. Remove from the heat; cool to room temperature.
2. Working in batches if necessary, place the sugar mixture, watermelon, honeydew, mint, lime juice and salt in a food processor. Cover and process until smooth. Refrigerate for at least 2 hours.
3. Combine sour cream and sugar. Garnish each serving with topping.

EAT SMART FAST FIX ▶

BLT Bow Tie Pasta Salad

I first had this summery salad at a family reunion, and it's become one of my husband's favorite dinners. Sometimes, we leave out the chicken and serve it as a side dish instead.

—**JENNIFER MADSEN** REXBURG, ID

START TO FINISH: 25 MIN.
MAKES: 8 SERVINGS

- 2½ cups uncooked bow tie pasta
- 6 cups torn romaine
- 1½ cups cubed cooked chicken breast
- 1 medium tomato, diced
- 4 bacon strips, cooked and crumbled
- ⅓ cup reduced-fat mayonnaise
- ¼ cup water
- 1 tablespoon barbecue sauce
- 1½ teaspoons white vinegar
- ¼ teaspoon pepper

1. Cook the pasta according to package directions. Drain and rinse under cold water. In a large bowl, combine romaine, chicken, tomato, bacon and pasta.
2. In a small bowl, whisk mayonnaise, water, barbecue sauce, vinegar and pepper. Pour over salad; toss to coat. Serve immediately.
PER SERVING *189 cal., 6 g fat (1 g sat. fat), 28 mg chol., 192 mg sodium, 20 g carb., 2 g fiber, 13 g pro.* **Diabetic Exchanges:** *1 starch, 1 lean meat, 1 vegetable, 1 fat.*

WATERMELON GAZPACHO

Cheddar-Bacon Burgers

You won't believe how juicy these burgers are. The secret is the apple cider; it's just enough to keep everything moist. Everyone enjoys the flavor, but no one can put a finger on what the ingredient is.
—**SHELLY BEVINGTON** HERMISTON, OR

START TO FINISH: 30 MIN.
MAKES: 6 SERVINGS

- 1 cup (4 ounces) shredded cheddar cheese
- ½ cup apple cider or juice
- 3 bacon strips, cooked and crumbled
- 1 tablespoon Worcestershire sauce
- 2 teaspoons Montreal steak seasoning
- 1 pound lean ground beef (90% lean)
- 1 pound bulk pork sausage
- 6 onion rolls, split
- ⅓ cup mayonnaise
- 6 slices onion
- 6 romaine leaves

1. In a large bowl, combine the first five ingredients. Add beef and sausage; mix lightly but thoroughly. Shape into six patties.
2. In a large skillet, cook burgers over medium heat 5-7 minutes on each side or until a thermometer reads 160°. Spread rolls with mayonnaise; top with burgers, onion and romaine.

Mediterranean Tuna Salad

You'll love the fresh flavors in this crispy salad, which is surprisingly quick to prepare.
—**RENEE NASH** SNOQUALMIE, WA

START TO FINISH: 25 MIN.
MAKES: 4 SERVINGS

- 1 can (15 ounces) garbanzo beans or chickpeas, rinsed and drained
- 3 celery ribs, chopped
- 1 small sweet red pepper, chopped
- 4 green onions, chopped
- 2 tablespoons olive oil
- 2 tablespoons balsamic vinegar
- 2 tablespoons spicy brown mustard
- ½ teaspoon dried basil
- ¼ teaspoon salt
- ¼ teaspoon pepper
- 2 cans (5 ounces each) albacore white tuna in water
- 4 cups shredded lettuce
- ½ cup crumbled feta or blue cheese, optional

In a large bowl, combine the beans, celery, red pepper and green onions. In a small bowl, whisk the oil, vinegar, mustard, basil, salt and pepper. Pour over bean mixture; toss to coat. Gently stir in tuna. Serve over lettuce. Sprinkle with cheese if desired.
PER SERVING *282 cal., 11 g fat (2 g sat. fat), 30 mg chol., 682 mg sodium, 23 g carb., 6 g fiber, 23 g pro.* ***Diabetic Exchanges:*** *3 lean meat, 1 starch, 1 vegetable, 1 fat.*

PESTO-DIJON EGG SALAD SANDWICHES

FAST FIX
Chicken, Pecan & Cherry Salad

Precooked chicken strips make this an easy meal when I'm trying to get dinner on the table in a hurry. A rotisserie chicken from the grocery store is another option when time is short.
—**KELLIE MULLEAVY** LAMBERTVILLE, MI

START TO FINISH: 10 MIN.
MAKES: 4 SERVINGS

- 8 cups torn mixed salad greens
- 2 packages (6 ounces each) ready-to-use grilled chicken breast strips
- ⅓ cup chopped pecans, toasted
- 2 tablespoons crumbled blue cheese
- 2 tablespoons dried cherries

VINAIGRETTE
- 2 tablespoons balsamic vinegar
- 1½ teaspoons Dijon mustard
- ½ teaspoon sugar
- ½ teaspoon seasoned salt
- ¼ teaspoon garlic powder
- ¼ teaspoon pepper
- 6 tablespoons olive oil

In a large bowl, combine the first five ingredients. In a small bowl, whisk the first six vinaigrette ingredients; gradually whisk in oil until blended. Pour over salad; toss to coat.
NOTE *To toast nuts, spread in a 15x10x1-in. baking pan. Bake at 350° for 5-10 minutes or until lightly browned, stirring occasionally. Or, spread in a dry nonstick skillet and heat over low heat until lightly browned, stirring occasionally.*

CHICKEN, PECAN & CHERRY SALAD

FAST FIX
Pesto-Dijon Egg Salad Sandwiches

Turn your old-standby egg salad into your new lunch favorite. Honey Dijon mustard and pesto add a sensational spin, and crisp veggies give it crunch.
—**CARRIE KENNEY** BATAVIA, OH

START TO FINISH: 20 MIN.
MAKES: 4 SERVINGS

- ½ cup mayonnaise
- ¼ cup finely chopped celery
- ¼ cup finely chopped red onion
- 2 tablespoons honey Dijon mustard
- 4 teaspoons prepared pesto
- 1 garlic clove, minced
- ½ teaspoon salt
- ¼ teaspoon pepper
- 8 hard-cooked eggs, chopped
- 8 slices whole wheat bread, toasted
- 4 romaine leaves
- 4 slices tomato or ½ cup roasted sweet red peppers, cut into strips

Combine the first eight ingredients in a small bowl. Gently stir in eggs. Spread over four toast slices; top with lettuce, tomato and remaining toast.

⑤ INGREDIENTS FAST FIX
Italian Grilled Cheese Sandwiches

I made up this recipe for the students in the foods and nutrition class that I teach. The kids like it so much, they often go home and fix it for their families.
—**BETH HIOTT** YORK, SC

START TO FINISH: 25 MIN.
MAKES: 4 SERVINGS

- 8 slices Italian bread
- 4 tablespoons prepared pesto
- 4 slices provolone cheese
- 4 slices part-skim mozzarella cheese
- 5 teaspoons olive oil
  Marinara sauce warmed, optional

1. Spread four bread slices with pesto. Layer with cheeses; top with remaining bread. Spread outsides of sandwiches with oil.
2. In a large skillet over medium heat, toast sandwiches for 3-4 minutes on each side or until cheese is melted. Serve with marinara if desired.

BLUEBERRY CHICKEN SALAD

Fruited Turkey Wraps

This colorful wrap tastes great and is great for you, too. It's packed with lean protein, fresh fruit and veggies and wrapped in whole-grain goodness.
—LISA RENSHAW KANSAS CITY, MO

START TO FINISH: 15 MIN.
MAKES: 4 SERVINGS

- ½ cup fat-free mayonnaise
- 1 tablespoon orange juice
- 1 teaspoon grated orange peel
- ¾ teaspoon curry powder
- 4 whole wheat tortillas (8 inches), room temperature
- 2 cups finely shredded Chinese or napa cabbage
- 1 small red onion, thinly sliced
- 1 can (11 ounces) mandarin oranges, drained
- ⅔ cup dried cranberries
- ½ pound thinly sliced deli smoked turkey

Combine mayonnaise, orange juice, peel and curry; spread over tortillas. Top with cabbage, onion, oranges, cranberries and turkey. Roll up.

PER SERVING *332 cal., 5 g fat (trace sat. fat), 23 mg chol., 845 mg sodium, 54 g carb., 5 g fiber, 17 g pro.*

"On weekday mornings, I whip up this fun chicken and blueberry combo to take for lunch. It also works as a nice, light summer supper, and it's a cinch to double for a shower or potluck." —**KARI CAVEN** COEUR D'ALENE, ID

Blueberry Chicken Salad

PREP: 15 MIN. • **MAKES:** 4 SERVINGS

- 2 cups fresh blueberries
- 2 cups cubed cooked chicken breast
- ¾ cup chopped celery
- ½ cup diced sweet red pepper
- ½ cup thinly sliced green onions
- ¾ cup (6 ounces) lemon yogurt
- 3 tablespoons mayonnaise
- ½ teaspoon salt
  Bibb lettuce leaves, optional

1. Set aside a few blueberries for topping salad. In a large bowl, combine chicken, celery, red pepper, green onions and remaining blueberries. In a small bowl, mix yogurt, mayonnaise and salt. Add to chicken mixture; gently toss to coat.
2. Refrigerate until serving. If desired, serve over lettuce. Top salad with reserved blueberries.
PER SERVING *277 cal., 11 g fat (2 g sat. fat), 60 mg chol., 441 mg sodium, 21 g carb., 3 g fiber, 23 g pro.* **Diabetic Exchanges:** *3 lean meat, 1 starch, 1 fat, ½ fruit.*

FRUITED TURKEY WRAPS

CRAB MELTS

Crab Melts

Two types of cheese melted over a savory crab mixture make these open-faced sandwiches special. I usually serve them for dinner, but they also make great appetizers when you're entertaining. Simply cut each piece in half.

—**DONNA BENNETT** BRAMALEA, ON

START TO FINISH: 15 MIN.
MAKES: 2 SERVINGS

- 1 can (6 ounces) crabmeat, drained, flaked and cartilage removed
- 3 tablespoons mayonnaise
- 5 teaspoons finely chopped celery
- 1 tablespoon minced green onion
- 2 English muffins, split
- 4 slices tomato
- 4 thin slices cheddar cheese
- 4 thin slices Monterey Jack cheese
  Paprika

1. Preheat broiler. In a small bowl, combine the crab, mayonnaise, celery and green onion until blended. Place the muffin halves on an ungreased baking sheet.
2. Broil 4-6 in. from heat until toasted. Spread muffin halves with crab mixture. Top with tomato and cheeses; sprinkle with paprika. Broil until bubbly.

Mushroom Cheeseburgers

Instead of topping cheeseburgers with sauteed mushrooms, include the savory mushrooms right in the meat mixture for a new twist. Folks will be pleasantly surprised by these deluxe sandwiches... bite after bite.

—**TASTE OF HOME TEST KITCHEN**

START TO FINISH: 20 MIN.
MAKES: 4 SERVINGS

- ¼ cup chopped canned mushrooms
- ¼ cup finely chopped onion
- 1 teaspoon dried oregano
- ½ teaspoon salt
- ½ teaspoon pepper
- 1 pound ground beef
- 4 slices process American cheese
- 4 hamburger buns, split
  Lettuce leaves, optional

1. In a large bowl, combine the mushrooms, onion, oregano, salt and pepper. Crumble beef over mixture and mix well. Shape into four patties.
2. Broil burgers 5 in. from the heat for 5-7 minutes on each side or until a thermometer reads 160° and juices run clear. Top with cheese. Serve on buns with lettuce if desired.

Fresh 'n' Fruity Salmon Salad

Celebrate spring with a nutritious salad perfect for a light lunch. If you like, customize the salad with a berry-flavored goat cheese.

—**SHELISA TERRY** HENDERSON, NV

START TO FINISH: 20 MIN.
MAKES: 2 SERVINGS

- 2 salmon fillets (6 ounces each)
- 2 tablespoons reduced-fat raspberry vinaigrette
- 3 cups fresh baby spinach
- ¾ cup sliced fresh strawberries
- 2 slices red onion, separated into rings
- 2 tablespoons crumbled goat cheese
- 2 tablespoons chopped pecans, toasted
  Additional reduced-fat raspberry vinaigrette

1. Place salmon on a broiler pan coated with cooking spray; drizzle with vinaigrette. Broil 3-4 in. from the heat for 10-15 minutes or until fish flakes easily with a fork.
2. Divide spinach between two serving plates. Top with strawberries, onion, cheese and pecans. Flake the salmon; sprinkle over salads. Drizzle with additional vinaigrette.

FRESH 'N' FRUITY SALMON SALAD

TURKEY TACO SALAD

EAT SMART **FAST FIX**
Turkey Taco Salad

START TO FINISH: 30 MIN.
MAKES: 4 SERVINGS

- 12 ounces ground turkey
- 1 medium sweet red pepper, chopped
- 1 small sweet yellow pepper, chopped
- ⅓ cup chopped onion
- 3 garlic cloves, minced
- 1½ cups salsa
- ½ cup canned kidney beans, rinsed and drained
- 2 teaspoons chili powder
- 1 teaspoon ground cumin
- 8 cups torn romaine
- 2 tablespoons fresh cilantro leaves
  Optional toppings: chopped tomatoes, shredded cheddar cheese and crushed tortilla chips

1. In a large skillet, cook turkey, peppers, onion and garlic over medium heat 6-8 minutes or until turkey is no longer pink and vegetables are tender, breaking up turkey into crumbles; drain.
2. Stir in salsa, beans, chili powder and cumin; heat through. Divide romaine among four plates. Top with turkey mixture; sprinkle with cilantro and toppings of your choice. Serve immediately.
PER SERVING *275 cal., 13 g fat (4 g sat. fat), 58 mg chol., 525 mg sodium, 21 g carb., 6 g fiber, 18 g pro.* **Diabetic Exchanges:** *2 medium-fat meat, 1½ starch.*

FAST FIX
Chicken Sausage Gyros

Surprise your family after a day at the beach with this fast, filling meal in minutes. Casual and hearty, the whole wheat pitas are packed with veggies—and flavor.
—KERRI GEORGE BERNE, IN

START TO FINISH: 20 MIN.
MAKES: 4 SERVINGS

- 1 package (12 ounces) fully cooked spinach and feta chicken sausage links or flavor of your choice, cut into ¼-inch slices
- 1 cup (8 ounces) reduced-fat sour cream
- ¼ cup finely chopped cucumber
- 1½ teaspoons red wine vinegar
- 1½ teaspoons olive oil
- ½ teaspoon garlic powder
- 4 whole wheat pita breads (6 inches)
- 1 plum tomato, sliced
- ½ small onion, thinly sliced

1. In a large skillet coated with cooking spray, cook sausage over medium heat until heated through.
2. Meanwhile, in a small bowl, combine the sour cream, cucumber, vinegar, oil and garlic powder. Serve chicken sausage on pita breads with tomato, onion and cucumber sauce.

CHICKEN SAUSAGE GYROS

FAST FIX

Smoked Turkey and Apple Salad

An eye-catching dish, this satisfying salad is a great main course for a summer lunch or light dinner. Dijon dressing pairs nicely with the turkey, while apples and walnuts add crunch.

—**CAROLYN NACE** WINTER HAVEN, FL

START TO FINISH: 20 MIN.
MAKES: 4 SERVINGS

DRESSING
- 5 tablespoons olive oil
- 2 tablespoons cider vinegar
- 1 tablespoon Dijon mustard
- 1 teaspoon lemon-pepper seasoning
- ½ teaspoon salt, optional

SALAD
- 6 to 8 cups torn watercress or romaine
- 1 medium carrot, julienned
- 10 cherry tomatoes, halved
- 8 ounces smoked turkey, julienned
- 4 unpeeled apples, sliced
- ⅓ cup chopped walnuts, toasted

1. Whisk together the dressing ingredients; set aside.
2. Just before serving, arrange salad greens on a platter or individual plates. Top with carrot, tomatoes, turkey and apples. Drizzle dressing over salad; toss to coat. Sprinkle with walnuts.

FAST FIX

Easy Low-Fat Chili

Here's a simple chili that will really warm you on cool fall days. It's so quick to make that you can enjoy it any time.

—**JANET MOORE** OGDENSBURG, NY

START TO FINISH: 30 MIN.
MAKES: 7 SERVINGS

- 1 medium onion, chopped
- ¼ cup chopped green pepper
- 2 cups water, divided
- 1 can (15½ ounces) great northern beans, rinsed and drained
- 1 can (15 ounces) navy beans, rinsed and drained
- 1 can (14½ ounces) reduced-salt diced tomatoes, undrained
- 1 can (6 ounces) salt-free tomato paste
- 2 to 4 teaspoons chili powder
- 1 teaspoon salt, optional
- ½ teaspoon pepper

In a large saucepan, cook the onion and green pepper in ½ cup water until tender. Add beans, tomatoes and tomato paste. Stir in chili powder, salt if desired, pepper and remaining water; bring to a boil. Reduce heat; cover and simmer for 20 minutes.

FAST FIX

Spinach Pastrami Wraps

Instead of using tortillas, you can simply wrap the meat around the other ingredients and fasten with a toothpick. Either way, the wraps can be sliced and served as appetizers or eaten whole.

—**RHONDA WILKINSON** LEVITTOWN, PA

START TO FINISH: 20 MIN.
MAKES: 4 SERVINGS

- 4 flour tortillas (10 inches), room temperature
- 4 ounces cream cheese, softened
- ¾ cup shredded cheddar cheese
- ¼ cup chopped red onion
- ¼ cup sliced Greek olives
- ½ pound thinly sliced deli pastrami
- 1½ cups fresh baby spinach

Spread tortillas with cream cheese; sprinkle with cheddar cheese, onion and olives. Top with pastrami and spinach. Roll up tightly; secure with toothpicks.

SPINACH PASTRAMI WRAPS

Patricia Nieh's
Scallops with Citrus Glaze
PAGE 159

Express Entrees

Turn to this popular chapter when you need to create a fabulous dinner ... fast! Discover dozens of stovetop and microwave dishes, all of them table-ready in 30 minutes or less!

Adam Gaylord's Pork Quesadillas with Fresh Salsa
PAGE 136

Lily Julow's Fresh Corn Fettuccine
PAGE 140

Mary Lou Cook's Cornmeal Catfish with Avocado Sauce
PAGE 144

Pork Quesadillas with Fresh Salsa

I threw this together one night when I was in the mood for quesadillas but didn't feel like going out. The homemade salsa is so delicious, you'll absolutely want to double the recipe.

—ADAM GAYLORD NATICK, MA

START TO FINISH: 30 MIN.
MAKES: 4 SERVINGS (¾ CUP SALSA)

- 1 tablespoon olive oil
- 1 each small green, sweet red and orange peppers, sliced
- 1 medium red onion, sliced
- ¾ pound thinly sliced cooked pork (about 3 cups)
- ¼ teaspoon salt
- ⅛ teaspoon pepper

SALSA
- 2 medium tomatoes, seeded and chopped
- 1 tablespoon chopped red onion
- 1 tablespoon minced fresh cilantro
- 2 teaspoons olive oil
- 1 to 2 teaspoons chopped seeded jalapeno pepper
- 1 teaspoon cider vinegar
- ⅛ teaspoon salt
  Dash pepper

QUESADILLLAS
- 4 flour tortillas (10 inches)
- 1½ cups (6 ounces) shredded part-skim mozzarella cheese

1. In a large skillet, heat oil over medium-high heat. Add peppers and onion; cook 4-5 minutes or until tender, stirring occasionally. Stir in pork, salt and pepper; heat through. Meanwhile, in a small bowl, combine salsa ingredients.

2. Place tortillas on a griddle. Layer one-half of each tortilla with ¼ cup cheese, 1 cup pork mixture and 2 tablespoons cheese; fold other half over filling.

3. Cook over medium heat 1-2 minutes on each side or until golden brown and cheese is melted. Cut into wedges. Serve with salsa.

NOTE *Wear disposable gloves when cutting hot peppers; the oils can burn skin. Avoid touching your face.*

SIMPLE SHRIMP PAD THAI

Simple Shrimp Pad Thai

Stir in soy sauce and brown sugar, add a sprinkle of cilantro and roasted peanuts, and no one will guess the secret ingredient in this dish is marinara sauce.

—ERIN CHILCOAT CENTRAL ISLIP, NY

START TO FINISH: 30 MIN.
MAKES: 4 SERVINGS

- 8 ounces uncooked thick rice noodles
- 1 pound uncooked medium shrimp, peeled and deveined
- 3 garlic cloves, minced
- 2 tablespoons canola oil
- 2 eggs, beaten
- 1 cup marinara sauce
- ¼ cup reduced-sodium soy sauce
- 2 tablespoons brown sugar
- ¼ cup chopped dry roasted peanuts
  Fresh cilantro leaves
- 1 medium lime, cut into wedges
  Sriracha Asian hot chili sauce or hot pepper sauce, optional

1. Cook rice noodles according to package directions.

2. Meanwhile, stir-fry shrimp and garlic in oil in a large nonstick skillet or wok until shrimp turn pink; remove and keep warm. Add eggs to skillet; cook and stir until set.

3. Add the marinara, soy sauce and brown sugar; heat through. Return shrimp to the pan. Drain noodles; toss with shrimp mixture.

4. Sprinkle with peanuts and cilantro. Serve with lime and Sriracha if desired.

PORK QUESADILLAS WITH FRESH SALSA

Apricot Pork Medallions

START TO FINISH: 20 MIN.
MAKES: 4 SERVINGS

- **1** pork tenderloin (1 pound), cut into eight slices
- **1** tablespoon plus 1 teaspoon butter, divided
- **½** cup apricot preserves
- **2** green onions, sliced
- **1** tablespoon cider vinegar
- **¼** teaspoon ground mustard

1. Pound pork slices with a meat mallet to ½-in. thickness. In a large skillet, heat 1 tablespoon butter over medium heat. Brown pork on each side. Remove pork from the pan, reserving drippings.

2. Add preserves, green onions, vinegar, mustard and remaining butter to pan; bring just to a boil, stirring to loosen browned bits from pan. Reduce heat; simmer, covered, 3-4 minutes to allow flavors to blend.

3. Return pork to the pan; cook until pork is tender. Let stand for 5 minutes before serving.

"There's no supper we like more in our house than a great pork dish, and this recipe is up there with the best of them. Apricot preserves gives the pork just the right amount of sweetness." —**CRYSTAL JO BRUNS** ILIFF, CO

APRICOT PORK MEDALLIONS

SOUPY CHICKEN NOODLE SUPPER

Soupy Chicken Noodle Supper

At least once a week my 6-year-old son, also known as Doctor John, hands me a "prescription" for chicken noodle soup. I'm always happy to fill it.

—**HEIDI HALL** NORTH ST. PAUL, MN

START TO FINISH: 30 MIN.
MAKES: 4 SERVINGS

- **1** tablespoon butter
- **1** medium carrot, sliced
- **1** celery rib, sliced
- **1** small onion, chopped
- **4** cups water
- **4** teaspoons chicken bouillon granules
- **1½** teaspoons dried parsley flakes
- **¼** teaspoon Italian seasoning
- **⅛** teaspoon celery seed
- **⅛** teaspoon pepper
- **3** cups uncooked wide egg noodles
- **1½** cups cubed rotisserie chicken
- **1** can (10¾ ounces) condensed cream of chicken soup, undiluted
- **½** cup sour cream
   Hot cooked stuffing, optional

1. In a large saucepan, heat butter over medium-high heat. Add carrot, celery and onion; cook and stir 6-8 minutes or until tender.

2. Stir in water, bouillon and seasonings; bring to a boil. Add noodles; cook, uncovered, 5-7 minutes or until tender. Stir in chicken, soup and sour cream; heat through. If desired, serve with stuffing.

"My quesadillas are versatile enough to serve as a meal or to win big points as a snack while the big game is on TV. Feel free to sub in your favorite flavor of tortillas. Or kick up the spice factor with pepper jack cheese instead of the Mexican cheese blend." —**CRYSTAL SCHLUETER** NORTHGLENN, CO

BUFFALO CHICKEN QUESADILLAS

Buffalo Chicken Quesadillas

START TO FINISH: 25 MIN.
MAKES: 4 SERVINGS

- 2 **cups shredded rotisserie chicken**
- ½ **cup buffalo wing sauce**
- 2 **teaspoons canola oil**
- 1 **cup chopped sweet onion**
- 2 **celery ribs, chopped**
- ¼ **teaspoon salt**
- ⅛ **teaspoon pepper**
- 4 **tomato-flavored flour tortillas (10 inches)**
- 2 **cups (8 ounces) shredded Mexican cheese blend**
- ¼ **cup finely chopped pitted green olives**
- ⅔ **cup sour cream**
- ½ **cup crumbled blue cheese**
- 2 **tablespoons chopped celery leaves**

Additional buffalo wing sauce, optional

1. Preheat oven to 350°. In a small bowl, toss chicken with wing sauce; set aside. In a large skillet, heat oil over medium-high heat. Add onion, celery, salt and pepper; cook and stir until onion is tender.

2. Place two tortillas on an ungreased baking sheet; top with chicken and onion mixtures. Sprinkle with Mexican cheese blend and olives. Top with remaining tortillas. Bake 8-10 minutes or until golden brown and cheese is melted.

3. In a small bowl, mix sour cream and blue cheese. Serve quesadillas with celery leaves, blue cheese sauce and, if desired, additional wing sauce.

EAT SMART

Mexican Beans and Rice

This skillet supper is terrific for a cold or rainy day. It's easy, comforting and really fills the tummy. Sometimes I subsitute pinto beans for the kidney beans, or white rice for brown.
—**LORRAINE CALAND** SHUNIAH, ON

START TO FINISH: 30 MIN.
MAKES: 4 SERVINGS

- 1 **tablespoon canola oil**
- 2 **celery ribs, chopped**
- 1 **medium green pepper, chopped**
- 1 **medium onion, chopped**
- 1 **can (28 ounces) diced tomatoes, undrained**
- 1 **can (16 ounces) kidney beans, rinsed and drained**
- 2 **cups cooked brown rice**
- 2 **teaspoons Worcestershire sauce**
- 1½ **teaspoons chili powder**
- ¼ **teaspoon pepper**
- ¼ **cup shredded cheddar cheese**
- ¼ **cup reduced-fat sour cream**
- 2 **green onions, chopped**

1. In a large nonstick skillet, heat oil over medium-high heat. Add celery, green pepper and onion; cook and stir until tender.

2. Stir in tomatoes, beans, rice, Worcestershire sauce, chili powder and pepper; bring to a boil. Reduce heat; simmer, covered, 7-9 minutes or until heated through. Top with cheese, sour cream and green onions.

PER SERVING *354 cal., 8 g fat (3 g sat. fat), 13 mg chol., 549 mg sodium, 58 g carb., 12 g fiber, 15 g pro.*

MEXICAN BEANS AND RICE

PORK CHOPS WITH MUSHROOM-TARRAGON SAUCE

Savory Beef and Noodles

Few can resist a hearty entree like this; it's comfort food at its finest. The recipe only calls for ½ cup gravy. Refrigerate the remainder and serve it with potatoes or leftover roast beef at another meal.
—TASTE OF HOME TEST KITCHEN

START TO FINISH: 20 MIN.
MAKES: 4 SERVINGS

- 1 pound ground beef
- 1 can (10½ ounces) condensed French onion soup, undiluted
- ½ cup beef gravy
- 1 can (4 ounces) mushroom stems and pieces, drained
- 1 tablespoon all-purpose flour
- 1 tablespoon cold water
  Hot cooked noodles
  Minced fresh parsley, optional

1. In a large skillet, cook beef over medium heat until no longer pink; drain. Stir in the soup, gravy and mushrooms. Bring to a boil. Reduce heat; cover and simmer for 5 minutes.
2. In a small bowl, combine flour and water until smooth; stir into beef mixture. Bring to a boil; cook and stir for 2 minutes or until thickened. Serve mixture over hot noodles. Sprinkle with parsley if desired.

SAVORY BEEF AND NOODLES

Pork Chops with Mushroom-Tarragon Sauce

Nothing says decadent like fresh mushrooms, wine and tarragon. The combo turns pork chops into a special entree.
—MELISSA JELINEK MENOMONEE FALLS, WI

START TO FINISH: 30 MIN.
MAKES: 4 SERVINGS

- 4 boneless pork loin chops (¾ inch thick and 6 ounces each)
- ¼ teaspoon garlic salt
- ¼ teaspoon pepper
- 2 teaspoons olive oil, divided
- ¾ pound sliced fresh mushrooms
- 1 medium onion, chopped
- 2 garlic cloves, minced
- ⅓ cup white wine or reduced-sodium chicken broth
- ¼ cup all-purpose flour
- 1 cup reduced-sodium chicken broth
- 2 teaspoons minced fresh tarragon or ½ teaspoon dried tarragon
- 2 teaspoons butter

1. Sprinkle pork chops with garlic salt and pepper. In a large nonstick skillet coated with cooking spray, brown chops in 1 teaspoon oil. Remove and keep warm. In the same pan, saute mushrooms and onion in remaining oil until almost tender. Add garlic; cook 1 minute longer.
2. Stir in wine. Bring to a boil; cook until liquid is almost evaporated. Combine flour and broth until smooth. Stir into pan. Bring to a boil; cook and stir for 2 minutes or until thickened. Return pork chops to pan and add tarragon. Cover and cook for 6-8 minutes or until a thermometer reads 145°. Stir in butter until melted. Let stand 5 minutes before serving.
PER SERVING *342 cal., 14 g fat (5 g sat. fat), 87 mg chol., 322 mg sodium, 14 g carb., 2 g fiber, 37 g pro.* **Diabetic Exchanges:** *5 lean meat, 1 vegetable, 1 fat, ½ starch.*

ROSEMARY CHICKEN WITH SPINACH & BEANS

EAT SMART

Rosemary Chicken with Spinach & Beans

With two young boys constantly on the go, I always look for tricks to simplify meals. Since this recipe uses just one pan, it's a cinch to prepare when I only have half an hour to make dinner for a hungry family.

—SARA RICHARDSON LITTLETON, CO

START TO FINISH: 30 MIN.
MAKES: 4 SERVINGS

- 1 **can (14½ ounces) stewed tomatoes**
- 4 **boneless skinless chicken breast halves (6 ounces each)**
- 2 **teaspoons dried rosemary, crushed**
- ½ **teaspoon salt**
- ½ **teaspoon pepper**
- 4 **teaspoons olive oil, divided**
- 1 **package (6 ounces) fresh baby spinach**
- 2 **garlic cloves, minced**
- 1 **can (15 ounces) white kidney or cannellini beans, rinsed and drained**

1. Drain tomatoes, reserving juice; coarsely chop tomatoes. Pound chicken with a meat mallet to ¼-in. thickness. Rub with rosemary, salt and pepper. In a large skillet, heat 2 teaspoons oil over medium heat. Add chicken; cook 5-6 minutes on each side or until no longer pink. Remove and keep warm.

2. In same pan, heat remaining oil over medium-high heat. Add spinach and garlic; cook and stir 2-3 minutes or until spinach is wilted. Stir in beans, tomatoes and reserved juice; heat through. Serve with chicken.

PER SERVING *348 cal., 9 g fat (2 g sat. fat), 94 mg chol., 729 mg sodium, 25 g carb., 6 g fiber, 41 g pro.* **Diabetic Exchanges:** *5 lean meat, 2 vegetable, 1 starch, 1 fat.*

Jiffy Pork & Penne

Some people call it "dinner hour," but many of us call it "rush hour." With this quick, easy meal, you can pause to enjoy dinner hour again. The only thing you'll have left over is time to share with your family at the table.

—BRIGITTE SCHALLER FLEMINGTON, MO

START TO FINISH: 30 MIN.
MAKES: 5 SERVINGS

- 1½ **cups uncooked penne pasta**
- 1 **pound ground pork**
- ½ **cup chopped onion**
- 1 **can (14½ ounces) stewed tomatoes, undrained**
- 1 **can (8 ounces) tomato sauce**
- 1 **teaspoon Italian seasoning**
- 1 **medium zucchini, cut into ¼-inch slices**

1. Cook pasta according to package directions. Meanwhile, in a large skillet, cook pork and onion over medium heat until meat is no longer pink; drain. Add the tomatoes, tomato sauce and Italian seasoning. Bring to a boil. Reduce heat; cover and cook for 5 minutes to allow flavors to blend.

2. Drain pasta; add to skillet. Stir in zucchini. Cover and cook for 3-5 minutes or until the zucchini is crisp-tender.

Fresh Corn Fettuccine

I love corn so it wasn't much of a leap to figure out that with the help of a food processor, I could turn fresh corn kernels into an ideal pasta sauce.

—LILY JULOW LAWRENCEVILLE, GA

START TO FINISH: 30 MIN.
MAKES: 6 SERVINGS

- 12 **ounces uncooked fettuccine**
- 4 **thick-sliced bacon strips, chopped**
- 4 **cups fresh or frozen corn, thawed**
- 3 **garlic cloves, minced**
- ¼ **teaspoon salt**
- ⅛ **teaspoon pepper**
- ½ **cup grated Parmesan cheese**
- ⅓ **cup blanched almonds**
- ⅓ **cup olive oil**
- 1 **cup thinly sliced fresh basil, divided**
  Halved grape tomatoes and additional grated Parmesan cheese, optional

1. Cook fettuccine according to package directions.

2. Meanwhile, in a large skillet, cook bacon over medium heat until crisp. Remove with a slotted spoon; drain on paper towels. Discard drippings, reserving 2 teaspoons.

3. Add corn, garlic, salt and pepper to drippings; cook and stir over medium-high heat until corn is tender. Remove ¾ cup corn from pan. Transfer remaining corn to a food processor; add cheese, almonds and oil. Process until blended. Return to skillet; add reserved corn and heat through.

4. Drain fettuccine, reserving ½ cup pasta water. Add pasta, three-fourths of the bacon and ¾ cup basil to corn mixture. Add enough reserved pasta water to reach desired consistency, tossing to coat. Sprinkle with remaining bacon and basil. If desired, top with tomatoes and additional cheese.

FRESH CORN FETTUCCINE

GARBANZO-VEGETABLE GREEN CURRY

Turkey Tortellini Toss

One night I had frozen tortellini on hand and didn't have a clue what I was going to make. I scanned my cupboards and refrigerator, and soon I was happily cooking away. Fresh-tasting and simple, this recipe is now a favorite.

—**LEO PARR** NEW ORLEANS, LA

START TO FINISH: 30 MIN.
MAKES: 4 SERVINGS

- 2 **cups frozen cheese tortellini (about 8 ounces)**
- 1 **pound ground turkey**
- 2 **medium zucchini, halved lengthwise and sliced**
- 2 **garlic cloves, minced**
- 1½ **cups cherry tomatoes, halved**
- 1 **teaspoon dried oregano**
- ½ **teaspoon salt**
- ¼ **teaspoon crushed red pepper flakes**
- 1 **cup shredded Asiago cheese, divided**
- 1 **tablespoon olive oil**

1. Cook tortellini according to package directions.
2. Meanwhile, in a large skillet, cook turkey, zucchini and garlic over medium heat 7-9 minutes or until turkey is no longer pink, breaking up turkey into crumbles; drain. Add tomatoes, oregano, salt and pepper flakes; cook 2 minutes longer. Stir in ¾ cup cheese.
3. Drain tortellini; add to skillet and toss to combine. Drizzle with oil; sprinkle with remaining cheese.

Garbanzo-Vegetable Green Curry

START TO FINISH: 20 MIN.
MAKES: 6 SERVINGS

- 3 **cups frozen cauliflower**
- 2 **cans (15 ounces each) garbanzo beans or chickpeas, rinsed and drained**
- 1 **can (13.66 ounces) coconut milk**
- ¼ **cup green curry paste**
- ½ **teaspoon salt**
- 2 **teaspoons cornstarch**
- 1 **tablespoon cold water**
- 1½ **cups frozen peas**
- 2 **packages (8.8 ounces each) ready-to-serve long grain rice**
- ½ **cup lightly salted cashews**

1. In a large skillet, combine cauliflower, beans, coconut milk, curry paste and salt. Bring to a boil; cook, uncovered, 5-6 minutes or until cauliflower is tender.
2. Combine cornstarch and water until smooth; gradually stir into the pan. Stir in peas. Bring to a boil; cook and stir 2 minutes or until thickened.
3. Meanwhile, prepare rice according to package directions. Sprinkle cauliflower mixture with cashews. Serve with rice.

TURKEY TORTELLINI TOSS

CALIFORNIA QUINOA

California Quinoa

I'm always changing up how I make quinoa. Here, I use tomato, zucchini and olives for a Greek-inspired dish. Try tossing in any fresh veggies you know your family will like.

—**ELIZABETH LUBIN** HUNTINGTON BEACH, CA

START TO FINISH: 30 MIN.
MAKES: 4 SERVINGS

- 1 tablespoon olive oil
- 1 cup quinoa, rinsed and well drained
- 2 garlic cloves, minced
- 1 medium zucchini, chopped
- 2 cups water
- ¾ cup garbanzo beans or chickpeas, rinsed and drained
- 1 medium tomato, finely chopped
- ½ cup crumbled feta cheese
- ¼ cup finely chopped Greek olives
- 2 tablespoons minced fresh basil
- ¼ teaspoon pepper

1. In a large saucepan, heat oil over medium-high heat. Add quinoa and garlic; cook and stir 2-3 minutes or until quinoa is lightly browned.
2. Stir in zucchini and water; bring to a boil. Reduce heat; simmer, covered, 12-15 minutes or until liquid is absorbed. Stir in remaining ingredients and heat through.
PER SERVING *310 cal., 11 g fat (3 g sat. fat), 8 mg chol., 353 mg sodium, 42 g carb., 6 g fiber, 11 g pro.* **Diabetic Exchanges:** *2 starch, 1½ fat, 1 lean meat, 1 vegetable.*

top tip · Get To Know Quinoa

Quinoa (pronounced KEEN-wah) is an ancient South American grain. It's often referred to as "the perfect grain" because, unlike other grains, it offers a complete protein. This makes quinoa an excellent choice for vegetarian and vegan meals, which sometimes tend to be low in protein.

Gnocchi with White Beans

Here's one of those no-muss, no-fuss recipes you can toss together in a single pan. It's also good with crumbled Italian chicken sausage if you need to please the meat lovers in your house.

—**JULIANNE MEYERS** HINESVILLE, GA

START TO FINISH: 30 MIN.
MAKES: 6 SERVINGS

- 1 tablespoon olive oil
- 1 medium onion, chopped
- 2 garlic cloves, minced
- 1 package (16 ounces) potato gnocchi
- 1 can (15 ounces) white kidney or cannellini beans, rinsed and drained
- 1 can (14½ ounces) Italian diced tomatoes, undrained
- 1 package (6 ounces) fresh baby spinach
- ¼ teaspoon pepper
- ½ cup shredded part-skim mozzarella cheese
- 3 tablespoons grated Parmesan cheese

1. In a large skillet, heat oil over medium-high heat. Add onion; cook and stir until tender. Add garlic; cook 1 minute longer. Add gnocchi; cook and stir 5-6 minutes or until golden brown. Stir in beans, tomatoes, spinach and pepper; heat through.
2. Sprinkle with cheeses; cover and remove from heat. Let stand 3-4 minutes or until cheese is melted.
NOTE *Look for potato gnocchi in the pasta or frozen foods section.*
PER SERVING *307 cal., 6 g fat (2 g sat. fat), 13 mg chol., 789 mg sodium, 50 g carb., 6 g fiber, 13 g pro.*

GNOCCHI WITH WHITE BEANS

Apple Chutney Chops

START TO FINISH: 25 MIN.
MAKES: 4 SERVINGS

- 4 cups chopped peeled apples (3 to 4 apples)
- ½ cup golden raisins
- ½ cup honey
- 3 tablespoons cider vinegar
- ½ teaspoon salt
- ½ teaspoon ground ginger
- ½ teaspoon ground mustard
- ½ teaspoon curry powder
- 1 tablespoon canola oil
- 4 boneless pork loin chops (¾ inch thick and 6 ounces each)

1. For chutney, in a large saucepan, combine the first eight ingredients; bring to a boil. Reduce heat; simmer, uncovered, 10-15 minutes or until apples are tender, stirring occasionally.

2. Meanwhile, in a large skillet, heat oil over medium-high heat. Add pork chops; cook 4-5 minutes on each side or until a thermometer reads 145°. Let stand 5 minutes before serving. Serve with chutney.

"When my husband and I lived in South Carolina for a year, some good friends served us these delicious pork chops. They instantly became a family favorite. They're especially good with basmati rice."

—**CHER ANJEMA** EAST ST. PAUL, MB

CORNMEAL CATFISH WITH AVOCADO SAUCE

APPLE CHUTNEY CHOPS

Cornmeal Catfish with Avocado Sauce

When I was growing up in California, my mother often made catfish. Now I cook it with my own twist. When only frozen catfish fillets are available, I thaw them in the refrigerator overnight, and they work just as well as fresh.

—**MARY LOU COOK** WELCHES, OR

START TO FINISH: 25 MIN.
MAKES: 4 SERVINGS (¾ CUP SAUCE)

- 1 medium ripe avocado, peeled and cubed
- ⅓ cup reduced-fat mayonnaise
- ¼ cup fresh cilantro leaves
- 2 tablespoons lime juice
- ½ teaspoon garlic salt
- ¼ cup cornmeal
- 1 teaspoon seafood seasoning
- 4 catfish fillets (6 ounces each)
- 3 tablespoons canola oil
- 1 medium tomato, chopped

1. Place the first five ingredients in a food processor; process until blended.

2. In a shallow bowl, mix cornmeal and seafood seasoning. Dip catfish in cornmeal mixture to coat both sides; shake off excess.

3. In a large skillet, heat oil over medium heat. Add catfish in batches; cook 4-5 minutes on each side or until fish flakes easily with a fork. Top with avocado sauce and chopped tomato.

Tuna Zucchini Cakes

Here's a great combination of seafood and garden vegetables. People like the color and texture in these skillet cakes... and their wonderful flavor!

—**BILLIE BLANTON** KINGSPORT, TN

START TO FINISH: 25 MIN.
MAKES: 3 SERVINGS

- 1 tablespoon butter
- ½ cup finely chopped onion
- 1 pouch (6.4 ounces) light tuna in water
- 1 cup seasoned bread crumbs, divided
- 1 cup shredded zucchini
- 2 eggs, lightly beaten
- ⅓ cup minced fresh parsley
- 1 teaspoon lemon juice
- ½ teaspoon salt
- ⅛ teaspoon pepper
- 2 tablespoons canola oil

1. In a large saucepan, heat butter over medium-high heat. Add onion; cook and stir until tender. Remove from heat.

2. Add tuna, ½ cup bread crumbs, zucchini, eggs, parsley, lemon juice, salt and pepper to onion mixture; mix lightly but thoroughly. Shape into six ½-in.-thick patties; coat with remaining bread crumbs.

3. In a large skillet, heat oil over medium heat. Add patties; cook 3 minutes on each side or until golden brown and heated through.

TUNA ZUCCHINI CAKES

BEEF & SPINACH LO MEIN

Beef & Spinach Lo Mein

If you like a good stir-fry, this dish definitely satisfies. I discovered the new favorite at an international luncheon.

—**DENISE PATTERSON** BAINBRIDGE, OH

START TO FINISH: 30 MIN.
MAKES: 5 SERVINGS

- ¼ cup hoisin sauce
- 2 tablespoons soy sauce
- 1 tablespoon water
- 2 teaspoons sesame oil
- 2 garlic cloves, minced
- ¼ teaspoon crushed red pepper flakes
- 1 pound beef top round steak, thinly sliced
- 6 ounces uncooked spaghetti
- 4 teaspoons canola oil, divided
- 1 can (8 ounces) sliced water chestnuts, drained
- 2 green onions, sliced
- 1 package (10 ounces) fresh spinach, coarsely chopped
- 1 red chili pepper, seeded and thinly sliced

1. In a small bowl, mix the first six ingredients. Remove ¼ cup mixture to a large bowl; add beef and toss to coat. Marinate at room temperature 10 minutes.

2. Cook spaghetti according to package directions. Meanwhile, in a large skillet, heat 1½ teaspoons canola oil. Add half of the beef mixture; stir-fry 1-2 minutes or until no longer pink. Remove from pan. Repeat with an additional 1½ teaspoons of oil and the remaining beef mixture.

3. Stir-fry water chestnuts and green onions in remaining canola oil 30 seconds. Stir in spinach and remaining hoisin mixture; cook until spinach is wilted. Return beef to the pan and heat through.

4. Drain spaghetti; add to beef mixture and toss to combine. Sprinkle with chili pepper.

NOTE *Wear disposable gloves when cutting hot peppers; the oils can burn skin. Avoid touching your face.*

PER SERVING *363 cal., 10 g fat (2 g sat. fat), 51 mg chol., 652 mg sodium, 40 g carb., 4 g fiber, 28 g pro.*

Pork & Ramen Stir-Fry

START TO FINISH: 30 MIN.
MAKES: 4 SERVINGS

- ¼ cup reduced-sodium soy sauce
- 2 tablespoons ketchup
- 2 tablespoons Worcestershire sauce
- 2 teaspoons sugar
- ¼ teaspoon crushed red pepper flakes
- 3 teaspoons canola oil, divided
- 1 pound boneless pork loin chops, cut into ½-inch strips
- 1 cup fresh broccoli florets
- 4 cups coleslaw mix
- 1 can (8 ounces) bamboo shoots, drained
- 4 garlic cloves, minced
- 2 packages (3 ounces each) ramen noodles

1. In a small bowl, whisk the first five ingredients until blended. In a large skillet, heat 2 teaspoons oil over medium-high heat. Add pork; stir-fry pork 2-3 minutes or until no longer pink. Remove from pan.

2. In same pan, stir-fry broccoli in remaining oil 3 minutes. Add coleslaw mix, bamboo shoots and garlic; stir-fry 3-4 minutes longer or until broccoli is crisp-tender. Stir in soy sauce mixture and pork; heat through.

3. Meanwhile, cook noodles according to package directions, discarding or saving seasoning packets for another use. Drain; add noodles to pork mixture, tossing to combine.

"I put a bit of a spin on stir-fry that you'd normally serve over rice. Ramen noodles are quick to sub in for the rice, and bagged coleslaw mix gives the dish an instant crisp-tender bite."

—**BARBARA PLETZKE** HERNDON, VA

PORK & RAMEN STIR-FRY

EAT SMART

Seafood Pasta Delight

I once made this dish while visiting friends. These days, whenever I eat it, the meal feels like a festive occasion.

—**DEBBIE CAMPBELL** DARTMOUTH, NS

START TO FINISH: 30 MIN.
MAKES: 6 SERVINGS

- ½ cup chicken broth
- ½ cup dry white wine or additional chicken broth
- ¼ cup reduced-sodium soy sauce
- 2 tablespoons cornstarch
- 1 teaspoon sugar
- ½ teaspoon salt
  Dash pepper
- 12 ounces uncooked vermicelli
- 4 teaspoons olive oil, divided
- ½ pound sea scallops
- ½ pound uncooked medium shrimp, peeled and deveined
- 1 medium sweet red pepper, julienned
- 1 medium sweet yellow pepper, julienned
- 1 cup fresh or frozen sugar snap peas
- 2 to 3 garlic cloves, minced
- 1 teaspoon minced fresh gingerroot
- 2 teaspoons sesame oil

1. In a small bowl, mix the first seven ingredients until smooth. Cook vermicelli according to package directions.

2. Meanwhile, in a large nonstick skillet, heat 2 teaspoons olive oil over medium-high heat. Add scallops and shrimp; stir-fry 3-4 minutes or until scallops are firm and opaque and shrimp turn pink. Remove from pan.

3. Stir-fry peppers, snap peas, garlic and ginger in remaining olive oil 3-5 minutes or just until vegetables are crisp-tender. Stir cornstarch mixture and add to pan. Bring to a boil; cook and stir 1-2 minutes or until sauce is thickened.

4. Return seafood to pan; heat through. Stir in sesame oil. Drain the vermicelli; add to pan and toss to combine.

PER SERVING *372 cal., 6 g fat (1 g sat. fat), 59 mg chol., 892 mg sodium, 53 g carb., 3 g fiber, 22 g pro.*

Chicken with Tarragon Sauce

This is comfort food at its finest. I cook it at least once a week and usually serve it with homemade mashed potatoes and sauteed green beans.

—CHER SCHWARTZ ELLISVILLE, MO

START TO FINISH: 30 MIN.
MAKES: 4 SERVINGS

- 4 **boneless skinless chicken breast halves (5 ounces each)**
- ¾ **teaspoon salt, divided**
- ¼ **teaspoon pepper**
- 1 **tablespoon butter**
- 1 **tablespoon olive oil**
- 1 **shallot, chopped**
- ¾ **cup heavy whipping cream**
- 3 **teaspoons minced fresh tarragon, divided**
- 2 **teaspoons lemon juice**

1. Pound chicken breasts with a meat mallet to ½-in. thickness. Sprinkle chicken with ½ teaspoon salt and pepper.
2. In a large skillet, heat butter and oil over medium heat. Add chicken; cook 4-5 minutes on each side or until no longer pink. Remove chicken from pan; keep warm.
3. Add shallot to same pan; cook and stir over medium heat until tender. Add cream, stirring to loosen browned bits from pan. Increase heat to medium-high; cook until slightly thickened. Stir in 2 teaspoons tarragon, lemon juice and remaining salt. Serve with chicken. Sprinkle with remaining tarragon.

CHICKEN WITH TARRAGON SAUCE

Angel Hair Primavera

I love to make pasta primavera when summer is in full swing and the vegetables are at their best. You can toss in almost any vegetable that's in season. At my house, this dish is rarely the same twice.

—TRE BALCHOWSKY SAUSALITO, CA

START TO FINISH: 30 MIN.
MAKES: 4 SERVINGS

- 1 **tablespoon olive oil**
- 2 **medium zucchini, coarsely chopped**
- 1 **cup fresh baby carrots, halved lengthwise**
- 1 **cup fresh or frozen corn**
- 1 **small red onion, cut into thin wedges**
- 1 **cup cherry tomatoes, halved**
- 2 **garlic cloves, minced**
- 1 **package (4.8 ounces) Pasta Roni angel hair pasta with herbs**
- ½ **cup chopped walnuts, toasted**
- ¼ **cup shredded Parmesan cheese Coarsely ground pepper**

1. In a large skillet, heat oil over medium-high heat. Add zucchini, carrots, corn and onion; cook and stir 10-12 minutes or until carrots are tender. Stir in tomatoes and garlic; cook 1 minute longer.
2. Meanwhile, prepare pasta mix according to package directions. Add to vegetable mixture and toss to combine. Sprinkle with walnuts, cheese and pepper.
NOTE *To toast nuts, spread in a 15x10x1-in. baking pan. Bake at 350° for 5-10 minutes or until lightly browned, stirring occasionally. Or, spread in a dry nonstick skillet and heat over low heat until lightly browned, stirring occasionally.*

QUICK MUSHROOM BEEF STEW

Quick Mushroom Beef Stew

Forget beef stew that takes all day to prepare. This version is just as tasty and it's ready to eat in a fraction of the time. You'll love the quick-cooking beef tips and loads of fresh veggies.

—TASTE OF HOME TEST KITCHEN

START TO FINISH: 30 MIN.
MAKES: 8 SERVINGS

- 1 **pound sliced baby portobello mushrooms**
- 1 **pound fresh baby carrots, sliced**
- 1 **large onion, chopped**
- 3 **tablespoons butter**
- 3 **garlic cloves, minced**
- 1 **teaspoon dried rosemary, crushed**
- 3 **tablespoons all-purpose flour**
- 1 **teaspoon pepper**
- 4 **cups water**
- 4 **teaspoons beef base**
- 2 **packages (17 ounces each) refrigerated beef tips with gravy**
   Hot cooked egg noodles and crumbled blue cheese

1. Saute the mushrooms, carrots and onion in butter in a Dutch oven until tender. Add garlic and rosemary; cook 1 minute longer. Stir in flour and pepper until blended; gradually add water. Stir in beef base.

2. Bring to a boil; cook and stir for 2 minutes or until thickened. Add beef tips with gravy; heat through. Serve with noodles and cheese.

NOTE *Look for beef base near the broth and bouillon.*

Texas Tacos

I created this recipe by combining a bunch of ingredients that my kids like. I often keep the beef mixture warm in a slow cooker so the kids can quickly stuff it into taco shells after an afternoon of rigorous soccer practice.

—SUSAN SCULLY MASON, OH

START TO FINISH: 30 MIN.
MAKES: 10 SERVINGS

- 1½ **pounds lean ground beef (90% lean)**
- 1 **medium sweet red pepper, chopped**
- 1 **small onion, chopped**
- 1 **can (14½ ounces) diced tomatoes, drained**
- 1⅓ **cups frozen corn, thawed**
- 1 **can (8 ounces) tomato sauce**
- 2 **tablespoons chili powder**
- ½ **teaspoon salt**
- 1 **package (8.8 ounces) ready-to-serve brown rice**
- 20 **taco shells**
   Optional toppings: shredded lettuce, chopped fresh tomatoes and reduced-fat sour cream

1. In a Dutch oven, cook beef, red pepper and onion over medium heat 8-10 minutes or until beef is no longer pink and vegetables are tender, breaking up beef into crumbles. Drain.

2. Stir in tomatoes, corn, tomato sauce, chili powder and salt; bring to a boil. Add rice; heat through. Serve mixture in taco shells with the toppings of your choice.

PER SERVING *294 cal., 11 g fat (4 g sat. fat), 42 mg chol., 420 mg sodium, 30 g carb., 3 g fiber, 17 g pro.* **Diabetic Exchanges:** *2 starch, 2 lean meat.*

Creamy Shrimp Pasta

Whip up a restaurant favorite at home with our simple-to-make recipe. Jarred Alfredo sauce makes it a snap!

—TASTE OF HOME TEST KITCHEN

START TO FINISH: 20 MIN.
MAKES: 4 SERVINGS

- 1 **package (9 ounces) refrigerated fettuccine**
- ½ **pound sliced fresh mushrooms**
- ½ **cup chopped onion**
- 1 **tablespoon butter**
- 1 **jar (15 ounces) Alfredo sauce**
- 1 **package (10 ounces) fresh baby spinach, chopped**
- 1 **pound peeled and deveined cooked medium shrimp**

Cook fettuccine to package directions. Saute mushrooms and onion in butter in a large skillet until tender. Stir in Alfredo sauce, spinach and shrimp; heat through. Drain fettuccine; add to sauce and toss to coat.

TEXAS TACOS

PEAR & TURKEY SAUSAGE RIGATONI

Cheeseburger Macaroni Skillet

This is the ultimate in simple dinners, using items that I typically have in the cupboard. And cleanup's a snap since I cook it all in one skillet.

—JULI MEYERS HINESVILLE, GA

START TO FINISH: 30 MIN.
MAKES: 6 SERVINGS

- 1 **pound lean ground beef (90% lean)**
- 8 **ounces uncooked whole wheat elbow macaroni**
- 3 **cups reduced-sodium beef broth**
- ¾ **cup fat-free milk**
- 3 **tablespoons ketchup**
- 2 **teaspoons Montreal steak seasoning**
- 1 **teaspoon prepared mustard**
- ¼ **teaspoon onion powder**
- 1 **cup (4 ounces) shredded reduced-fat cheddar cheese**
  Minced chives

1. In a large skillet, cook beef over medium heat 6-8 minutes or until no longer pink, breaking the meat into crumbles; drain.
2. Stir in macaroni, broth, milk, ketchup, steak seasoning, mustard and onion powder; bring to a boil. Reduce heat; simmer, uncovered, 10-15 minutes or until macaroni is tender. Stir in cheese until melted. Sprinkle with chives.

CHEESEBURGER MACARONI SKILLET

"The sweet pear, salty sausage and creamy blue cheese make a wonderful combination in this one-pot supper. Now we don't have to go to an elegant restaurant to enjoy something similar." **—DEBBY HARDEN** WILLIAMSTON, MI

EAT SMART
Pear & Turkey Sausage Rigatoni

START TO FINISH: 30 MIN.
MAKES: 6 SERVINGS

- 8 **ounces uncooked rigatoni or large tube pasta**
- 2 **Italian turkey sausage links (4 ounces each), casings removed**
- 2 **medium pears, sliced**
- 2 **cups fresh baby spinach**
- ½ **cup half-and-half cream**
- ½ **cup crumbled blue cheese, divided**
  Toasted sliced almonds, optional

1. Cook the rigatoni according to package directions.
2. Meanwhile, in a Dutch oven, cook sausage over medium heat 6-8 minutes or until no longer pink, breaking into large crumbles. Add pears; cook and stir 3-5 minutes or until lightly browned.
3. Drain rigatoni; add to sausage mixture. Add spinach, cream and ¼ cup cheese; cook 3-4 minutes or until spinach is wilted, stirring occasionally. Top with remaining cheese. If desired, sprinkle with almonds.

NOTE *To toast nuts, spread in a 15x10x1-in. baking pan. Bake at 350° for 5-10 minutes or until lightly browned, stirring occasionally. Or, spread in a dry nonstick skillet and heat over low heat until lightly browned, stirring occasionally.*
PER SERVING *273 cal., 9 g fat (4 g sat. fat), 32 mg chol., 333 mg sodium, 37 g carb., 3 g fiber, 13 g pro.* **Diabetic Exchanges:** *2½ starch, 2 medium-fat meat.*

SALSA SPAGHETTI SQUASH

Salsa Spaghetti Squash

This colorful and satisfying dish is one of my favorite ways to use spaghetti squash. You'll love how quickly it comes together.

—CLARA COULSON MINNEY
WASHINGTON COURT HOUSE, OH

START TO FINISH: 30 MIN.
MAKES: 4 SERVINGS

- 1 medium spaghetti squash
- 1 medium onion, chopped
- 2 cups salsa
- 1 can (15 ounces) black beans, rinsed and drained
- 3 tablespoons minced fresh cilantro
- 1 medium ripe avocado, peeled and cubed

1. Cut squash in half lengthwise; discard seeds. Place squash on a microwave-safe plate, cut side down. Microwave, uncovered, on high for 15-18 minutes or until tender.
2. Meanwhile, in a nonstick skillet coated with cooking spray, cook and stir onion over medium heat until tender. Stir in salsa, beans and cilantro; heat through. Gently stir in avocado; cook 1 minute longer.
3. When squash is cool enough to handle, use a fork to separate strands. Serve squash topped with salsa mixture.
NOTE *This recipe was tested in a 1,100-watt microwave.*
PER SERVING *308 cal., 9 g fat (2 g sat. fat), 0 chol., 822 mg sodium, 46 g carb., 16 g fiber, 8 g pro.*

Roasted Pepper Tortellini

Convenient ingredients like refrigerated tortellini and ready-to-go pizza sauce get a special treatment with roasted sweet red pepper puree.

—TASTE OF HOME TEST KITCHEN

START TO FINISH: 25 MIN.
MAKES: 6 SERVINGS

- 1 package (20 ounces) refrigerated cheese tortellini
- 1 pound bulk Italian sausage
- ½ cup chopped onion
- 2 jars (7 ounces each) roasted sweet red peppers, drained
- 1 can (15 ounces) pizza sauce
  Shredded part-skim mozzarella cheese

1. Cook tortellini according to package directions. Meanwhile, cook sausage and onion in a large skillet over medium heat until meat is no longer pink; drain.
2. Process the peppers in a food processor until smooth. Add the peppers, pizza sauce and drained tortellini to the skillet; heat through. Sprinkle with mozzarella cheese.

Asian Noodle Toss

We bet you'll love this fresh and easy pasta with an Asian spin. Leftovers are great in the lunch box, too.

—TASTE OF HOME TEST KITCHEN

START TO FINISH: 20 MIN.
MAKES: 4 SERVINGS

- 1 package (9 ounces) refrigerated angel hair pasta
- 1 package (10 ounces) julienned carrots
- 1 package (6 ounces) snow peas
- 2 cups cubed cooked chicken
- 1 can (11 ounces) mandarin oranges, undrained
- ⅔ cup stir-fry sauce
  Chopped green onion

1. Cook pasta according to package directions in a Dutch oven, adding carrots, snow peas and pasta at the same time; drain.
2. Add chicken, oranges and stir-fry sauce; heat through. Top with chopped green onion.

ROASTED PEPPER TORTELLINI

Pronto Vegetarian Peppers

In the summer I like to serve these stuffed peppers with salad and rolls. Near the end of summer, I freeze them for cold months when produce costs are high. For a hot meal on a cold day, I love to serve them with a side of warm pasta tossed with olive oil.

—**RENEE HOLLOBAUGH** ALTOONA, PA

START TO FINISH: 25 MIN.
MAKES: 2 SERVINGS

- 2 **large sweet red peppers**
- 1 **cup canned stewed tomatoes**
- ⅓ **cup instant brown rice**
- 2 **tablespoons hot water**
- ¾ **cup canned kidney beans, rinsed and drained**
- ½ **cup frozen corn, thawed**
- 2 **green onions, thinly sliced**
- ⅛ **teaspoon crushed red pepper flakes**
- ½ **cup shredded part-skim mozzarella cheese**
- 1 **tablespoon grated Parmesan cheese**

1. Cut peppers in half lengthwise; remove seeds. Place peppers in an ungreased shallow microwave-safe dish. Cover and microwave on high for 3-4 minutes or until tender.

2. Combine the tomatoes, rice and water in a small microwave-safe bowl. Cover and microwave on high for 5-6 minutes or until rice is tender. Stir in the beans, corn, onions and pepper flakes; spoon into peppers.

3. Sprinkle with cheeses. Microwave, uncovered, for 3-4 minutes or until heated through.

NOTE *This recipe was tested in a 1,100-watt microwave.*

PER SERVING *341 cal., 7 g fat (3 g sat. fat), 19 mg chol., 556 mg sodium, 56 g carb., 11 g fiber, 19 g pro.*

THAI RED CHICKEN CURRY

PRONTO VEGETARIAN PEPPERS

Thai Red Chicken Curry

I re-created a favorite dish from a restaurant, and now I cook it almost every week for my family. On a busy night, frozen stir-fry veggies really help speed things up.

—**MARY SHENK** DEKALB, IL

START TO FINISH: 25 MIN.
MAKES: 4 SERVINGS

- 1 **can (13.66 ounces) coconut milk**
- ⅓ **cup chicken broth**
- 2 **tablespoons brown sugar**
- 2 **tablespoons fish sauce**
- 1 **tablespoon red curry paste**
- 2 **cups frozen stir-fry vegetable blend**
- 3 **cups cubed cooked chicken breast**
  Cooked jasmine rice
  Minced fresh cilantro, optional

1. Combine the first five ingredients in a large skillet. Bring to a boil; reduce heat and simmer 5 minutes.

2. Stir in vegetables; return to a boil. Reduce heat and simmer, uncovered, for 9-11 minutes or until vegetables are tender and sauce thickens slightly.

3. Add chicken; heat through. Serve with rice. Sprinkle with cilantro if desired.

Mediterranean Shrimp and Linguine

This nutritious pasta tastes like it came from an Italian restaurant. When I'm in a rush, I use jarred tomato sauce and omit the tomatoes and seasonings. You can make the sauce ahead of time and reheat it for convenience.

—**NANCY DEANS** ACTON, ME

START TO FINISH: 30 MIN.
MAKES: 6 SERVINGS

- 9 ounces uncooked linguine
- 2 tablespoons olive oil
- 1 cup sliced fresh mushrooms
- 1 pound uncooked medium shrimp, peeled and deveined
- 3 medium tomatoes, chopped
- 1 can (14 ounces) water-packed artichoke hearts, rinsed, drained and halved
- 1 can (6 ounces) pitted ripe olives, drained and halved
- 2 garlic cloves, minced
- 1 teaspoon dried oregano
- ½ teaspoon salt
- ½ teaspoon dried basil
- ⅛ teaspoon pepper

1. Cook linguine according to package directions. Meanwhile, in a large skillet, heat oil over medium-high heat. Add the mushrooms; cook and stir for 4 minutes. Add remaining ingredients; cook and stir 5 minutes or until heated through and shrimp turn pink.

2. Drain the linguine; serve with shrimp mixture.

PER SERVING *328 cal., 9 g fat (1 g sat. fat), 112 mg chol., 748 mg sodium, 41 g carb., 3 g fiber, 21 g pro.* **Diabetic Exchanges:** *2 starch, 2 lean meat, 1½ fat, 1 vegetable.*

Shrimp with Tomatoes & Feta

Any recipe that is special enough for company, but easy enough for a weeknight, is a star in my book. All you need to finish off the meal is a side salad and crusty French bread to sop up the delicious tomato broth.

—**SUSAN SEYMOUR** VALATIE, NY

START TO FINISH: 30 MIN.
MAKES: 6 SERVINGS

- 3 tablespoons olive oil
- 2 shallots, finely chopped
- 2 garlic cloves, minced
- 6 plum tomatoes, chopped
- ½ cup white wine or chicken broth
- 1 tablespoon dried oregano
- ½ teaspoon salt
- ½ teaspoon crushed red pepper flakes
- ¼ teaspoon sweet paprika
- 2 pounds uncooked large shrimp, peeled and deveined
- ⅔ cup crumbled feta cheese
- 2 teaspoons minced fresh mint
  Hot cooked rice

1. In a large skillet, heat oil over medium-high heat. Add shallots and garlic; cook and stir until tender. Add tomatoes, wine, oregano, salt, pepper flakes and paprika; bring to a boil. Reduce heat; simmer, uncovered, for 5 minutes.

2. Stir in shrimp and cheese; cook 5-6 minutes or until shrimp turn pink. Stir in mint. Serve with rice.

PER SERVING *261 cal., 11 g fat (3 g sat. fat), 191 mg chol., 502 mg sodium, 8 g carb., 2 g fiber, 28 g pro.* **Diabetic Exchanges:** *4 lean meat, 1 vegetable, 1 fat.*

SHRIMP WITH TOMATOES & FETA

GINGER STEAK FRIED RICE

Hearty Portobello Linguine

If you like Mediterranean cuisine, you'll enjoy this entree. Any night when it's on the menu instantly feels like a special occasion. I like to serve it with hot bread and a crisp white wine.

—**TRE BALCHOWSKY** SAUSALITO, CA

START TO FINISH: 25 MIN.
MAKES: 4 SERVINGS

- 1 **package (9 ounces) refrigerated linguine**
- ¼ **cup olive oil**
- 4 **large portobello mushroom caps (about ¾ pound), halved and thinly sliced**
- 3 **garlic cloves, minced**
- 3 **plum tomatoes, chopped**
- ⅓ **cup pitted Greek olives, halved**
- 1 **teaspoon Greek seasoning**
- ¾ **cup crumbled tomato and basil feta cheese**

1. Cook linguine according to package directions. Meanwhile, in a large skillet, heat oil over medium-high heat. Add mushrooms; cook and stir until tender. Add garlic; cook 1 minute longer.

2. Stir in the tomatoes, olives and seasoning; cook and stir 2 minutes longer. Drain linguine; add to the pan and toss to coat. Sprinkle with cheese.

HEARTY PORTOBELLO LINGUINE

Ginger Steak Fried Rice

Perfect for an end-of-the-week meal, this sensational dish comes together quickly with leftover rice. I learned a great tip for the steak recently: Partially freeze it, and it becomes so much easier to slice.

—**SIMONE GARZA** EVANSVILLE, IN

START TO FINISH: 30 MIN.
MAKES: 4 SERVINGS

- 2 **eggs, lightly beaten**
- 2 **teaspoons olive oil**
- 1 **beef top sirloin steak (¾ pound), cut into thin strips**
- 4 **tablespoons reduced-sodium soy sauce, divided**
- 1 **package (12 ounces) broccoli coleslaw mix**
- 1 **cup frozen peas**
- 2 **tablespoons grated fresh gingerroot**
- 3 **garlic cloves, minced**
- 2 **cups cold cooked brown rice**
- 4 **green onions, sliced**

1. In a large nonstick skillet coated with cooking spray, cook and stir eggs over medium heat until no liquid egg remains, breaking up eggs into small pieces. Remove from pan; wipe skillet clean if necessary.

2. In the same pan, heat oil over medium-high heat. Add beef; stir-fry 1-2 minutes or until no longer pink. Stir in 1 tablespoon soy sauce; remove from pan.

3. Add coleslaw mix, peas, ginger and garlic to the pan; cook and stir until coleslaw mix is crisp-tender. Add rice and remaining soy sauce, tossing to combine rice with vegetable mixture and heat through. Stir in cooked eggs, beef and green onions; heat through.

PER SERVING *346 cal., 9 g fat (3 g sat. fat), 140 mg chol., 732 mg sodium, 36 g carb., 6 g fiber, 29 g pro.* **Diabetic Exchanges:** *3 lean meat, 2 starch, 1 vegetable, ½ fat.*

EAT SMART
Chili Beef Pasta

START TO FINISH: 30 MIN.
MAKES: 6 SERVINGS

- 1 **pound lean ground beef (90% lean)**
- 2 **tablespoons dried minced onion**
- 2 **teaspoons dried oregano**
- 2 **teaspoons chili powder**
- ½ **teaspoon garlic powder**
- ⅛ **teaspoon salt**
- 3 **cups tomato juice**
- 2 **cups water**
- 1 **can (6 ounces) tomato paste**
- 1 **teaspoon sugar**
- 8 **ounces uncooked whole wheat spiral pasta**
  Chopped tomatoes and minced fresh oregano, optional

1. In a Dutch oven, cook beef over medium heat 6-8 minutes or until no longer pink, breaking into crumbles; drain. Stir in seasonings.

2. Add tomato juice, water, tomato paste and sugar to pan; bring to a boil. Stir in pasta. Reduce heat; simmer, covered, 20-22 minutes or until pasta is tender, stirring occasionally. If desired, top with tomatoes and oregano.

PER SERVING *319 cal., 7 g fat (2 g sat. fat), 47 mg chol., 442 mg sodium, 41 g carb., 6 g fiber, 24 g pro.* **Diabetic Exchanges:** *3 lean meat, 2 starch, 1 vegetable.*

EAT SMART
Sausage Zucchini Skillet

I began serving a version of this easy recipe as a side dish with my grilled salmon. I later added sausage and rice to make it a complete meal on its own.

—**DEBBY ABEL** FLAT ROCK, NC

START TO FINISH: 25 MIN.
MAKES: 4 SERVINGS

- 1 **pound Italian turkey sausage links, casings removed**
- 2 **large zucchini, chopped**
- 1 **large sweet onion, chopped**
- 2 **garlic cloves, minced**
- 1 **can (14½ ounces) no-salt-added diced tomatoes, undrained**
- ¼ **teaspoon pepper**
- 2 **cups hot cooked rice**

1. Crumble sausage into a large nonstick skillet coated with cooking spray. Add zucchini and onion; cook and stir over medium heat until meat is no longer pink. Add garlic; cook 1 minute longer. Drain.

2. Stir in tomatoes and pepper; bring to a boil. Reduce heat; simmer, uncovered, for 4-5 minutes or until liquid is evaporated. Serve with rice.

PER SERVING *329 cal., 11 g fat (2 g sat. fat), 68 mg chol., 724 mg sodium, 36 g carb., 5 g fiber, 23 g pro.* **Diabetic Exchanges:** *3 lean meat, 2 vegetable, 1½ starch.*

"Right after I got married, my aunt gave me her recipe for skillet spaghetti and told me it was ideal for a quick weeknight meal. Over the years, I've tinkered with the ingredients and played with the seasonings to make it a healthier dish that my family truly loves." —**KRISTEN KILLIAN** DEPEW, NY

CHILI BEEF PASTA

CREAMY NOODLE CASSEROLE

Asian Turkey Lettuce Cups

These lettuce wraps make a fantastic light lunch or fun appetizer. When I want to make it easier for my kids to eat, I mix it all up with shredded lettuce and serve it as a salad instead.

—DIANA RIOS LYTLE, TX

START TO FINISH: 30 MIN.
MAKES: 4 SERVINGS

- 3 tablespoons reduced-sodium soy sauce
- 2 teaspoons sugar
- 2 teaspoons sesame oil
- 1 teaspoon Thai chili sauce, optional
- 1 pound lean ground turkey
- 1 celery rib, chopped
- 1 tablespoon minced fresh gingerroot
- 1 garlic clove, minced
- 1 can (8 ounces) whole water chestnuts, drained and chopped
- 1 medium carrot, shredded
- 2 cups cooked brown rice
- 8 Bibb or Boston lettuce leaves

1. In a small bowl, whisk soy sauce, sugar, sesame oil and, if desired, chili sauce until blended. In a large skillet over medium heat, cook turkey and celery 6-9 minutes or until turkey is no longer pink, breaking up turkey into crumbles; drain.

2. Add ginger and garlic to turkey; cook 2 minutes. Stir in soy sauce mixture, water chestnuts and carrot; cook 2 minutes longer. Stir in rice; heat through. Serve in lettuce leaves.

PER SERVING *353 cal., 13 g fat (3 g sat. fat), 90 mg chol., 589 mg sodium, 35 g carb., 4 g fiber, 24 g pro.* ***Diabetic Exchanges:*** *3 lean meat, 2 starch, 1 vegetable, ½ fat.*

Bibb Lettuce Cups

With its small, round leaves and buttery taste, Bibb lettuce is ideal for lettuce cups. Try stuffing Bibb leaves with your favorite tuna salad, chicken strips or taco filling.

Creamy Noodle Casserole

My husband, Ronald, works long hours and frequently doesn't arrive home until after 7 p.m. But this casserole is still tasty after it has been warmed in the microwave.

—BARB MARSHALL PICKERINGTON, OH

START TO FINISH: 25 MIN.
MAKES: 8 SERVINGS

- 1 package (12 ounces) egg noodles
- 1 package (16 ounces) frozen broccoli cuts
- 3 cups cubed fully cooked ham
- 1 cup (4 ounces) shredded part-skim mozzarella cheese
- 1 cup (4 ounces) shredded Parmesan cheese
- ⅓ cup butter, cubed
- ½ cup half-and-half cream
- ¼ teaspoon each garlic powder, salt and pepper

1. In a Dutch oven, cook noodles in boiling water for 5 minutes. Add broccoli and ham; cook 5-10 minutes longer or until noodles are tender.

2. Drain; return to pan. Stir in the remaining ingredients. Cook and stir over low heat until butter is melted and mixture is heated through.

Speedy Shepherd's Pie

Turn mashed potatoes and a few pantry staples into cozy comfort food. This recipe is flexible. So if you have extra veggies on hand, such as corn or peppers, stir them into the beef mixture for even more goodness.

—SHARON TIPTON WINTER GARDEN, FL

START TO FINISH: 20 MIN.
MAKES: 4 SERVINGS

- 1½ pounds ground beef
- 1 medium onion, chopped
- 2 garlic cloves, minced
- ½ cup water
- 1 envelope taco seasoning
- 2 cups (8 ounces) shredded cheddar cheese, divided
- 3 cups leftover or refrigerated mashed potatoes, warmed

1. Preheat broiler. In a large ovenproof skillet, cook beef, onion and garlic over medium heat until beef is no longer pink, breaking up beef into crumbles; drain. Stir in water and taco seasoning; heat through. Stir in 1 cup cheese. Remove from heat.

2. In a bowl, mix mashed potatoes and remaining cheese; spread over beef mixture. Broil 4-6 in. from heat 5-6 minutes or until top is golden brown.

EAT SMART
Italian Turkey Skillet

I'm always up for the challenge of finding imaginative ways to use leftovers, especially turkey. Here's a favorite of mine that you can easily make ahead. Prepare the recipe as directed, then place in a casserole dish and stash it in the freezer for up to three months.

—**PATRICIA KILE** ELIZABETHTOWN, PA

START TO FINISH: 20 MIN.
MAKES: 8 SERVINGS

- 1 **package (16 ounces) linguine**
- 2 **tablespoons canola oil**
- ¾ **cup sliced fresh mushrooms**
- 1 **medium onion, chopped**
- 1 **celery rib, chopped**
- 1 **small green pepper, chopped**
- 2 **cups cubed cooked turkey**
- 1 **can (14½ ounces) diced tomatoes, drained**
- 1 **can (10¾ ounces) condensed tomato soup, undiluted**
- 1 **tablespoon Italian seasoning**
- 1 **tablespoon minced fresh parsley**
- ¼ **teaspoon pepper**
- ⅛ **teaspoon salt**
- 1 **cup (4 ounces) shredded cheddar cheese, optional**

1. Cook linguine according to package directions. Meanwhile, in a large skillet, heat oil over medium-high heat. Add mushrooms, onion, celery and green pepper; cook and stir until tender. Stir in turkey, tomatoes, soup and seasonings; heat through.

2. Drain linguine; add to turkey mixture and toss to combine. If desired, sprinkle with cheese and let stand, covered, until cheese is melted.

PER SERVING *338 cal., 7 g fat (1 g sat. fat), 27 mg chol., 362 mg sodium, 51 g carb., 4 g fiber, 19 g pro.*

ITALIAN TURKEY SKILLET

SCALLOPS WITH CITRUS GLAZE

Cheese Beef Burritos

START TO FINISH: 25 MIN.
MAKES: 6 SERVINGS

- 1 package (8½ ounces) ready-to-serve Santa Fe whole grain rice medley
- ½ pound lean ground beef (90% lean)
- ¾ cup frozen corn, thawed
- ¾ cup black beans, rinsed and drained
- 1 jar (12 ounces) salsa
- 4 ounces process cheese (Velveeta), thinly sliced
- 6 flour tortillas (10 inches), warmed
  Optional additional ingredients: torn leaf lettuce, chopped onion, chopped sweet red pepper, sour cream and shredded Mexican cheese blend

1. Heat rice according to package directions. Meanwhile, crumble beef into a 4-qt. microwave-safe dish. Add corn and beans; mix well. Microwave, covered, on high 4-5 minutes or until beef is no longer pink; drain. Stir in salsa and cheese; microwave 2-3 minutes longer or until cheese is melted. Stir in rice.

2. Spoon ¾ cup beef mixture near the center of each tortilla; add additional ingredients of your choice. Fold bottom and sides of tortilla over filling and roll up.

NOTE *This recipe was tested in a 1,100-watt microwave.*

Scallops with Citrus Glaze

These scallops are especially good when served on steamed rice with a green salad on the side.

—**PATRICIA NIEH** PORTOLA VALLEY, CA

START TO FINISH: 20 MIN.
MAKES: 4 SERVINGS

- 12 sea scallops (about 1½ pounds)
- ½ teaspoon pepper
- ¼ teaspoon salt
- 2 tablespoons olive oil, divided
- 4 garlic cloves, minced
- ½ cup orange juice
- ¼ cup lemon juice
- 1 tablespoon reduced-sodium soy sauce
- ½ teaspoon grated orange peel

1. Sprinkle scallops with pepper and salt. In a large skillet, saute scallops in 1 tablespoon oil until firm and opaque. Remove and keep warm.

2. In the same skillet, cook garlic in remaining oil for 1 minute. Add the juices, soy sauce and orange peel. Bring to a boil; cook and stir for 5 minutes or until thickened. Serve with scallops.

PER SERVING *235 cal., 8 g fat (1 g sat. fat), 56 mg chol., 574 mg sodium, 10 g carb., trace fiber, 29 g pro.* **Diabetic Exchanges:** *4 lean meat, 1½ fat.*

"After a busy day, I can always get this dish on the table fast. The recipe came about totally by accident: I started throwing ingredients together, and soon I had a winner! Everyone who has tried these burritos goes home with the recipe." —**AMANDA ALFORD** HOPEDALE, IL

CHEESE BEEF BURRITOS

**Wendy Gorton's
Parmesan Chicken with Mushroom Wild Rice**
PAGE 164

Casseroles & Oven Suppers

From tender Sunday roasts to homey, bubbling casseroles and potpies, hot dinners from the oven have a special place in the heart. The family-pleasing recipes that follow are quick to assemble and then bake hands-free.

Cleo Gonske's Oktoberfest Strudels
PAGE 166

Brittney House's Effortless Alfredo Pizza
PAGE 178

Lydia Garrod's Turkey Bundles
PAGE 181

CHICKEN TACO PIE

Chicken Taco Pie

This family fave comes to the rescue on busy nights when we've been rushing to soccer, swimming lessons or Scouts. I make it in the morning and just pop it in the oven when we get home.
—**KAREN LATIMER** WINNIPEG, MB

PREP: 20 MIN. • **BAKE:** 30 MIN.
MAKES: 6 SERVINGS

- 1 tube (8 ounces) refrigerated crescent rolls
- 1 pound ground chicken
- 1 envelope taco seasoning
- 1 can (4 ounces) chopped green chilies
- ½ cup water
- ½ cup salsa
- ½ cup shredded Mexican cheese blend
- 1 cup shredded lettuce
- 1 small sweet red pepper, chopped
- 1 small green pepper, chopped
- 1 medium tomato, seeded and chopped
- 1 green onion, thinly sliced
- 2 tablespoons pickled jalapeno slices
  Sour cream and additional salsa

1. Preheat oven to 350°. Unroll crescent dough and separate into triangles. Press onto bottom of a greased 9-in. pie plate to form a crust, sealing seams well. Bake 18-20 minutes or until golden brown.
2. Meanwhile, in a large skillet, cook chicken over medium heat 6-8 minutes or until no longer pink, breaking into crumbles; drain. Stir in taco seasoning, green chilies, water and salsa; bring to a boil.
3. Spoon into crust; sprinkle with cheese. Bake 8-10 minutes or until cheese is melted.
4. Top the pie with lettuce, peppers, tomato, green onion and pickled jalapeno. Serve with sour cream and additional salsa.

Ham and Broccoli Biscuit Bake

Whenever I cook this creamy dish, I'm on alert to make sure my husband doesn't nibble before I bring it to the table. I chide him, but really, who can resist the rich ham filling and golden biscuit crust?
—**AMY WHEELER** BALTIMORE, MD

PREP: 20 MIN. • **BAKE:** 25 MIN.
MAKES: 6 SERVINGS

- 2½ cups frozen chopped broccoli
- 1 can (10¾ ounces) condensed cream of potato soup, undiluted
- 1¼ cups 2% milk, divided
- 1 teaspoon garlic pepper blend
- ½ teaspoon crushed red pepper flakes
- ¼ teaspoon pepper
- 2 cups cubed fully cooked ham
- 1 cup (4 ounces) shredded cheddar-Monterey Jack cheese
- 1½ cups biscuit/baking mix
- 1 egg

1. Preheat oven to 350°. Combine broccoli, soup, ¾ cup milk and seasonings in a large saucepan; bring to a boil. Reduce heat; add ham and cheese. Cook and stir until cheese is melted. Pour into a greased 11x7-in. baking dish.
2. Combine biscuit mix, egg and the remaining milk in a small bowl just until moistened. Drop dough by tablespoonfuls over ham mixture; spread gently.
3. Bake, uncovered, 25-30 minutes or until golden brown.

Cobre Valley Casserole

We live in southeastern Arizona, in a part of the state known as Cobre Valley. Cobre is a Spanish word for copper, which is mined here. Variations of this recipe have been enjoyed in this area for many years.
—**CAROLYN DEMING** MIAMI, AZ

PREP: 15 MIN. • **BAKE:** 30 MIN.
MAKES: 8 SERVINGS

- 1 pound ground beef
- 1 medium onion, chopped
- 1 celery rib, chopped
- 1 envelope taco seasoning
- ¼ cup water
- 2 cans (16 ounces each) refried beans
- 1 can (4 ounces) chopped green chilies, optional
- 1 cup (4 ounces) shredded cheddar cheese
- 2 green onions, sliced
- 1 large tomato, peeled, seeded and chopped
- ⅓ cup sliced ripe olives
- 1½ cups crushed tortilla chips

1. In a large skillet, cook the beef, onion and celery over medium heat until meat is no longer pink; drain. Stir in the taco seasoning, water, beans and green chilies if desired.
2. Transfer to a greased 11-in. x 7-in. baking dish. Bake, uncovered, at 350° for 30 minutes or until heated through. Top with cheese, green onions, tomato, olives and chips.

COBRE VALLEY CASSEROLE

TURKEY & SPINACH STUFFING CASSEROLE

Sunday Pork Loin

My mom often made this roast, covered with thick homemade barbecue sauce, for our Sunday dinner. When it was in the oven, the aroma filled the whole house.

—**MARI ANNE WARREN** MILTON, WI

PREP: 15 MIN.
BAKE: 2¼ HOURS + STANDING
MAKES: 8 SERVINGS

- 1 boneless pork loin roast (4 to 5 pounds)
- ⅓ cup chopped onion
- ⅓ cup chopped celery
- 1 garlic clove, minced
- 1 teaspoon canola oil
- 1 can (10¾ ounces) condensed tomato soup, undiluted
- ⅓ cup water
- 2 tablespoons brown sugar
- 2 tablespoons lemon juice
- 2 tablespoons Worcestershire sauce
- 2 tablespoons Dijon mustard
- ⅛ to ¼ teaspoon hot pepper sauce

1. Place roast on a greased rack in a shallow roasting pan. Bake, uncovered, at 325° for 1½ hours. In a skillet, saute the onion, celery and garlic in oil until tender. Stir in the remaining ingredients.
2. Spoon 1 cup sauce over roast. Bake 45-55 minutes longer or until a thermometer reads 145°. Let stand for 10-15 minutes before slicing. Serve with the remaining sauce.

SUNDAY PORK LOIN

"I know dried cranberries may seem like an odd ingredient to include in this dish, but they add just a hint of sweetness that makes the casserole special."
—**GILDA LESTER** MILLSBORO, DE

FAST FIX
Turkey & Spinach Stuffing Casserole

START TO FINISH: 25 MIN.
MAKES: 4 SERVINGS

- 1 can (14½ ounces) reduced-sodium chicken broth
- 3 tablespoons butter
- 3 cups stuffing mix
- 3 cups cubed cooked turkey
- 2 cups fresh baby spinach
- ½ cup dried cranberries
- ¾ cup shredded cheddar cheese

1. Preheat oven to 350°. In a large saucepan, bring broth and butter to a boil. Remove from heat. Add stuffing mix; stir until moistened. Stir in turkey, spinach and cranberries.
2. Transfer to a greased 11x7-in. baking dish. Sprinkle with cheese. Bake, uncovered, 10-15 minutes or until cheese is melted.

PARMESAN CHICKEN WITH MUSHROOM WILD RICE

Creamy Ham & Cheese Casserole

I felt so proud when I created this recipe, which my husband loved. Handy cream of chicken soup and refrigerated cooking creme make an easy, delicious sauce for noodle casserole.

—**BETSY HOWARD** ST. LOUIS, MO

PREP: 15 MIN. • **BAKE:** 20 MIN.
MAKES: 4 SERVINGS

- 8 ounces uncooked wide egg noodles
- 3 cups cubed fully cooked ham
- 1 can (10¾ ounces) condensed cream of chicken soup, undiluted
- 1 carton (10 ounces) Philadelphia original cooking creme
- 1 cup 2% milk
- ½ teaspoon garlic-herb seasoning blend
- ¼ teaspoon pepper
- 2 cups (8 ounces) shredded Monterey Jack cheese

1. Cook noodles according to package directions. Meanwhile, combine the ham, soup, cooking creme, milk and seasonings in a large bowl.
2. Drain noodles and add to ham mixture; mix well. Transfer to a 13-in. x 9-in. baking dish coated with cooking spray; sprinkle with cheese.
3. Bake, uncovered, at 350° for 20-25 minutes or until heated through.

CREAMY HAM & CHEESE CASSEROLE

Parmesan Chicken with Mushroom Wild Rice

We call this dish OMG Chicken! Frozen veggies and rice make this hearty meal in one both quick and delicious, and we love the easy prep and cleanup.

—**WENDY GORTON** OAK HARBOR, OH

PREP: 15 MIN. • **BAKE:** 45 MIN.
MAKES: 6 SERVINGS

- ½ pound sliced fresh mushrooms
- 1 tablespoon canola oil
- ½ cup grated Parmesan cheese
- ½ cup mayonnaise
- ½ teaspoon Italian seasoning
- 2 packages (10 ounces each) frozen brown and wild rice with broccoli and carrots
- ¼ teaspoon salt
- ⅛ teaspoon pepper
- 6 boneless skinless chicken thighs

1. Saute mushrooms in oil in a large skillet until tender. Meanwhile, combine the cheese, mayonnaise and Italian seasoning in a small bowl; set mixture aside.
2. Place frozen rice mixture in a greased 13-in. x 9-in. baking dish; sprinkle with salt and pepper. Top with mushrooms and chicken. Spread cheese mixture over chicken.
3. Bake, uncovered, at 325° for 45-50 minutes or until a thermometer reads 170°.

FAST FIX ▸
Mini Hawaiian Burgers

These are great burgers for a luau or any backyard gathering. I came up with these little treats while trying to find something new that my husband would enjoy. He had no idea they were turkey burgers, and now he asks for them all the time!

—KATHLEEN MANASIAN WHITMORE LAKE, MI

START TO FINISH: 25 MIN.
MAKES: 12 SERVINGS

- 1 can (8 ounces) unsweetened crushed pineapple
- 1 green onion, finely chopped
- 1 teaspoon Worcestershire sauce
- ½ teaspoon salt
- ½ teaspoon garlic powder
- ½ teaspoon salt-free seasoning blend
- ½ teaspoon pepper
- 1 pound ground turkey
- ½ pound uncooked chorizo or bulk spicy pork sausage
- ⅔ cup ketchup
- 12 Hawaiian sweet rolls, split
- 6 lettuce leaves, cut in half
- 12 slices tomato

1. Drain pineapple, reserving ½ cup juice. In a large bowl, combine the pineapple, onion, Worcestershire sauce and seasonings. Add turkey and chorizo; mix lightly but thoroughly. Shape into twelve ½-in.-thick patties.
2. Place on a broiler pan. Broil burgers 4 in. from heat 4-5 minutes on each side or until a thermometer reads 165°.
3. Meanwhile, in a small bowl, mix ketchup and reserved pineapple juice. Serve burgers on rolls with lettuce, tomato and ketchup mixture.

Creamy Lasagna

When I make lasagna, I blend an 8-ounce package of softened cream cheese into the ricotta and egg mixture. Sometimes I also add a little chopped fresh spinach, basil or parsley.

—DONNA M. NEWTON FALLS, OH

Sausage Ravioli Lasagna

Here's a hearty entree that'll have guests kissing the cook! You can easily alter it to please any palate—substituting ground beef or turkey for the sausage or using beef ravioli instead of cheese.

—NICOLE GAZZO BONDURANT, IA

PREP: 20 MIN. • **BAKE:** 35 MIN. + STANDING
MAKES: 8 SERVINGS

- 1 package (25 ounces) frozen cheese ravioli
- 1½ pounds bulk Italian sausage
- 1 container (15 ounces) ricotta cheese
- 1 egg, lightly beaten
- 1 teaspoon dried basil
- ½ teaspoon Italian seasoning
- 2 jars (one 26 ounces, one 14 ounces) spaghetti sauce
- 2 cups (8 ounces) shredded Italian cheese blend

1. Cook ravioli according to package directions. Meanwhile, in a large skillet, cook sausage over medium heat until no longer pink; drain. In a small bowl, combine the ricotta cheese, egg, basil and Italian seasoning; set aside. Drain ravioli.
2. Spoon 1⅓ cups spaghetti sauce into a greased 13-in. x 9-in. baking dish. Layer with half of the ravioli and sausage. Spoon ricotta mixture over sausage; top with 1⅓ cups sauce. Layer with remaining ravioli and sausage. Spread remaining sauce over top; sprinkle with shredded cheese.
3. Cover and bake at 350° for 30 minutes. Uncover and bake 5-10 minutes longer or until cheese is melted. Let stand for 10 minutes before cutting.

Oktoberfest Strudels

My husband was born and raised in Wisconsin, and he loves bratwurst. I tweaked this savory strudel filling to include some of his favorite hometown ingredients. Serve the strudels with extra mustard for dipping.
—**CLEO GONSKE** REDDING, CA

PREP: 30 MIN. • **BAKE:** 25 MIN. + STANDING
MAKES: 2 STRUDELS (3 SERVINGS EACH)

- 1 **tablespoon butter**
- 5 **fully cooked bratwurst links, chopped**
- 1 **medium onion, chopped**
- 1 **can (14 ounces) sauerkraut, rinsed and well drained**
- ½ **cup sour cream**
- 3 **tablespoons Dijon mustard**
- 2½ **teaspoons caraway seeds, divided**
- 1 **package (17.3 ounces) frozen puff pastry, thawed**
- 1 **cup (4 ounces) shredded Muenster cheese**
- 1 **cup (4 ounces) shredded sharp cheddar cheese**

1. Preheat oven to 400°. In a large skillet, heat butter over medium heat. Add bratwurst and onion; cook and stir 8-10 minutes or until onion is tender. Stir in sauerkraut; cool slightly.

2. In a small bowl, mix sour cream, mustard and ½ teaspoon caraway seeds. Unfold one sheet of puff pastry. Spread with ⅓ cup sour cream mixture to within ½ in. of edges. Spoon 2½ cups sausage mixture down center of pastry; sprinkle with ½ cup each Muenster and cheddar cheeses.

3. Lightly brush edges of pastry with water; bring edges together, pinching to seal. Transfer to an ungreased baking sheet, seam side down; pinch ends and fold under. Repeat with remaining ingredients.

4. Brush tops with water; sprinkle with remaining caraway seeds. Cut slits in pastry. Bake 25-30 minutes or until golden brown. Let stand 10 minutes before slicing.

SALMON WITH BALSAMIC-HONEY GLAZE

FAST FIX

Salmon with Balsamic-Honey Glaze

Look no further—you've just found the first, last and only way you'll ever want to fix salmon again. The sweet and tangy flavors blend beautifully in this easy-to-remember recipe.
—**MARY LOU TIMPSON** CENTENNIAL PARK, AZ

START TO FINISH: 30 MIN.
MAKES: 8 SERVINGS

- ½ **cup balsamic vinegar**
- 2 **tablespoons white wine or chicken broth**
- 2 **tablespoons Dijon mustard**
- 2 **tablespoons honey**
- 5 **garlic cloves, minced**
- 1 **tablespoon olive oil**
- 8 **salmon fillets (6 ounces each)**
- ½ **teaspoon salt**
- ½ **teaspoon pepper**
- 1 **tablespoon minced fresh oregano**

1. Combine the first six ingredients in a small saucepan. Bring to a boil; cook and stir for 4-5 minutes or until mixture is thickened.

2. Place salmon skin side down on a greased 15-in. x 10-in. x 1-in. baking pan. Sprinkle with salt and pepper. Spoon glaze over salmon; sprinkle with oregano.

3. Bake, uncovered, at 400° for 12-15 minutes or until fish flakes easily with a fork.

OKTOBERFEST STRUDELS

Chicken Caesar Pizza

Dressed greens on top of warm pizza may sound a little strange, but trust me: The result is fantastic.

—TRACY YOUNGMAN POST FALLS, ID

START TO FINISH: 30 MIN.
MAKES: 6 SERVINGS

- 1 **tube (13.8 ounces) refrigerated pizza crust**
- 1 **tablespoon olive oil**
- 1 **pound boneless skinless chicken breasts, cut into ½-inch cubes**
- 1½ **teaspoons minced garlic, divided**
- 6 **tablespoons creamy Caesar salad dressing, divided**
- 2 **cups (8 ounces) shredded Monterey Jack cheese, divided**
- ½ **cup grated Parmesan cheese, divided**
- 2 **cups hearts of romaine salad mix**
- 2 **green onions, thinly sliced**
- 2 **plum tomatoes, chopped**

1. Preheat oven to 400°. Unroll pizza crust and press to fit into a greased 15x10x1-in. baking pan, pinching edges to form a rim. Bake 10 minutes or until edges are lightly browned.
2. Meanwhile, in a large skillet, heat oil over medium-high heat. Add chicken and ½ teaspoon garlic; cook and stir until chicken is no longer pink. Remove from the heat and stir in 2 tablespoons of salad dressing.
3. Spread crust with 3 tablespoons salad dressing; sprinkle with remaining garlic. Top with half of the cheeses and all of the chicken. Sprinkle with remaining cheeses. Bake for 10-15 minutes or until crust is golden brown and cheese is melted.
4. In a small bowl, toss salad mix and green onions with remaining dressing. Just before serving, top pizza with salad and tomatoes.

CHICKEN CAESAR PIZZA

All-American Meat Loaf

There are many variations on meat loaf, but my family loves it when I keep to this classic version.

—MARGIE WILLIAMS MT. JULIET, TN

PREP: 30 MIN. **• BAKE:** 50 MIN. + STANDING
MAKES: 2 LOAVES (8 SERVINGS EACH)

- 1 **large green pepper, chopped**
- 1 **large onion, chopped**
- 2 **teaspoons olive oil**
- 4 **garlic cloves, minced**
- 2 **eggs, lightly beaten**
- 1 **cup 2% milk**
- 6 **slices bread, cubed**
- 1½ **cups (6 ounces) shredded cheddar cheese**
- 2¼ **teaspoons dried rosemary, crushed**
- 2 **teaspoons salt**
- 1 **teaspoon pepper**
- 2 **pounds lean ground beef (90% lean)**
- 1 **pound ground pork**
- 1½ **cups ketchup**
- ¼ **cup packed brown sugar**
- 2 **teaspoons cider vinegar**

1. Saute green pepper and onion in oil in a large skillet until tender. Add garlic; cook 1 minute longer. Transfer to a large bowl; cool to room temperature.
2. Add the eggs, milk, bread, cheese, rosemary, salt and pepper. Crumble beef and pork over the mixture and mix well.
3. Pat into two greased 9-in. x 5-in. loaf pans. Combine ketchup, brown sugar and vinegar in a small bowl. Spread over tops. Cover and freeze one meat loaf for up to 3 months.
4. Bake the remaining loaf, uncovered, at 350° for 50-55 minutes or until no pink remains and a thermometer reads 160°. Let stand 10 minutes before slicing.
TO USE FROZEN MEAT LOAF *Bake frozen meat loaf as directed, increasing time to 1¼ to 1½ hours.*

CREOLE BLACKENED CHICKEN

Lemon Parsley Swordfish

This dish looks impressive and it's easy to prepare—a winner in my book. I like that it comes together fast enough for a family weeknight meal, but it's special enough to serve guests for Sunday dinner.

—**NATHAN LEOPOLD** MECHANICSBURG, PA

START TO FINISH: 25 MIN.
MAKES: 4 SERVINGS

- 4 **swordfish steaks (7 ounces each)**
- ½ **teaspoon salt**
- ½ **cup minced fresh parsley, divided**
- ⅓ **cup olive oil**
- 1 **tablespoon lemon juice**
- 2 **teaspoons minced garlic**
- ¼ **teaspoon crushed red pepper flakes**

1. Preheat oven to 425°. Place fish in a greased 13x9-in. baking dish; sprinkle with salt. In a small bowl, combine ¼ cup parsley, oil, lemon juice, garlic and pepper flakes; spoon over fish.
2. Bake, uncovered, 15-20 minutes or until fish flakes easily with a fork, basting occasionally. Sprinkle with remaining parsley.

LEMON PARSLEY SWORDFISH

"I love blackened chicken and was thrilled to discover I can cook it at home. I adjusted the original recipe, making it spicier to suit my taste. If you prefer a milder chicken, reduce or omit the cayenne pepper."

—**LAUREN HARDY** JACKSONVILLE, FL

FAST FIX
Creole Blackened Chicken

START TO FINISH: 30 MIN.
MAKES: 8 SERVINGS

- 2 **tablespoons ground cumin**
- 2 **tablespoons Creole seasoning**
- 2 **tablespoons salt-free Southwest chipotle seasoning blend**
- 4 **teaspoons lemon-pepper seasoning**
- 1 **teaspoon cayenne pepper**
- 8 **boneless skinless chicken breast halves (6 ounces each)**
- 2 **tablespoons canola oil**

1. Preheat oven to 350°. Mix the first five ingredients; sprinkle over chicken. In a large skillet, heat oil over medium-high heat. Brown chicken in batches on both sides; transfer to a greased 15x10x1-in. baking pan.
2. Bake, uncovered, 12-15 minutes or until a thermometer reads 165°.

GLAZED BBQ RIBS

Glazed BBQ Ribs

After trying a fruit salad at a backyard barbecue, I wanted to make a rib sauce that tasted as sweet. Everyone loves the raspberry-red wine sauce combo.
—**STEPHEN MARINO** NUTLEY, NJ

PREP: 2 HOURS • **BROIL:** 10 MIN.
MAKES: 4 SERVINGS

- 4 **pounds pork baby back ribs**
- ½ **cup olive oil**
- 2 **teaspoons salt**
- 2 **teaspoons pepper**
- 1 **bottle (18 ounces) barbecue sauce**
- 1 **cup seedless raspberry preserves**
- ¼ **cup dry red wine**
- ½ **teaspoon onion powder**
- ½ **teaspoon cayenne pepper**

1. Preheat oven to 325°. Place ribs in a shallow roasting pan, bone side down. In a small bowl, mix oil, salt and pepper; rub over ribs. Bake, covered, 1½ to 2 hours or until tender; drain.
2. In another bowl, mix remaining ingredients; reserve ¾ cup for serving with ribs. Brush some of the remaining sauce over ribs. Bake, uncovered, 25-30 minutes or until ribs are glazed,

basting occasionally with the additional sauce.
3. Transfer ribs to a broiler pan, bone side down. Broil 4-5 in. from heat 8-10 minutes or until browned. Serve with reserved sauce.

Creamy Cavatappi & Cheese

Dive fork first into oodles of noodles cloaked in delectable sharp cheddar. Hot pepper sauce lends a mild heat that complements the smoky bacon topping in this grown-up version of macaroni and cheese.
—**BARBARA COLUCCI** ROCKLEDGE, FL

PREP: 30 MIN. • **BAKE:** 20 MIN.
MAKES: 10 SERVINGS

- 6 **cups uncooked cavatappi or spiral pasta**
- 3 **garlic cloves, minced**
- ⅓ **cup butter**
- ¼ **cup all-purpose flour**
- 1 **tablespoon hot pepper sauce**
- 4 **cups 2% milk**
- 6 **cups (24 ounces) shredded sharp cheddar cheese**
- 1 **cup cubed process cheese (Velveeta)**
- 3 **green onions, chopped**

TOPPINGS
- ½ **cup panko (Japanese) bread crumbs**
- 3 **thick-sliced bacon strips, cooked and coarsley crumbled**
- 1 **tablespoon butter, melted**
- 1 **green onion, chopped**
  Coarsely ground pepper, optional

1. Cook cavatappi according to package directions.
2. Meanwhile, saute garlic in butter in a Dutch oven. Stir in flour and pepper sauce until blended; gradually add milk. Bring to a boil; cook and stir for 2 minutes or until thickened.
3. Stir in cheeses until melted; add green onions. Drain cavatappi; stir into cheese mixture.
4. Transfer to a greased 13-in. x 9-in. baking dish. Combine the bread crumbs, bacon and melted butter; sprinkle over top.
5. Bake, uncovered, at 350° for 20-25 minutes or until bubbly. Sprinkle with green onion and, if desired, pepper.

FAST FIX ▶

Lime-Ginger Chicken Tenders

We cook chicken breasts often because they're low in fat, high in protein, and almost always a good price at the grocery store. To keep things exciting, I add a few of our favorites to the mix like jalapenos, lime and fresh ginger.
—**SAMANTHA ANDERSON** FORT WORTH, TX

START TO FINISH: 30 MIN.
MAKES: 4 SERVINGS

- ⅓ **cup minced fresh cilantro**
- 1 **jalapeno pepper, seeded and minced**
- 2 **tablespoons lime juice**
- 2 **tablespoons olive oil**
- 3 **garlic cloves, minced**
- 1½ **teaspoons minced fresh gingerroot**
- 1½ **teaspoons grated lime peel**
- ½ **teaspoon salt**
- ½ **teaspoon ground cumin**
- 1½ **pounds chicken tenderloins**

Preheat oven to 375°. In a large bowl, mix the first nine ingredients. Add chicken; toss to coat. Transfer to a greased 15x10x1-in. baking pan. Bake, uncovered, 20-25 minutes or until chicken is no longer pink.
NOTE *Wear disposable gloves when cutting hot peppers; the oils can burn skin. Avoid touching your face.*

LIME-GINGER CHICKEN TENDERS

FAST FIX ▶
Salsa Verde Chicken Casserole

Here's a rich and tasty rendition of all my favorite Tex-Mex dishes rolled into one beautiful casserole. Best of all, it's ready in almost no time!

—**JANET MCCORMICK** PROCTORVILLE, OH

START TO FINISH: 30 MIN.
MAKES: 6 SERVINGS

- 2 **cups shredded rotisserie chicken**
- 1 **cup (8 ounces) sour cream**
- 1½ **cups salsa verde, divided**
- 8 **corn tortillas (6 inches)**
- 2 **cups chopped tomatoes**
- ¼ **cup minced fresh cilantro**
- 2 **cups (8 ounces) shredded Monterey Jack cheese**
  Optional toppings: avocado slices, thinly sliced green onions or fresh cilantro leaves

1. Combine the chicken, sour cream and ¾ cup salsa in a small bowl. Spread ¼ cup salsa on the bottom of a greased 8-in. square baking dish.
2. Layer with half of the tortillas and chicken mixture; sprinkle with the tomatoes, minced cilantro and half of the cheese. Repeat layers with remaining tortillas, chicken mixture and cheese.
3. Bake, uncovered, at 400° for 20-25 minutes or until bubbly. Serve with remaining salsa and, if desired, optional toppings.

Barbecue Chicken Pizza

My husband and I like barbeque chicken pizza, but I decided to take it up a notch by adding other toppings that we love, including smoky bacon and creamy Gorgonzola. My mouth starts to water just thinking about it!

—**MEGAN CROW** LINCOLN, NE

PREP: 40 MIN. • **BAKE:** 20 MIN.
MAKES: 8 SERVINGS

- 2 **tablespoons olive oil**
- 1 **medium red onion, sliced**
- 1 **tube (13.8 ounces) refrigerated pizza crust**
- ¾ **cup barbecue sauce**
- 2 **cups shredded cooked chicken breast**
- 6 **bacon strips, cooked and crumbled**
- ¼ **cup crumbled Gorgonzola cheese**
- 2 **jalapeno peppers, seeded and minced**
- 1 **teaspoon paprika**
- 1 **teaspoon garlic powder**
- 2 **cups (8 ounces) shredded part-skim mozzarella cheese**

1. Preheat oven to 425°. In a large skillet, heat oil over medium heat. Add onion; cook and stir 4-6 minutes or until softened. Reduce heat to medium-low; cook 20-25 minutes or until deep golden brown, stirring occasionally.
2. Unroll and press dough onto bottom and ½-in. up sides of a greased 15x10x1-in. baking pan. Bake 8 minutes.

RANCH-MARINATED CHICKEN BREASTS

3. Spread barbecue sauce over dough; top with chicken, cooked onion, bacon, Gorgonzola cheese and jalapenos. Sprinkle with paprika and garlic powder; top with mozzarella cheese.
4. Bake 8-10 minutes or until crust is golden and cheese is melted.
NOTE *Wear disposable gloves when cutting hot peppers; the oils can burn skin. Avoid touching your face.*

Ranch-Marinated Chicken Breasts

With a little prep time the night before, you can have these savory chicken breasts ready in about half an hour.

—**BARBEE DECKER** WHISPERING PINES, NC

PREP: 10 MIN. + MARINATING
BAKE: 25 MIN. • **MAKES:** 6 SERVINGS

- 2 **cups (16 ounces) sour cream**
- 1 **envelope ranch salad dressing mix**
- 4 **teaspoons lemon juice**
- 4 **teaspoons Worcestershire sauce**
- 2 **teaspoons celery salt**
- 2 **teaspoons paprika**
- 1 **teaspoon garlic salt**
- 1 **teaspoon pepper**
- 6 **boneless skinless chicken breast halves (6 ounces each)**
- ¼ **cup butter, melted**

1. Combine the first eight ingredients in a large resealable plastic bag; add chicken. Seal bag and turn to coat; refrigerate for 8 hours or overnight.
2. Drain chicken and discard marinade. Place chicken breasts in a greased 15-in. x 10-in. x 1-in. baking pan. Drizzle with butter. Bake, uncovered, at 350° for 25-30 minutes or until juices run clear.

SALSA VERDE CHICKEN CASSEROLE

Tortellini Spinach Casserole

This casserole's fresh taste will delight even those who say they don't like spinach. In fact, people are often surprised at just how good it is! Whenever I bring it to a gathering, it doesn't sit around long.

—BARBARA KELLEN ANTIOCH, IL

PREP: 20 MIN. • **BAKE:** 20 MIN.
MAKES: 12 SERVINGS

- 2 packages (10 ounces each) frozen cheese tortellini
- 1 pound sliced fresh mushrooms
- 1 teaspoon garlic powder
- ¼ teaspoon onion powder
- ¼ teaspoon pepper
- ½ cup butter, divided
- 1 can (12 ounces) evaporated milk
- 1 block (8 ounces) brick cheese, cubed
- 3 packages (10 ounces each) frozen chopped spinach, thawed and squeezed dry
- 2 cups (8 ounces) shredded part-skim mozzarella cheese

1. Cook tortellini according to package directions. Meanwhile, in a large skillet, saute the mushrooms, garlic powder, onion powder and pepper in ¼ cup butter until mushrooms are tender. Remove and keep warm.

2. In the same skillet, combine milk and remaining butter. Bring to a gentle boil; stir in brick cheese. Cook and stir until smooth. Drain tortellini; place in a large bowl. Stir in the mushroom mixture and spinach. Add cheese sauce and toss to coat.

3. Transfer to a greased 13-in. x 9-in. baking dish; sprinkle with mozzarella cheese. Cover and bake at 350° for 15 minutes. Uncover; bake 5-10 minutes longer or until heated through and cheese is melted.

Italian Pizza Meat Loaf

If you have kids who protest when they hear meat loaf is on the menu, just try keeping them away from this saucy creation packed with pizza flavors. One bite and there's no turning back!

—HANNAH KLEINHANS MILWAUKEE, WI

PREP: 20 MIN. • **BAKE:** 50 MIN. + STANDING
MAKES: 2 LOAVES (8 SERVINGS EACH)

- 3 eggs, lightly beaten
- ⅔ cup 2% milk
- ⅔ cup jarred pizza sauce
- 2 tablespoons Worcestershire sauce
- 1 large onion, finely chopped
- 2 cans (2¼ ounces each) sliced ripe olives, drained
- ¾ cup dry bread crumbs
- 2½ teaspoons dried oregano
- 2½ teaspoons dried basil
- 1½ teaspoons pepper
- 1¼ teaspoons salt
- 3 pounds lean ground beef (90% lean)
  Optional toppings: shredded mozzarella cheese and additional warmed pizza sauce

1. Combine the first 11 ingredients in a large bowl. Crumble beef over mixture and mix well. Pat into two greased 9-in. x 5-in. loaf pans.

2. Cover and freeze one meat loaf for up to 3 months. Bake the remaining loaf, uncovered, at 350° for 50-55 minutes until no pink remains and a thermometer reads 160°. Top with cheese and additional pizza sauce if desired. Let stand for 10 minutes before slicing.

TO USE FROZEN MEAT LOAF *Bake frozen meat loaf as directed, increasing time to 1¼ to 1½ hours. Top with pizza sauce and cheese if desired.*

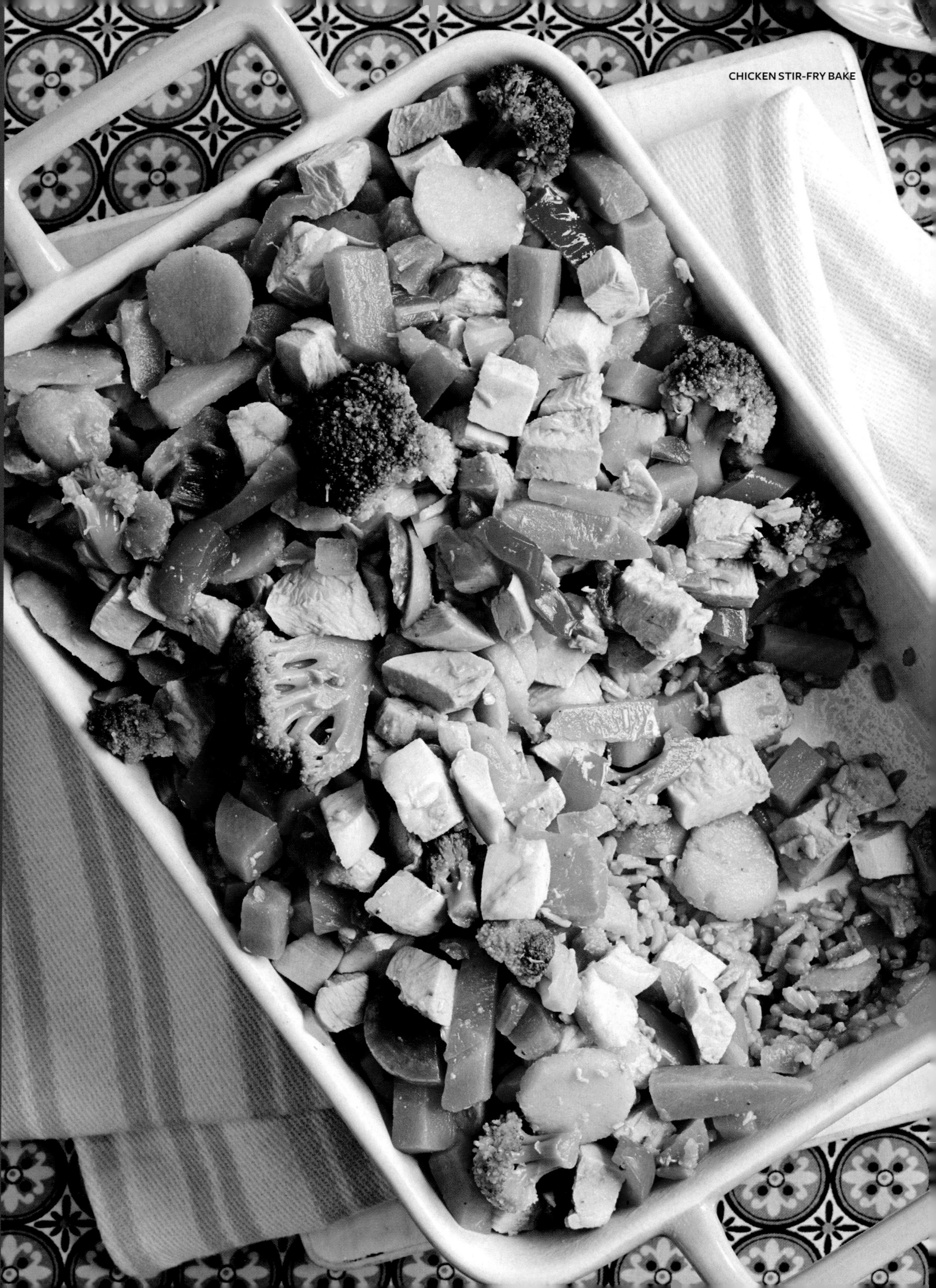

CHICKEN STIR-FRY BAKE

Chicken Stir-Fry Bake

One night I decided to use frozen vegetables in my chicken stir-fry. Not wanting to stand watch over the stovetop, I baked the entree in the oven. People say this tastes like it's hot from the wok.

—CARLY CARTER NASHVILLE, TN

PREP: 10 MIN. • **BAKE:** 25 MIN.
MAKES: 4 SERVINGS

- 2 cups uncooked instant rice
- 1 can (8 ounces) sliced water chestnuts, drained
- 2 cups cubed cooked chicken
- 1 package (16 ounces) frozen stir-fry vegetables, thawed
- 1 can (14½ ounces) chicken broth
- ¼ cup soy sauce
- 1 garlic clove, minced
- ½ to ¾ teaspoon ground ginger

Place rice in a greased 11-in. x 7-in. baking dish. Layer with the water chestnuts, chicken and vegetables. Combine remaining ingredients; pour over top. Cover and bake at 375° for 25 minutes or until rice is tender.

Baked Creole Tilapia

We think the champagne dressing in this recipe is delicious on almost anything, but it's excellent with this mild-flavored fish. The tilapia is nice in tacos, too.

—BERNADETTE BENNETT WACO, TX

PREP: 10 MIN. + MARINATING
BAKE: 20 MIN. • **MAKES:** 6 SERVINGS

- 1 cup champagne salad dressing
- 2 tablespoons lemon juice
- 1 tablespoon Creole seasoning
- 1 teaspoon dried parsley flakes
- 1 teaspoon dill weed
- 6 tilapia fillets (6 ounces each)

1. Combine the first five ingredients in a small bowl. Pour marinade into a large resealable plastic bag. Add tilapia; seal bag and turn to coat. Refrigerate for 15 minutes.
2. Drain and discard marinade. Place fillets in a greased 15-in. x 10-in. x 1-in. baking pan.
3. Bake, uncovered, at 375° for 20-25 minutes or until fish flakes easily with a fork.
NOTE *The following spices may be substituted for 1 teaspoon Creole*

seasoning: ¼ teaspoon each salt, garlic powder and paprika; and a pinch each of dried thyme, ground cumin and cayenne pepper.

FAST FIX ▶
Smoked Gouda Spinach Pizza

My daughter created this fabulous pizza and serves it as an appetizer, but it also makes an excellent main dish. Leftovers pack beautifully for a workday lunch.

—MARIE HATTRUP SPARKS, NV

START TO FINISH: 30 MIN.
MAKES: 10 PIECES

- 1 tube (13.8 ounces) refrigerated pizza crust
- ½ pound sliced fresh mushrooms
- 1 small red onion, chopped
- 2 tablespoons butter
- 2 garlic cloves, minced
- 1 cup Alfredo sauce
- ½ teaspoon dried thyme
- 1 package (6 ounces) fresh baby spinach
- ½ pound fully cooked Italian chicken sausage links, sliced
- 2 cups (8 ounces) shredded smoked Gouda cheese

1. Unroll dough into a greased 15-in. x 10-in. x 1-in. baking pan; flatten dough and build up edges slightly. Bake at 425° for 10-12 minutes or until lightly browned.
2. Meanwhile, saute mushrooms and onion in butter in a large skillet until tender. Add garlic; cook 1 minute longer. Stir in Alfredo sauce and thyme. Spread over crust. Top with spinach, sausage and cheese.
3. Bake for 10-15 minutes or until crust and cheese are lightly browned.

SMOKED GOUDA SPINACH PIZZA

LEMONY PARSLEY BAKED COD

Mexi-Mac Casserole

Here's one of my favorite all-in-one meals that uses items I typically have in the pantry. Green chilies and spicy tomatoes give it just a little heat.

—**JAN CONKLIN** STEVENSVILLE, MT

PREP: 25 MIN. • **BAKE:** 30 MIN.
MAKES: 8 SERVINGS

- 1 package (7¼ ounces) macaroni and cheese dinner mix
- 1½ pounds lean ground beef (90% lean)
- 1 medium onion, finely chopped
- 2 garlic cloves, minced
- 1 can (14½ ounces) diced tomatoes with mild green chilies
- 1 can (4 ounces) chopped green chilies
- 1 envelope reduced-sodium taco seasoning
- 2½ cups (10 ounces) shredded Mexican cheese blend, divided
- 1 can (16 ounces) kidney beans, rinsed and drained
- 1 can (15¼ ounces) whole kernel corn, drained
- 1 can (7¾ ounces) Mexican-style hot tomato sauce
- ½ cup crushed tortilla chips

1. Prepare macaroni and cheese mix according to package directions.
2. Meanwhile, cook the beef, onion and garlic in a Dutch oven over medium heat until meat is no longer pink; drain.
3. Add diced tomatoes, green chilies and taco seasoning. Stir in 2 cups cheese, beans, corn, tomato sauce and the prepared macaroni and cheese.

4. Transfer to a greased 13-in. x 9-in. baking dish; sprinkle with chips and remaining cheese.
5. Bake, uncovered, at 350° for 30-35 minutes or until bubbly.

Lemony Parsley Baked Cod

If there's one thing I hate, it's overcooking a good piece of fish. The trick is to cook it at a high temperature for just a short time. It keeps the fish moist and tender.

—**SHERRY DAY** PINCKNEY, MI

START TO FINISH: 25 MIN.
MAKES: 4 SERVINGS

- 3 tablespoons minced fresh parsley
- 2 tablespoons lemon juice
- 1 tablespoon grated lemon peel
- 1 tablespoon olive oil
- 2 garlic cloves, minced
- ¼ teaspoon salt
- ⅛ teaspoon pepper
- 4 cod fillets (6 ounces each)
- 2 green onions, chopped

Preheat oven to 400°. In a small bowl, mix the first seven ingredients. Place cod in an ungreased 11x7-in. baking dish; top with parsley mixture. Sprinkle with green onions. Bake, covered, 10-15 minutes or until fish flakes easily with a fork.
PER SERVING *161 cal., 4 g fat (1 g sat. fat), 65 mg chol., 95 mg sodium, 2 g carb., 1 g fiber, 27 g pro.* **Diabetic Exchanges:** *4 lean meat, ½ fat.*

Glazed Ham with Sweet Potatoes

I took a class at a local junior college on cooking for singles. This recipe is the perfect size for me. I can reheat the second serving for lunch the next day.

—**ELOISE SMITH** WILLOWBROOK, IL

START TO FINISH: 15 MIN.
MAKES: 2 SERVINGS

- 2 tablespoons apricot jam
- 1 teaspoon Dijon mustard
- 1 boneless fully cooked ham steak (about 8 ounces)
- 1 can (15¾ ounces) sweet potatoes, drained
- 1 can (8½ ounces) sliced peaches, drained
- 2 tablespoons maple syrup, divided

1. In a small microwave-safe bowl, combine jam and mustard. Microwave, uncovered, on high for 15-30 seconds or until jam is melted; stir until blended. Set aside.
2. Place ham steak in an ovenproof skillet. Arrange sweet potatoes and peaches around ham. Drizzle with 1 tablespoon syrup. Broil 3-4 in. from the heat for 5 minutes. Turn ham, peaches and potatoes. Brush ham with jam mixture; drizzle peaches and potatoes with remaining syrup. Broil 5 minutes longer or until heated through.

GLAZED HAM WITH SWEET POTATOES

OVEN-BARBECUED SALMON

EAT SMART **FAST FIX**

Margherita Pita Pizzas

My husband plants the garden and I harvest and cook the fruits of his labor. My favorite way to use plum tomatoes is this easy Margherita Pita Pizza. It is so good!

—ROSEMARIE WELESKI NATRONA HEIGHTS, PA

START TO FINISH: 20 MIN.
MAKES: 4 SERVINGS

- 4 pita breads (6 inches)
- 2 teaspoons olive oil
- 2 garlic cloves, minced
- 2 cups (8 ounces) shredded part-skim mozzarella cheese
- 3 plum tomatoes, thinly sliced
- ¼ teaspoon garlic powder
- 1 teaspoon Italian seasoning
  Thinly sliced fresh basil, optional

1. Place pita breads on an ungreased baking sheet; brush with oil. Top with garlic, 1 cup cheese, tomatoes, garlic powder and remaining cheese; sprinkle with Italian seasoning.
2. Bake at 425° for 10-12 minutes or until cheese is melted. Top with basil if desired.
PER SERVING *340 cal., 12 g fat (6 g sat. fat), 33 mg chol., 588 mg sodium, 38 g carb., 2 g fiber, 20 g pro.* **Diabetic Exchanges:** *2 starch, 2 medium-fat meat, ½ fat.*

MARGHERITA PITA PIZZAS

"Late last summer, the South Carolina heat drove me indoors and away from my grill. So I changed my favorite over-the-coals recipe to be baked in the oven with results that are just as tasty." —**MANDY RIVERS** LEXINGTON, SC

EAT SMART **FAST FIX**

Oven-Barbecued Salmon

START TO FINISH: 25 MIN.
MAKES: 5 SERVINGS

- 5 salmon fillets (6 ounces each)
- 3 tablespoons orange juice
- 2 tablespoons lemon juice
- 2 tablespoons brown sugar
- 1 tablespoon chili powder
- 1 tablespoon paprika
- ½ teaspoon salt
- ½ teaspoon garlic powder
- ½ teaspoon ground cumin

1. Preheat oven to 425°. Place salmon in a greased 15x10x1-in. baking pan; drizzle with orange and lemon juices.
2. In a small bowl, mix remaining ingredients; sprinkle over fillets. Bake 13-15 minutes or until fish flakes easily with a fork.
PER SERVING *301 cal., 16 g fat (3 g sat. fat), 85 mg chol., 340 mg sodium, 9 g carb., 1 g fiber, 29 g pro.* **Diabetic Exchanges:** *5 lean meat, ½ starch.*

Bubbly & Golden Mexican Beef Cobbler

Add whatever you like to this recipe to make it yours: black beans, sour cream, even guacamole.

—**MARY BROOKS** CLAY, MI

PREP: 20 MIN. • **BAKE:** 35 MIN.
MAKES: 6 SERVINGS

- 1 **pound ground beef**
- 1 **envelope taco seasoning**
- ¾ **cup water**
- 1 **jar (16 ounces) salsa**
- 1 **can (8¾ ounces) whole kernel corn, drained**
- 2 **cups (8 ounces) shredded sharp cheddar cheese**
- 3⅓ **cups biscuit/baking mix**
- 1⅓ **cups 2% milk**
- ⅛ **teaspoon salt**
- ⅛ **teaspoon pepper**

1. In a large skillet, cook beef over medium heat for 6-8 minutes or until no longer pink, breaking into crumbles; drain. Stir in taco seasoning and water. Bring to a boil; cook until liquid is evaporated. Transfer to an 11-in. x 7-in. baking dish; layer with salsa, corn and cheese.

2. In a large bowl, mix biscuit mix and milk just until blended; drop by tablespoonfuls over cheese (dish will be full). Sprinkle with salt and pepper.

3. Bake, uncovered, at 350° for 35-45 minutes or until bubbly and topping is golden brown.

Company Pot Roast

The aroma of this roast slowly cooking in the oven is absolutely mouthwatering. It gives the home such a cozy feeling, even on the chilliest winter days.

—**ANITA OSBORNE** THOMASBURG, ON

PREP: 20 MIN. • **BAKE:** 2¾ HOURS
MAKES: 6 SERVINGS

- 1 **boneless beef chuck roast (3 to 4 pounds)**
- 2 **tablespoons olive oil**
- 1 **cup sherry or beef broth**
- ½ **cup reduced-sodium soy sauce**
- ¼ **cup sugar**
- 2 **teaspoons beef bouillon granules**
- 1 **cinnamon stick (3 inches)**
- 8 **medium carrots, cut into 2-inch pieces**
- 6 **medium potatoes, peeled and cut into 1½-inch pieces**
- 1 **medium onion, sliced**
- 2 **tablespoons cornstarch**
- 2 **tablespoons cold water**

1. Brown roast in oil in a Dutch oven on all sides; drain. Combine the sherry, soy sauce, sugar, bouillon and cinnamon stick; pour over roast.

2. Cover and bake at 325° for 2¾ to 3¼ hours or until meat and vegetables are tender, adding the carrots, potatoes and onion during the last 30 minutes of cooking.

3. Remove roast and vegetables to a serving platter; keep warm. Combine cornstarch and water until smooth. Stir into pan. Bring to a boil; cook and stir for 2 minutes or until thickened. Serve with roast and vegetables.

BUBBLY & GOLDEN MEXICAN BEEF COBBLER

TASTY TUNA CASSEROLE

Sausage and Pepperoni Pizza Pasta

Spaghetti sauce mix helps you get this meat-lover's pizza casserole on the table pronto. It's great for potlucks, too, as it's easy and economical to double the recipe.

—JULIE GLISSON ZDERO RACINE, WI

PREP: 25 MIN. • **BAKE:** 25 MIN.
MAKES: 8 SERVINGS

- 4 cups uncooked penne pasta
- 3 Italian sausage links, cut into ½-inch slices
- 1 cup sliced fresh mushrooms
- 1 medium green pepper, chopped
- 1 medium onion, chopped
- 1 package (3½ ounces) sliced pepperoni
- 3½ cups water
- 2 cans (6 ounces each) tomato paste
- 2 envelopes thick and zesty spaghetti sauce mix
- 1 can (2¼ ounces) sliced ripe olives, drained
- ¼ cup olive oil
- ½ teaspoon garlic salt
- 1 cup (4 ounces) shredded part-skim mozzarella cheese

1. Cook penne according to package directions. Meanwhile, in a Dutch oven, cook the sausage, mushrooms, pepper and onion over medium heat until meat is no longer pink and the vegetables are tender; drain and remove from pan.

2. Cook pepperoni in the same pan until heated through. Return sausage mixture to the pan.

3. Stir in the water, tomato paste, spaghetti sauce mix, olives, oil and garlic salt. Bring to a boil. Reduce heat; simmer, uncovered, for 4-5 minutes to allow flavors to blend.

4. Drain pasta; stir into sausage mixture. Transfer to a greased 13-in. x 9-in. baking dish. Sprinkle with cheese.

5. Bake, uncovered, at 350° for 25-30 minutes or until bubbly.

Tasty Tuna Casserole

This is not your usual tuna casserole. The macaroni and tuna are coated in a rich and creamy sauce with a hint of tomato.

—ELSIE EPP NEWTON, KS

PREP: 20 MIN. • **BAKE:** 20 MIN.
MAKES: 4 SERVINGS

- 2 cups uncooked elbow macaroni
- 1 can (12 ounces) albacore white tuna in water
- 1 can (8 ounces) tomato sauce
- 4 ounces reduced-fat cream cheese, cubed
- 1 small onion, finely chopped
- ¼ teaspoon salt
- ½ teaspoon dried oregano

1. Cook macaroni according to package directions. Meanwhile, in a large bowl, combine the remaining ingredients. Drain macaroni; stir into tuna mixture.

2. Transfer to a 2-qt. baking dish coated with cooking spray. Cover and bake at 350° for 20-25 minutes or until heated through.

PER SERVING *334 cal., 9 g fat (5 g sat. fat), 56 mg chol., 851 mg sodium, 33 g carb., 2 g fiber, 29 g pro.* **Diabetic Exchanges:** *3 lean meat, 2 starch, 1 fat.*

SAUSAGE AND PEPPERONI PIZZA PASTA

EFFORTLESS ALFREDO PIZZA

EAT SMART

Texas Oven-Roasted Beef Brisket

I was once a brisket novice, but now I cook up a classic dish with the taste of Texas. Thanks to a zesty spice rub, the end result is a fork-tender cut with a crispy crust.

—AUDRIA AUSBERN TAHOKA, TX

PREP: 20 MIN. • **BAKE:** 3¼ HOURS
MAKES: 10 SERVINGS

- 2 tablespoons chili powder
- 1 tablespoon sugar
- 1 tablespoon onion powder
- 1 tablespoon garlic powder
- 1 tablespoon pepper
- 2 teaspoons ground mustard
- ½ teaspoon salt
- 1 fresh beef brisket (4 pounds), halved
- 1 tablespoon canola oil
- 1½ cups beef broth
- 1 bay leaf

1. Combine the first seven ingredients; rub over brisket. In an ovenproof Dutch oven, brown meat in oil in batches. Add broth and bay leaf. Bring to a boil.
2. Cover and bake at 325° for 3¼ to 3¾ hours or until meat is tender. Remove brisket to a serving platter. Skim fat from cooking juices; discard bay leaf. Thinly slice meat across the grain. Serve with cooking juices.
NOTE This is a fresh beef brisket, not corned beef.
PER SERVING 263 cal., 10 g fat (3 g sat. fat), 77 mg chol., 328 mg sodium, 4 g carb., 1 g fiber, 38 g pro. **Diabetic Exchange:** 5 lean meat.

TEXAS OVEN-ROASTED BEEF BRISKET

EAT SMART
Effortless Alfredo Pizza

Here's a light and scrumptious twist for pizza night. The recipe makes good use of leftovers and convenience items, so I don't have to spend much time in the kitchen. I occasionally use collard greens instead of spinach.

—BRITTNEY HOUSE LOCKPORT, IL

START TO FINISH: 20 MIN.
MAKES: 6 SLICES

- 1 package (10 ounces) frozen chopped spinach, thawed and squeezed dry
- 1 cup shredded cooked turkey breast
- 2 teaspoons lemon juice
- ¼ teaspoon salt
- ¼ teaspoon pepper
- 1 prebaked 12-inch pizza crust
- 1 garlic clove, peeled and halved
- ½ cup reduced-fat Alfredo sauce
- ¾ cup shredded fontina cheese
- ½ teaspoon crushed red pepper flakes

1. Preheat oven to 450°. In a large bowl, mix the first five ingredients until blended.
2. Place crust on an ungreased 12-in. pizza pan; rub with cut sides of garlic. Discard garlic. Spread Alfredo sauce over crust. Top with spinach mixture, cheese and pepper flakes. Bake 8-12 minutes or until crust is lightly browned.
PER SERVING 302 cal., 10 g fat (4 g sat. fat), 45 mg chol., 756 mg sodium, 33 g carb., 1 g fiber, 20 g pro. **Diabetic Exchanges:** 2 starch, 2 lean meat, ½ fat.

FAST FIX
Chicken Potpies

This cute pair of potpies is perfect for any busy night.

—SHIRLEA ANN ROMAN JAMESTOWN, NY

START TO FINISH: 30 MIN.
MAKES: 2 SERVINGS

- ⅓ cup biscuit/baking mix
- 2 tablespoons plus 1½ teaspoons 2% milk
- 1 teaspoon dried parsley flakes
- 1 envelope chicken gravy mix
- 1¼ cups cubed cooked chicken
- 1 cup frozen mixed vegetables

1. In a small bowl, combine the biscuit mix, milk and parsley just until moistened; set aside. In a saucepan, prepare gravy mix according to package directions. Add the chicken and vegetables; cook for 1-2 minutes or until heated through.
2. Pour into two ungreased 4½-in. deep-dish pie plates. Drop biscuit dough over chicken mixture. Bake at 350° for 20-25 minutes or until bubbly.

Chickpea Potpies

My family loves potpies, and with this recipe, no one—not even my carnivores—misses the meat. Hungry teens and adults gobble up these individual potpies.

—**ANNETTE WOOFENDEN** MIDDLEBORO, MA

PREP: 15 MIN. • **BAKE:** 25 MIN.
MAKES: 4 SERVINGS

- 1 small onion, chopped
- 6 tablespoons butter
- 2 garlic cloves, minced
- 6 tablespoons all-purpose flour
- ½ teaspoon salt
- ¼ teaspoon pepper
- 3 cups vegetable broth
- 2 cups frozen mixed vegetables, thawed
- 1 can (15 ounces) garbanzo beans or chickpeas, rinsed and drained
- 1¼ cups frozen cubed hash brown potatoes
- ¼ cup heavy whipping cream
- ¾ teaspoon Italian seasoning
- 1 sheet refrigerated pie pastry

1. Saute onion in butter in a large saucepan until tender. Add garlic; cook 1 minute longer. Stir in the flour, salt and pepper until blended. Gradually add broth; bring to a boil. Cook and stir for 2 minutes or until thickened.
2. Stir in the vegetables, garbanzo beans, potatoes, cream and Italian seasoning. Divide mixture among four ungreased 10-oz. ramekins.
3. Unroll pastry; divide into four portions. Roll out each portion to fit ramekins; place over filling. Trim, seal and flute edges. Cut slits in pastry. Place ramekins on a baking sheet.
4. Bake at 400° for 25-30 minutes or until pastry is golden brown.

Taco Bubble Pizza

Your entire family's going to be requesting this meal! Lucky for you, it's a cinch with tomato soup, taco seasoning and refrigerated biscuits. Set up a taco bar and let everyone add their favorite toppings.

—**DAWN SCHUTTER** TITONKA, IA

PREP: 20 MIN. • **BAKE:** 30 MIN.
MAKES: 8 SERVINGS

- 1½ pounds lean ground beef (90% lean)
- 1 can (10¾ ounces) condensed tomato soup, undiluted
- ¾ cup water
- 1 envelope taco seasoning
- 1 can (12 ounces) refrigerated buttermilk biscuits
- 2 cups (8 ounces) shredded cheddar cheese

TOPPINGS

- 2 cups torn leaf lettuce
- 2 medium tomatoes, seeded and chopped
- 1 cup salsa
- 1 cup (8 ounces) sour cream
- 1 can (2¼ ounces) sliced ripe olives, drained
- Green onions, optional

1. Cook beef in a large skillet over medium heat until no longer pink; drain. Stir in the soup, water and taco seasoning; bring to a boil. Reduce heat; simmer, uncovered, for 3 minutes.
2. Meanwhile, cut each biscuit into 8 pieces; set aside. Remove beef mixture from heat and gently stir in biscuits. Transfer to an ungreased 13-in. x 9-in. baking dish.
3. Bake, uncovered, at 375° for 20-25 minutes or until biscuits are golden brown. Sprinkle with cheese; bake 8-10 minutes longer or until cheese is melted. Serve with toppings.

TACO BUBBLE PIZZA

FAST FIX

Parmesan-Broiled Tilapia

START TO FINISH: 15 MIN.
MAKES: 4 SERVINGS

- ½ cup grated Parmesan cheese
- 3 tablespoons butter, softened
- 2 tablespoons mayonnaise
- ¼ teaspoon dried basil
- ¼ teaspoon pepper
- ⅛ teaspoon onion powder
- ⅛ teaspoon celery salt
- 4 tilapia fillets (6 ounces each)
- 4 lemon wedges

1. In a small bowl, mix the first seven ingredients. Arrange fillets in a 15x10x1-in. baking pan coated with cooking spray. Spread cheese mixture over fish.

2. Broil 4 in. from heat 4-5 minutes or until topping is lightly browned and fish flakes easily with a fork, rotating pan halfway for more even browning. Serve with lemon wedges.

"I love how Parmesan cheese brings rich flavor to an otherwise mild-tasting fish. This is one dish where leftovers are never a problem." —TRACY LOCKEN GILLETTE, WY

PARMESAN-BROILED TILAPIA

French Meat Pie

Some time ago, a co-worker brought a meat pie to lunch. The aroma was familiar...and after one taste, I was amazed to discover it was the same pie my grandmother used to serve when I was a youngster! My friend shared the recipe, and I have been enjoying it ever since.
—RITA WINTERBERGER HUSON, MT

PREP: 20 MIN. • **BAKE:** 30 MIN.
MAKES: 8 SERVINGS

- 1 large onion, thinly sliced
- 2 tablespoons canola oil
- 1 pound ground beef
- 1 pound ground pork
- 1 cup mashed potatoes
- 1 can (8 ounces) mixed vegetables, drained
- 2 teaspoons ground allspice
- 1 teaspoon salt
- ¼ teaspoon pepper
  Pastry for double-crust pie (9 inches)
- 1 egg, lightly beaten, optional

1. In a large skillet, saute onion in oil until tender. Remove and set aside. Brown beef and pork together; drain. Combine onion, meat, potatoes, vegetables and seasonings.

2. Line pie plate with pastry; fill with meat mixture. Top with crust; seal and flute edges. Make slits in top crust. Brush with egg if desired.

3. Bake at 375° for 30-35 minutes or until golden brown.

Curried Chicken and Grits Casserole

I moved to the South about seven years ago from Ohio. I've been creating recipes with grits recently and feel like I'm finally getting the Southern vibe! This recipe turns out beautifully with the mix of veggies, golden sauce and cheese-crusted grits on top.

—LORI SHAMSZADEH FAIRHOPE, AL

PREP: 25 MIN. • **BAKE:** 50 MIN.
MAKES: 8 SERVINGS

- 1 cup water
- 1½ cups chicken broth, divided
- ¼ teaspoon salt
- ½ cup quick-cooking grits
- 2 eggs, beaten
- 2 cups (8 ounces) shredded cheddar cheese, divided
- 3 tablespoons butter, cubed
- 1 can (10¾ ounces) condensed cream of chicken and mushroom soup, undiluted
- 1½ cups mayonnaise
- 2 teaspoons curry powder
- 1 package (16 ounces) frozen broccoli-cauliflower blend
- 2 cups cubed cooked chicken
- 2 cups refrigerated diced potatoes with onion

TURKEY BUNDLES

CURRIED CHICKEN AND GRITS CASSEROLE

1. Bring water, 1 cup broth and salt to a boil in a large saucepan. Slowly stir in grits. Reduce heat; cook and stir for 5-6 minutes or until thickened. Remove from the heat; stir a small amount of grits into eggs. Return all to the pan, stirring constantly. Add 1½ cups cheese and butter; stir until melted.
2. Combine the soup, mayonnaise, curry powder and remaining broth in a large bowl. Add the vegetable blend, chicken and potatoes; toss to coat. Transfer to a greased 13-in. x 9-in. baking dish. Top with grits; sprinkle with remaining cheese.
3. Bake, uncovered, at 350° for 50-55 minutes or until heated through.

FAST FIX
Turkey Bundles

This simple recipe is a must-try. Crescent roll dough is wrapped around creamy turkey filling to form cute bundles. I usually double the recipe so I have extras for lunch the next day.
—LYDIA GARROD TACOMA, WA

START TO FINISH: 30 MIN.
MAKES: 6 SERVINGS

- 4 ounces cream cheese, softened
- 2 tablespoons milk

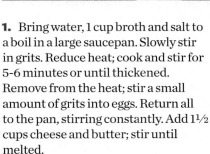

- ½ teaspoon dill weed
- ¼ teaspoon celery salt
- ¼ teaspoon pepper
- 2 cups cubed cooked turkey
- ¼ cup chopped water chestnuts
- 1 green onion, chopped
- 2 tubes (one 8 ounces, one 4 ounces) refrigerated crescent rolls
- 2 tablespoons butter, melted
- 2 tablespoons seasoned bread crumbs

1. Preheat oven to 375°. In a large bowl, beat the first five ingredients until smooth. Stir in turkey, water chestnuts and green onion.
2. Unroll both tubes of crescent dough and separate dough into six rectangles; press perforations to seal. Place ⅓ cup turkey mixture in center of each rectangle. Bring four corners of dough together above filling; twist and pinch seams to seal.
3. Place on a baking sheet. Brush tops with butter; sprinkle with bread crumbs. Bake 15-20 minutes or until golden brown.

LAYERED TORTILLA PIE

Layered Tortilla Pie

My sister served tortilla pie at the hunting and fishing lodge she used to operate in Colorado. It was sure to win compliments from the men who came in cold and hungry after spending the day tramping through the woods.

—DELMA SNYDER MCCOOK, NE

PREP: 20 MIN. • **BAKE:** 20 MIN.
MAKES: 4-6 SERVINGS

- 1 **pound ground beef**
- 1 **medium onion, chopped**
- 1 **can (8 ounces) tomato sauce**
- 1 **garlic clove, minced**
- 1 **tablespoon chili powder**
- ½ **teaspoon salt**
- ¼ **teaspoon pepper**
- 1 **can (2¼ ounces) sliced ripe olives, drained, optional**
- 1 **tablespoon butter**
- 6 **corn tortillas (6 inches)**
- 2 **cups (8 ounces) shredded cheddar cheese**
- ¼ **cup water**

1. In a large skillet, cook beef and onion until meat is no longer pink; drain. Add the tomato sauce, garlic, chili powder, salt, pepper and, if desired, olives. Bring to a boil. Reduce heat; simmer for 5 minutes or until mixture is thickened.

2. Lightly butter tortillas on one side; place one tortilla, buttered side down, in a 2-qt. round casserole. Top with about ½ cup meat mixture and ⅓ cup cheese. Repeat layers, ending with cheese.

3. Pour water around the sides of casserole (not over top). Cover and bake at 400° for 20 minutes or until heated through. Let stand 5 minutes before cutting.

Barbecue Turkey Meat Loaf

I have no trouble getting my girls to lend a hand with this turkey loaf. And topping it with my husband's favorite barbecue sauce always gets him to clean his plate!

—ROBYN YOUNG INDIANAPOLIS, IN

PREP: 20 MIN. • **BAKE:** 50 MIN. + STANDING
MAKES: 2 LOAVES (8 SERVINGS EACH)

- 2 eggs, lightly beaten
- ½ cup barbecue sauce
- ⅓ cup 2% milk
- 2 tablespoons Worcestershire sauce
- 2 teaspoons prepared mustard
- 1⅓ cups seasoned bread crumbs
- 1 small onion, finely chopped
- 2 garlic cloves, minced
- 1 teaspoon salt
- 1 teaspoon rubbed sage
- 2 pounds extra-lean ground turkey
- 1 pound Italian turkey sausage links, casings removed

TOPPING

- 1 cup barbecue sauce
- ½ cup packed brown sugar
- 2 teaspoons prepared mustard

1. Combine the first 10 ingredients in a large bowl. Crumble ground turkey and sausage over mixture and mix well. Pat into two greased 9-in. x 5-in. loaf pans. Combine the topping ingredients in a small bowl; spread over tops.

2. Cover and freeze one meat loaf for up to 3 months. Bake the remaining loaf, uncovered, at 350° for 50-55 minutes or until no pink remains and a thermometer reads 165°. Let stand 10 minutes before slicing.

TO USE FROZEN MEAT LOAF *Bake frozen meat loaf as directed, increasing time to 1¼ to 1½ hours.*

BARBECUE TURKEY MEAT LOAF

**Trisha Kruse's
Chicago-Style Beef Rolls**
PAGE 194

Slow-Cooked Sensations

After a busy day, come home to the welcoming aroma of a hot dinner waiting! For comfort food made easy and down-home favorites that fit your schedule, slow-cooked recipes are simply the best.

**Estella Peterson's
Pepperoni Pizza Soup**
PAGE 187

**Lisa Varner's
Butterscotch-Pecan Bread Pudding**
PAGE 207

**Roxanne Chan's
Pork Roast Cubano**
PAGE 188

Soy-Ginger Chicken

This is the first recipe I ever tried making without a cookbook, and it came out tender and delicious. Garlic, ginger and spices give the rich sauce plenty of authentic Asian flavor.

—KAEL HARVEY BROOKLYN, NY

PREP: 25 MIN. • **COOK:** 5 HOURS
MAKES: 4 SERVINGS

- 4 **bone-in chicken thighs (about 1½ pounds), skin removed**
- 4 **chicken drumsticks (about 1 pound), skin removed**
- 2 **medium carrots, sliced**
- 4 **green onions, thinly sliced**
- ⅓ **cup soy sauce**
- 2 **tablespoons brown sugar**
- 1 **piece fresh gingerroot (about 2 inches), peeled and thinly sliced**
- 5 **garlic cloves, minced**
- 1 **tablespoon balsamic vinegar**
- 1 **teaspoon ground coriander**
- ½ **teaspoon pepper**
- 1 **tablespoon cornstarch**
- 1 **tablespoon cold water**
  Hot cooked rice and minced fresh cilantro

1. Place chicken, carrots and green onions in a 3-qt. slow cooker. Combine the soy sauce, brown sugar, ginger, garlic, vinegar, coriander and pepper in a small bowl. Pour over top. Cover and cook on low for 5-6 hours or until chicken is tender.

2. Remove chicken to a serving platter; keep warm. Pour juices into a small saucepan. Bring to a boil. Combine the cornstarch and water until smooth; gradually stir into pan. Bring to a boil; cook and stir for 1-2 minutes or until thickened. Serve with chicken and rice; sprinkle each serving with cilantro.

CHICKEN MOLE

Chicken Mole

If you're not familiar with mole, don't be afraid to try this versatile Mexican sauce. I love sharing the recipe because it's a tasty, simple introduction to mole.

—DARLENE MORRIS FRANKLINTON, LA

PREP: 25 MIN. • **COOK:** 6 HOURS
MAKES: 12 SERVINGS

- 12 **bone-in chicken thighs (about 4½ pounds), skin removed**
- 1 **teaspoon salt**

MOLE SAUCE

- 1 **can (28 ounces) whole tomatoes, drained**
- 1 **medium onion, chopped**
- 2 **dried ancho chilies, stems and seeds removed**
- ½ **cup sliced almonds, toasted**
- ¼ **cup raisins**
- 3 **ounces bittersweet chocolate, chopped**
- 3 **tablespoons olive oil**
- 1 **chipotle pepper in adobo sauce**
- 3 **garlic cloves, peeled and halved**
- ¾ **teaspoon ground cumin**
- ½ **teaspoon ground cinnamon**
  Fresh cilantro leaves, optional

1. Sprinkle chicken with salt; place in a 5- or 6-qt. slow cooker. Place the tomatoes, onion, chilies, almonds, raisins, chocolate, oil, chipotle pepper, garlic, cumin and cinnamon in a food processor; cover and process until blended. Pour over chicken.

2. Cover and cook on low for 6-8 hours or until chicken is tender; skim fat. Serve chicken with sauce and sprinkle with cilantro if desired.

SOY-GINGER CHICKEN

Pepperoni Pizza Soup

PREP: 20 MIN. • **COOK:** 8¼ HOURS
MAKES: 6 SERVINGS (2¼ QUARTS)

- 2 cans (14½ ounces each) Italian stewed tomatoes, undrained
- 2 cans (14½ ounces each) reduced-sodium beef broth
- 1 small onion, chopped
- 1 small green pepper, chopped
- ½ cup sliced fresh mushrooms
- ½ cup sliced pepperoni, halved
- 1½ teaspoons dried oregano
- ⅛ teaspoon pepper
- 1 package (9 ounces) refrigerated cheese ravioli
  Shredded part-skim mozzarella cheese and sliced ripe olives

1. In a 4-qt. slow cooker, combine the first eight ingredients. Cook, covered, on low 8-9 hours.

2. Stir in ravioli; cook, covered, on low 15-30 minutes or until pasta is tender. Top servings with cheese and olives.

"Once upon a time, my husband and I owned a pizzeria, where this dish was always popular. We've since sold the restaurant, but I still make the soup for potlucks and other gatherings."

—ESTELLA PETERSON MADRAS, OR

PEPPERONI PIZZA SOUP

MEAT SAUCE FOR SPAGHETTI

Meat Sauce for Spaghetti

Here's a thick and hearty sauce that turns ordinary spaghetti and garlic bread into a feast. When I'm in a hurry, I make the recipe in an electric frying pan instead of the slow cooker.

—MARY TALLMAN ARBOR VITAE, WI

PREP: 30 MIN. • **COOK:** 8 HOURS
MAKES: 9 SERVINGS

- 1 pound ground beef
- 1 pound bulk Italian sausage
- 1 can (28 ounces) crushed tomatoes, undrained
- 1 medium green pepper, chopped
- 1 medium onion, chopped
- 2 medium carrots, finely chopped
- 1 cup water
- 1 can (8 ounces) tomato sauce
- 1 can (6 ounces) tomato paste
- 1 tablespoon brown sugar
- 1 tablespoon Italian seasoning
- 2 garlic cloves, minced
- ½ teaspoon salt
- ¼ teaspoon pepper
  Hot cooked spaghetti

1. In a large skillet, cook beef and sausage over medium heat until no longer pink; drain.

2. Transfer to a 5-qt. slow cooker. Stir in the tomatoes, green pepper, onion, carrots, water, tomato sauce, tomato paste, brown sugar, Italian seasoning, garlic, salt and pepper. Cover and cook on low for 8-10 hours or until bubbly. Serve with spaghetti.

Pork Roast Cubano

It takes me only a few minutes to get this recipe started, and the slow cooker does the rest. It's a one-dish meal that's real comfort food for my family.
—ROXANNE CHAN ALBANY, CA

PREP: 30 MIN. • **COOK:** 7 HOURS
MAKES: 8 SERVINGS

- 3 pounds boneless pork shoulder butt roast
- 2 tablespoons olive oil
- 1 can (15 ounces) black beans, rinsed and drained
- 1 medium sweet potato, cut into ½-inch cubes
- 1 small sweet red pepper, cubed
- 1 can (13.66 ounces) light coconut milk
- ½ cup salsa verde
- 1 teaspoon minced fresh gingerroot
- 2 green onions, thinly sliced
  Sliced papaya

1. In a large skillet, brown roast in oil on all sides. Transfer to a 5-qt. slow cooker. Add black beans, sweet potato and red pepper. In a small bowl, mix coconut milk, salsa and ginger; pour over top.

2. Cook, covered, on low 7-9 hours or until pork is tender. Sprinkle with green onions; serve with papaya.

BUSY-DAY CHICKEN FAJITAS

PORK ROAST CUBANO

Busy-Day Chicken Fajitas

When I don't have much time to cook supper, chicken fajitas from the slow cooker are a flavorful way to keep my family full and satisfied. If you aren't cooking for youngsters, try spicing things up with medium or hot picante sauce.
—MICHELE FURRY PLAINS, MT

PREP: 20 MIN. • **COOK:** 4 HOURS
MAKES: 6 SERVINGS

- 1 pound boneless skinless chicken breasts
- 1 can (15 ounces) black beans, rinsed and drained
- 1 medium green pepper, cut into strips
- 1 large onion, sliced
- 1½ cups picante sauce
- ½ teaspoon garlic powder
- ½ teaspoon ground cumin
- 12 flour tortillas (6 inches), warmed
- 2 cups (8 ounces) shredded cheddar cheese
  Optional toppings: sour cream, sliced ripe olives and thinly sliced green onions

1. Place chicken in a 4-qt. slow cooker; add black beans, pepper and onion. In a small bowl, mix picante sauce, garlic powder and cumin; pour over top. Cook, covered, on low 4-5 hours or until chicken is tender.

2. Remove chicken and cool slightly. Shred meat with two forks and return to slow cooker; heat through. Serve with tortillas, cheese and toppings of your choice.

Green Chile Chicken Chili

This easy chili is loaded with chicken and beans. The spicy heat can be tamed a bit with cool sour cream.

—**FRED LOCKWOOD** PLANO, TX

PREP: 25 MIN. • **COOK:** 5 HOURS
MAKES: 10 SERVINGS (3½ QUARTS)

- 4 **bone-in chicken breast halves (14 ounces each)**
- 2 **medium onions, chopped**
- 2 **medium green peppers, chopped**
- 1 **cup pickled jalapeno slices**
- 1 **can (4 ounces) chopped green chilies**
- 2 **jars (16 ounces each) salsa verde**
- 2 **cans (15½ ounces each) navy beans, rinsed and drained**
- 1 **cup (8 ounces) sour cream**
- ½ **cup minced fresh cilantro**
  Optional toppings: shredded Colby-Monterey Jack cheese, sour cream and tortilla chips

1. Place the first five ingredients in a 5- or 6-qt. slow cooker. Pour salsa over top. Cover and cook on low for 5-6 hours or until chicken is tender.
2. Remove chicken; cool slightly. Shred with two forks, discarding skin and bones; return meat to slow cooker. Stir in beans, sour cream and cilantro; heat through. Serve with toppings.
NOTE *Wear disposable gloves when cutting hot pepper, the oils can burn skin. Avoid touching your face.*

SLOW COOKER TZIMMES

"Tzimmes is a sweet Jewish dish consisting of a variety of fruits and vegetables that may or may not include meat. Traditionally (as it is here), it's tossed with honey and cinnamon and slowly cooked to meld the flavors."

—**LISA RENSHAW** KANSAS CITY, MO

GREEN CHILE CHICKEN CHILI

Slow Cooker Tzimmes

PREP: 20 MIN. • **COOK:** 5 HOURS
MAKES: 12 SERVINGS (⅔ CUP EACH)

- ½ **medium butternut squash, peeled and cubed**
- 2 **medium sweet potatoes, peeled and cubed**
- 6 **medium carrots, sliced**
- 2 **medium tart apples, peeled and sliced**
- 1 **cup chopped sweet onion**
- 1 **cup chopped dried apricots**
- 1 **cup golden raisins**
- ½ **cup orange juice**
- ¼ **cup honey**
- 2 **tablespoons finely chopped crystallized ginger**
- 3 **teaspoons ground cinnamon**
- 3 **teaspoons pumpkin pie spice**
- 2 **teaspoons grated orange peel**
- 1 **teaspoon salt**
  Vanilla yogurt, optional

1. Place the first seven ingredients in a 5- or 6-qt. slow cooker. Combine the orange juice, honey, ginger, cinnamon, pie spice, orange peel and salt; pour over top and mix well.
2. Cover and cook on low for 5-6 hours or until vegetables are tender. Dollop servings with yogurt if desired.

PORK SATAY WITH RICE NOODLES

Pork Satay with Rice Noodles

I love the addition of peanut butter to savory recipes, such as this Thai-inspired dish. Ramp up the flavor by sprinkling minced fresh cilantro and chopped peanuts over the top.
—**STEPHANIE ANDERSON** HORSEHEADS, NY

PREP: 20 MIN. • **COOK:** 4 HOURS
MAKES: 6 SERVINGS

- 1½ **pounds boneless pork loin chops, cut into 2-inch pieces**
- ¼ **teaspoon pepper**
- 1 **medium onion, halved and sliced**
- ⅓ **cup creamy peanut butter**
- ¼ **cup reduced-sodium soy sauce**
- ½ **teaspoon onion powder**
- ½ **teaspoon garlic powder**
- ½ **teaspoon hot pepper sauce**
- 1 **can (14½ ounces) reduced-sodium chicken broth**
- 3 **tablespoons cornstarch**
- 3 **tablespoons water**
- 9 **ounces uncooked thick rice noodles**
  Minced fresh cilantro and chopped peanuts, optional

1. Sprinkle pork with pepper. Place in a 3-qt. slow cooker; top with onion. In a small bowl, mix peanut butter, soy sauce, onion powder, garlic powder and pepper sauce; gradually add broth. Pour over onion. Cook, covered, on low 4-6 hours or until pork is tender.
2. Remove pork from slow cooker and keep warm. Skim fat from cooking juices; transfer cooking juices to a large skillet. Bring to a boil. In a small bowl, mix cornstarch and water until smooth and add to pan. Return to a boil; cook and stir 2 minutes or until thickened. Add pork; heat through.
3. Meanwhile, cook noodles according to package directions; drain. Serve with pork mixture. If desired, sprinkle with cilantro and peanuts.
NOTE *Reduced-fat peanut butter is not recommended for this recipe.*
PER SERVING *411 cal., 14 g fat (4 g sat. fat), 55 mg chol., 700 mg sodium, 41 g carb., 2 g fiber, 30 g pro.* **Diabetic Exchanges:** *3 lean meat, 2½ starch, 1 fat.*

Slow Cooker Italian Sloppy Joes

I wanted to make sloppy joes for a work potluck without using canned sloppy joe sauce. I had a few ingredients on hand, and this recipe was born. It's also good over pasta.
—**HOPE WASYLENKI** GAHANNA, OH

PREP: 30 MIN. • **COOK:** 4 HOURS
MAKES: 36 SERVINGS

- 2 **pounds lean ground beef (90% lean)**
- 2 **pounds bulk Italian sausage**
- 2 **medium green peppers, chopped**
- 1 **large onion, chopped**
- 4 **cups spaghetti sauce**
- 1 **can (28 ounces) diced tomatoes, undrained**
- ½ **pound sliced fresh mushrooms**
- 1 **can (6 ounces) tomato paste**
- 2 **garlic cloves, minced**
- 2 **bay leaves**
- 36 **hamburger buns, split**

1. Cook the beef, sausage, peppers and onion in a Dutch oven over medium heat until meat is no longer pink; drain. Transfer to a 6-qt. slow cooker. Stir in the spaghetti sauce, tomatoes, mushrooms, tomato paste, garlic and bay leaves.
2. Cover and cook on high for 4-5 hours or until flavors are blended. Discard bay leaves. Serve on buns.

Mom's Scalloped Potatoes and Ham

Mom's friend gave her this recipe years ago, and she shared it with me. When we have leftover ham to use up, it's the most-requested recipe at my house.
—**KELLY GRAHAM** ST. THOMAS, ON

PREP: 20 MIN. • **COOK:** 8 HOURS
MAKES: 9 SERVINGS

- 10 **medium potatoes, peeled and thinly sliced**
- 3 **cups cubed fully cooked ham**
- 2 **large onions, thinly sliced**
- 2 **cups (8 ounces) shredded cheddar cheese**
- 1 **can (10¾ ounces) condensed cream of mushroom soup, undiluted**
- ½ **teaspoon paprika**
- ¼ **teaspoon pepper**

1. In a greased 6-qt. slow cooker, layer half of the potatoes, ham, onions and cheese. Repeat layers. Pour soup over top. Sprinkle with paprika and pepper.
2. Cover and cook on low for 8-10 hours or until potatoes are tender.

MOM'S SCALLOPED POTATOES AND HAM

Hawaiian Meatballs

PREP: 20 MIN. • **COOK:** 6¼ HOURS
MAKES: 8 SERVINGS

- 1 can (20 ounces) unsweetened pineapple chunks, undrained
- ½ cup packed brown sugar
- ¼ cup cornstarch
- ½ cup cider vinegar
- 1 package (32 ounces) frozen fully cooked homestyle meatballs
- 2 medium green peppers, cut into 1-inch pieces
- 1 jar (10 ounces) maraschino cherries, drained
  Salt and pepper to taste
  Hot cooked rice, optional

1. Drain pineapple, reserving juice in a 2-cup measuring cup; add enough water to measure 2 cups. In a small saucepan, mix brown sugar, cornstarch, vinegar and juice mixture until blended. Bring to a boil; cook and stir until thickened.

2. In a 3-qt. slow cooker, combine meatballs, peppers, drained pineapple and sauce. Cook, covered, on low 6-8 hours or until meatballs are heated through and peppers are tender.

3. Stir in cherries; cook, covered, on low 15-30 minutes longer or until heated through. Season with salt and pepper to taste. If desired, serve meatballs with rice.

LENTIL AND PASTA STEW

Lentil and Pasta Stew

Warm up with a big bowl of this stick-to-your-ribs stew. Loaded with chopped smoked sausage, hearty veggies and tender lentils, it's terrific with bread fresh from the oven.

—GERALDINE SAUCIER ALBUQUERQUE, NM

PREP: 25 MIN. • **COOK:** 8 HOURS
MAKES: 8 SERVINGS

- ½ pound smoked kielbasa or Polish sausage, chopped
- 3 tablespoons olive oil
- 3 tablespoons butter
- 1 cup cubed peeled potatoes
- ¾ cup sliced fresh carrots
- 1 celery rib, sliced
- 1 small onion, finely chopped
- 5 cups beef broth
- 1 cup dried lentils, rinsed
- 1 cup canned diced tomatoes
- 1 bay leaf
- 1 teaspoon coarsely ground pepper
- ¼ teaspoon salt
- 1 cup uncooked ditalini or other small pasta
  Shredded Romano cheese

1. Brown kielbasa in oil and butter in a large skillet. Add the potatoes, carrots, celery and onion. Cook and stir for 3 minutes over medium heat. Transfer to a 4- or 5-qt. slow cooker. Stir in the broth, lentils, tomatoes, bay leaf, pepper and salt.

2. Cover and cook on low for 8-10 hours or until lentils are tender. Cook pasta according to package directions; drain. Stir pasta into slow cooker. Discard bay leaf. Sprinkle servings with cheese.

"Talk about one easy dish with an amazing sweet and sour sauce! You can serve the meatballs over rice for dinner, or as a tasty addition to the appetizer buffet."

—JULIE SCHIEFER NAPPANEE, IN

SAVORY MUSTARD PORK ROAST

Savory Mustard Pork Roast

The mustard sauce for this tender pork roast has a kiss of honey and molasses. Even though the recipe makes a large batch, I rarely have leftovers when I serve this family favorite.

—EZRA ELKON CHARLES TOWN, WV

PREP: 20 MIN.
COOK: 6 HOURS + STANDING
MAKES: 8 SERVINGS

- 1 boneless pork shoulder butt roast (3 to 4 pounds)
- ¾ teaspoon salt
- ½ teaspoon pepper
- 1 tablespoon canola oil
- 1 can (14½ ounces) diced tomatoes, drained
- 1 medium onion, chopped
- 1 can (14½ ounces) beef broth
- ½ cup dry red wine
- ⅜ cup stone-ground mustard
- 6 garlic cloves, minced
- 2 tablespoons honey
- 2 tablespoons molasses
- 1 teaspoon dried thyme
- 2 tablespoons cornstarch
- 2 tablespoons cold water

1. Sprinkle roast with salt and pepper; brown in oil in a large skillet on all sides. Transfer to a 5-qt. slow cooker. Add tomatoes and onion; pour broth and wine around meat. Combine the mustard, garlic, honey, molasses and thyme; pour over pork. Cover and cook on low for 6-7 hours or until the meat is tender.

2. Remove roast; cover and let stand for 15 minutes before slicing. Meanwhile, skim fat from cooking juices; transfer juices to a small saucepan. Bring to a boil. Combine cornstarch and water until smooth; gradually stir into the pan. Bring to a boil; cook and stir for 2 minutes or until thickened. Slice pork and serve with sauce.

top tip

Easy Cleanup

When measuring sticky ingredients like honey and molasses, spritz the measuring cup or spoon with cooking spray before you measure. For the pork roast recipe, fill a ¼-cup measure half-full with honey, then top off with the molasses.

Chicago-Style Beef Rolls

I have fond memories of eating these big, messy sandwiches at a neighbor's house when I was growing up. Freeze extras and save for another meal, too!

—**TRISHA KRUSE** EAGLE, ID

PREP: 20 MIN. • **COOK:** 8 HOURS
MAKES: 16 SERVINGS

1   boneless beef chuck roast (4 to 5 pounds)
1   tablespoon olive oil
3   cups beef broth
1   medium onion, chopped
1   package Italian salad dressing mix
3   garlic cloves, minced
1   tablespoon Italian seasoning
½   teaspoon crushed red pepper flakes
16   sourdough rolls, split
Sliced pepperoncini and pickled red pepper rings, optional

1. Brown roast in oil on all sides in a large skillet; drain. Transfer to a 5-qt. slow cooker. Combine the broth, onion, dressing mix, garlic, Italian seasoning and pepper flakes in a large bowl; pour over roast.

2. Cover and cook on low for 8-10 hours or until tender. Remove meat; cool slightly. Skim fat from cooking juices. Shred beef with two forks and return to slow cooker; heat through. Place ½ cup on each roll, using a slotted spoon. Top sandwiches with pepperoncini and pepper rings, if desired.

Potato and Leek Soup

Chock-full of veggies and bacon with just a little tanginess from sour cream, bowls of this comforting soup taste just as terrific with a sandwich as they do with crackers!

—**MELANIE WOODEN** RENO, NV

PREP: 20 MIN. • **COOK:** 8 HOURS
MAKES: 8 SERVINGS (2 QUARTS)

4   cups chicken broth
3   medium potatoes, peeled and cubed
1½   cups chopped cabbage
2   medium carrots, chopped
1   medium leek (white portion only), chopped
1   medium onion, chopped
¼   cup minced fresh parsley
½   teaspoon salt
½   teaspoon caraway seeds
½   teaspoon pepper
1   bay leaf
½   cup sour cream
1   pound bacon strips, cooked and crumbled

1. Combine the first 11 ingredients in a 4- or 5-qt. slow cooker. Cover and cook on low for 8-10 hours or until vegetables are tender.

2. Before serving, combine sour cream with 1 cup soup; return all to the slow cooker. Stir in bacon and discard bay leaf.

POTATO AND LEEK SOUP

CHICAGO-STYLE BEEF ROLLS

SLOW-COOKED SENSATIONS

MOROCCAN BRAISED BEEF

Asian Ribs

My husband adores this dish, and I love how good it makes the house smell as it simmers away! The tangy, sweet-salty sauce with fresh ginger and garlic is delicious with rice or noodles.

—JULIE KO ROGERS, AR

PREP: 15 MIN. • **COOK:** 6 HOURS
MAKES: 6 SERVINGS

- 6 **pounds pork baby back ribs, cut into serving-size pieces**
- 1⅓ **cups packed brown sugar**
- 1 **cup reduced-sodium soy sauce**
- ¼ **cup rice vinegar**
- ¼ **cup sesame oil**
- ¼ **cup minced fresh gingerroot**
- 6 **garlic cloves, minced**
- 1 **teaspoon crushed red pepper flakes**
- ¼ **cup cornstarch**
- ¼ **cup cold water**
   Thinly sliced green onions and sesame seeds, optional

1. Place ribs in a 6-qt. slow cooker. In a small bowl, combine the brown sugar, soy sauce, vinegar, oil, ginger, garlic and pepper flakes; pour over ribs. Cover and cook on low for 6-7 hours or until meat is tender.

2. Remove meat to a serving platter; keep warm. Skim fat from cooking juices; transfer to a small saucepan. Bring to a boil.

3. Combine cornstarch and water until smooth. Gradually stir into the pan. Bring to a boil; cook and stir for 2 minutes or until thickened. Serve with ribs. Garnish with onions and sesame seeds if desired.

Moroccan Braised Beef

Curry powder is a blend of up to 20 spices, herbs and seeds. Add a pinch of curry to your favorite soups, stews, salads and even rice for an exotic flavor. In this Moroccan stew, begin with 2 teaspoons curry, then add more to your taste.

—TASTE OF HOME TEST KITCHEN

PREP: 20 MIN. • **COOK:** 7 HOURS
MAKES: 6 SERVINGS

- ⅓ **cup all-purpose flour**
- 2 **pounds boneless beef chuck roast, cut into 1-inch cubes**
- 3 **tablespoons olive oil**
- 2 **cans (14½ ounces each) beef broth**
- 2 **cups chopped onions**
- 1 **can (14½ ounces) diced tomatoes, undrained**
- 1 **cup dry red wine**
- 1 **tablespoon curry powder**
- 1 **tablespoon paprika**
- 1 **teaspoon salt**
- 1 **teaspoon ground cumin**
- 1 **teaspoon ground coriander**
- ½ **teaspoon cayenne pepper**
- 1½ **cups golden raisins**
   Hot cooked couscous, optional

1. Place flour in a large resealable plastic bag; add beef and toss to coat. In a large skillet, brown beef in oil. Transfer to a 5-qt. slow cooker. Stir in the broth, onions, tomatoes, wine and seasonings. Cover and cook on low for 7-8 hours or until the meat is tender.

2. During the last 30 minutes of cooking, stir in raisins. Serve with couscous if desired.

ASIAN RIBS

Slow Cooker Calico Beans

PREP: 20 MIN. • **COOK:** 5 HOURS
MAKES: 15 SERVINGS (¾ CUP EACH)

- 2 teaspoons canola oil
- 1 large sweet onion, chopped
- 1 medium sweet red pepper, chopped
- 2 cans (28 ounces each) vegetarian baked beans
- 1 can (16 ounces) butter beans, rinsed and drained
- 1 can (16 ounces) kidney beans, rinsed and drained
- 1 can (14½ ounces) fire-roasted diced tomatoes, undrained
- ½ cup ketchup
- ⅓ cup packed brown sugar
- 1 tablespoon ground mustard
- 1 tablespoon cider vinegar
- 1 teaspoon salt
- 1 teaspoon Worcestershire sauce

In a large skillet, heat oil over medium-high heat. Add onion and pepper; cook and stir until tender. Transfer to a 5-qt. slow cooker; stir in remaining ingredients. Cook, covered, on low 5-6 hours or until heated through.

SLOW COOKER CALICO BEANS

"With so many folks moving to meatless or healthier food choices, I decided to remove the meat from my original recipe but turn up the flavor. Sweet onion and pepper add a savory crunch to these beans."

—**DAVID DIXON** SHAKER HEIGHTS, OH

HOMINY BEEF CHILI

Hominy Beef Chili

Hunker down in the cold of winter with this hearty chili. Loaded with pantry staples, it's an easy supper. Great with warm tortillas or chips.

—**STEVE WESTPHAL** WIND LAKE, WI

PREP: 25 MIN. • **COOK:** 6 HOURS
MAKES: 8 SERVINGS (3 QUARTS)

- 1 boneless beef chuck roast (3 to 4 pounds), cut into 1-inch pieces
- 2 tablespoons canola oil
- 1 can (15½ ounces) hominy, rinsed and drained
- 1 can (14½ ounces) reduced-sodium beef broth
- 1 can (14½ ounces) diced tomatoes, undrained
- ½ cup chopped onion
- 1 large sweet red pepper, diced
- 1 can (4 ounces) chopped green chilies
- 1 tablespoon chili powder
- 1 tablespoon paprika
- 2 teaspoons ground cumin
- 2 garlic cloves, minced
- ½ teaspoon salt
- ½ teaspoon pepper
- 1½ cups frozen corn
  Shredded cheddar cheese and sour cream, optional

1. Brown meat in oil on all sides in a large skillet; drain. Transfer to a 5-qt. slow cooker.
2. Stir in the hominy, broth, tomatoes, onion, red pepper, chilies and seasonings. Cover and cook on low for 6-7 hours or until meat is tender. Stir in the corn; heat through. Serve with cheese and sour cream, if desired.

Ginger Applesauce

This is my favorite way to prepare applesauce. It's simple to do and makes the whole house smell like fall.

—**RENEE PAJESTKA** BRUNSWICK, OH

PREP: 25 MIN. • **COOK:** 4 HOURS
MAKES: ABOUT 5 CUPS

- **4 pounds apples (about 12 medium), peeled and cubed**
- **¼ cup water**
- **2 tablespoons brown sugar**
- **2 teaspoons ground cinnamon**
- **2 teaspoons minced fresh gingerroot**
- **2 teaspoons vanilla extract**

1. Place all ingredients in a 4-qt. slow cooker; stir until combined.

2. Cover and cook on low for 4-5 hours or until apples are tender. Mash if desired. Refrigerate leftovers.

Pepperoni Extreme Dip

Set it and forget it! This awesome dip is hot and cheesy, simple to make and loved by all. Just 10 minutes of prep time and it's ready for the slow cooker.

—**LAURA STONESIFER** HOULTON, WI

PREP: 10 MIN. • **COOK:** 3 HOURS
MAKES: 2¼ QUARTS

- **4 cups (16 ounces) shredded cheddar cheese**
- **3½ cups spaghetti sauce**
- **2 cups mayonnaise**
- **1 package (8 ounces) sliced pepperoni, chopped**
- **1 can (6 ounces) pitted ripe olives, chopped**
- **1 jar (5¾ ounces) sliced green olives with pimientos, drained and chopped**
  Tortilla chips

Combine the first six ingredients in a 4-qt. slow cooker coated with cooking spray. Cover and cook on low for 1½ hours; stir. Cover and cook 1½ hours longer or until cheese is melted. Serve with tortilla chips.

PEPPERONI EXTREME DIP

EASY PHILLY CHEESESTEAKS

Easy Philly Cheesesteaks

Since we live in a rural area where there aren't any restaurants to speak of, I thought it would be fun to make this classic sandwich at home. For an extra flavor boost, try a splash of steak sauce.
—**LENETTE A. BENNETT** COMO, CO

PREP: 20 MIN. • **COOK:** 6 HOURS
MAKES: 6 SERVINGS

- 2 medium onions, halved and sliced
- 2 medium sweet red or green peppers, halved and sliced
- 1 beef top sirloin steak (1½ pounds), cut into thin strips
- 1 envelope onion soup mix
- 1 can (14½ ounces) reduced-sodium beef broth
- 6 hoagie buns, split
- 12 slices provolone cheese, halved
  Pickled hot cherry peppers, optional

1. Place onions and red peppers in a 4- or 5-qt. slow cooker. Add beef, soup mix and broth. Cook, covered, on low 6-8 hours or until meat is tender.
2. Arrange buns on a baking sheet, cut side up. Using tongs, place meat mixture on bun bottoms; top with cheese.
3. Broil 2-3 in. from heat 30-60 seconds or until cheese is melted and bun tops are toasted. If desired, serve with cherry peppers.

Creamy Chicken & Broccoli Stew

This recipe is so easy to make, but no one would ever guess. My husband, who doesn't like many chicken dishes, requests this one regularly.
—**MARY WATKINS** LITTLE ELM, TX

PREP: 15 MIN. • **COOK:** 6 HOURS
MAKES: 8 SERVINGS

- 8 bone-in chicken thighs, skin removed (about 3 pounds)
- 1 cup Italian salad dressing
- ½ cup white wine or chicken broth
- 6 tablespoons butter, melted, divided
- 1 tablespoon dried minced onion
- 1 tablespoon garlic powder
- 1 tablespoon Italian seasoning
- ¾ teaspoon salt, divided
- ¾ teaspoon pepper, divided
- 1 can (10¾ ounces) condensed cream of mushroom soup, undiluted
- 1 package (8 ounces) cream cheese, softened
- 2 cups frozen broccoli florets, thawed
- 2 pounds red potatoes, quartered

1. Place chicken in a 4-qt. slow cooker. Combine the salad dressing, wine, 4 tablespoons butter, onion, garlic powder, Italian seasoning, ½ teaspoon salt and ½ teaspoon pepper in a small bowl; pour over chicken.
2. Cover and cook on low for 5 hours. Skim fat. Combine the soup, cream cheese and 2 cups of liquid from slow cooker in a small bowl until blended; add to slow cooker.
3. Cover and cook 45 minutes longer or until chicken is tender, adding the broccoli during the last 30 minutes of cooking.
4. Meanwhile, place potatoes in a large saucepan and cover with water. Bring to a boil. Reduce heat; cover and simmer for 15-20 minutes or until tender. Drain and return to pan. Mash potatoes with the remaining butter, salt and pepper. Serve with chicken and broccoli mixture.

CREAMY CHICKEN & BROCCOLI STEW

HAM WITH CRANBERRY PINEAPPLE SAUCE

Spinach Alfredo Lasagna

With ground beef, spinach, two types of sauce and three kinds of cheese, this super-hearty dish goes beyond the expected. When serving, be sure to scoop all the way down to the bottom of the slow cooker so that you get a good sampling of all the layers.

—DEBORAH BRUNO MIRA LOMA, CA

PREP: 20 MIN. • **COOK:** 4 HOURS
MAKES: 8 SERVINGS

- 1 **pound ground beef**
- 1 **medium onion, chopped**
- 2 **garlic cloves, minced**
- 1 **jar (24 ounces) spaghetti sauce**
- 1 **carton (15 ounces) ricotta cheese**
- ½ **cup grated Parmesan cheese**
- 2 **tablespoons minced fresh parsley**
- ½ **teaspoon pepper**
- 1 **package (8 ounces) no-cook lasagna noodles**
- 8 **cups (32 ounces) shredded part-skim mozzarella cheese**
- 1 **package (10 ounces) frozen chopped spinach, thawed and squeezed dry**
- 1 **jar (15 ounces) Alfredo sauce**

1. In a large skillet, cook beef, onion and garlic over medium heat 6-8 minutes or until beef is no longer pink, breaking up beef into crumbles; drain. Stir in spaghetti sauce.
2. In a small bowl, mix ricotta cheese, Parmesan cheese, parsley and pepper. Spread 1 cup meat mixture onto the bottom of an ungreased 5- or 6-qt. slow cooker. Arrange four noodles over sauce, breaking noodles to fit if necessary; layer with half of the ricotta mixture, 2 cups mozzarella cheese and 1 cup meat mixture.
3. Top with four noodles, spinach, Alfredo sauce and 2 cups mozzarella cheese. Continue layering with four noodles, remaining ricotta mixture, 2 cups mozzarella cheese and 1 cup meat mixture. Add any remaining noodles; top with remaining meat mixture and mozzarella cheese.
4. Cook, covered, on low 4-5 hours or until noodles are tender.

" Flag this dish for when you want an unusual and mouthwatering combo—cranberry, pineapple and stone-ground mustard served with smoky boneless ham."
—CAROLE RESNICK CLEVELAND, OH

Ham with Cranberry-Pineapple Sauce

PREP: 15 MIN. • **COOK:** 5 HOURS
MAKES: 20 SERVINGS (4½ CUPS SAUCE)

- 1 **fully cooked boneless ham (5 to 6 pounds)**
- 12 **whole cloves**
- 1 **can (20 ounces) crushed pineapple, undrained**
- 1 **can (14 ounces) whole-berry cranberry sauce**
- 2 **garlic cloves, minced**
- 2 **tablespoons stone-ground mustard**
- ½ **teaspoon coarsely ground pepper**
- 2 **tablespoons cornstarch**
- 2 **tablespoons cold water**

1. Score the ham, making ½-in.-deep diamond shapes; insert a clove in each diamond. Place ham in a 5-qt. slow cooker. In a large bowl, combine the pineapple, cranberry sauce, garlic, mustard and pepper; pour over ham.
2. Cover and cook on low for 5-6 hours or until a thermometer reads 140°. Remove meat to a cutting board and keep warm; remove and discard the cloves.
3. Transfer sauce to a small saucepan. Bring to a boil. Combine cornstarch and water until smooth; gradually stir into pan. Bring to a boil; cook and stir for 2 minutes or until thickened. Slice ham and serve with sauce.

Mexican Beef & Bean Stew

I like that this stew makes up quickly. The beans, veggies and spices taste great together, and it really warms me up on blustery days.

—TACY FLEURY CLINTON, SC

PREP: 20 MIN. • **COOK:** 8 HOURS
MAKES: 10 SERVINGS (2½ QUARTS)

- 1 cup all-purpose flour
- ¼ teaspoon salt
- ⅛ teaspoon pepper
- 1 pound beef stew meat, cut into 1-inch cubes
- 2 tablespoons canola oil
- 1 can (16 ounces) kidney beans, rinsed and drained
- 1 can (15¼ ounces) whole kernel corn, drained
- 2 medium potatoes, cubed
- 2 small carrots, sliced
- 2 celery ribs, sliced
- 1 small onion, chopped
- 2 cans (15 ounces each) tomato sauce
- 1 cup water
- 1 envelope taco seasoning
- ½ teaspoon ground cumin
  Tortilla chips and shredded cheddar cheese

1. Combine the flour, salt and pepper in a large resealable plastic bag. Add beef, a few pieces at a time, and shake to coat.

2. Brown meat in batches in oil in a large skillet; drain. Transfer to a 5-qt. slow cooker. Add the beans, corn, potatoes, carrots, celery and onion.

3. Whisk the tomato sauce, water, taco seasoning and cumin; pour over top. Cover and cook on low for 8-10 hours or until meat is tender. Serve with tortilla chips and cheese.

MEXICAN BEEF & BEAN STEW

All-Day Meatball Stew

I had some frozen meatballs and I wanted to use my new slow cooker, so I created this easy recipe using what I had on hand. It smells great while it's cooking. A terrific one-dish meal.

—ANITA HOFFMAN HOLLAND, PA

PREP: 20 MIN. • **COOK:** 8½ HOURS
MAKES: 8 SERVINGS (3 QUARTS)

- 2 packages (12 ounces each) frozen fully cooked Italian meatballs
- 5 medium potatoes, peeled and cubed
- 1 pound fresh baby carrots
- 1 medium onion, halved and sliced
- 1 jar (4½ ounces) sliced mushrooms, drained
- 2 cans (8 ounces each) tomato sauce
- 1 can (10½ ounces) condensed beef broth, undiluted
- ¾ cup water
- ¾ cup dry red wine or beef broth
- ½ teaspoon garlic powder
- ¼ teaspoon pepper
- 2 tablespoons all-purpose flour
- ½ cup cold water

1. Place the meatballs, potatoes, carrots, onion and mushrooms in a 5- or 6-qt. slow cooker. In a large bowl, combine the tomato sauce, broth, water, wine, garlic powder and pepper; pour over top.

2. Cover and cook on low for 8-10 hours or until vegetables are tender.

3. Combine flour and water until smooth; gradually stir into stew. Cover and cook on high for 30 minutes or until thickened.

top tip Freezer Lunches

Freeze soups, stews and chili for future lunches in handy single-serving bags. Line a measuring cup with a resealable plastic freezer bag to hold the bag upright and steady, then fill with chili. Freeze the bags flat, then stack them for efficient storage.

TURKEY WITH CRANBERRY SAUCE

Carolina-Style Pork Barbecue

PREP: 30 MIN. • **COOK:** 6 HOURS
MAKES: 14 SERVINGS

- 1 boneless pork shoulder butt roast (4 to 5 pounds)
- 2 tablespoons brown sugar
- 2 teaspoons salt
- 1 teaspoon paprika
- ½ teaspoon pepper
- 2 medium onions, quartered
- ¾ cup cider vinegar
- 4 teaspoons Worcestershire sauce
- 1 tablespoon sugar
- 1 tablespoon crushed red pepper flakes
- 1 teaspoon garlic salt
- 1 teaspoon ground mustard
- ½ teaspoon cayenne pepper
- 14 hamburger buns, split
- 1¾ pounds deli coleslaw

1. Cut roast into quarters. Mix brown sugar, salt, paprika and pepper; rub over meat. Place meat and onions in a 5-qt. slow cooker.

2. In a small bowl, whisk vinegar, Worcestershire sauce, sugar and seasonings; pour over roast. Cook, covered, on low 6-8 hours or until meat is tender.

3. Remove roast; cool slightly. Reserve 1½ cups cooking juices; discard remaining juices. Skim fat from reserved juices. Shred pork with two forks. Return pork and reserved juices to slow cooker; heat through. Serve on buns with coleslaw.

"I am originally from North Carolina, where swine are divine, and this recipe for the slow cooker is a family favorite. My husband swears my authentic Carolina 'cue is the best BBQ he has ever eaten!"

—**KATHRYN RANSOM WILLIAMS** SPARKS, NV

⑤ INGREDIENTS
Turkey with Cranberry Sauce

Here's a tasty and easy way to cook turkey breast in the slow cooker. Ideal for holiday potlucks, the sweet cranberry sauce complements the turkey nicely.

—**MARIE RAMSDEN** FAIRGROVE, MI

PREP: 15 MIN. • **COOK:** 4 HOURS
MAKES: 15 SERVINGS

- 2 boneless skinless turkey breast halves (3 pounds each)
- 1 can (14 ounces) jellied cranberry sauce
- ½ cup plus 2 tablespoons water, divided
- 1 envelope onion soup mix
- 2 tablespoons cornstarch

1. Place turkey breasts in a 5-qt. slow cooker. In a small bowl, combine the cranberry sauce, ½ cup water and soup mix. Pour over turkey.

2. Cover and cook on low for 4-6 hours or until meat is tender. Remove turkey and keep warm.

3. Transfer cooking juices to a large saucepan. Combine the cornstarch and remaining water until smooth. Bring cranberry mixture to a boil; gradually stir in cornstarch mixture. Cook and stir for 2 minutes or until thickened. Serve sauce with turkey.

CAROLINA-STYLE PORK BARBECUE

Italian Shredded Pork Stew

Need a warm meal for a blustery night? Throw together this slow-cooked stew loaded with nutritious sweet potatoes, white beans and kale. The recipe freezes well for a quick meal later.

—ROBIN JUNGERS CAMPBELLSPORT, WI

PREP: 20 MIN. • **COOK:** 8 HOURS
MAKES: 9 SERVINGS (3½ QUARTS)

- 2 **medium sweet potatoes, peeled and cubed**
- 2 **cups chopped fresh kale**
- 1 **large onion, chopped**
- 3 **garlic cloves, minced**
- 1 **boneless pork shoulder butt roast (2½ to 3½ pounds)**
- 1 **can (14 ounces) white kidney or cannellini beans, rinsed and drained**
- 1½ **teaspoons Italian seasoning**
- ½ **teaspoon salt**
- ½ **teaspoon pepper**
- 3 **cans (14½ ounces each) chicken broth**
  Sour cream, optional

1. Place the sweet potatoes, kale, onion and garlic in a 5-qt. slow cooker. Place roast on vegetables. Add the beans and seasonings. Pour broth over top. Cover and cook on low for 8-10 hours or until meat is tender.
2. Remove meat; cool slightly. Skim fat from cooking juices. Shred pork with two forks and return to slow cooker; heat through. Garnish servings with sour cream if desired.

ITALIAN SHREDDED PORK STEW

Split Pea and Sausage Soup

A big bowl of satisfying soup is the perfect antidote to cold weather. Whether it's a family meal or an informal get-together, I pull out my tried-and-true soup recipe and simply relax.

—TRISHA KRUSE EAGLE, ID

PREP: 25 MIN. • **COOK:** 7 HOURS
MAKES: 6 SERVINGS (2¼ QUARTS)

- 1 **pound smoked sausage, sliced**
- 1 **medium potato, peeled and cubed**
- 2 **medium carrots, thinly sliced**
- 2 **celery ribs, thinly sliced**
- 1 **medium onion, chopped**
- 2 **tablespoons butter**
- 3 **garlic cloves, minced**
- ¼ **teaspoon dried oregano**
- 1 **cup dried green split peas**
- 2½ **teaspoons chicken bouillon granules**
- 1 **bay leaf**
- 5 **cups water**

1. Saute the sausage, potato, carrots, celery and onion in butter in a large skillet until vegetables are crisp-tender. Add garlic and oregano; cook 2 minutes longer.
2. Transfer to a 5-qt. slow cooker. Add the peas, bouillon, bay leaf and water. Cover and cook on low for 7-8 hours or until peas are tender. Discard bay leaf.

LIP SMACKIN' RIBS

Lip Smackin' Ribs

No matter what time of year you enjoy them, these ribs taste like summer. It's feel-good food!

—RON BYNAKER LEBANON, PA

PREP: 20 MIN. • **COOK:** 6 HOURS
MAKES: 8 SERVINGS

- 3 **tablespoons butter**
- 3 **pounds boneless country-style pork ribs**
- 1 **can (15 ounces) tomato sauce**
- 1 **cup packed brown sugar**
- 1 **cup ketchup**
- ¼ **cup prepared mustard**
- 2 **tablespoons honey**
- 3 **teaspoons pepper**
- 2 **teaspoons dried savory**
- 1 **teaspoon salt**

In a large skillet, heat butter over medium heat. Brown ribs in batches; transfer to a 5-qt. slow cooker. Add remaining ingredients. Cook, covered, on low 6-8 hours or until meat is tender.

Slow Cooker Beef Vegetable Stew

This is based on my mom's wonderful recipe, though I adapted it to cook in the slow cooker. Add a sprinkle of Parmesan to each bowl for a finishing touch.

—MARCELLA WEST WASHBURN, IL

PREP: 20 MIN. • **COOK:** 6½ HOURS
MAKES: 8 SERVINGS (3 QUARTS)

- 1½ **pounds boneless beef chuck roast, cut into 1-inch cubes**
- 3 **medium potatoes, peeled and cubed**
- 3 **cups hot water**

- 1½ **cups fresh baby carrots**
- 1 **can (10¾ ounces) condensed tomato soup, undiluted**
- 1 **medium onion, chopped**
- 1 **celery rib, chopped**
- 2 **tablespoons Worcestershire sauce**
- 1 **tablespoon browning sauce, optional**
- 2 **teaspoons beef bouillon granules**
- 1 **garlic clove, minced**
- 1 **teaspoon sugar**
- ¾ **teaspoon salt**
- ¼ **teaspoon pepper**
- ¼ **cup cornstarch**
- ¾ **cup cold water**
- 2 **cups frozen peas, thawed**

1. Place the roast, potatoes, hot water, carrots, soup, onion, celery, Worcestershire sauce, browning sauce if desired, bouillon granules, garlic, sugar, salt and pepper in a 5- or 6-qt. slow cooker. Cover and cook on low for 6-8 hours or until meat is tender.
2. Combine cornstarch and cold water in a small bowl until smooth; gradually stir into stew. Add peas. Cover and cook on high for 30 minutes or until thickened.

Barbecued Party Starters

These sweet and tangy bites are sure to tide everyone over until dinner. At the buffet, set out party picks to make for easy nibbling.

—ANASTASIA WEISS PUNXSUTAWNEY, PA

PREP: 30 MIN. • **COOK:** 2¼ HOURS
MAKES: 18 SERVINGS (⅓ CUP EACH)

- 1 **pound ground beef**
- ¼ **cup finely chopped onion**
- 1 **package (16 ounces) miniature hot dogs, drained**
- 1 **jar (12 ounces) apricot preserves**
- 1 **cup barbecue sauce**
- 1 **can (20 ounces) pineapple chunks, drained**

1. In a small bowl, combine beef and onion. Shape into 1-in. balls. In a large skillet, cook meatballs in batches until no longer pink; drain.
2. Place in a 3-qt. slow cooker; add hot dogs, preserves and barbecue sauce. Cover and cook on high 2-3 hours or until heated through. Stir in pineapple; cook, covered, 15-20 minutes longer or until heated through.

BARBECUED PARTY STARTERS

CANTONESE SWEET AND SOUR PORK

Cantonese Sweet and Sour Pork

Step away from the takeout menu. There'll be no reason to dial up delivery once you taste my easy, economical sweet and sour pork. The tender vegetables, juicy pork and flavorful sauce are delicious with hot white rice.
—**NANCY TEWS** ANTIGO, WI

PREP: 20 MIN. • **COOK:** 7½ HOURS
MAKES: 6 SERVINGS

- 1 can (15 ounces) tomato sauce
- 1 medium onion, halved and sliced
- 1 medium green pepper, cut into strips
- 1 can (4½ ounces) sliced mushrooms, drained
- 3 tablespoons brown sugar
- 4½ teaspoons white vinegar
- 2 teaspoons steak sauce
- 1 teaspoon salt
- 1½ pounds pork tenderloin, cut into 1-inch cubes
- 1 tablespoon olive oil
- 1 can (8 ounces) unsweetened pineapple chunks, drained
  Hot cooked rice

1. In a large bowl, combine the first eight ingredients; set aside.
2. In a large skillet, brown pork in oil in batches. Transfer to a 3- or 4-qt. slow cooker. Pour tomato sauce mixture over pork. Cover and cook on low for 7-8 hours or until meat is tender.
3. Add pineapple; cover and cook 30 minutes longer or until heated through. Serve with rice.

Slow Cooker French Dip Sandwiches

These sandwiches make a standout addition to any buffet line. Make sure to have plenty of small cups of broth for individual servings. Dipping perfection!
—**HOLLY NEUHARTH** MESA, AZ

PREP: 15 MIN. • **COOK:** 8 HOURS
MAKES: 12 SERVINGS

- 1 beef rump or bottom round roast (3 pounds)
- 1½ teaspoons onion powder
- 1½ teaspoons garlic powder
- ½ teaspoon Creole seasoning
- 1 carton (26 ounces) beef stock
- 12 whole wheat hoagie buns, split
- 6 ounces Havarti cheese, cut into 12 slices

1. Cut roast in half. Mix onion powder, garlic powder and Creole seasoning; rub onto beef. Place in a 5-qt. slow cooker; add stock. Cook, covered, on low 8-10 hours or until meat is tender.
2. Remove beef; cool slightly. Skim fat from cooking juices. Shred beef with two forks and return to slow cooker.
3. Place buns on baking sheets, cut side up. Using tongs, place beef on bun bottoms. Place cheese on bun tops. Broil 3-4 in. from heat 1-2 minutes or until cheese is melted. Close sandwiches; serve with cooking juices.
NOTE *The following spices may be substituted for 1 tablespoon Creole seasoning: ¾ teaspoon each salt, garlic powder and paprika; and a pinch each of dried thyme, ground cumin and cayenne.*

Machaca Beef Dip Sandwiches

The winning combination of beef, cumin, chili powder and chipotles make these sandwiches a game-day star!
—**KAROL CHANDLER-EZELL** NACOGDOCHES, TX

PREP: 20 MIN. • **COOK:** 8 HOURS
MAKES: 6 SERVINGS

- 1 boneless beef chuck roast (2 to 3 pounds)
- 1 large sweet onion, thinly sliced
- 1 can (14½ ounces) reduced-sodium beef broth
- ½ cup water
- 3 chipotle peppers in adobo sauce, chopped
- 1 tablespoon adobo sauce
- 1 envelope au jus gravy mix
- 1 tablespoon Creole seasoning
- 1 tablespoon chili powder
- 2 teaspoons ground cumin
- 6 French rolls, split
  Guacamole and salsa, optional

1. Place roast in a 3- to 4-qt. slow cooker; top with onion. Combine the broth, water, chipotle peppers, adobo sauce, gravy mix, Creole seasoning, chili powder and cumin; pour over meat. Cover and cook on low for 8-10 hours or until meat is tender.
2. Remove roast; cool slightly. Skim fat from cooking juices. Shred beef with two forks and return to slow cooker; heat through. Using a slotted spoon, place meat on rolls. Serve sandwiches with cooking juices and, if desired, guacamole or salsa.
NOTE *Wear disposable gloves when cutting hot peppers; the oils can burn skin. Avoid touching your face. The following spices may be substituted for 1 tablespoon Creole seasoning: ¾ teaspoon each salt, garlic powder and paprika; and a pinch each of dried thyme, ground cumin and cayenne.*

MACHACA BEEF DIP SANDWICHES

Spinach and Sausage Lasagna

Dig into the rich layers of this hearty lasagna that features plenty of Italian sausage and gooey cheese. No-cook noodles, frozen spinach and jarred spaghetti sauce simplify the prep. But it tastes far from ordinary!

—**KATHLEEN MORROW** HUBBARD, OH

PREP: 25 MIN. • **COOK:** 3 HOURS
MAKES: 8 SERVINGS

- 1 pound bulk Italian sausage
- 1 jar (24 ounces) garden-style spaghetti sauce
- ½ cup water
- 1 teaspoon Italian seasoning
- ½ teaspoon salt
- 1 carton (15 ounces) ricotta cheese
- 1 package (10 ounces) frozen chopped spinach, thawed and squeezed dry
- 2 cups (8 ounces) shredded part-skim mozzarella cheese, divided
- 9 no-cook lasagna noodles
  Grated Parmesan cheese

1. Cook sausage in a large skillet over medium heat until no longer pink; drain. Stir in the spaghetti sauce, water, Italian seasoning and salt. Combine ricotta, spinach and 1 cup mozzarella cheese in a small bowl.

2. Spread 1 cup sauce mixture in a greased oval 5-qt. slow cooker. Layer with three noodles (breaking noodles if necessary to fit), 1¼ cups sauce mixture and half of the cheese mixture. Repeat layers. Layer with remaining noodles and sauce mixture; sprinkle with remaining mozzarella cheese.

3. Cover and cook on low for 3-4 hours or until noodles are tender. Sprinkle servings with Parmesan cheese.

(5) INGREDIENTS
Cola Beef Brisket

This fork-tender beef is perfect for summertime because using the slow cooker helps keep your kitchen cool. Leftovers make delicious sandwiches the next day.

—**STEPHANIE STRONG** MT. JULIET, TN

PREP: 10 MIN. • **COOK:** 6 HOURS
MAKES: 7 SERVINGS (2 CUPS GRAVY)

- 1 fresh beef brisket (3 pounds)
- 1 cup chili sauce
- 1 cup cola
- 1 envelope onion soup mix
- 1 tablespoon cornstarch
- 1 tablespoon cold water

1. Cut brisket in half and place in a 5-qt. slow cooker. Combine chili sauce, cola and soup mix; pour over brisket. Cover and cook on low for 6-7 hours or until meat is tender.

2. Remove meat to a serving platter and keep warm. Skim fat from cooking juices; transfer to a small saucepan. Bring liquid to a boil.

3. Combine cornstarch and cold water until smooth. Gradually stir into the pan. Bring to a boil; cook and stir for 2 minutes or until thickened. Thinly slice meat across the grain; serve with gravy.

NOTE *This is a fresh beef brisket, not corned beef.*

SPINACH AND SAUSAGE LASAGNA

BUTTERSCOTCH-PECAN BREAD PUDDING

German Potato Salad with Sausage

Main-dish satisfying, this potato salad is an old family recipe. I updated it to use canned soup for easy preparation. Sauerkraut gives it special zip.

—TERESA MCGILL TROTWOOD, OH

PREP: 30 MIN. • **COOK:** 6 HOURS
MAKES: 5 SERVINGS

- 8 bacon strips, finely chopped
- 1 large onion, chopped
- 1 pound smoked kielbasa or Polish sausage, halved and cut into ½-inch slices
- 2 pounds medium red potatoes, cut into chunks
- 1 can (10¾ ounces) condensed cream of potato soup, undiluted
- 1 cup sauerkraut, rinsed and well drained
- ½ cup water
- ¼ cup cider vinegar
- 1 tablespoon sugar
- ½ teaspoon salt
- ½ teaspoon coarsely ground pepper

1. In a large skillet, cook bacon over medium heat until crisp. Remove to paper towels with a slotted spoon to drain. Saute onion in drippings for 1 minute. Add sausage; cook until lightly browned. Add potatoes; cook 2 minutes longer. Drain.

2. Transfer sausage mixture to a 3-qt. slow cooker. In a small bowl, combine the soup, sauerkraut, water, vinegar, sugar, salt and pepper. Pour over sausage mixture. Sprinkle with bacon. Cover and cook on low for 6-7 hours or until potatoes are tender.

"Bread pudding fans just might hoard this delicious butterscotch version. Toppings like whipped cream and butterscotch drizzle make this dessert irresistible."

—LISA VARNER EL PASO, TX

Butterscotch-Pecan Bread Pudding

PREP: 15 MIN. • **COOK:** 3 HOURS
MAKES: 8 SERVINGS

- 8 slices white bread, cubed
- ½ cup chopped pecans
- ½ cup butterscotch chips
- 4 eggs
- 2 cups half-and-half cream
- ½ cup packed brown sugar
- ½ cup butter, melted
- 1 teaspoon vanilla extract
  Whipped cream and butterscotch ice cream topping

1. Place the bread, pecans and butterscotch chips in a greased 4-qt. slow cooker. In a large bowl, whisk the eggs, cream, brown sugar, butter and vanilla. Pour over top.

2. Cover and cook on low for 3-4 hours or until a knife inserted in the center comes out clean.

3. Serve warm with whipped cream and butterscotch topping.

GERMAN POTATO SALAD WITH SAUSAGE

**Michelle Glassmeyer Wunsch's
Creamy Herb Grilled Salmon**
PAGE 217

Hot Off the Grill

Hone your grill skills with fresh takes on juicy burgers, amazing fish, classic steaks, smoky sides and delicious desserts. Celebrate summer with these fun, fuss-free recipes.

**Susan Nordin's
Grilled Potatoes & Peppers**
PAGE 211

**Angela Spengler's
Molasses-Glazed Pork Chops**
PAGE 221

**Judy Puskas'
Greek-Style Chicken Burgers**
PAGE 221

Barbecued Chicken

Every summer, we have a neighborhood cookout. I always take this chicken and watch it quickly disappear! My family loves the zesty seasoning blend and homemade barbecue sauce.

—**LINDA SCOTT** HAHIRA, GA

PREP: 10 MIN. • **GRILL:** 40 MIN.
MAKES: 8 SERVINGS

- 2 broiler/fryer chickens (3 to 4 pounds each), cut up

SPICE RUB
- 2 tablespoons onion powder
- 4 teaspoons salt or salt substitute
- 1 tablespoon paprika
- 2 teaspoons garlic powder
- 1½ teaspoons chili powder
- 1½ teaspoons pepper
- ¼ teaspoon ground turmeric
  Pinch cayenne pepper

SAUCE
- 2 cups ketchup
- 3 tablespoons brown sugar
- 2 tablespoons dried minced onion
- 2 tablespoons thawed orange juice concentrate
- ½ teaspoon liquid smoke, optional

1. Pat chicken pieces dry. In a small bowl, mix spice rub ingredients; reserve 1 tablespoon spice rub for sauce. Rub remaining spice rub on all sides of chicken.

2. Grill chicken, uncovered, over medium heat 20 minutes, skin side down. Meanwhile, combine all sauce ingredients; stir in reserved spice rub. Turn chicken; grill 20-30 minutes longer or until juices run clear, basting frequently with sauce.

ROSEMARY-LEMON GRILLED CHICKEN

BARBECUED CHICKEN

(5)INGREDIENTS FAST FIX

Rosemary-Lemon Grilled Chicken

Here's a simple dish with big, bold flavors from only a few ingredients. It's great by itself, but can also be served atop salad greens as another dinner option.

—**DEBBIE CARTER** KINGSBURG, CA

START TO FINISH: 25 MIN.
MAKES: 4 SERVINGS

- 1 medium lemon
- ⅓ cup butter, cubed
- 4 teaspoons minced fresh rosemary or 1 teaspoon dried rosemary, crushed
- 2 garlic cloves, minced
- ¼ teaspoon salt
- ¼ teaspoon pepper
- 4 boneless skinless chicken breast halves (6 ounces each)

1. Finely grate peel from lemon; juice lemon. In a microwave, melt butter. Stir in lemon juice and peel, rosemary, garlic, salt and pepper.

2. Grill chicken, covered, over medium heat or broil 4 in. from heat 5-7 minutes on each side or until a thermometer reads 165°, basting frequently with butter mixture during the last 5 minutes of cooking.

SUN-DRIED TOMATO TURKEY BURGERS

Grilled Potatoes & Peppers

PREP: 20 MIN. • **GRILL:** 40 MIN.
MAKES: 10 SERVINGS

- 8 **medium red potatoes, cut into wedges**
- 2 **medium green peppers, sliced**
- 1 **medium onion, cut into thin wedges**
- 2 **tablespoons olive oil**
- 5 **garlic cloves, thinly sliced**
- 1 **teaspoon paprika**
- 1 **teaspoon Montreal steak seasoning**
- 1 **teaspoon Italian seasoning**
- ¼ **teaspoon salt**
- ¼ **teaspoon pepper**

1. In a large bowl, combine all ingredients. Divide between two pieces of heavy-duty foil (about 18 in. square). Fold foil around potato mixture and crimp edges to seal.
2. Grill, covered, over medium heat 40-45 minutes or until potatoes are tender. Open foil carefully to allow steam to escape.
PER SERVING *103 cal., 3 g fat (trace sat. fat), 0 chol., 134 mg sodium, 18 g carb., 2 g fiber, 2 g pro.* **Diabetic Exchanges:** *1 starch, ½ fat.*

"My husband, Matt, grills this recipe for both breakfast and dinner gatherings. The potatoes and the company are my favorite parts of these get-togethers."
—**SUSAN NORDIN** WARREN, PA

GRILLED POTATOES & PEPPERS

Sun-Dried Tomato Turkey Burgers

This recipe brings back memories of my mom's homemade sun-dried tomatoes in the summer. I've prepared the burgers with both ground beef and ground turkey. Either way, they taste great!
—**SAMMY STAAB** PENSACOLA, FL

START TO FINISH: 25 MIN.
MAKES: 6 SERVINGS

- 1 **large red onion**
- 1 **cup (4 ounces) crumbled feta cheese, divided**
- ⅔ **cup chopped oil-packed sun-dried tomatoes**
- ¼ **teaspoon salt**
- ¼ **teaspoon pepper**
- 2 **pounds lean ground turkey**
- 6 **ciabatta rolls, split**

1. Cut onion in half. Finely chop one half and thinly slice the remaining half. Combine ½ cup feta, sun-dried tomatoes, chopped onion, salt and pepper in a large bowl. Crumble turkey over mixture and mix well. Shape into six patties.
2. Grill burgers, covered, over medium heat or broil 4 in. from the heat for 5-7 minutes on each side or until a thermometer reads 165° and juices run clear.
3. Meanwhile, saute sliced onion in a small nonstick skillet coated with cooking spray until tender. Serve burgers on buns with onion and remaining feta.

EAT SMART FAST FIX ▶
Pork Chops with Apricot Glaze

A quick homemade rub adds just the right amount of flavor to pork chops, and the apricot glaze offers a touch of sweetness. The glaze is also tasty on grilled chicken.

—KATHY HARDING RICHMOND, MO

START TO FINISH: 30 MIN.
MAKES: 6 SERVINGS

- 1½ teaspoons ground ginger
- 1 teaspoon salt
- ½ teaspoon garlic powder
- ½ teaspoon pepper
- 6 boneless pork loin chops (6 ounces each)
- 1 cup apricot preserves
- 2 tablespoons hoisin sauce
- ½ teaspoon crushed red pepper flakes
- 2 green onions, chopped
- 3 tablespoons chopped unsalted peanuts

1. Mix ginger, salt, garlic powder and pepper; rub onto both sides of chops. In a small saucepan, combine the preserves, hoisin sauce and pepper flakes; cook and stir over medium heat until blended. Reserve ½ cup for brushing chops after grilling.
2. Moisten a paper towel with cooking oil; using long-handled tongs, rub on grill rack to coat lightly. Grill pork, covered, over medium heat or broil 4 in. from heat 4-5 minutes on each side or until a thermometer reads 145°, basting chops frequently with remaining sauce during last 4 minutes of cooking. Let stand 5 minutes before serving. Brush chops with reserved sauce; sprinkle with green onions and peanuts.

PER SERVING *399 cal., 12 g fat (4 g sat. fat), 82 mg chol., 549 mg sodium, 39 g carb., 1 g fiber, 34 g pro.*

EAT SMART
Marinated Lamb Chops

These lamb chops are packed with the flavors of rosemary, ginger and mustard. Marinating makes them so tender. They're something special for spring.

—JILL HEATWOLE PITTSVILLE, MD

PREP: 10 MIN. + MARINATING
GRILL: 10 MIN. • **MAKES:** 4 SERVINGS

- 1 small onion, sliced
- 2 tablespoons red wine vinegar
- 1 tablespoon lemon juice
- 1 tablespoon olive oil
- 2 teaspoons minced fresh rosemary or ¾ teaspoon dried rosemary, crushed
- 2 teaspoons Dijon mustard
- 1 garlic clove, minced
- ½ teaspoon pepper
- ¼ teaspoon salt
- ¼ teaspoon ground ginger
- 8 lamb loin chops (3 ounces each)

1. In a large resealable plastic bag, combine the first 10 ingredients; add lamb chops. Seal bag and turn to coat; refrigerate chops for several hours or overnight.
2. Drain and discard marinade and onion. Moisten a paper towel with cooking oil; using long-handled tongs, rub on grill rack to coat lightly.
3. Grill the chops, covered, over medium heat or broil 4 in. from the heat for 5-7 minutes on each side or until meat reaches desired doneness (for medium-rare, a thermometer should read 145°; medium, 160°; well-done, 170°).

PER SERVING *164 cal., 8 g fat (3 g sat. fat), 68 mg chol., 112 mg sodium, trace carb., trace fiber, 21 g pro.* **Diabetic Exchange:** *3 lean meat.*

GRILLED SAUSAGES WITH PEPPERS

FAST FIX ▶
Grilled Sausages with Peppers

This is one of my family's favorite ways to have sausage on the grill. The sweet and sour vegetables make the perfect accompaniment to savory sausage.

—STEVEN SCHEND GRAND RAPIDS, MI

START TO FINISH: 25 MIN.
MAKES: 2 SERVINGS

- 2 teaspoons olive oil
- 1 small green pepper, julienned
- 1 small onion, thinly sliced
- 1 tablespoon brown sugar
- 1 tablespoon red wine vinegar
- 1 garlic clove, minced
  Dash salt
  Dash pepper
- 2 Italian sausage links (4 ounces each)
- 2 brat buns
  Spicy brown mustard, optional

1. In a large skillet, heat oil over medium-high heat. Add green pepper and onion; cook and stir until softened. Stir in the brown sugar, vinegar, garlic, salt and pepper. Reduce the heat to medium-low; cook, stirring vegetables occasionally, 12-15 minutes or until onion is golden brown.
2. Meanwhile, grill sausages, covered, over medium heat 12-15 minutes or until a thermometer reads 160°, turning occasionally. Serve in buns with pepper mixture; if desired, top with mustard.

PORK CHOPS WITH APRICOT GLAZE

Balsamic-Glazed Beef Skewers

With only five ingredients, these mouthwatering kabobs are a favorite to make and eat. To prevent wooden skewers from burning, soak them in water for 30 minutes before use.
—CAROLE FRASER TORONTO, ON

START TO FINISH: 25 MIN.
MAKES: 4 SERVINGS

- ¼ cup balsamic vinaigrette
- ¼ cup barbecue sauce
- 1 teaspoon Dijon mustard
- 1 beef top sirloin steak (1 pound), cut into 1-inch cubes
- 2 cups cherry tomatoes

1. In a large bowl, whisk vinaigrette, barbecue sauce and mustard until blended. Reserve ¼ cup of the marinade for basting. Add beef to remaining marinade; toss to coat.

2. Alternately thread beef and tomatoes on four metal or soaked wooden skewers. Moisten a paper towel with cooking oil; using long-handled tongs, rub on grill rack to coat lightly.

3. Grill skewers, covered, over medium heat or broil 4 in. from heat 6-9 minutes or until beef reaches desired doneness, turning them occasionally and basting frequently with reserved marinade during the last 3 minutes.
PER SERVING *194 cal., 7 g fat (2 g sat. fat), 46 mg chol., 288 mg sodium, 7 g carb., 1 g fiber, 25 g pro.* **Diabetic Exchanges:** *3 lean meat, 1½ fat, ½ starch.*

Grilled Mushrooms

Mushrooms cooked over hot coals are always good, but this easy recipe makes them taste fantastic.
—MELANIE KNOLL MARSHALLTOWN, IA

START TO FINISH: 15 MIN.
MAKES: 4 SERVINGS

- ½ pound medium fresh mushrooms
- ¼ cup butter, melted
- ½ teaspoon dill weed
- ½ teaspoon garlic salt

Thread mushrooms on four metal or soaked wooden skewers. Combine butter, dill and garlic salt; brush over mushrooms. Grill over medium-high heat for 10-15 minutes or until tender, basting and turning every 5 minutes.

BALSAMIC-GLAZED BEEF SKEWERS

PORK WITH STRAWBERRY-PORT SAUCE

Pork with Strawberry-Port Sauce

I never thought to add fruit to barbecue sauce, but after I saw a contest-winning recipe that featured the combination, I decided to try something similar. I'm glad I did. This turned out to be a family favorite!

—LILY JULOW LAWRENCEVILLE, GA

PREP: 25 MIN. • **GRILL:** 10 MIN.
MAKES: 8 SERVINGS (2 CUPS SAUCE)

- 2 tablespoons butter
- 2 medium onions, finely chopped
- 1¼ teaspoons salt, divided
- ½ teaspoon pepper, divided
- 1 cup strawberry spreadable fruit
- ¼ cup port wine or chicken broth
- 2 tablespoons balsamic vinegar
- ½ teaspoon ground mustard
- 1 cup grape tomatoes, halved
- 2 tablespoons minced fresh basil
- 2 teaspoons lime juice
- 8 pork rib chops (1 inch thick and 8 ounces each)

1. In a large skillet, heat butter over medium-high heat. Add onions, ¾ teaspoon salt and ¼ teaspoon pepper; cook and stir until tender. Stir in spreadable fruit, wine, vinegar and mustard. Bring to a boil; cook and stir until slightly thickened. Add tomatoes and cook 2-3 minutes longer or until softened. Stir in basil and lime juice.
2. Moisten a paper towel with cooking oil; using long-handled tongs, rub on grill rack to coat lightly. Sprinkle chops with remaining salt and pepper. Grill, covered, over medium heat or broil 4 in. from heat 4-6 minutes on each side or until a thermometer reads 145°. Let chops stand 5 minutes before serving. Serve with sauce.

top tip — Port Wine

Port wine is available in ruby (bright red and fruity) and tawny (amber-colored and nutty) styles. While either type will work fine in the sauce, you might prefer the fruity interplay of ruby port with the recipe's strawberry jam. And ruby is often less expensive than tawny port.

GRILLED WHISKEY CHOPS

"No one can believe that these fabulous chops are ready in half an hour! We love them for weeknights and family gatherings. The dollop of molasses butter on each chop is absolutely delish!" —KELLY HODSON ANDERSON, IN

FAST FIX
Grilled Whiskey Chops

START TO FINISH: 25 MIN.
MAKES: 4 SERVINGS

- ¼ cup butter, softened
- 1 tablespoon molasses
- ½ teaspoon ground cinnamon
- ½ teaspoon lemon juice
- 3 tablespoons coarsely ground pepper
- ⅓ cup whiskey
- ½ teaspoon salt
- 4 bone-in pork loin chops (¾ inch thick)

1. In a small bowl, mix the butter, molasses, cinnamon and lemon juice; refrigerate until serving.
2. Place pepper in a shallow bowl. In a separate shallow bowl, mix whiskey and salt. Dip chops in whiskey mixture, then in pepper.
3. Moisten a paper towel with cooking oil; using long-handled tongs, rub on grill rack to coat lightly. Grill chops, covered, over medium heat or broil 4 in. from heat 4-5 minutes on each side or until a thermometer reads 145°. Let stand 5 minutes. Serve chops with molasses butter.

CITRUS-MARINATED CHICKEN

Citrus-Marinated Chicken

This juicy, zesty chicken stars in many of my family's summer meals. While there are a million ways to dress up poultry, you'll find yourself turning to this recipe again and again. It's that quick and easy!

—DEBORAH GRETZINGER GREEN BAY, WI

PREP: 10 MIN. + MARINATING
GRILL: 10 MIN. • **MAKES:** 6 SERVINGS

- ½ cup lemon juice
- ½ cup orange juice
- 6 garlic cloves, minced
- 2 tablespoons canola oil
- 1 teaspoon salt
- 1 teaspoon ground ginger
- 1 teaspoon dried tarragon
- ¼ teaspoon pepper
- 6 boneless skinless chicken breast halves (6 ounces each)

1. Combine the first eight ingredients in a large resealable plastic bag. Add the chicken; seal bag and turn to coat. Refrigerate for at least 4 hours.
2. Drain and discard marinade. Grill chicken, covered, over medium heat or broil chicken 4 in. from the heat for 5-7 minutes on each side or until a thermometer reads 170°.

EAT SMART

Grilled Chicken with Black Bean Salsa

Black bean salsa with mango gives this dish a Mexican twist without too much heat. I like to slice the chicken and serve it over a long grain and wild rice mix.

—TERRI CLOUSE CONNOQUENESSING, PA

PREP: 15 MIN. + MARINATING
GRILL: 10 MIN. • **MAKES:** 5 SERVINGS

- 1 cup lime juice
- 2 tablespoons olive oil
- 2 teaspoons ground cumin
- 1 teaspoon salt
- 1 teaspoon dried oregano
- ½ teaspoon pepper
- 5 boneless skinless chicken breast halves (4 ounces each)

BLACK BEAN SALSA
- 1 can (15 ounces) black beans, rinsed and drained
- 1 mango, peeled and cubed
- ¼ cup minced fresh cilantro
- 3 tablespoons lime juice
- 1 tablespoon olive oil
- 2 teaspoons brown sugar
- 1 teaspoon minced jalapeno pepper

1. In a small bowl, whisk the first six ingredients. Pour ⅔ cup marinade into a large resealable plastic bag. Add chicken; seal bag and turn to coat. Refrigerate 1-2 hours. Reserve the remaining marinade for basting. In a small bowl, combine salsa ingredients; toss to combine.
2. Drain the chicken, discarding marinade. Grill chicken, covered, over medium heat or broil 4 in. from heat 5-6 minutes on each side or until a thermometer reads 165°, basting occasionally with reserved marinade during the last 4 minutes. Serve chicken with salsa.

NOTE *Wear disposable gloves when cutting hot peppers; the oils can burn skin. Avoid touching your face.*

PER SERVING *266 cal., 7 g fat (1 g sat. fat), 63 mg chol., 339 mg sodium, 23 g carb., 4 g fiber, 27 g pro.* **Diabetic Exchanges:** *3 lean meat, 1½ starch, 1 fat.*

GRILLED CHICKEN WITH BLACK BEAN SALSA

Creamy Herb Grilled Salmon

START TO FINISH: 30 MIN.
MAKES: 4 SERVINGS

- ½ cup sour cream
- ¼ cup minced fresh chives
- ¼ cup snipped fresh dill
- ¼ cup ranch salad dressing
- 3 tablespoons minced fresh parsley
- 1 garlic clove, minced
- ½ teaspoon seasoned salt
- ½ teaspoon pepper

- 1 salmon fillet (1 pound)
- 1 teaspoon olive oil

1. In a small bowl, mix the first eight ingredients. Brush skin side of salmon with oil.

2. Moisten a paper towel with cooking oil; using long-handled tongs, rub on grill rack to coat lightly. Place salmon on grill rack, skin side down; spread sour cream mixture over fish. Grill salmon, covered, over medium heat 12-14 minutes or until it flakes easily with a fork.

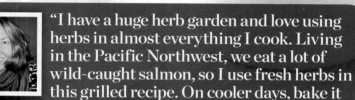

"I have a huge herb garden and love using herbs in almost everything I cook. Living in the Pacific Northwest, we eat a lot of wild-caught salmon, so I use fresh herbs in this grilled recipe. On cooler days, bake it instead." —**MICHELLE GLASSMEYER WUNSCH** BOTHELL, WA

CREAMY HERB GRILLED SALMON

Raspberry Turkey Tenderloins

Fast to prep and even quicker to grill, this dish is always a winner at my house. We love the raspberry-Dijon sauce. You can substitute chicken breasts for the turkey if you wish.
—**JOANN HANDLEY** MOUNT DORA, FL

PREP: 20 MIN. • **GRILL:** 15 MIN.
MAKES: 6 SERVINGS

- ½ cup seedless raspberry jam
- ⅓ cup cider vinegar
- ¼ cup Dijon mustard
- 1 teaspoon grated orange peel
- ½ teaspoon minced fresh thyme or ⅛ teaspoon dried thyme
- 4 turkey breast tenderloins (6 ounces each)
- ⅛ teaspoon salt

1. In a small saucepan, combine the first five ingredients. Cook and stir for 2-3 minutes or until heated through. Set aside ¼ cup for serving.

2. Sprinkle turkey with salt. Moisten a paper towel with cooking oil; using long-handled tongs, lightly coat the grill rack. Grill turkey, covered, over medium heat or broil 4 in. from the heat for 13-18 minutes or until a thermometer reads 170°, turning occasionally. Baste with remaining sauce during last 5 minutes of cooking.

3. Let stand for 5 minutes before slicing. Serve with reserved sauce.

PER SERVING *199 cal., 2 g fat (trace sat. fat), 56 mg chol., 351 mg sodium, 20 g carb., trace fiber, 26 g pro.*
***Diabetic Exchanges:** 3 lean meat, 1 starch.*

BLUE CHEESE FLAT IRON STEAK

GRILLED CHICKEN WITH HERBED STUFFING

Blue Cheese Flat Iron Steak

If you haven't already enjoyed the rich, creamy pairing of blue cheese with your favorite steak, stop reading and get cooking! I take it a step further by folding in a little butter to make the dish even more drool-worthy.

—**AMANDA MARTIN** MONSON, MA

PREP: 15 MIN. + MARINATING
GRILL: 10 MIN. • **MAKES:** 4 SERVINGS

- ¼ cup olive oil
- 2 tablespoons red wine vinegar
- 2 garlic cloves, minced
- 1 teaspoon dried oregano
- 1 teaspoon dried rosemary, crushed
- 1 teaspoon pepper
- ¼ teaspoon salt
- 1¼ pounds beef flat iron steak or top sirloin steak (1 inch thick)

BLUE CHEESE BUTTER

- ¼ cup crumbled blue cheese
- 3 tablespoons butter, softened
- 1 tablespoon minced fresh chives
- ⅛ teaspoon pepper

1. In a large resealable plastic bag, combine the first seven ingredients. Add beef; seal bag and turn to coat. Refrigerate 30 minutes.
2. In a small bowl, mix blue cheese, butter, chives and pepper; set aside. Drain beef, discarding marinade.
3. Grill steaks, covered, over medium heat or broil them 4 in. from heat for 5-7 minutes on each side or until meat reaches desired doneness (for medium-rare, a thermometer should read 145°; medium, 160°; well-done, 170°). Serve with blue cheese butter.

FAST FIX
Grilled Chicken with Herbed Stuffing

I like to dress up grilled chicken breasts by stuffing them with herbs, bread crumbs and garlic. They taste infinitely better this way, and the stuffing helps keep the chicken moist.

—**JOY MCMILLAN** THE WOODLANDS, TX

START TO FINISH: 30 MIN.
MAKES: 4 SERVINGS

- 5 teaspoons butter, divided
- ½ cup finely chopped onion
- 1 garlic clove, minced
- ½ cup soft bread crumbs
- 1 tablespoon minced fresh parsley
- ¼ teaspoon salt, divided
- ⅛ teaspoon dried marjoram
- ⅛ teaspoon dried thyme
- 4 boneless skinless chicken breast halves (6 ounces each)
- 1 teaspoon grated lemon peel

1. In a small nonstick skillet coated with cooking spray, heat 2 teaspoons butter. Add onion and garlic; cook and stir until tender. Stir in bread crumbs, parsley, ⅛ teaspoon salt, marjoram and thyme.
2. Cut a pocket in the thickest part of each chicken breast. Fill with the bread crumb mixture; secure with toothpicks. Sprinkle chicken with remaining salt. In a microwave, melt remaining butter; stir in lemon peel.
3. Moisten a paper towel with cooking oil; using long-handled tongs, rub on grill rack to coat lightly. Grill chicken over medium heat 6-9 minutes on each side or until chicken is no longer pink, brushing occasionally with the butter mixture during last 5 minutes of cooking. Discard the toothpicks before serving.

FAST FIX
Kathy's Herbed Corn

My husband and I agreed that the original recipe for this corn needed a little jazzing up, so I added thyme and cayenne pepper to suit our tastes. Now fresh corn makes a regular appearance on our grill.

—**KATHY VONKORFF** NORTH COLLEGE HILL, OH

START TO FINISH: 30 MIN.
MAKES: 8 SERVINGS

- ½ cup butter, softened
- 2 tablespoons minced fresh parsley
- 2 tablespoons minced fresh chives
- 1 teaspoon dried thyme
- ½ teaspoon salt
- ½ teaspoon cayenne pepper
- 8 ears sweet corn, husked

1. In a small bowl, beat the first six ingredients until blended. Spread 1 tablespoon mixture over each ear of corn. Wrap corn individually in heavy-duty foil.
2. Grill corn, covered, over medium heat 10-15 minutes or until tender, turning occasionally. Open foil carefully to allow steam to escape.

Spicy Chicken Tomato Pitas

I'm not sure if this is a Mediterranean dish with a Southwestern flair or the other way around. All I know is that it's ideal for a summer dinner. The tomato relish is yummy as an appetizer with tortilla chips, so you may want to double it.

—CORI COOPER BOISE, ID

START TO FINISH: 30 MIN.
MAKES: 4 SERVINGS

TOMATO RELISH

- ¼ cup lemon juice
- 1 tablespoon olive oil
- 1 teaspoon ground coriander
- 1 teaspoon ground cumin
- ¼ teaspoon crushed red pepper flakes
- 4 medium tomatoes, seeded and chopped
- 1 small onion, chopped
- ¼ cup minced fresh parsley

CHICKEN PITAS

- 1 tablespoon ground cumin
- 1 tablespoon paprika
- 1½ teaspoons dried oregano
- 1½ teaspoons ground coriander
- ½ teaspoon crushed red pepper flakes
- ¼ teaspoon salt
- 4 boneless skinless chicken breast halves (4 ounces each)
- 8 whole wheat pita pocket halves

1. In a bowl, whisk the first five ingredients. Add tomatoes, onion and parsley; toss to coat. Refrigerate relish until serving.

2. Moisten a paper towel with cooking oil; using long-handled tongs, rub on grill rack to coat lightly. Combine cumin, paprika, oregano, coriander, pepper flakes and salt; rub onto both sides of chicken. Grill chicken, covered, over medium heat or broil 4 in. from heat 4-7 minutes on each side or until a thermometer reads 165°.

3. Cut chicken into slices. Serve in pita halves with relish.

PER SERVING *383 cal., 9 g fat (2 g sat. fat), 63 mg chol., 558 mg sodium, 47 g carb., 9 g fiber, 32 g pro.*

Quick Seeded Tomatoes

To quickly seed a tomato, cut it into wedges. Swipe your finger over each wedge to remove the gel pockets and seeds. Then chop the wedges as desired. This fast technique is useful when you don't need the tomatoes to be picture-perfect.

SPICY CHICKEN TOMATO PITAS

MOLASSES-GLAZED PORK CHOPS

Molasses-Glazed Pork Chops

I serve these versatile chops for family meals and big backyard barbecues. I sometimes add a hint of chipotle to the sauce: It's my secret ingredient that lends a little extra pop.

—**ANGELA SPENGLER** CLOVIS, NM

START TO FINISH: 30 MIN.
MAKES: 4 SERVINGS

- ¼ cup molasses
- 1 tablespoon Worcestershire sauce
- 1½ teaspoons brown sugar
- 4 boneless pork loin chops (¾ inch thick and 5 ounces each)

1. In a small bowl, combine the molasses, Worcestershire sauce and brown sugar. Reserve 3 tablespoons sauce for serving.

2. Grill pork, covered, over medium heat or broil 4 in. from the heat for 4-5 minutes on each side or until a thermometer reads 145°, brushing with remaining sauce during the last 3 minutes of cooking. Let stand for 5 minutes before serving. Serve with reserved sauce.

PER SERVING *256 cal., 8 g fat (3 g sat. fat), 68 mg chol., 89 mg sodium, 17 g carb., 0 fiber, 27 g pro.* **Diabetic Exchanges:** *4 lean meat, 1 starch.*

Greek-Style Chicken Burgers

PREP: 25 MIN. • **GRILL:** 10 MIN.
MAKES: 4 SERVINGS

SAUCE

- ⅓ cup fat-free plain Greek yogurt
- ¼ cup chopped peeled cucumber
- ¼ cup crumbled reduced-fat feta cheese
- 1½ teaspoons snipped fresh dill
- 1½ teaspoons lemon juice
- 1 small garlic clove, minced

BURGERS

- 1 medium onion, finely chopped
- ¼ cup dry bread crumbs
- 1 tablespoon dried oregano
- 1 tablespoon lemon juice
- 2 garlic cloves, minced
- ½ teaspoon salt
- ¼ teaspoon pepper
- 1 pound ground chicken
- 4 hamburger buns, split
- 4 lettuce leaves
- 4 tomato slices

1. In a small bowl, mix the sauce ingredients; refrigerate until serving.

2. In a large bowl, combine the first seven burger ingredients. Add the chicken; mix lightly but thoroughly. Shape into four ½-in.-thick patties.

3. Moisten a paper towel with cooking oil; using long-handled tongs, rub on grill rack to coat lightly. Grill burgers, covered, over medium heat or broil 4 in. from heat 5-7 minutes on each side or until a thermometer reads 165°. Serve on buns with lettuce, tomato and sauce.

PER SERVING *350 cal., 12 g fat (4 g sat. fat), 78 mg chol., 732 mg sodium, 35 g carb., 3 g fiber, 27 g pro.* **Diabetic Exchanges:** *3 lean meat, 2 starch, 1 vegetable.*

"The original recipe for these burgers called for lamb or beef, but I decided to try ground chicken to decrease the fat. The sauce nicely doubles as a dip for veggies and toasted pita chips." —**JUDY PUSKAS** WALLACEBURG, ON

GREEK-STYLE CHICKEN BURGERS

Grilled Italian Burgers

When all I had available was ground beef and I was tired of plain-old hamburgers, I invented these. Italian seasonings and mozzarella cheese make them unique. They're great with homemade French fries.
—**REBEKAH BEYER** SABETHA, KS

START TO FINISH: 20 MIN.
MAKES: 4 SERVINGS

- 1 cup (4 ounces) shredded part-skim mozzarella cheese, divided
- 1 teaspoon Worcestershire sauce
- ¼ teaspoon Italian seasoning
- ⅛ teaspoon salt
- ⅛ teaspoon pepper
- 1 pound ground beef
  Marinara or spaghetti sauce, warmed

1. In a large bowl, combine ½ cup cheese and seasonings. Add beef; mix lightly but thoroughly. Shape into four ½-in.-thick patties.
2. Grill the burgers, covered, over medium heat or broil 4 in. from heat 4-5 minutes on each side or until a thermometer reads 160°. Sprinkle with remaining cheese; grill, covered, 1-2 minutes longer or until cheese is melted. Serve with marinara sauce.

SWEET-CHILI SALMON WITH BLACKBERRIES

Sweet-Chili Salmon with Blackberries

My garden is often my cooking inspiration. Because I have a large berry patch, I especially enjoy using just-picked berries in savory dishes. They add natural sweetness and a pop of tanginess.
—**ROXANNE CHAN** ALBANY, CA

START TO FINISH: 25 MIN.
MAKES: 4 SERVINGS

- 1 cup fresh or frozen blackberries, thawed
- 1 cup finely chopped English cucumber
- 1 green onion, finely chopped
- 2 tablespoons sweet chili sauce, divided
- 4 salmon fillets (6 ounces each)
- ½ teaspoon salt
- ½ teaspoon pepper

1. In a small bowl, combine the blackberries, cucumber, green onion and 1 tablespoon chili sauce; toss to coat. Moisten a paper towel with cooking oil; using long-handled tongs, rub on the grill rack to coat lightly. Sprinkle salmon with salt and pepper.
2. Place fillets on grill rack, skin side down. Grill, covered, over medium-high heat or broil 4 in. from heat for 10-12 minutes or until fish flakes easily with a fork, brushing with remaining chili sauce during the last 2-3 minutes of cooking. Serve with blackberry mixture.
PER SERVING *303 cal., 16 g fat (3 g sat. fat), 85 mg chol., 510 mg sodium, 9 g carb., 2 g fiber, 30 g pro.* **Diabetic Exchanges:** *5 lean meat, ½ starch.*

GRILLED ITALIAN BURGERS

SPICY PORK TENDERLOIN

Bacon-Wrapped Hamburgers

Since South Dakota summers are so short, we grill out as often as we can when the weather is warm. By mixing the cheese into the burger, I know I can get a little cheese in every delicious bite.

—DANA MATTHIES PARKER, SD

START TO FINISH: 25 MIN.
MAKES: 6 SERVINGS

- ½ **cup shredded cheddar cheese**
- ½ **cup finely chopped onion**
- 1 **egg, lightly beaten**
- 2 **tablespoons ketchup**
- 1 **tablespoon grated Parmesan cheese**
- 1 **tablespoon Worcestershire sauce**
- ½ **teaspoon salt**
- ⅛ **teaspoon pepper**
- 1 **pound ground beef**
- 6 **bacon strips**
- 6 **hamburger buns, split**

1. In a large bowl, combine the first eight ingredients. Add beef; mix thoroughly. Shape into six patties. Wrap a bacon strip around sides of each patty; secure with a toothpick.
2. Grill the burgers, covered, over medium heat or broil 4 in. from heat 5-6 minutes on each side or until a thermometer reads 160°. Discard toothpicks. Serve on buns.

BACON-WRAPPED HAMBURGERS

Spicy Pork Tenderloin

A friend shared this recipe for marvelously seasoned pork years ago. It really sparks up a barbecue and has been popular whenever I've served it.

—DIANA STEGER PROSPECT, KY

PREP: 5 MIN. + CHILLING • **GRILL:** 25 MIN.
MAKES: 8 SERVINGS

- 1 **to 3 tablespoon chili powder**
- 1 **teaspoon salt**
- ¼ **teaspoon ground ginger**
- ¼ **teaspoon ground thyme**
- ¼ **teaspoon pepper**
- 2 **pork tenderloins (about 1 pound each)**

1. Combine the first five ingredients; rub over tenderloins. Cover and refrigerate for 2-4 hours.
2. Grill, covered, over medium-hot indirect heat for 25-40 minutes or until a thermometer reads 145°. Let stand 5 minutes before slicing.
PER SERVING 135 cal., 4 g fat (1 g sat. fat), 63 mg chol., 350 mg sodium, 1 g carb., trace fiber, 23 g pro. **Diabetic Exchange:** 3½ lean meat.

GRILLED BANANAS FOSTER

FAST FIX
Curried Pork & Orange Kabobs

I love the sweet flavor of red, yellow and orange peppers. I always go for them in the summer when they're inexpensive and plentiful. They taste so much better than green ones.

—**LIV VORS** PETERBOROUGH, ON

START TO FINISH: 30 MIN.
MAKES: 4 SERVINGS

- ½ cup canola oil
- 2 tablespoons dried minced onion
- 1 garlic clove, minced
- 1 to 2 tablespoons curry powder
- ½ teaspoon each ground cumin, coriander and cinnamon
- 1½ pounds pork tenderloin
- 1 large sweet red pepper
- 1 large sweet yellow or orange pepper
- 1 small onion
- 1 large unpeeled navel orange

1. In a small bowl, mix oil, minced onion, garlic and spices; reserve half of the mixture for basting kabobs while cooking. Cut pork, peppers, onion and unpeeled orange into 1-in. pieces. On four metal or soaked wooden skewers, alternately thread pork, vegetables and orange; brush with remaining curry mixture.

2. Grill kabobs, covered, over medium heat 10-15 minutes or until the pork and vegetables are tender, turning occasionally. Baste frequently with reserved curry mixture during the last 4 minutes of cooking.

CURRIED PORK & ORANGE KABOBS

⑤INGREDIENTS FAST FIX
Grilled Bananas Foster

This wonderful version of the classic dessert is made on the grill. Just add ice cream and you have a heavenly treat without heating up your kitchen.

—**KATHLEEN HEDGER** FAIRVIEW HEIGHTS, IL

START TO FINISH: 20 MIN.
MAKES: 4 SERVINGS

- ⅓ cup packed brown sugar
- ¼ cup butter, melted
- 2 tablespoons rum or unsweetened apple juice
- 4 medium bananas
- 2 cups vanilla ice cream

1. In a small bowl, combine the brown sugar, butter and rum. Cut bananas into 1-in. slices; place each banana on a double thickness of heavy-duty foil (about 18 in. x 12 in.). Top with brown sugar mixture. Fold foil around banana mixture; seal packets tightly.

2. Grill, covered, over medium heat for 7-9 minutes or until bananas are tender. Open foil carefully to allow steam to escape. Serve with ice cream.

top tip

3-Ingredient Sweets

Grill up one of these sweet ideas to round out your next barbecue:

- Sandwich mini marshmallows and chocolate chips into frozen waffles; wrap in foil and grill.
- Grill sliced pound cake; serve with whipped cream and your favorite berry sauce.
- Peel tangerines; slice into thick wheels. Toss with orange liqueur, then grill. Serve with vanilla ice cream.

Favorite Chili Cheeseburgers

I like to experiment when making hamburgers. Stuffing them with sharp cheddar cheese makes them absolutely delicious. For lighter fare, I sometimes use a combination of lean ground beef and ground turkey.

—DEB WILLIAMS PEORIA, AZ

START TO FINISH: 20 MIN.
MAKES: 4 SERVINGS

- 1 **pound ground beef**
- 2 **tablespoons chili sauce**
- 1 **tablespoon chili powder**
- ½ **cup shredded cheddar cheese**
- 4 **hamburger-size pretzel buns or hamburger buns, split**
- ½ **cup nacho cheese sauce, warmed**

1. In a large bowl, combine the beef, chili sauce and chili powder, mixing lightly but thoroughly. Shape the mixture into eight ¼-in.-thick patties. Place 2 tablespoons cheese on the center of each of four patties. Top with remaining patties; press edges firmly to seal.

2. Grill burgers, covered, over medium heat or broil 4 in. from heat 4-6 minutes on each side or until a thermometer reads 160°. Serve on buns with cheese sauce.

GRILLED PEACHES 'N' BERRIES

FAVORITE CHILI CHEESEBURGERS

EAT SMART **(5)INGREDIENTS FAST FIX**
Grilled Peaches 'n' Berries

Highlight the natural sweetness of peak summertime fruit with brown sugar, butter and a squeeze of lemon juice. Foil packets make this a go-anywhere dessert.

—SHARON BICKETT CHESTER, SC

START TO FINISH: 30 MIN.
MAKES: 2 SERVINGS

- 2 **medium ripe peaches, halved and pitted**
- ½ **cup fresh blueberries**
- 1 **tablespoon brown sugar**
- 2 **teaspoons lemon juice**
- 4 **teaspoons butter**

1. Place two peach halves, cut side up, on each of two double thicknesses of heavy-duty foil (12 in. square). Sprinkle each with blueberries, brown sugar and lemon juice; dot with butter. Fold foil around peaches and seal tightly.

2. Grill, covered, over medium-low heat for 18-20 minutes or until tender. Open foil carefully to allow steam to escape.

PER SERVING *156 cal., 8 g fat (5 g sat. fat), 20 mg chol., 57 mg sodium, 23 g carb., 2 g fiber, 1 g pro.* **Diabetic Exchanges:** *1 fruit, 1 fat, ½ starch.*

Steve Cayford's
Beernana Bread
PAGE 239

Sides & More

Jazz up your meal with nutritious veggies, shortcut breads, crisp salads, pretty pastas and more. No matter what's for dinner, find the perfect companion right here.

**Blair Lonergan's
Roasted Potato &
Green Bean Salad**
PAGE 232

**Marcy Griffith's
Mojito Marinated Fruit**
PAGE 228

**Kris Bristol's
Blueberry Romaine Salad**
PAGE 231

Greek Three-Bean Salad

Green, kidney and wax beans combine for a summer classic with a tasty twist. Thanks to some bold Mediterranean flavors, it's not hard to close your eyes and imagine yourself on a Greek island.
—VIVIAN LEVINE SUMMERFIELD, FL

START TO FINISH: 25 MIN.
MAKES: 10 SERVINGS

- 2 cups frozen cut green beans, thawed
- 1 can (16 ounces) kidney beans, rinsed and drained
- 1 can (14½ ounces) cut wax beans, drained
- 1 medium red onion, halved and sliced
- 1 can (6 ounces) pitted ripe olives, drained
- ½ cup julienned green pepper
- ½ cup peeled, seeded and chopped cucumber
- ¾ cup bottled Greek vinaigrette
- 1 cup (4 ounces) crumbled feta cheese

Combine the first seven ingredients in a large salad bowl. Drizzle with vinaigrette; toss to coat. Chill until serving and sprinkle with cheese. Serve with a slotted spoon.

GREEK THREE-BEAN SALAD

MOJITO MARINATED FRUIT

Mojito Marinated Fruit

All the flavors of the popular Mojito cocktail are featured in this fantastic salad. After you eat the fruit, you'll want to sip the luscious syrup!
—MARCY GRIFFITH EXCELSIOR, MN

PREP: 20 MIN. + CHILLING
MAKES: 8 SERVINGS

- ⅔ cup sugar
- ⅓ cup water
- ½ cup light rum
- 2 tablespoons lime juice
- 1 teaspoon grated lime peel
- 2 cups each cantaloupe, honeydew and seedless watermelon balls
- 2 cups cubed fresh pineapple
- 3 mint sprigs
  Fresh mint leaves, optional

1. In a small saucepan, combine sugar and water; cook and stir over medium heat until sugar is dissolved. Remove from heat. Stir in rum, lime juice and peel. Cool completely.

2. In a large bowl, combine melons, pineapple and mint sprigs. Add rum mixture; toss to coat. Refrigerate, covered, overnight.

3. Discard mint sprigs. Spoon fruit with syrup into serving dishes. If desired, top with mint.

RIGATONI CHARD TOSS

"I had to get my firefighter husband to eat more fruits and veggies to lower his cholesterol and triglycerides. Fresh chard adds fiber and vitamins, but we love it for the flavor. While he would never admit to eating health food around the firehouse, this dish is one of many that made his trips to the doctor much more pleasant!"

—CAROLYN KUMPE EL DORADO, CA

Quick Cheesy Onion Focaccia

Turn an everyday dinner into a special meal with oven-fresh cheese bread that starts with convenient bread dough.

—TASTE OF HOME TEST KITCHEN

START TO FINISH: 30 MIN.
MAKES: 12 SERVINGS

- 2 medium onions, halved and thinly sliced
- 3 tablespoons butter
- 3 garlic cloves, minced
- 2 teaspoons Italian seasoning
- 2 teaspoons brown sugar
- 1 loaf (1 pound) frozen bread dough, thawed
- 1 cup (4 ounces) shredded cheddar cheese
- 2 tablespoons grated Parmesan cheese

1. Saute onions in butter in a large skillet until tender. Add the garlic, Italian seasoning and brown sugar; cook 2 minutes longer.
2. Pat dough into a 10-in. circle on an ungreased 12-in. pizza pan. Build up edges slightly. Make indentations at 1-in. intervals with a wooden spoon handle. Top with onion mixture and cheeses.
3. Bake at 425° for 10-15 minutes or until golden brown. Cut into wedges; serve warm.

Rigatoni Chard Toss

PREP: 25 MIN. • **COOK:** 20 MIN.
MAKES: 11 SERVINGS

- 8 ounces uncooked rigatoni or large tube pasta
- 2 tablespoons olive oil
- 1 bunch Swiss chard, coarsely chopped
- 1 small onion, thinly sliced
- 2 garlic cloves, minced
- 3 medium tomatoes, chopped
- 1 can (15 ounces) white kidney or cannellini beans, rinsed and drained
- ½ teaspoon salt
- ⅛ teaspoon crushed red pepper flakes
- ⅛ teaspoon fennel seed, crushed
- ⅛ teaspoon pepper
- ¼ cup minced fresh basil
- ½ cup grated Parmesan cheese

1. Cook the rigatoni according to package directions.
2. Meanwhile, in a large skillet, heat oil over medium-high heat. Add Swiss chard and onion; cook and stir 4 minutes. Add garlic; cook 2 minutes longer. Stir in tomatoes, beans, salt, pepper flakes, fennel seed and pepper. Cook 3-4 minutes longer or until chard is tender.
3. Drain rigatoni, reserving ¼ cup pasta water. Add rigatoni, pasta water and basil to skillet; toss to combine. Serve with cheese.

PER SERVING *159 cal., 4 g fat (1 g sat. fat), 3 mg chol., 291 mg sodium, 24 g carb., 3 g fiber, 7 g pro.* **Diabetic Exchanges:** *1½ starch, ½ fat.*

QUICK CHEESY ONION FOCACCIA

Mushroom & Onion Crescents

I knew these stuffed crescents were keepers when my husband ate most of the filling before I could roll it into the dough. I've had to get sneaky now when I make them.

—CARRIE POMMIER LAKEVILLE, MN

PREP: 25 MIN. • **BAKE:** 25 MIN.
MAKES: 8 ROLLS

- **3 tablespoons butter, divided**
- **1 cup sliced baby portobello mushrooms**
- **1 medium onion, halved and sliced**
- **3 garlic cloves, minced**
- **⅓ cup grated Parmesan cheese**
- **1 tablespoon minced fresh parsley**
- **1 tube (8 ounces) refrigerated reduced-fat crescent rolls**
- **½ cup shredded part-skim mozzarella cheese**

1. Preheat oven to 375°. In a large skillet, heat 2 tablespoons butter over medium-high heat. Add mushrooms and onion; cook and stir 2-3 minutes or until softened. Reduce heat to medium-low; cook and stir 10-12 minutes or until onion is golden. Add garlic; cook 1 minute longer. Remove from heat; stir in Parmesan cheese and parsley.

2. Unroll crescent dough; separate into triangles. Place 1 tablespoon mushroom mixture at the wide end of each triangle; top with 1 tablespoon mozzarella cheese. Roll up and seal edges. Place 2 in. apart on an ungreased baking sheet, point side down; curve ends to form a crescent. Melt remaining butter; brush over tops.

3. Bake 10-12 minutes or until golden brown. Refrigerate leftovers.

Sour Cream Potatoes

This is an old recipe from Mom with a few of my updates. Paprika gives the potatoes gorgeous color and just a hint of spice. One year, my aunt made these potatoes at a family gathering and grabbed the cayenne pepper instead of the paprika. When we all sat down to eat, our mouths were on fire from the unexpected heat!

—KRISTA KLIEBENSTEIN
HIGHLANDS RANCH, CO

PREP: 30 MIN. • **BAKE:** 30 MIN.
MAKES: 10 SERVINGS

- 10 medium red potatoes, peeled and quartered
- 1 package (8 ounces) cream cheese, cubed
- 1 cup (8 ounces) sour cream
- ¼ cup 2% milk
- 2 tablespoons butter, divided
- 1 tablespoon dried parsley flakes
- 1¼ teaspoons garlic salt
- ¼ teaspoon paprika

1. Place potatoes in a large saucepan and cover with water. Bring to a boil. Reduce heat; cover and cook for 15-20 minutes or until tender. Drain.
2. In a large bowl, mash the potatoes. Add the cream cheese, sour cream, milk, 1 tablespoon butter, parsley and garlic salt; beat until smooth.
3. Spoon into a greased 2-qt. baking dish. Dot with remaining butter; sprinkle with paprika. Bake, uncovered, at 350° for 30-40 minutes or until heated through.

SOUR CREAM POTATOES

BLUEBERRY ROMAINE SALAD

FAST FIX ▸
Blueberry Romaine Salad

I love to bring this salad to school functions. The homemade vinaigrette couldn't be simpler. I make the dressing in advance and give everything a quick toss when I get to the event.

—KRIS BRISTOL CHARLOTTE, MI

START TO FINISH: 15 MIN.
MAKES: 8 SERVINGS

- ⅓ cup white vinegar
- ¼ cup sugar
- 1 tablespoon chopped red onion
- 2 teaspoons poppy seeds
- 1 teaspoon ground mustard
- ½ teaspoon salt
- ¼ teaspoon pepper
  Dash Worcestershire sauce
- 1 cup canola oil

SALAD
- 1 package (10 ounces) hearts of romaine salad mix
- 1 cup unsalted cashews
- 1 cup (4 ounces) shredded Swiss cheese
- 1 cup fresh blueberries

In a small bowl, whisk the first eight ingredients. Gradually whisk in oil. In a large bowl, combine salad ingredients. To serve, pour dressing over salad; toss to coat.

top tip
Potatoes with Pop

Instead of adding butter and cream to my mashed potatoes, I use flavored cream cheese—usually chive and onion. This really enhances the potatoes.

—MARGARET M.
CLINTON TOWNSHIP, MI

Roasted Potato & Green Bean Salad

I made this salad to take advantage of in-season potatoes, onions and green beans. It's a fresh twist on the tangy German potato salad my mom used to make.

—BLAIR LONERGAN ROCHELLE, VA

PREP: 15 MIN. • **BAKE:** 25 MIN.
MAKES: 7 SERVINGS

- 6 medium red potatoes, cut into 1-inch cubes
- 1 large red onion, cut into 1-inch pieces
- ¼ pound fresh green beans, trimmed and halved
- 2 tablespoons olive oil
- 8 bacon strips, cooked and crumbled

VINAIGRETTE
- 2 tablespoons cider vinegar
- 1 tablespoon minced fresh thyme or 1 teaspoon dried thyme
- 1 tablespoon lemon juice
- 1 tablespoon Dijon mustard
- ½ teaspoon salt
- ¼ teaspoon pepper
- ¼ cup olive oil

1. Preheat oven to 425°. Place potatoes, onion and green beans in a greased 15x10x1-in. baking pan. Drizzle with oil; toss to coat.

2. Roast 25-30 minutes or until tender, stirring twice. Transfer to a large bowl; add bacon. In a small bowl, whisk the first six vinaigrette ingredients. Gradually whisk in oil until blended. Pour over potato mixture; toss to coat. Serve warm.

ROASTED POTATO & GREEN BEAN SALAD

KASHA VARNISHKES

Kasha Varnishkes

This is one of the great Jewish comfort foods. It's easy to put together, and leftovers make a surprisingly delicious breakfast. Find kasha with other grains or in the kosher foods section.

—JOANNE WEINTRAUB MILWAUKEE, WI

PREP: 10 MIN. • **COOK:** 25 MIN.
MAKES: 8 SERVINGS

- 4 cups uncooked bow tie pasta
- 2 large onions, chopped
- 1 cup sliced fresh mushrooms
- 2 tablespoons canola oil
- 1 cup roasted whole grain buckwheat groats (kasha)
- 1 egg, lightly beaten
- 2 cups chicken broth, heated
- ½ teaspoon salt
  Dash pepper
  Minced fresh parsley

1. Cook pasta according to package directions. Meanwhile, saute onions and mushrooms in oil in a large skillet until lightly browned, about 9 minutes. Remove from pan and set aside.

2. Combine buckwheat groats and egg in a small bowl; add to the same skillet. Cook and stir over high heat for 2-4 minutes or until buckwheat is browned, separating grains with the back of a spoon. Add the hot broth, salt and pepper.

3. Bring to a boil; add onion mixture. Reduce heat; cover and simmer for 10-12 minutes or until liquid is absorbed. Drain pasta; add to pan and heat through. Sprinkle with parsley.

VEGETABLE AND BARLEY PILAF

EAT SMART | FAST FIX

Feta Romaine Salad

My friend Cathy, who is of Greek heritage, prepared this simple salad for me. She served it with lamb chops and pitas to create a classic Mediterranean meal.

—MICHAEL VOLPATT SAN FRANCISCO, CA

START TO FINISH: 15 MIN.
MAKES: 6 SERVINGS

- 1 bunch romaine, chopped
- 3 plum tomatoes, seeded and chopped
- 1 cup (4 ounces) crumbled feta cheese
- 1 cup chopped seeded cucumber
- ½ cup Greek olives, chopped
- 2 tablespoons minced fresh parsley
- 2 tablespoons minced fresh cilantro
- 3 tablespoons lemon juice
- 2 tablespoons olive oil
- ¼ teaspoon pepper

In a large bowl, combine the first seven ingredients. In a small bowl, whisk the remaining ingredients. Drizzle over salad; toss to coat. Serve immediately.
PER SERVING *139 cal., 11 g fat (3 g sat. fat), 10 mg chol., 375 mg sodium, 6 g carb., 3 g fiber, 5 g pro.* **Diabetic Exchanges:** *2 fat, 1 vegetable.*

FETA ROMAINE SALAD

EAT SMART

Caraway Coleslaw with Citrus Mayonnaise

I always get requests to bring a big batch of this unique coleslaw to potlucks—proof that it's a keeper. I like to make it a day ahead so the flavors can blend.

—LILY JULOW LAWRENCEVILLE, GA

PREP: 20 MIN. + CHILLING
MAKES: 12 SERVINGS (⅔ CUP EACH)

- 1 medium head cabbage, finely shredded
- 1 tablespoon sugar
- 2 teaspoons salt

DRESSING

- ⅔ cup reduced-fat mayonnaise
- ⅓ cup orange juice
- 3 tablespoons cider vinegar
- 2 tablespoons caraway seeds
- 2 teaspoons grated orange peel
- ¼ teaspoon salt
- ¼ teaspoon pepper

1. Place cabbage in a colander over a plate. Sprinkle with sugar and salt; toss to coat. Let stand 1 hour.
2. In a small bowl, whisk the dressing ingredients until blended. Rinse cabbage and drain well; place in a large bowl. Add dressing; toss to coat. Refrigerate, covered, overnight.
PER SERVING *75 cal., 5 g fat (1 g sat. fat), 5 mg chol., 366 mg sodium, 8 g carb., 2 g fiber, 1 g pro.* **Diabetic Exchanges:** *1 vegetable, 1 fat.*

EAT SMART | FAST FIX

Vegetable and Barley Pilaf

My nutritious dish features barley, which is a good source of soluble fiber. You should feel free to toss in whatever fresh vegetables you have on hand.

—JESSE KLAUSMEIER BURBANK, CA

START TO FINISH: 30 MIN.
MAKES: 4 SERVINGS

- 1 large zucchini, quartered and sliced
- 1 large carrot, chopped
- 1 tablespoon butter
- 2 cups reduced-sodium chicken broth
- 1 cup quick-cooking barley
- 2 green onions, chopped
- ½ teaspoon dried marjoram
- ¼ teaspoon salt
- ⅛ teaspoon pepper

1. Saute the zucchini and carrot in butter in a large saucepan until crisp-tender. Add broth; bring to a boil. Stir in barley. Reduce heat; cover and simmer for 10-12 minutes or until barley is tender.
2. Stir in the onions, marjoram, salt and pepper. Remove from the heat; cover and let stand for 5 minutes.
PER SERVING *219 cal., 4 g fat (2 g sat. fat), 8 mg chol., 480 mg sodium, 39 g carb., 10 g fiber, 9 g pro.*

LOADED POTATO SALAD

Loaded Potato Salad

Get a load of this: sour cream, bacon, shredded cheddar, green onions and more come together to give you all the richness of restaurant potato skins at your next picnic.

—**MONIQUE BOULANGER** GREENWOOD, NS

PREP: 30 MIN. + CHILLING
MAKES: 8 SERVINGS

- 2 pounds red potatoes, quartered
- ½ pound bacon strips, chopped
- ½ cup mayonnaise
- ¼ cup creamy Caesar salad dressing
- ¼ cup ranch salad dressing
- 3 tablespoons sour cream
- 1 tablespoon Dijon mustard
- 3 green onions, chopped
- ¼ cup shredded cheddar cheese
   Coarsely ground pepper, optional

1. Place potatoes in a large saucepan and cover with water. Bring to a boil. Reduce heat; cover and cook 15-20 minutes or until tender.
2. Meanwhile, cook bacon in a large skillet over medium heat until crisp. Remove to paper towels; drain, reserving 3 tablespoons drippings.
3. Drain potatoes and place in a large bowl. Add bacon and reserved drippings; toss to coat. Refrigerate until chilled.
4. Whisk the mayonnaise, dressings, sour cream and mustard in a small bowl. Pour over potato mixture; toss to coat. Stir in onions and cheese. Sprinkle with pepper if desired.

⑤ INGREDIENTS

French Onion Pan Rolls

A crusty topping of Parmesan cheese and onion soup mix adds lots of flavor to these golden brown rolls. They're great with a bowl of soup or a salad. I often use frozen rolls to make preparation even easier.

—**ANNE PRINCE** ELKHORN, WI

PREP: 30 MIN. + RISING • **BAKE:** 30 MIN.
MAKES: 20 ROLLS

- 2 loaves (1 pound each) frozen bread dough, thawed
- 1 cup grated Parmesan cheese
- 1 envelope onion soup mix
- ½ cup butter, melted

HERBED NOODLES WITH EDAMAME

1. Divide the bread dough into 20 portions; shape each into a ball. In a shallow bowl, combine cheese and soup mix. Place butter in another shallow bowl.
2. Roll each ball in butter, then in the cheese mixture. Arrange in a greased 13-in. x 9-in. baking dish. Cover and let rise in a warm place until doubled, about 45 minutes.

Bake at 350° for 30-35 minutes or until golden brown. Remove from dish to wire rack. Serve warm.

EAT SMART FAST FIX

Herbed Noodles with Edamame

Serve this side dish and you'll give your meal flavor and color! All the fresh herbs make it feel extra-special.

—**MARIE RIZZIO** INTERLOCHEN, MI

START TO FINISH: 30 MIN.
MAKES: 4 SERVINGS

- 3½ cups uncooked egg noodles
- 2 tablespoons butter
- 1 green onion, sliced
- 1 tablespoon finely chopped sweet red pepper
- ½ cup frozen shelled edamame, thawed
- ¼ cup reduced-sodium chicken broth
- 1 tablespoon minced fresh parsley
- 1½ teaspoons minced fresh marjoram
- 1½ teaspoons minced fresh chives
- 1 tablespoon olive oil
- ¼ cup grated Romano cheese

1. Cook noodles according to package directions. Meanwhile, in a large skillet, heat butter over medium-high heat. Add onion and red pepper; cook and stir until tender. Stir in edamame and broth; heat through. Add herbs.
2. Drain noodles and add to skillet; toss to combine. Transfer to a serving plate. Drizzle with oil and sprinkle with cheese.
PER SERVING *264 cal., 14 g fat (6 g sat. fat), 50 mg chol., 214 mg sodium, 26 g carb., 2 g fiber, 10 g pro.*

Tossed Pepperoni Pizza Salad

START TO FINISH: 20 MIN
MAKES: 5 SERVINGS

- ¼ **cup sun-dried tomatoes (not packed in oil)**
- 1 **cup boiling water**
- 3 **cups torn leaf lettuce**
- ¾ **cup cubed part-skim mozzarella cheese**
- 2 **ounces sliced pepperoni, quartered (about ½ cup)**
- 6 **slices red onion, separated into rings**
- ½ **cup chopped green pepper**
- ½ **cup chopped sweet red pepper**
- ½ **cup grape tomatoes, halved**
- ¼ **cup grated Parmesan cheese**
- ¼ **cup sun-dried tomato salad dressing**
- 1 **teaspoon Italian seasoning**
- ½ **teaspoon garlic powder**

1. In a small bowl, combine sun-dried tomatoes and boiling water. Let stand 5 minutes; drain.
2. In a large bowl, combine lettuce, mozzarella cheese, pepperoni, onion, peppers, grape tomatoes, Parmesan cheese and sun-dried tomatoes. In a small bowl, whisk salad dressing, Italian seasoning and garlic powder; drizzle over salad and toss to coat. Serve immediately.
PER SERVING *183 cal., 12 g fat (5 g sat. fat), 24 mg chol., 580 mg sodium, 9 g carb., 2 g fiber, 10 g pro.* **Diabetic Exchanges:** *1 medium-fat meat, 1 vegetable, 1 fat.*

"Sun-dried tomato dressing is a perfect complement to the peppers, cheese and pepperoni in this pizzalicious salad. For a change of pace, I sometimes omit the dressing and drizzle the mozzarella cubes with olive oil instead." —LISA DEMARSH MOUNT SOLON, VA

TOSSED PEPPERONI PIZZA SALAD

LEMON COUSCOUS WITH BROCCOLI

Lemon Couscous with Broccoli

I combined two recipes to create this side dish of broccoli and pasta. The splash of lemon adds nice flavor. Instead of toasted almonds, you could sprinkle servings with grated Parmesan cheese.
—**BETH DAUENHAUER** PUEBLO, CO

START TO FINISH: 25 MIN.
MAKES: 6 SERVINGS

- 1 **tablespoon olive oil**
- 4 **cups fresh broccoli florets, cut into small pieces**
- 1 **cup uncooked whole wheat couscous**
- 2 **garlic cloves, minced**
- 1¼ **cups reduced-sodium chicken broth**
- 1 **teaspoon grated lemon peel**
- 1 **teaspoon lemon juice**
- ½ **teaspoon salt**
- ½ **teaspoon dried basil**
- ¼ **teaspoon coarsely ground pepper**
- 1 **tablespoon slivered almonds, toasted**

1. In a large skillet, heat oil over medium-high heat. Add broccoli; cook and stir until crisp-tender.
2. Add couscous and garlic; cook and stir 1-2 minutes longer. Stir in broth and seasonings; bring to a boil. Remove from heat; let stand, covered, 5-10 minutes or until broth is absorbed. Fluff with a fork. Sprinkle with almonds.
PER SERVING *115 cal., 3 g fat (trace sat. fat), 0 chol., 328 mg sodium, 18 g carb., 4 g fiber, 5 g pro.* **Diabetic Exchanges:** *1 starch, ½ fat.*

(5)INGREDIENTS
Garlic-Chive Baked Fries

No one can resist crispy, golden-brown fries seasoned with garlic and fresh chives. They're great with a steak.

—STEVE WESTPHAL WIND LAKE, WI

PREP: 15 MIN. • **BAKE:** 20 MIN.
MAKES: 4 SERVINGS

- 4 medium russet potatoes
- 1 tablespoon olive oil
- 4 teaspoons dried minced chives
- ½ teaspoon salt
- ½ teaspoon garlic powder
- ¼ teaspoon pepper

1. Cut potatoes into ¼-in. julienne strips. Rinse well and pat dry.
2. Transfer potatoes to a large bowl. Drizzle with oil; sprinkle with the remaining ingredients. Toss to coat. Arrange in a single layer on two 15-in. x 10-in. x 1-in. baking pans coated with cooking spray.
3. Bake at 450° for 20-25 minutes or until lightly browned, turning once.

MOZZARELLA PEPPERONI BREAD

GARLIC-CHIVE BAKED FRIES

(5)INGREDIENTS FAST FIX
Mozzarella Pepperoni Bread

My family enjoys this tempting bread as an appetizer when we have company and as a quick meal on hectic evenings. With five children at home, all involved in sports, we have this hot snack sandwich often.

—TERRI TOTI SAN ANTONIO, TX

START TO FINISH: 30 MIN.
MAKES: 18 SLICES

- 1 loaf (1 pound) French bread
- 3 tablespoons butter, melted
- 3 ounces sliced turkey pepperoni
- 1½ cups (6 ounces) shredded part-skim mozzarella cheese
- 3 tablespoons minced fresh parsley

1. Cut loaf of bread in half widthwise; cut each half into 1-in. slices, leaving slices attached at bottom. Brush butter on both sides of each slice. Arrange pepperoni between slices; sprinkle with cheese and parsley.
2. Place on an ungreased baking sheet. Bake at 350° for 12-15 minutes or until cheese is melted.

(5)INGREDIENTS FAST FIX
Holiday Peas

My mom used to dress up peas with buttery cracker crumbs on top when I was a little girl, and it remains one of my favorite dishes. Just about any type of savory cracker can be used in this irresistible dish.

—SUE GRONHOLZ BEAVER DAM, WI

START TO FINISH: 20 MIN.
MAKES: 12 SERVINGS

- 2 packages (16 ounces each) frozen peas
- 2 teaspoons salt
- 1 cup finely crushed wheat crackers
- 2 tablespoons grated Parmesan cheese
- 2 tablespoons butter, melted

1. Place peas in a large saucepan; add salt. Cover with water. Bring to a boil. Reduce heat; cover and simmer for 5-6 minutes or until tender.
2. Meanwhile, toss the cracker crumbs, cheese and butter. Drain peas and place in a serving bowl; top with crumb mixture.

SWISS & CARAWAY FLATBREADS

Swiss & Caraway Flatbreads

My mom came across this rustic-looking flatbread recipe many years ago and always made it on Christmas Eve. Now I make it for my own family, especially during the holidays. It's easy to double or cut in half, depending on how many you're serving.

—**DIANE BERGER** SEQUIM, WA

PREP: 20 MIN. + RISING • **BAKE:** 10 MIN.
MAKES: 2 LOAVES (16 PIECES EACH)

- 2 **loaves (1 pound each) frozen bread dough, thawed**
- ¼ **cup butter, melted**
- ¼ **cup canola oil**
- 1 **tablespoon dried minced onion**
- 1 **tablespoon Dijon mustard**
- 2 **teaspoons caraway seeds**
- 1 **teaspoon Worcestershire sauce**
- 1 **tablespoon dry sherry, optional**
- 2 **cups (8 ounces) shredded Swiss cheese**

1. On a lightly floured surface, roll each portion of dough into a 15x10-in. rectangle. Transfer to two greased 15x10x1-in. baking pans. Cover with kitchen towels; let rise in a warm place until doubled, about 45 minutes.
2. Preheat oven to 425°. Using fingertips, press several dimples into dough. In a small bowl, whisk melted butter, oil, onion, mustard, caraway seeds, Worcestershire sauce and, if desired, sherry until blended; brush over dough. Sprinkle with cheese. Bake 10-15 minutes or until golden brown. Serve warm.

Tangy Baked Apples

When the weather turns cooler in fall, these baked apples are sure to warm you up. Our family enjoys them with turkey, pork, even meat loaf. My husband and I like to add a bit more horseradish for extra zip. I got the recipe from my mom.

—**DEE POPPIE** GILMAN, IL

PREP: 10 MIN. • **BAKE:** 30 MIN.
MAKES: 6 SERVINGS

- 3 **medium tart apples**
- 2 **teaspoons lemon juice, divided**
- ⅓ **cup packed brown sugar**
- ⅓ **cup ketchup**
- 2 **tablespoons butter, softened**
- 2 **tablespoons prepared horseradish**
- ¼ **cup water**

1. Cut apples in half lengthwise; remove cores. Brush with 1 teaspoon lemon juice. Place in an ungreased 11-in. x 7-in. baking dish. Combine the brown sugar, ketchup, butter, horseradish and remaining lemon juice. Top each apple half with 2 tablespoons ketchup mixture. Pour water around apples.
2. Bake, uncovered, at 325° for 30 minutes or until apples are tender. Serve warm.

Bacon Caprese Salad

In summer, I am always looking for ways to use the fresh basil and tomatoes that grow in my garden. This recipe combines the two flavors in a wonderful salad.

—**MARY ANN TURK** JOPLIN, MO

START TO FINISH: 15 MIN.
MAKES: 12 SERVINGS

- 1 **pound fresh mozzarella cheese, cut into ¼-inch slices**
- 3 **plum tomatoes, cut into ¼-inch slices**
- 1½ **cups fresh baby spinach**
- 8 **bacon strips, cooked and crumbled**
- ½ **cup minced fresh basil**
- 2 **green onions, chopped**
- ¼ **cup balsamic vinaigrette**
- ½ **teaspoon salt**
- ¼ **teaspoon coarsely ground pepper**

Arrange cheese, tomatoes and spinach on a large serving platter; top with bacon, basil and green onions. Just before serving, drizzle salad with vinaigrette; sprinkle with salt and pepper.

TANGY BAKED APPLES

KIWI-STRAWBERRY SPINACH SALAD

Beernana Bread

Really, it's simple arithmetic...or something like that: Beer is good. Banana bread is good. Beernana bread is great! Even guys who don't know their way around the kitchen can pull this one off.

—STEVE CAYFORD DUBUQUE, IA

PREP: 15 MIN. • **BAKE:** 55 MIN. + COOLING
MAKES: 1 LOAF (16 SLICES)

- 3 **cups self-rising flour**
- ¾ **cup quick-cooking oats**
- ½ **cup packed brown sugar**
- 1½ **cups mashed ripe bananas (about 3 medium)**
- 1 **bottle (12 ounces) wheat beer**
- ¼ **cup maple syrup**
- 2 **tablespoons olive oil**
- 1 **tablespoon sesame seeds**
- ¼ **teaspoon kosher salt**

1. Preheat oven to 375°. In a large bowl, mix flour, oats and brown sugar. In another bowl, mix bananas, beer and maple syrup until blended. Add to flour mixture; stir just until moistened.

2. Transfer to a greased 9x5-in. loaf pan. Drizzle with oil; sprinkle with sesame seeds and salt. Bake 55-60 minutes or until a toothpick inserted in center comes out clean. Cool in pan 10 minutes before removing to wire rack to cool.

EAT SMART FAST FIX ▶
Kiwi-Strawberry Spinach Salad

This pretty salad is always a hit when I serve it. The recipe came from a cookbook, but I personalized it. Sometimes just a small change in ingredients can make a big difference.

—LAURA POUNDS ANDOVER, KS

START TO FINISH: 20 MIN.
MAKES: 12 SERVINGS (1 CUP EACH)

- ¼ **cup canola oil**
- ¼ **cup raspberry vinegar**
- ¼ **teaspoon Worcestershire sauce**
- ⅓ **cup sugar**
- ¼ **teaspoon paprika**
- 2 **green onions, chopped**
- 2 **tablespoons sesame seeds, toasted**
- 1 **tablespoon poppy seeds**
- 12 **cups torn fresh spinach (about 9 ounces)**
- 2 **pints fresh strawberries, halved**
- 4 **kiwifruit, peeled and sliced**

1. Place the first five ingredients in a blender; cover and process 30 seconds or until blended. Transfer to a bowl; stir in green onions, sesame seeds and poppy seeds.

2. In a large bowl, combine spinach, strawberries and kiwi. Drizzle with dressing; toss to coat.

PER SERVING *121 cal., 6 g fat (trace sat. fat), 0 chol., 64 mg sodium, 16 g carb., 4 g fiber, 3 g pro.* **Diabetic Exchanges:** *1 vegetable, 1 fat, ½ fruit.*

BEERNANA BREAD

COLORFUL BROCCOLI RICE

(5) INGREDIENTS
Parmesan-Ranch Pan Rolls

My mom taught me this easy recipe, which is great for feeding a crowd. There is never a crumb left over. Mom made her own bread dough, but using frozen dough is my shortcut.

—TRISHA KRUSE EAGLE, ID

PREP: 30 MIN. + RISING • **BAKE:** 20 MIN.
MAKES: 1½ DOZEN

- 2 loaves (1 pound each) frozen bread dough, thawed
- 1 cup grated Parmesan cheese
- ½ cup butter, melted
- 1 envelope buttermilk ranch salad dressing mix
- 1 small onion, finely chopped

1. On a lightly floured surface, divide dough into 18 portions; shape each into a ball. In a small bowl, combine the cheese, butter and ranch dressing mix.

2. Roll balls in cheese mixture; arrange in two greased 9-in. square baking pans. Sprinkle with onion. Cover and let rise in a warm place until doubled, about 45 minutes.

3. Bake at 350° for 20-25 minutes or until golden brown. Remove from pans to wire racks.

PARMESAN-RANCH PAN ROLLS

EAT SMART (5) INGREDIENTS FAST FIX
Colorful Broccoli Rice

I discovered this quick rice dish years ago. It's a favorite with many meals. The fresh flavor makes it a great accompaniment to all kinds of meats.

—GALE LALMOND DEERING, NH

START TO FINISH: 15 MIN.
MAKES: 2 SERVINGS

- ⅔ cup water
- 2 teaspoons butter
- 1 teaspoon reduced-sodium chicken bouillon granules
- 1 cup coarsely chopped fresh broccoli
- ½ cup instant brown rice
- 2 tablespoons chopped sweet red pepper

1. In a small microwave-safe bowl, combine the water, butter and bouillon. Cover and microwave on high for 1-2 minutes; stir until blended. Add the broccoli, rice and red pepper. Cover and cook 6-7 minutes longer or until broccoli is crisp-tender.

2. Let rice stand for 5 minutes. Fluff with a fork.

NOTE *This recipe was tested in a 1,100-watt microwave.*

PER SERVING *136 cal., 5 g fat (2 g sat. fat), 10 mg chol., 197 mg sodium, 20 g carb., 2 g fiber, 3 g pro.* **Diabetic Exchanges:** *1 starch, 1 fat.*

top tip
Flavorful Rice

Everyone loves it when I make instant rice with a can of beef consomme instead of water. Since I use equal amounts of consomme and rice, the soup can makes a handy measure for the rice.

—MARSHA G. CASS CITY, MI

MARMALADE CANDIED CARROTS

Marmalade Candied Carrots

Crisp-tender carrots with crunchy pecans and a sweet citrus glaze are perfect for special occasions. This is my favorite carrot recipe.

—**HEATHER CLEMMONS** SUPPLY, NC

START TO FINISH: 30 MIN.
MAKES: 8 SERVINGS

- 2 **pounds fresh baby carrots**
- ⅔ **cup orange marmalade**
- 3 **tablespoons brown sugar**
- 2 **tablespoons butter**
- ½ **cup chopped pecans, toasted**
- 1 **teaspoon rum extract**

1. In a large saucepan, place steamer basket over 1 in. of water. Place carrots in basket. Bring water to a boil. Reduce heat to maintain a low boil; steam, covered, 12-15 minutes or until carrots are crisp-tender.

2. Meanwhile, in a small saucepan, combine marmalade, brown sugar and butter; cook and stir over medium heat until mixture is thickened and reduced to about ½ cup. Stir in pecans and extract.

3. Place carrots in a large bowl. Add marmalade mixture and stir to coat.

Garlic Herb Bread

This bread needs just 10 minutes of prep and the bread machine does the rest. You'll love the aroma that fills your house as it bakes.

—**TRISHA KRUSE** EAGLE, ID

PREP: 10 MIN. • **BAKE:** 3 HOURS
MAKES: 1 LOAF (1½ POUNDS, 16 SLICES)

- 1 **cup warm water (70° to 80°)**
- ¼ **cup evaporated milk**
- 2 **tablespoons olive oil**
- 3 **garlic cloves, minced**
- 4½ **teaspoons dried parsley flakes**
- 1 **tablespoon nonfat dry milk powder**
- 1 **tablespoon sugar**
- 1½ **teaspoons salt**
- 1 **teaspoon dried rosemary, crushed**
- ½ **teaspoon dried oregano**
- 3 **cups bread flour**
- 1 **package (¼ ounce) active dry yeast**

1. Place all of the ingredients in order suggested by manufacturer in bread machine pan. Select basic bread setting. Choose crust color and loaf size if available.

2. Bake according to bread machine directions. Check the dough after 5 minutes of mixing; add 1 to 2 tablespoons of water or flour if needed.

Pineapple-Stuffed Sweet Potatoes

Here's an unusual way to serve sweet potatoes, but if your family is like mine, they'll love it. It's a regular on our menu throughout the holiday season.

—**JOY MCMILLAN** THE WOODLANDS, TX

PREP: 15 MIN. • **BAKE:** 55 MIN.
MAKES: 2 SERVINGS

- 2 **small sweet potatoes**
- ½ **cup canned crushed pineapple**
- 4½ **teaspoons brown sugar**
- 1 **tablespoon butter**
- ⅛ **teaspoon salt**
- 1 **tablespoon dried cranberries**
- 2 **tablespoons chopped pecans, divided**

1. Wrap potatoes in foil and bake at 400° for 45-50 minutes or until tender. Let stand until cool enough to handle. Cut a thin slice off the top of each potato and discard. Scoop out the pulp, leaving a thin shell.

2. In a small bowl, mash the pulp; add the pineapple, brown sugar, butter and salt. Stir in the dried cranberries and 1 tablespoon of pecans. Spoon into potato shells. Sprinkle with remaining pecans. Place on a baking sheet. Bake at 400° for 8-12 minutes or until heated through.

PINEAPPLE-STUFFED SWEET POTATOES

Katherine White's
Apple Caramel Cheesecake Bars
PAGE 254

Delectable Desserts

Make any day a celebration with these irresistible treats. Create showstopping tortes, cute cookie-jar favorites, even 10-minute pies! These reader recipes are so quick and easy, you won't need a special occasion to whip them up.

**Meryl Herr's
Citrus Berry Shortcake**
PAGE 245

**Kandy Bingham's
Apple-Cinnamon Mini Pies**
PAGE 249

**Jeff King's
Quadruple Chocolate
Chunk Cookies**
PAGE 255

CHOCOLATE HAZELNUT MOUSSE CUPS

Sugar-Cone Chocolate Chip Cookies

If I could make a batch of cookies a day, I'd be in baking heaven. I made these for my boys when they were growing up, and now I treat my grandkids, too.

—PAULA MARCHESI LENHARTSVILLE, PA

PREP: 25 MIN. • **BAKE:** 10 MIN./BATCH
MAKES: 6 DOZEN

- 1 cup butter, softened
- ¾ cup sugar
- ¾ cup packed brown sugar
- 2 eggs
- 3 teaspoons vanilla extract
- 2¼ cups all-purpose flour
- 1 teaspoon baking soda
- ½ teaspoon salt
- 2 cups milk chocolate chips
- 2 cups coarsely crushed ice cream sugar cones (about 16)
- 1 cup sprinkles

1. Preheat oven to 375°. In a large bowl, cream butter and sugars until light and fluffy. Beat in eggs and vanilla. In another bowl, whisk flour, baking soda and salt; gradually beat into creamed mixture. Stir in chips, crushed sugar cones and sprinkles.
2. Drop by tablespoonfuls 2 in. apart onto ungreased baking sheets. Bake 8-10 minutes or until golden brown. Remove cookies from pans to wire racks to cool.

Chocolate Hazelnut Mousse Cups

Three of my favorite foods–chocolate, hazelnuts and puff pastry–come together for an impressive dessert. Dress them up with a drizzle of melted chocolate and sprinkling of chopped nuts.

—ROXANNE CHAN ALBANY, CA

PREP: 30 MIN. + COOLING
MAKES: 6 SERVINGS

- 1 package (10 ounces) frozen puff pastry shells, thawed
- ½ cup heavy whipping cream
- 1 to 2 tablespoons confectioners' sugar
- ¼ teaspoon vanilla extract
- ½ cup mascarpone cheese
- ½ cup Nutella
- ¼ teaspoon ground cinnamon
- 2 tablespoons miniature semisweet chocolate chips
  Additional miniature semisweet chocolate chips, melted, optional
- 2 tablespoons chopped hazelnuts, toasted

1. Bake pastry shells according to package directions. Cool completely.
2. In a small bowl, beat the cream until it begins to thicken. Add confectioners' sugar and vanilla; beat until soft peaks form.
3. In another bowl, beat mascarpone cheese, Nutella and cinnamon until blended. Fold in whipped cream and chocolate chips. Spoon into pastry shells. If desired, drizzle with melted chocolate. Sprinkle with hazelnuts. Refrigerate until serving.
NOTE *To toast nuts, spread in a 15x10x1-in. baking pan. Bake at 350° for 5-10 minutes or until lightly browned, stirring occasionally. Or, spread in a dry nonstick skillet and heat over low heat until lightly browned, stirring occasionally.*

SUGAR-CONE CHOCOLATE CHIP COOKIES

CITRUS BERRY SHORTCAKE

Pumpkin Pie Bars

These bars taste like a cross between pumpkin pie and pecan pie–yum! If you can't find butter cake mix, yellow cake mix will work.

—SUE DRAHEIM WATERFORD, WI

PREP: 15 MIN. • **BAKE:** 50 MIN. + CHILLING
MAKES: 16 SERVINGS

- 1 can (29 ounces) solid-pack pumpkin
- 1 can (12 ounces) evaporated milk
- 1½ cups sugar
- 4 eggs
- 2 teaspoons ground cinnamon
- 1 teaspoon ground ginger
- ½ teaspoon ground nutmeg
- 1 package butter recipe golden cake mix (regular size)
- 1 cup butter, melted
- 1 cup chopped pecans
  Whipped topping, optional

1. Preheat oven to 350°. In a large bowl, beat the first seven ingredients on medium speed until smooth. Pour into an ungreased 13x9-in. baking pan. Sprinkle with dry cake mix. Drizzle with butter ; sprinkle with pecans.
2. Bake 50-60 minutes or until a toothpick inserted in center comes out clean. Cool 1 hour on a wire rack.
3. Refrigerate 3 hours or overnight. Remove from refrigerator 15 minutes before serving. If desired, serve with whipped topping.

PUMPKIN PIE BARS

Citrus Berry Shortcake

PREP: 30 MIN. • **BAKE:** 20 MIN. + COOLING
MAKES: 8 SERVINGS

- 1⅓ cups all-purpose flour
- ½ cup sugar
- 2 teaspoons baking powder
- ¼ teaspoon salt
- ⅔ cup buttermilk
- ¼ cup butter, melted
- 1 egg
- 1 tablespoon orange juice
- 1 teaspoon grated orange peel
- 1 teaspoon vanilla extract
- 1 cup sliced fresh strawberries

TOPPING
- 1½ cups sliced fresh strawberries
- 1 tablespoon lemon juice
- 1 teaspoon sugar
- 2 cups whipped topping
- 2 teaspoons orange liqueur or orange juice

1. Preheat oven to 350°. Line bottom of a greased 9-in. round baking pan with parchment paper; grease paper.
2. In a large bowl, whisk flour, sugar, baking powder and salt. In another bowl, whisk buttermilk, melted butter, egg, orange juice, orange peel and vanilla. Stir into dry ingredients just until moistened. Fold in 1 cup sliced strawberries. Transfer to the prepared pan.
3. Bake 20-25 minutes or until a toothpick inserted in center comes out clean. Cool in pan 10 minutes before removing from pan to a wire rack; remove paper. Cool completely.
4. For topping, in a small bowl, toss strawberries with lemon juice and sugar. Refrigerate until serving. In another bowl, mix whipped topping and liqueur; spread over cake. Drain strawberries; arrange over top.

Chewy Chocolate-Cherry Bars

Colorful dried cranberries and pistachios are in this new take on seven-layer bars. For other variations, try cinnamon or chocolate graham cracker crumbs instead of plain and substitute pecans or walnuts for the pistachios.

—TASTE OF HOME TEST KITCHEN

PREP: 10 MIN. • **BAKE:** 25 MIN. + COOLING
MAKES: 3 DOZEN

- 1½ cups graham cracker crumbs
- ½ cup butter, melted
- 1½ cups semisweet chocolate chips
- 1½ cups dried cherries
- 1 can (14 ounces) sweetened condensed milk
- 1 cup flaked coconut
- 1 cup pistachios, chopped

1. Preheat oven to 350°. In a small bowl, mix cracker crumbs and butter. Press into a greased 13x9-in. baking pan. In a large bowl, mix remaining ingredients until blended; carefully spread over crust.
2. Bake 25-28 minutes or until edges are golden brown. Cool in pan on a wire rack. Cut into bars.

CHEWY CHOCOLATE-CHERRY BARS

Apple Kuchen Bars

This recipe is about family, comfort and simplicity. My mom made these and now I bake them in my own kitchen. I double batches to pass on the love!

—ELIZABETH MONFORT CELINA, OH

PREP: 35 MIN.
BAKE: 1 HOUR + COOLING
MAKES: 2 DOZEN

- 3 cups all-purpose flour, divided
- ¼ teaspoon salt
- 1½ cups cold butter, divided
- 4 to 5 tablespoons ice water
- 8 cups thinly sliced peeled tart apples (about 8 medium)
- 2 cups sugar, divided
- 2 teaspoons ground cinnamon

1. Preheat oven to 350°. Place 2 cups flour and salt in a food processor; pulse until blended. Add 1 cup butter; pulse until butter is the size of peas. While pulsing, add just enough ice water to form moist crumbs. Press mixture into a greased 13x9-in. baking pan. Bake 20-25 minutes or until edges are lightly browned. Cool on a wire rack.
2. In a large bowl, combine apples, 1 cup sugar and cinnamon; toss to coat. Spoon over crust. Place remaining flour, butter and sugar in food processor; pulse until coarse crumbs form. Sprinkle over apples. Bake 60-70 minutes or until golden brown and apples are tender. Cool completely on a wire rack. Cut into bars.

Quick Blue-Ribbon Peanut Butter Torte

No one will guess that this majestic cake isn't completely homemade. Chunky peanut butter is stirred into both the cake batter and the decadent chocolate ganache, giving each layer an amazing from-scratch taste.

—TASTE OF HOME TEST KITCHEN

PREP: 25 MIN. + CHILLING
BAKE: 20 MIN. + COOLING
MAKES: 14 SERVINGS

- 1 package yellow cake mix (regular size)
- 1¼ cups water
- 1 cup chunky peanut butter, divided

QUICK BLUE-RIBBON PEANUT BUTTER TORTE

- 3 eggs
- ⅓ cup canola oil
- 1 teaspoon vanilla extract
- 1 package (10 ounces) 60% cacao bittersweet chocolate baking chips
- 2¼ cups heavy whipping cream
- ½ cup packed brown sugar
- 2 cans (16 ounces each) cream cheese frosting
- 2 Butterfinger candy bars (2.1 ounces each), coarsely chopped
- ⅓ cup chopped honey-roasted peanuts

1. Grease and flour three 9-in. round baking pans; set aside. Combine the cake mix, water, ½ cup peanut butter, eggs, oil and vanilla in a large bowl; beat on low speed for 30 seconds. Beat on medium for 2 minutes. Pour batter into prepared pans (pans will have a shallow fill).
2. Bake at 350° for 17-20 minutes or until a toothpick inserted in the center comes out clean. Cool for 10 minutes before removing from pans to wire racks.
3. Place chocolate chips in a large bowl. Bring cream and brown sugar to a boil in a small heavy saucepan over medium heat, stirring occasionally. Reduce heat; simmer for 1-2 minutes or until sugar is dissolved.
4. Pour cream mixture over chocolate; whisk until smooth. Stir in remaining peanut butter until blended. Chill until mixture reaches a spreading consistency. Spread between layers.
5. Frost top and sides of cake. Garnish with chopped candy bars and peanuts. Store in the refrigerator.
NOTE *Reduced-fat peanut butter is not recommended for this recipe.*

Butterfinger Cookie Bars

PREP: 20 MIN. • **BAKE:** 25 MIN. + COOLING
MAKES: 3 DOZEN

- 1 package dark chocolate cake mix (regular size)
- 1 cup all-purpose flour
- 1 package (3.9 ounces) instant chocolate pudding mix
- 1 tablespoon baking cocoa
- ½ cup 2% milk
- ⅓ cup canola oil
- ⅓ cup butter, melted
- 2 eggs
- 6 Butterfinger candy bars (2.1 ounces each), divided
- 1½ cups chunky peanut butter
- 1 teaspoon vanilla extract
- 1½ cups semisweet chocolate chips, divided

1. Preheat oven to 350°. In a large bowl, combine cake mix, flour, pudding mix and cocoa. In another bowl, whisk milk, oil, butter and 1 egg until blended. Add to dry ingredients; stir just until moistened. Press half of the mixture into a greased 15x10x1-in. baking pan. Bake 10 minutes.

2. Meanwhile, chop two candy bars. Stir peanut butter, vanilla and remaining egg into remaining cake mix mixture. Fold in chopped bars and 1 cup chocolate chips.

3. Chop three additional candy bars; sprinkle over warm crust and press down gently. Cover with cake mix mixture; press down firmly with a metal spatula. Crush remaining candy bar; sprinkle crushed bar and remaining chocolate chips over top.

4. Bake 25-30 minutes or until a toothpick inserted in center comes out clean. Cool on a wire rack. Cut into bars. Store in an airtight container.

"My boys went through a phase where they loved Butterfingers. We made Butterfinger shakes, muffins, cookies and experimented with different bars. This one was voted the best of the bunch." —**BARBARA LEIGHTY** SIMI VALLEY, CA

BUTTERFINGER COOKIE BARS

DOUBLE CHOCOLATE COCONUT BROWNIES

Double Chocolate Coconut Brownies

Thanks to a head start from a mix, it's easy to bake up these crowd-pleasing treats. It's hard to stop at one, but don't worry, my recipe makes 30 servings!
—**BRENDA MELANCON** MCCOMB, MS

PREP: 15 MIN. • **BAKE:** 40 MIN. + COOLING
MAKES: 2½ DOZEN

- 1 package fudge brownie mix (13-inch x 9-inch pan size)
- ½ cup canola oil
- ¼ cup water
- 3 eggs
- ½ cup semisweet chocolate chips
- ½ cup white baking chips
- ½ cup chopped walnuts
- 1 can (14 ounces) sweetened condensed milk
- 2½ cups flaked coconut

FROSTING

- ¼ cup butter, softened
- ¼ cup evaporated milk
- 2 tablespoons baking cocoa
- 2 cups confectioners' sugar
- 1 teaspoon vanilla extract

1. Beat the brownie mix, oil, water and eggs on medium speed in a large bowl until blended; stir in chips and walnuts. Pour into a greased 13x9-in. baking pan.

2. Bake at 350° for 20 minutes. Remove from oven. Combine condensed milk and coconut in a small bowl; spread over top. Bake 20-25 minutes longer or until center is set. Cool on a wire rack.

3. Place frosting ingredients in a small bowl; beat until smooth. Spread over cooled brownies.

Cream Cheese Frosted Pumpkin Bars

These tender bars are a welcome treat. Biscuit mix speeds up the batter, and the from-scratch frosting is divine. This recipe feeds a bunch.

—**ESTHER THYS** BELLE PLAINE, IA

PREP: 15 MIN. • **BAKE:** 25 MIN. + COOLING
MAKES: ABOUT 3 DOZEN

- 1 **can (15 ounces) solid-pack pumpkin**
- 2 **cups sugar**
- 4 **eggs**
- ½ **cup canola oil**
- 2 **cups biscuit/baking mix**
- 2 **teaspoons ground cinnamon**
- ½ **cup raisins**

CREAM CHEESE FROSTING

- 1 **package (3 ounces) cream cheese, softened**
- ⅓ **cup butter, softened**
- 1 **tablespoon 2% milk**
- 1 **teaspoon vanilla extract**
- 2 **cups confectioners' sugar**

1. Beat the pumpkin, sugar, eggs and oil in a large bowl. Combine biscuit mix and cinnamon; gradually add to pumpkin mixture and mix well. Stir in raisins.
2. Pour into a greased 15-in. x 10-in. x 1-in. baking pan. Bake at 350° for 25-30 minutes or until a toothpick inserted near the center comes out clean. Cool on a wire rack.
3. Meanwhile, in a large bowl, beat cream cheese and butter until fluffy. Add milk and vanilla. Gradually beat in confectioners' sugar until smooth. Spread over bars. Store in the refrigerator.

top tip | Instant Winner

I blend an 8-ounce package of cream cheese into a 16-ounce can of prepared frosting. It enhances the flavor, reduces the sweetness and increases the amount of frosting. Try it with any flavor.

—**EDITH B.** PEORIA, IL

Mocha Macaroon Cookies

Here's a sophisticated version of an old favorite. The combination of chocolate, coffee and cinnamon is delicious. For a smart finishing touch, I top them with chocolate-covered coffee beans.

—**JEANNE HOLT** MENDOTA HEIGHTS, MN

PREP: 15 MIN. • **BAKE:** 10 MIN./BATCH
MAKES: 4 DOZEN

- 2 **teaspoons instant coffee granules**
- 2 **teaspoons hot water**
- 1 **can (14 ounces) sweetened condensed milk**
- 2 **ounces unsweetened chocolate, melted**
- 1 **teaspoon vanilla extract**
- ¼ **teaspoon ground cinnamon**
- ⅛ **teaspoon salt**
- 1 **package (14 ounces) flaked coconut**
- ⅔ **cup white baking chips, melted Plain or chocolate-covered coffee beans**

1. Preheat oven to 350°. In a large bowl, dissolve coffee granules in hot water. Stir in condensed milk, melted chocolate, vanilla, cinnamon and salt until blended. Stir in coconut. Drop by rounded teaspoonfuls 2 in. apart onto parchment paper-lined baking sheets.
2. Bake 10-12 minutes or until set. Cool on pans 1 minute. Remove to wire racks to cool completely.
3. Drizzle tops with melted baking chips; top with coffee beans.

[5 INGREDIENTS] Apple-Cinnamon Mini Pies

PREP: 20 MIN. • **BAKE:** 15 MIN.
MAKES: 1 DOZEN

- 1 **package (14.1 ounces) refrigerated pie pastry**
- ½ **cup chunky applesauce**
- 3 **teaspoons cinnamon-sugar, divided**
- 2 **tablespoons butter, cut into 12 pieces**
- 1 **tablespoon 2% milk, divided**

1. Preheat oven to 350°. On a lightly floured surface, unroll pastry sheets. Using a floured 3½-in. round cookie cutter, cut six circles from each sheet.

2. In a small bowl, mix applesauce with 1½ teaspoons cinnamon-sugar. Place 2 teaspoons applesauce mixture on one half of each circle; dot with butter. Moisten pastry edges with some of the milk. Fold pastry over filling; press edges with a fork to seal.

3. Transfer to ungreased baking sheets. Brush tops with remaining milk; sprinkle with remaining cinnamon-sugar. Bake 12-15 minutes or until golden brown. Remove from pans to wire racks. Serve warm or at room temperature.

MINT BROWNIE CHEESECAKE CUPS

Mint Brownie Cheesecake Cups

Set several plates of these fuss-free brownie cheesecake bites around the house for guests to munch on as they mingle. Bursting with mint chocolate, they'll be the talk of the party.
—**JANET PAYNE** LAWRENCEVILLE, GA

PREP: 20 MIN. • **BAKE:** 25 MIN. + COOLING
MAKES: 2½ DOZEN

- ½ **cup crushed chocolate cream-filled chocolate sandwich cookies (about 7 cookies)**
- 1 **package (4.67 ounces) Andes mint candies or 1 cup Andes creme de menthe baking chips**
- 1 **package (8 ounces) cream cheese, softened**
- ¼ **cup sugar**
- 1 **egg**
- ½ **teaspoon vanilla extract**
  Additional Andes mint candies or Andes creme de menthe baking chips, melted

1. Grease or paper-line miniature muffin cups. Press 1 teaspoon cookie crumbs onto the bottom of each muffin cup; set aside.

2. Heat candies on high in a microwave-safe bowl for 30-60 seconds or until melted, stirring every 15 seconds. Cool to room temperature.

3. Beat cream cheese and sugar in a small bowl until smooth. Beat in egg and vanilla. Stir in melted candies.

4. Spoon 1 tablespoon mixture into each cup. Bake at 350° for 25-30 minutes or until tops appear dry and begin to crack. Cool for 1 minute before removing to wire racks to cool completely. Drizzle with additional melted candies. Store in the refrigerator.

"I came up with the idea for these little pies while snacking on applesauce one night and thought it would make a quick and delicious pie filling. What's better than an apple pie that you can actually hold in your hand to eat?" —**KANDY BINGHAM** GREEN RIVER, WY

APPLE-CINAMON MINI PIES

(5) INGREDIENTS
S'mores-Dipped Apples

For me, the flavor combination of marshmallows, graham crackers and apples just can't be beat. Others must think the same thing. Whenever I take these to a bake sale, they sell out in a flash.
—**MARIA REGAKIS** SOMERVILLE, MA

PREP: 20 MIN. • **COOK:** 10 MIN. + CHILLING
MAKES: 8 SERVINGS

- 8 **large Granny Smith apples**
- 8 **wooden pop sticks**
- 2 **tablespoons butter**
- 2 **packages (16 ounces each) large marshmallows**
- 2 **cups coarsely crushed graham crackers**
- 1 **package (11½ ounces) milk chocolate chips**

S'MORES-DIPPED APPLES

1. Line a baking sheet with waxed paper; generously coat waxed paper with cooking spray. Wash and dry apples; remove stems. Insert pop sticks into apples.
2. In a large heavy saucepan, melt butter over medium heat. Add marshmallows; stir until melted. Dip apples, one at a time, into warm marshmallow mixture, allowing excess to drip off. Place on prepared baking sheet and refrigerate until set, about 15 minutes.
3. Place graham cracker crumbs in a shallow dish. In top of a double boiler or a metal bowl over barely simmering water, melt chocolate chips; stir until smooth. Dip bottom half of apples in chocolate; dip bottoms in cracker crumbs. Place on baking sheet. Refrigerate until set.

FAST FIX
Mini Rum Cakes

Mom often kept sponge cakes in her freezer and pudding in the pantry. We tried many rum cakes to find the best one. We think this has the most flavor.
—**DONA HOFFMAN** ADDISON, IL

START TO FINISH: 10 MIN.
MAKES: 6 SERVINGS

- 2 **cups cold 2% milk**
- 1 **package (3.4 ounces) instant vanilla pudding mix**
- 1 **teaspoon rum extract**
- 6 **individual round sponge cakes**
- 1½ **cups whipped topping**
  Fresh or frozen raspberries

1. In a small bowl, whisk milk and pudding mix for 2 minutes; stir in extract. Let stand for 2 minutes or until soft-set.
2. Place sponge cakes on dessert plates; top with pudding. Garnish with whipped topping and raspberries.

(5) INGREDIENTS
Blueberry Angel Dessert

Use angel food cake, pie filling and whipped topping to create a light and crowd-pleasing dessert that doesn't keep you in the kitchen for hours. It's the perfect way to end a summer meal.
—**CAROL JOHNSON** TYLER, TX

PREP: 10 MIN. + CHILLING
MAKES: 12 SERVINGS

- 1 **package (8 ounces) cream cheese, softened**
- 1 **cup confectioners' sugar**
- 1 **carton (8 ounces) frozen whipped topping, thawed**
- 1 **prepared angel food cake (8 to 10 ounces), cut into 1-inch cubes**
- 2 **cans (21 ounces each) blueberry pie filling**

In a large bowl, beat cream cheese and confectioners' sugar until smooth; fold in whipped topping and cake cubes. Spread evenly into an ungreased 13x9-in. dish; top with pie filling. Refrigerate, covered, at least 2 hours before serving.

"When asked to bring a dessert for my boys' football team to share, I whipped up these unique blondies and was instantly named 'the greatest mom.' They're a surefire hit." —**VALONDA SEWARD** COARSEGOLD, CA

SNICKERDOODLE BLONDIE BARS

Lemon Cupcakes with Strawberry Frosting

I sometimes call these my Triple Lemon Whammy Cupcakes because they take full advantage of vibrant citrus flavor. Sweet strawberries nudge them over the top!
—**EMMA SISK** PLYMOUTH, MN

PREP: 20 MIN. • **BAKE:** 25 MIN. + COOLING
MAKES: 2 DOZEN

- 1 **package white cake mix (regular size)**
- ¼ **cup lemon curd**
- 3 **tablespoons lemon juice**
- 3 **teaspoons grated lemon peel**
- ½ **cup butter, softened**
- 3½ **cups confectioners' sugar**
- ¼ **cup seedless strawberry jam**
- 2 **tablespoons 2% milk**
- 1 **cup sliced fresh strawberries**

1. Line 24 muffin cups with paper liners. Prepare cake mix batter according to package directions, decreasing water by 1 tablespoon and adding lemon curd, lemon juice and lemon peel before mixing batter. Fill prepared cups two-thirds full. Bake and cool cupcakes as package directs.
2. In a large bowl, beat butter, confectioners' sugar, jam and milk until smooth. Frost the cooled cupcakes; top with strawberries. Refrigerate leftovers.

LEMON CUPCAKES WITH STRAWBERRY FROSTING

Snickerdoodle Blondie Bars

PREP: 15 MIN. • **BAKE:** 40 MIN. + COOLING
MAKES: 20 SERVINGS

- 1 **cup butter, softened**
- 2 **cups packed brown sugar**
- 2 **eggs**
- 3 **teaspoons vanilla extract**
- 2⅔ **cups all-purpose flour**
- 2 **teaspoons baking powder**
- 1 **teaspoon ground cinnamon**
- ¼ **teaspoon ground nutmeg**
- ½ **teaspoon salt**

TOPPING
- 1½ **teaspoons sugar**
- ½ **teaspoon ground cinnamon**

1. Preheat oven to 350°. In a large bowl, cream butter and brown sugar until fluffy. Beat in eggs and vanilla. In another bowl, whisk flour, baking powder, spices and salt; gradually beat into creamed mixture. Spread into a greased 9-in.-square baking pan.
2. Mix topping ingredients; sprinkle over top. Bake 35-40 minutes or until set and golden brown. Cool in pan on a wire rack. Cut into bars. Store in an airtight container.

BLACK & WHITE CEREAL TREATS

Black & White Cereal Treats

When my daughter was just 7 years old, she had the brilliant idea of adding Oreo cookies to cereal treats. Now 24, she still asks me to make these on occasion; they're that good.

—**TAMMY PHOENIX** AVA, IL

PREP: 10 MIN. • **COOK:** 10 MIN. + COOLING
MAKES: 2 DOZEN

¼ cup butter, cubed

8 cups miniature marshmallows

6 cups Rice Krispies

2½ cups chopped double-stuffed Oreo cookies (about 16), divided

1⅓ cups white baking chips, melted

1. In a Dutch oven, melt butter over medium heat. Stir in marshmallows until melted. Remove from heat. Stir in cereal and 2 cups Oreos. Press into a greased 13x9-in. baking pan.

2. Spread melted baking chips over top; sprinkle with remaining Oreos, pressing gently to adhere. Cool to room temperature. Cut into bars.

Chocolate Delight Dessert

My three children loved this dessert so much that they begged me to get the recipe. It's easy to make and tastes good. And making it ahead of time frees your hands and your time for other to-do's.

—**RUTH DYCK** FOREST, ON

PREP: 30 MIN. + FREEZING
MAKES: 12 SERVINGS

---

1 cup crushed saltines

½ cup graham cracker crumbs

⅓ cup butter, melted

2 cups milk

1 package (3.9 ounces) instant chocolate pudding mix

1 package (3.4 ounces) instant vanilla pudding mix

1½ quarts cookies and cream ice cream, softened

1 carton (12 ounces) frozen whipped topping, thawed

3 Heath candy bars (1.4 ounces each), crushed

1. In a small bowl, combine saltine and graham cracker crumbs; stir in butter. Press onto the bottom of a greased 13x9-in. baking pan. Refrigerate 15 minutes.

2. Meanwhile, in a large bowl, whisk milk and pudding mixes 2 minutes. Fold in ice cream. Spread over crust. Top with whipped topping; sprinkle with crushed candy bars. Freeze, covered, until firm. Remove from freezer 30 minutes before serving.

Apple Caramel Cheesecake Bars

It's a caramel apple, cheesecake and streusel-topped apple pie all rolled into one irresistible bar. Arrange the bars on a serving platter so no one will know you sneaked a piece beforehand.

—KATHERINE WHITE CLEMMONS, NC

PREP: 30 MIN. • **BAKE:** 25 MIN. + CHILLING
MAKES: 3 DOZEN

- 2 **cups all-purpose flour**
- ½ **cup packed brown sugar**
- ¾ **cup cold butter, cubed**
- 2 **packages (8 ounces each) cream cheese, softened**
- ½ **cup plus 2 tablespoons sugar, divided**
- 1 **teaspoon vanilla extract**
- 2 **eggs, lightly beaten**
- 3 **medium tart apples, peeled and finely chopped**
- ½ **teaspoon ground cinnamon**
- ¼ **teaspoon ground nutmeg**

STREUSEL

- ¾ **cup all-purpose flour**
- ¾ **cup packed brown sugar**
- ½ **cup quick-cooking oats**
- ⅓ **cup cold butter, cubed**
- ⅓ **cup hot caramel ice cream topping**

1. Preheat oven to 350°. In a small bowl, combine flour and brown sugar; cut in butter until crumbly. Press into a well-greased 13x9-in. baking pan. Bake 15-18 minutes or until lightly browned.

2. Meanwhile, in a large bowl, beat cream cheese, ½ cup sugar and vanilla until smooth. Add eggs; beat on low speed just until combined. Spread over crust.

3. In a small bowl, toss apples with cinnamon, nutmeg and remaining sugar; spoon over cream cheese layer. In another bowl, mix flour, brown sugar and oats; cut in butter until crumbly. Sprinkle over apple layer.

4. Bake 25-30 minutes or until filling is set. Drizzle with caramel topping; cool in pan on a wire rack 1 hour. Refrigerate for at least 2 hours. Cut into bars.

LEMON ANGEL CAKE BARS

APPLE CARAMEL CHEESECAKE BARS

Lemon Angel Cake Bars

A neighbor shared this recipe with me years ago, and it's been in my baking rotation ever since. It can be prepared ahead and serves a bunch, making it perfect for parties and potlucks.

—MARINA CASTLE CANYON COUNTRY, CA

PREP: 15 MIN. • **BAKE:** 20 MIN. + CHILLING
MAKES: 4 DOZEN

- 1 **package (16 ounces) angel food cake mix**
- 1 **can (15¾ ounces) lemon pie filling**
- 1 **cup finely shredded unsweetened coconut**

FROSTING

- 1 **package (8 ounces) cream cheese, softened**
- ½ **cup butter, softened**
- 1 **teaspoon vanilla extract**
- 2½ **cups confectioners' sugar**
- 3 **teaspoons grated lemon peel**

1. Preheat oven to 350°. In a large bowl, mix cake mix, pie filling and coconut until blended; spread into a greased 15x10x1-in. baking pan.

2. Bake 20-25 minutes or until a toothpick inserted in center comes out clean. Cool completely in pan on a wire rack.

3. Meanwhile, in a large bowl, beat cream cheese, butter and vanilla until smooth. Gradually beat in confectioners' sugar. Spread over cooled bars; sprinkle with lemon peel. Refrigerate at least 4 hours. Cut into bars or triangles.

NOTE *Look for unsweetened coconut in the baking or health food section.*

Cranberry-Pear Tart with Hazelnut Topping

Treat your family to a fruity, nutty tart that starts with convenient store-bought pastry. Festive ruby-red cranberries, succulent pears and crunchy hazelnuts make an unforgettable dessert.

—SHELISA TERRY HENDERSON, NV

PREP: 15 MIN. • **BAKE:** 30 MIN. + COOLING
MAKES: 14 SERVINGS

- 1 sheet refrigerated pie pastry
- 2 cups fresh or frozen cranberries, coarsely chopped
- 3 medium ripe pears, peeled and coarsely chopped
- 1 cup chopped hazelnuts
- 1¼ cups packed brown sugar
- 2 tablespoons all-purpose flour
- ½ teaspoon ground cinnamon
- ½ teaspoon vanilla extract
- 2 tablespoons butter
- 2 tablespoons hazelnut liqueur
- 1 carton (8 ounces) frozen whipped topping, thawed

1. Roll pastry into a 13-in. circle on a lightly floured surface. Press onto the bottom and up the sides of an ungreased 11-in. fluted tart pan with removable bottom.
2. Combine the cranberries, pears, hazelnuts, brown sugar, flour, cinnamon and vanilla in a large bowl; transfer to crust. Dot with butter.
3. Place tart pan on a baking sheet. Bake at 425° for 30-35 minutes or until filling is hot and bubbly and crust is golden. Cool on a wire rack.
4. Stir liqueur into whipped topping; serve with tart.

QUADRUPLE CHOCOLATE CHUNK COOKIES

Quadruple Chocolate Chunk Cookies

When your cookies feature Oreos, candy bars and all the other goodies that go into a sweet treat, you're guaranteed a winner.

—JEFF KING DULUTH, MN

PREP: 25 MIN. • **BAKE:** 10 MIN./BATCH
MAKES: 8 DOZEN

- 1 cup butter, softened
- 1 cup sugar
- 1 cup packed brown sugar
- 2 eggs
- 2 teaspoons vanilla extract
- 2½ cups all-purpose flour
- ¾ cup Dutch-processed cocoa
- 1 teaspoon baking soda
- ¼ teaspoon salt
- 1 cup white baking chips, chopped
- 1 cup semisweet chocolate chips, chopped
- 1 cup chopped Oreo cookies (about 10 cookies)
- 1 Hershey's cookies and cream candy bar (1.55 ounces), chopped

1. Preheat oven to 375°. In a large bowl, cream butter, sugar and brown sugar until light and fluffy. Beat in eggs and vanilla. In another bowl, whisk flour, cocoa, baking soda and salt; gradually beat into creamed mixture. Stir in remaining ingredients.
2. Drop by tablespoonfuls 2 in. apart onto greased baking sheets. Bake 6-8 minutes or until set. Cool on pans 1 minute. Remove to wire racks to cool completely. Store cookies in an airtight container.

CRANBERRY-PEAR TART WITH HAZELNUT TOPPING

CHERRY BARS

Cherry Bars

Whip up a pan of these festive bars with pantry staples. They're destined to become a holiday classic for your family, as they have for mine.

—JANE KAMP GRAND RAPIDS, MI

PREP: 20 MIN. • **BAKE:** 30 MIN. + COOLING
MAKES: 5 DOZEN

- 1 cup butter, softened
- 2 cups sugar
- 1 teaspoon salt
- 4 eggs
- 1 teaspoon vanilla extract
- ¼ teaspoon almond extract
- 3 cups all-purpose flour
- 2 cans (21 ounces each) cherry pie filling

GLAZE

- 1 cup confectioners' sugar
- ½ teaspoon vanilla extract
- ½ teaspoon almond extract
- 2 to 3 tablespoons milk

1. Preheat oven to 350°. In a large bowl, cream butter, sugar and salt until light and fluffy. Add eggs, one at a time, beating well after each addition. Beat in the extracts. Gradually add flour; beat just until blended.

2. Spread 3 cups batter into a greased 15x10x1-in. baking pan. Spread with pie filling. Drop remaining batter by teaspoonfuls over filling.

3. Bake 30-35 minutes or until golden brown. Cool completely in pan on a wire rack.

4. In a small bowl, mix confectioners' sugar, extracts and enough milk to reach desired consistency. Drizzle over top.

top tip Double-Duty Pie Filling

When a recipe calls for canned cherry pie filling, I like to hold back a few tablespoons of the thickened syrup. It makes a tasty sundae topping for another time.

—LORRAINE S. BEMIDJI, MN

Honey Nut & Cream Cheese Baklava

PREP: 30 MIN. • **BAKE:** 35 MIN. + COOLING
MAKES: 3 DOZEN

- Butter-flavored cooking spray
- ½ cup spreadable honey nut cream cheese
- 1¼ cups sugar, divided
- 3 cups chopped walnuts
- 1 package (16 ounces, 14x9-inch sheets) frozen phyllo dough, thawed
- 1 cup water
- ½ cup honey

1. Preheat oven to 350°. Coat a 13x9-in. baking pan with cooking spray. In a large bowl, mix cream cheese and ¼ cup sugar until blended. Stir in walnuts.

2. Unroll phyllo dough; trim to fit into pan. Layer 20 sheets of phyllo in prepared pan, spritzing each with cooking spray. Keep remaining phyllo covered with plastic wrap and a damp towel to prevent it from drying out.

3. Spread with half of the walnut mixture. Layer with five more phyllo sheets, spritzing each with cooking spray. Spread remaining walnut mixture over phyllo. Top with remaining phyllo sheets, spritzing each with cooking spray.

4. Cut into 1½-in. diamonds. Bake 35-40 minutes or until golden brown. Meanwhile, in a saucepan, combine water, honey and remaining sugar; bring to a boil, stirring to dissolve sugar. Reduce heat; simmer, uncovered, 10 minutes. Pour over warm baklava.

5. Cool completely in pan on a wire rack. Refrigerate, covered, until serving.

"I love serving desserts that look like you spent hours in the kitchen when, in reality, they're easy to make. This is one of those recipes." **—CHERYL SNAVELY** HAGERSTOWN, MD

HONEY NUT & CREAM CHEESE BAKLAVA

CARAMEL-CHOCOLATE CHIP
SANDWICH COOKIES

Caramel-Chocolate Chip Sandwich Cookies

These cake treats are a nice change from chewy chocolate chip cookies. I've been known to add a little peanut butter to the filling, too.

—LAUREN REIFF EAST EARL, PA

PREP: 30 MIN.
BAKE: 10 MIN./BATCH + COOLING
MAKES: 2½ DOZEN

- ½ cup butter, softened
- 1 cup packed brown sugar
- 2 eggs
- ¼ cup honey
- 1 teaspoon vanilla extract
- 2¾ cups all-purpose flour
- 1 teaspoon baking soda
- 1 teaspoon baking powder
- ½ teaspoon salt
- 1½ cups semisweet chocolate chips

FILLING
- 6 tablespoons butter, cubed
- ¾ cup packed brown sugar
- 3 tablespoons 2% milk
- 1⅓ to 1½ cups confectioners' sugar

1. Preheat oven to 350°. In a large bowl, cream butter and sugar until light and fluffy. Beat in eggs, then honey and vanilla. In another bowl, whisk flour, baking soda, baking powder and salt; gradually beat into creamed mixture. Stir in chocolate chips.

2. Drop by tablespoonfuls 2 in. apart onto ungreased baking sheets. Bake 8-10 minutes or until golden brown. Remove from pans to wire racks to cool completely.

3. For filling, in a small saucepan, melt butter over medium heat. Stir in brown sugar and milk; bring to a boil. Reduce heat to low; cook and stir until sugar is dissolved. Remove from heat; cool to room temperature.

4. Beat in enough confectioners' sugar to reach desired consistency. Spread 1½ teaspoons filling onto bottoms of half of the cookies; cover with remaining cookies.

Minty Chocolate Cream Cheese Bars

I always looked forward to my grandma's rich cream cheese bars when I was growing up. This version includes mint, which is one of my favorite flavors.

—JILL LUTZ WOODBURY, MN

PREP: 15 MIN. • **BAKE:** 30 MIN. + COOLING
MAKES: 2 DOZEN

- 1 package chocolate cake mix (regular size)
- ½ cup butter, softened
- 1 teaspoon vanilla extract
- 1 teaspoon almond extract
- 4 eggs, divided
- 1 package (10 ounces) Andes creme de menthe baking chips, divided
- 1 package (8 ounces) cream cheese, softened
- 1⅔ cups confectioners' sugar

1. Preheat oven to 350°. In a large bowl, beat cake mix, butter, extracts and 2 eggs until blended. Spread into a greased 13x9-in. baking pan. Sprinkle with ¾ cup chips.

2. In a small bowl, beat cream cheese and confectioners' sugar until smooth. Add remaining eggs; beat on low speed just until blended. Pour over chocolate layer, spreading evenly; sprinkle with remaining chips.

3. Bake 30-35 minutes or until edges begin to brown. Cool in pan on a wire rack. Cut into bars. Refrigerate leftovers.

(5) INGREDIENTS
Cool Coffee Gels

If you like coffee, you'll love this cute dessert idea. It makes a big impression.

—LILY JULOW LAWRENCEVILLE, GA

PREP: 20 MIN. + CHILLING
MAKES: 4 SERVINGS

- 1 envelope unflavored gelatin
- ¼ cup cold water
- 1½ cups hot brewed coffee
- ¼ cup plus 2 tablespoons sugar, divided
- ½ cup heavy whipping cream
  Instant espresso powder and chocolate-covered coffee beans, optional

1. In a small saucepan, sprinkle gelatin over cold water; let stand for 1 minute. Stir in coffee and ¼ cup sugar. Heat over low heat, stirring until gelatin is completely dissolved.

2. Pour into four Irish coffee mugs or 4-oz. custard cups. Cover and refrigerate until set.

3. In a large bowl, beat cream until it begins to thicken. Add remaining sugar; beat until stiff peaks form. Serve with gelatin. Garnish with espresso powder and coffee beans if desired.

COOL COFFEE GELS

THICK SUGAR COOKIES

Thick Sugar Cookies

Thicker than the norm, this sugar cookie is like one you might find at a good bakery. My children often request these for their birthdays. They love to decorate them.

—**HEATHER BIEDLER** MARTINSBURG, WV

PREP: 25 MIN. + CHILLING
BAKE: 10 MIN./BATCH + COOLING
MAKES: ABOUT 3 DOZEN

- 1 **cup butter, softened**
- 1 **cup sugar**
- 2 **eggs**
- 3 **egg yolks**
- 1½ **teaspoons vanilla extract**
- ¾ **teaspoon almond extract**
- 3½ **cups all-purpose flour**
- 1½ **teaspoons baking powder**
- ¼ **teaspoon salt**

FROSTING
- 4 **cups confectioners' sugar**
- ½ **cup butter, softened**
- ½ **cup shortening**
- 1 **teaspoon vanilla extract**
- ½ **teaspoon almond extract**
- 2 **to 3 tablespoons 2% milk**
  Assorted colored nonpareils, optional

1. In a large bowl, cream butter and sugar until light and fluffy. Beat in eggs, egg yolks and extracts. In another bowl, whisk the flour, baking powder and salt; gradually beat into creamed mixture until blended. Shape into a disk; wrap in plastic wrap. Refrigerate the dough for 1 hour or until firm enough to roll.

2. Preheat oven to 375°. On a lightly floured surface, roll dough to ½-in. thickness. Cut with a floured 2-in. cookie cutter. Place 1 in. apart on ungreased baking sheets.

3. Bake 10-12 minutes or until edges begin to brown. Cool on pans 5 minutes. Remove to wire racks to cool completely.

4. For frosting, in a large bowl, beat confectioners' sugar, butter, shortening, extracts and enough milk to achieve desired consistency. Spread the frosting over cookies. If desired, sprinkle with nonpareils.

Root Beer Float Fudge

PREP: 15 MIN. • **COOK:** 15 MIN. + CHILLING
MAKES: ABOUT 3 POUNDS

- 1 teaspoon plus ¾ cup butter, divided
- 3 cups sugar
- 1 can (5 ounces) evaporated milk
- 1 package (10 to 12 ounces) white baking chips
- 1 jar (7 ounces) marshmallow creme
- ½ teaspoon vanilla extract
- 2 teaspoons root beer concentrate

1. Line a 9-in.-square baking pan with foil; grease foil with 1 teaspoon butter. In a large heavy saucepan, combine sugar, milk and remaining butter. Bring to a rapid boil over medium heat, stirring constantly. Cook and stir for 4 minutes.

2. Remove from heat. Stir in baking chips and marshmallow creme until melted. Pour one-third of the mixture into a small bowl; stir in vanilla.

3. To remaining mixture, stir in root beer concentrate; immediately spread into prepared pan. Spread vanilla mixture over top. Refrigerate 1 hour or until firm.

4. Using foil, lift fudge out of pan. Remove foil; cut fudge into 1-in. squares. Store between layers of waxed paper in an airtight container in the refrigerator.

NOTE *This recipe was tested with McCormick root beer concentrate.*

"My children have always loved root beer floats, so I came up with this fudgy treat just for them. Sweet and creamy with that nostalgic root beer flavor, it's always a best-seller at bake sales." —**JENNIFER FISHER** AUSTIN, TX

PEANUT BUTTER CHOCOLATE PRETZELS

ROOT BEER FLOAT FUDGE

⑤ INGREDIENTS

Peanut Butter Chocolate Pretzels

Chocolate and peanut butter, sweet and salty, crunchy and smooth—what's not to love? These dipped and drizzled pretzels are sure to bring a smile to everyone on your list.

—**MARCIA PORCH** WINTER PARK, FL

PREP: 30 MIN. + STANDING
MAKES: ABOUT 3 DOZEN

- 2 cups (12 ounces) semisweet chocolate chips
- 4 teaspoons canola oil, divided
- 35 to 40 pretzels
- ½ cup peanut butter chips

1. In a microwave, melt chocolate chips and 3 teaspoons oil; stir until smooth. Dip pretzels in chocolate; allow excess to drip off. Place on waxed paper-lined baking sheets to set.

2. Melt peanut butter chips and remaining oil; transfer to a small resealable plastic bag. Cut a small hole in a corner of bag; drizzle over pretzels. Let stand until set. Store in airtight containers.

Cranberry Bars with Cream Cheese Frosting

When I place a pan of these bars in the teachers' lounge and come back after the last bell, the pan is always empty. White chocolate chips and cranberries make them impossible to pass by.

—MIRELLA HACKETT CHANDLER, AZ

PREP: 30 MIN. • BAKE: 25 MIN. + COOLING
MAKES: 4 DOZEN

- ¾ cup butter, softened
- 1 cup sugar
- 2 eggs
- ¾ cup sour cream
- ½ teaspoon almond extract
- ½ teaspoon vanilla extract
- 1½ cups all-purpose flour
- 1 teaspoon baking powder
- ⅛ teaspoon salt
- 1 cup white baking chips
- 1 cup dried cranberries
- ½ cup chopped walnuts

FROSTING
- 2 packages (8 ounces each) cream cheese, softened
- ¼ cup butter, softened
- 1 teaspoon vanilla extract
- 2 cups confectioners' sugar
- ½ cup dried cranberries, chopped

1. Preheat oven to 350°. In a large bowl, cream butter and sugar until light and fluffy. Gradually beat in eggs, sour cream and extracts. In a small bowl, whisk flour, baking powder and salt; gradually beat into creamed mixture. Fold in baking chips, cranberries and walnuts. Spread into a greased 15x10x1-in. baking pan.

2. Bake 25-30 minutes or until a toothpick inserted in center comes out clean. Cool completely in pan on a wire rack.

3. For frosting, in a small bowl, beat cream cheese, butter and vanilla until smooth. Beat in confectioners' sugar; spread over top. Sprinkle with cranberries. Cut into bars or triangles. Refrigerate leftovers.

FRESH BLUEBERRY PIE

Fresh Blueberry Pie

I've been making this dessert for decades. It represents our state well because Michigan is the leader in blueberry production. Nothing says summer like a piece of fresh blueberry pie!

—LINDA KERNAN MASON, MI

PREP: 15 MIN. + COOLING
MAKES: 8 SERVINGS

- ¾ cup sugar
- 3 tablespoons cornstarch
- ⅛ teaspoon salt
- ¼ cup cold water
- 5 cups fresh blueberries, divided
- 1 tablespoon butter
- 1 tablespoon lemon juice
- 1 pastry shell (9 inches), baked

1. In a saucepan over medium heat, combine sugar, cornstarch, salt and water until smooth. Add 3 cups blueberries. Bring to a boil; cook and stir for 2 minutes or until thickened and bubbly.

2. Remove from the heat. Add butter, lemon juice and remaining berries; stir until butter is melted. Cool. Pour into pastry shell. Chill until serving.

CRANBERRY BARS WITH CREAM CHEESE FROSTING

top tip My Secret Ingredient

I found an excellent sweet-and-tart twist for blueberry pie. I slightly decrease the sugar and stir in black raspberry jelly. This really brightens up the pie.

—ALYCE S. TOLEDO, OH

PUMPKIN SPICE CAKE WITH MAPLE GLAZE

Pumpkin Spice Cake with Maple Glaze

Serve up some fun with my delicious cake that's especially nice during the holiday season. The traditional pumpkin, spices and maple glaze give it an amazing homemade taste.

—**BARBARA ELLIOTT** TYLER, TX

PREP: 20 MIN. • **BAKE:** 45 MIN. + COOLING
MAKES: 12 SERVINGS

- 1 **package yellow cake mix (regular size)**
- 1 **can (15 ounces) solid-pack pumpkin**
- 4 **eggs**
- ½ **cup canola oil**
- ⅓ **cup sugar**
- 2 **tablespoons ground cinnamon**
- 1 **teaspoon ground ginger**
- 1 **teaspoon ground allspice**
- 1 **teaspoon ground nutmeg**
- ¼ **teaspoon ground cloves**

GLAZE

- 2 **cups confectioners' sugar**
- ¼ **cup 2% milk**
- 2 **tablespoons maple syrup**
- ½ **teaspoon maple flavoring**
- ½ **cup chopped pecans, toasted**

1. Place the first 10 ingredients in a large bowl; beat on low speed for 30 seconds. Beat on medium for 2 minutes. Pour into a greased and floured 10-in. fluted tube pan.

2. Bake at 350° for 45-50 minutes or until a toothpick inserted near the center comes out clean. Cool for 10 minutes before removing from pan to a wire rack to cool completely.

3. Whisk the confectioners' sugar, milk, syrup and maple flavoring until smooth. Drizzle over cake and sprinkle with pecans.

Banana Cream Pie

This fluffy no-bake pie is full of old-fashioned flavor, but with only a fraction of the work. Because it uses instant pudding , it's ready in just minutes.

—**PERLENE HOEKEMA** LYNDEN, WA

START TO FINISH: 10 MIN.
MAKES: 8 SERVINGS

- 1 **cup cold 2% milk**
- ½ **teaspoon vanilla extract**
- 1 **package (3.4 ounces) instant vanilla pudding mix**
- 1 **carton (12 ounces) frozen whipped topping, thawed, divided**
- 1 **graham cracker crust (9 inches)**
- 2 **medium firm bananas, sliced Additional banana slices, optional**

1. In a large bowl, whisk milk, vanilla and pudding mix for 2 minutes (mixture will be thick). Fold in 3 cups whipped topping.

2. Pour 1⅓ cups of pudding mixture into pie crust. Layer with banana slices and remaining pudding mixture. Top with remaining whipped topping. Garnish with additional banana slices if desired. Refrigerate until serving.

BANANA CREAM PIE

Strawberry Poke Cake

Strawberry shortcake takes on a wonderful twist with my super-simple layered cake. Strawberries liven up each pretty slice.

—**MARY JO GRIGGS** WEST BEND, WI

PREP: 25 MIN. • **BAKE:** 25 MIN. + CHILLING
MAKES: 12 SERVINGS

- 1 package white cake mix (regular size)
- 1¼ cups water
- 2 eggs
- ¼ cup canola oil
- 2 packages (10 ounces each) frozen sweetened sliced strawberries, thawed
- 2 packages (3 ounces each) strawberry gelatin
- 1 carton (12 ounces) frozen whipped topping, thawed, divided
  Fresh strawberries, optional

1. In a large bowl, combine the cake mix, water, eggs and oil; beat on low speed for 30 seconds. Beat on medium for 2 minutes.

2. Pour into two greased and floured 9-in. round baking pans. Bake at 350° for 25-35 minutes or until a toothpick inserted near the center comes out clean. Cool for 10 minutes; remove from pans to wire racks to cool completely.

3. Using a serrated knife, level tops of cakes if necessary. Return layers, top side up, to two clean 9-in. round baking pans. Pierce the cakes with a meat fork or wooden skewer at ½-in. intervals.

4. Drain juice from strawberries into a 2-cup measuring cup; refrigerate berries. Add water to juice to measure 2 cups; pour into a small saucepan. Bring to a boil; stir in gelatin until dissolved. Chill for 30 minutes. Gently spoon over each cake layer. Chill for 2-3 hours.

5. Dip bottom of one pan in warm water for 10 seconds. Invert cake onto a serving platter. Top with reserved strawberries and 1 cup whipped topping. Place the second cake layer over topping.

6. Frost cake with remaining whipped topping. Chill for at least 1 hour. Serve with fresh berries if desired. Refrigerate leftovers.

NOTE *This cake was tested with Pillsbury white cake mix.*

Calgary Nanaimo Bars

This version may claim roots in Alberta, but the original was said to be dreamed up in a Nanaimo, British Columbia, kitchen. Either way, they're three delicious layers of Canadian goodness.

—**CAROL HILLIER** CALGARY, AB

PREP: 25 MIN. + CHILLING
MAKES: 3½ DOZEN

- ¼ cup sugar
- ¼ cup baking cocoa
- ¾ cup butter, cubed
- 2 eggs, beaten
- 2 cups graham cracker crumbs
- 1 cup flaked coconut
- ½ cup chopped almonds, optional

FILLING
- 2 cups confectioners' sugar
- 2 tablespoons instant vanilla pudding mix
- ¼ cup butter, melted
- 3 tablespoons 2% milk

GLAZE
- 3 ounces semisweet chocolate, chopped
- 1 tablespoon butter

1. Line an 8-in.-square baking pan with foil, letting ends extend over sides by 1 in. In a large heavy saucepan, combine sugar and cocoa; add butter. Cook and stir over medium-low heat until butter is melted. Whisk a small amount of hot mixture into eggs. Return all to the pan, whisking constantly. Cook and stir until mixture reaches 160°. Remove from heat.

2. Stir in cracker crumbs, coconut and, if desired, almonds. Press into prepared pan. Refrigerate 30 minutes or until set.

3. For filling, in a small bowl, beat confectioners' sugar, pudding mix, butter and milk until smooth; spread over crust.

4. In a microwave, melt chocolate and butter; stir until smooth. Spread over top. Refrigerate until set. Using foil, lift bars out of pan. Discard foil; cut dessert into bars.

CALGARY NANAIMO BARS

Peter Halferty's
Bacon-Wrapped Hot Dogs
PAGE 281

Holiday &
Seasonal Pleasers

For fun get-togethers and holiday feasts, turn to the cherished recipes in this giant chapter. Gatherings are a simple joy with the menus, snacks, gifts and treats you'll find here.

Ruth Bolduc's
Poppy Seed Pecan Muffins
PAGE 273

Tami Voltz's
Alfredo-Pancetta Stuffed Shells
PAGE 274

Anne Keenan's
Cranberry Almond Coffee Cake
PAGE 295

FIVE-SPICE CHICKEN WINGS
MEAT LOVERS' SNACK MIX
BEER-CHEESE APPETIZERS

Five-Spice Chicken Wings

Bird is the word when it comes to these wings. They're baked to a perfect golden brown and hum with mild Asian spices. Thanks to an overnight marinade, the chicken inside stays tender while the skin maintains that signature crunch.

—**CRYSTAL JO BRUNS** ILIFF, CO

PREP: 15 MIN. + MARINATING
BAKE: 25 MIN. • **MAKES:** ABOUT 3 DOZEN

- 3½ pounds chicken wings
- 3 green onions, chopped
- 2 tablespoons sweet chili sauce
- 2 tablespoons reduced-sodium soy sauce
- 2 tablespoons fish sauce or additional soy sauce
- 4 garlic cloves, minced
- 1 tablespoon sugar
- 1 tablespoon Chinese five-spice powder
- 2 medium limes, cut into wedges

1. Cut chicken wings into three sections and discard the wing tip sections.
2. Combine the onions, chili sauce, soy sauce, fish sauce, garlic, sugar and five-spice powder in a large resealable plastic bag. Add wings; seal bag and toss to coat. Refrigerate 8 hours or overnight.
3. Drain and discard marinade. Place wings in a greased 15-in. x 10-in. x 1-in. baking pan.
4. Bake at 425° for 25-30 minutes or until no longer pink, turning every 10 minutes. Squeeze lime over wings.
NOTE *Uncooked chicken wing sections (wingettes) may be substituted for whole chicken wings.*

Meat Lovers' Snack Mix

Admittedly, this crunchy appetizer might skew toward the dudes. But everyone will go wild for this go-to on game day! My husband loves that it features all of his favorite foods: salted meats, salted nuts and hot sauce.

—**GINA MYHILL-JONES** 100 MILE HOUSE, BC

PREP: 15 MIN. • **BAKE:** 50 MIN. + COOLING
MAKES: 6 CUPS

- 1¼ cups wasabi-coated green peas
- ¾ cup salted peanuts
- 3 pepperoni-flavored meat snack sticks (1½ ounces each), cut into bite-size pieces
- 2 ounces beef jerky, cut into bite-size pieces
- ½ cup corn nuts
- ½ cup Rice Chex
- ½ cup Multi Grain Cheerios
- ½ cup crunchy cheese puff snacks
- 2 tablespoons chopped sun-dried tomatoes (not packed in oil)
- ⅓ cup canola oil
- 1½ teaspoons chili powder
- 1½ teaspoons onion powder
- ½ teaspoon hot pepper sauce
- ½ teaspoon soy sauce
- ¼ teaspoon seasoned salt

1. Combine the first nine ingredients in a large bowl. In a small bowl, whisk the oil, chili powder, onion powder, pepper sauce, soy sauce and seasoned salt. Drizzle over cereal mixture and toss to coat.
2. Spread into a greased 15-in. x 10-in. x 1-in. baking pan. Bake at 250° for 50 minutes, stirring every 10 minutes. Cool completely on a wire rack. Store in an airtight container.

Beer-Cheese Appetizers

It's hard to stop eating these amazing treats that feature a classic pairing of beer and hot melted cheese. They disappear fast on game day.

—**KRISTY WILSHIRE** PITTSBURGH, PA

PREP: 25 MIN. • **BAKE:** 5 MIN./BATCH
MAKES: 80 APPETIZERS (1¾ CUPS SAUCE)

- 2 cups biscuit/baking mix
- ½ cup shredded cheddar cheese
- ½ cup beer or nonalcoholic beer
- 2 tablespoons butter, melted
  Sesame and/or poppy seeds
- **CHEESE SAUCE**
- 1 package (8 ounces) process cheese (Velveeta), cubed
- ½ cup refried beans
- 2 jalapeno peppers, seeded and chopped
- ¼ cup sour cream
- ¼ cup salsa

1. Combine biscuit mix and cheese in a large bowl. Stir in beer until a soft dough forms. Turn onto a floured surface; knead 5 times. Roll into a 16-in. x 10-in. rectangle. Cut into 2-in. squares; cut each square in half diagonally.
2. Place 1 in. apart on greased baking sheets. Brush with butter; sprinkle with seeds. Bake at 450° for 6-8 minutes or until lightly browned. Remove to wire racks to cool.
3. For sauce, combine the remaining ingredients in a small saucepan. Cook and stir over medium heat until cheese is melted. Serve immediately with triangles.
NOTE *Wear disposable gloves when cutting hot peppers; the oils can burn skin. Avoid touching your face.*

FAST FIX
Party Time Popcorn

Irresistible and addicting: that's how friends will describe this cheesy twist on regular popped popcorn.

—**TASTE OF HOME TEST KITCHEN**

START TO FINISH: 10 MIN.
MAKES: 3½ QUARTS

- ¼ cup grated Parmesan cheese
- 2 tablespoons ranch salad dressing mix
- 1 teaspoon dried parsley
- ¼ teaspoon onion powder
- ⅓ cup butter
- 3½ quarts popped popcorn

Combine Parmesan cheese, dressing mix, parsley and onion powder. Melt butter; drizzle over popcorn and toss. Sprinkle with cheese mixture; toss.

PARTY TIME POPCORN

BERRY MINI CHEESECAKES

Berry Mini Cheesecakes

There's always room for dessert when it's just a bite!

—TASTE OF HOME TEST KITCHEN

PREP: 30 MIN. + CHILLING
MAKES: 1½ DOZEN

- 1 cup graham cracker crumbs
- 3 tablespoons butter, melted
- 1 package (8 ounces) cream cheese, softened
- ⅓ cup sugar
- 1 teaspoon vanilla extract
- 1 egg, lightly beaten
- 18 fresh raspberries

1. In a small bowl, combine graham cracker crumbs and butter. Press gently onto the bottom of 18 paper-lined miniature muffin cups. In another small bowl, beat the cream cheese, sugar and vanilla until smooth. Add egg; beat on low speed just until combined. Spoon over crusts.

2. Bake at 350° for 12-14 minutes or until centers are set. Cool for 10 minutes before removing from pan to a wire rack to cool completely. Refrigerate for at least 1 hour.

3. To serve, remove paper liners; top cheesecakes with raspberries.

Black Forest Cake

When my daughter went to Germany on a backpacking trip, she said the streets were lined with pastry shops. Here's my easy take on one of the country's most popular desserts. It's delicious.

—PATRICIA RUTHERFORD WINCHESTER, IL

PREP: 10 MIN. • **BAKE:** 25 MIN. + CHILLING
MAKES: 6-8 SERVINGS

- 1 package (9 ounces) devil's food cake mix
- ½ cup water
- 1 egg
- 1 package (3 ounces) cream cheese, softened
- 2 tablespoons sugar
- 1 carton (8 ounces) frozen whipped topping, thawed
- 1 can (21 ounces) cherry pie filling

1. In a small bowl, beat the cake mix, water and egg on medium speed for 3-4 minutes. Pour into a greased 9-in. springform pan; place the pan on a baking sheet.

2. Bake at 350° for 23-25 minutes or until cake springs back when lightly touched. Cool on a wire rack.

3. In a small bowl, beat cream cheese and sugar until fluffy; fold in whipped topping. Spread pie filling over cake; top with cream cheese mixture. Cover and refrigerate for 4 hours. Remove sides of pan.

BLACK FOREST CAKE

RASPBERRY TRUFFLE COCKTAIL

Valentine Heart Brownies

Steal hearts this Valentine's Day with brownies that have cute frosting centers. They're sweet!

—TASTE OF HOME TEST KITCHEN

PREP: 35 MIN. • **BAKE:** 20 MIN. + COOLING
MAKES: 15 SERVINGS

- 1 package fudge brownie mix (13-inch x 9-inch pan size)
- ¼ teaspoon mint extract
- ½ cup butter, softened
- 1½ cups confectioners' sugar
- ¼ teaspoon vanilla extract
  Red paste food coloring, optional
- ¼ cup baking cocoa

1. Prepare brownie mix according to package directions, adding mint extract to batter. Transfer to a greased 13-in. x 9-in. baking pan. Bake at 350° for 20-25 minutes or until a toothpick inserted near the center comes out clean. Cool completely on a wire rack.

2. Meanwhile, in a small bowl, cream the butter, confectioners' sugar, vanilla and, if desired, food coloring until light and fluffy. Place in a heavy-duty resealable plastic bag; cut a small hole in a corner of bag. Set aside.

3. Line a baking sheet with parchment paper. Dust with cocoa; set aside. Cut brownies into 15 rectangles. Using a 1½-in. heart-shaped cookie cutter, cut out a heart from the center of each brownie. Reserve cutout centers for another use. Place brownies on prepared baking sheet. Pipe frosting into centers of brownies.

Raspberry Truffle Cocktail

This adults-only hot chocolate is a decadent addition to any holiday gathering. You can easily adapt it to dairy lovers' tastes by using regular milk instead of the almond products.

—MELANIE MILHORAT NEW YORK, NY

START TO FINISH: 10 MIN.
MAKES: 1 SERVING

- 1 cup chocolate almond milk or 2% chocolate milk
- 1 ounce vodka
- ½ ounce raspberry liqueur
- ¼ cup cold vanilla almond milk or fat-free milk
  Baking cocoa, optional

1. Place chocolate almond milk in a small saucepan; heat through. Add vodka and raspberry liqueur; transfer to a mug.

2. Pour vanilla almond milk into a small bowl. With a milk frother, blend until foamy. Spoon foam into mug. Sprinkle with cocoa if desired.

VALENTINE HEART BROWNIES

PEANUT BUTTER CUP NAPOLEONS

"Top layers of puff pastry and peanut butter ice cream with a warm, sweet drizzle the whole family will love! These are terrific last-minute treats. Or make them a day in advance and pop them in the freezer."

—**JEANNE HOLT** MENDOTA HEIGHTS, MN

⑤ INGREDIENTS

Peanut Butter Cup Napoleons

PREP: 10 MIN. • **BAKE:** 15 MIN. + COOLING
MAKES: 4 SERVINGS

- 1 sheet frozen puff pastry, thawed
- 2 cups peanut butter ice cream with peanut butter cup pieces, softened
- ¾ cup butterscotch-caramel ice cream topping
- 3 tablespoons creamy peanut butter
- ¼ cup chopped chocolate-covered peanuts

1. Unfold puff pastry. Cut into eight 4½-in. x 2¼-in. rectangles. Place on a greased baking sheet. Bake at 400° for 12-15 minutes or until golden brown. Cool completely on a wire rack.
2. Scoop ½ cup ice cream onto each of four pastries. Top with remaining pastries. Freeze until serving.
3. Combine ice cream topping and peanut butter in a small microwave-safe bowl. Cover and cook on high for 30-45 seconds or until warmed. Drizzle over napoleons and sprinkle with peanuts.

⑤ INGREDIENTS | FAST FIX ▶

Honey-Soy Asparagus

It's love at first bite when you get a delectable burst of sweet-and-salty flavor with just the right amount of garlic in this crisp-tender side. Just toss the asparagus into the pan, and it's ready to eat in the blink of an eye.

—**LISA DANIELL** LOVELAND, CO

START TO FINISH: 15 MIN.
MAKES: 4 SERVINGS

- ¼ cup butter
- 2 tablespoons reduced-sodium soy sauce
- 2 tablespoons honey
- 2 garlic cloves, minced
- 1 pound fresh asparagus, trimmed

In a large skillet, melt butter. Stir in the soy sauce, honey and garlic. Add asparagus; saute until crisp-tender.

⑤ INGREDIENTS | FAST FIX ▶

Chive Red Potatoes

With a vegetable peeler, remove a small strip from around each potato to add an artful touch to these simpe spuds. Their pretty appearance and light garlic taste will enhance many different entrees.

—**TASTE OF HOME TEST KITCHEN**

START TO FINISH: 25 MIN.
MAKES: 6 SERVINGS

- 2 pounds small red potatoes
- ⅓ cup butter, melted
- 2 tablespoons minced chives
- ½ teaspoon salt
- ¼ teaspoon garlic powder

1. Peel a narrow strip around the middle of each potato. Place potatoes in a large saucepan and cover with water. Bring to a boil. Reduce heat; cover and cook for 15-20 minutes or until tender.
2. Combine the butter, chives, salt and garlic powder in a small bowl. Drain potatoes; drizzle with butter mixture and toss gently to coat.

⑤ INGREDIENTS

Crab & Herb Cheese Filet Mignon

Save the money you'd spend on going out for surf and turf. Instead, treat yourself to thick-cut steaks stuffed with garlic-herb cheese and fresh crabmeat. It's a home-cooked entree that looks and tastes like it came from a four-star restaurant!

—**TASTE OF HOME TEST KITCHEN**

PREP: 15 MIN. • **BROIL:** 20 MIN.
MAKES: 4 SERVINGS

- 1½ cups fresh crabmeat
- 1 package (6½ ounces) garlic-herb spreadable cheese, divided
- 4 beef tenderloin steaks (1 inch thick and 8 ounces each)
- ¼ teaspoon salt
- ¼ teaspoon pepper

1. Combine crab and ¾ cup spreadable cheese in a small bowl.
2. Cut a horizontal pocket in each steak. Fill each pocket with ⅓ cup crab mixture. Place steaks on a greased broiler pan. Sprinkle with salt and pepper.
3. Broil 4 in. from the heat for 10 minutes on each side or until meat reaches desired doneness (for medium-rare, a thermometer should read 145°; medium, 160°; well-done, 170°), spooning the remaining cheese over steaks during the last 2 minutes of broiling. Let stand for 5 minutes before serving.

HOLIDAY & SEASONAL PLEASERS

HONEY-SOY ASPARGUS
CHIVE RED POTATOES
CRAB & HERB CHEESE FILET MIGNON

HONEY-LIME YOGURT DIP
SPICED BACON TWISTS
CHILI & CHEESE HAM STRATA

Honey-Lime Yogurt Dip

When it comes to this tangy fruit dip, I don't mind my kids playing with their food. We like to dip strawberries, bananas, pears and more.

—SHELLY BEVINGTON HERMISTON, OR

START TO FINISH: 5 MIN.
MAKES: 2 CUPS

- 2 cups (16 ounces) plain yogurt
- ¼ cup honey
- 2 tablespoons lime juice
- ½ teaspoon grated lime peel
  Assorted fresh fruit

Whisk the yogurt, honey, lime juice and lime peel in a small bowl. Refrigerate until serving. Serve with assorted fruit.

Spiced Bacon Twists

Whenever I share this recipe, I also issue a caveat that you might find bacon even more addictive once you've had these sweet little twists. Don't say I didn't warn you!

—GLENDA EVANS WITTNER JOPLIN, MO

PREP: 10 MIN. • **BAKE:** 25 MIN.
MAKES: 5 SERVINGS

- ¼ cup packed brown sugar
- 1½ teaspoons ground mustard
- ⅛ teaspoon ground cinnamon
- ⅛ teaspoon ground nutmeg
  Dash cayenne pepper
- 10 center-cut bacon strips

1. Combine the first five ingredients; rub over bacon on both sides. Twist bacon; place on a rack in a 15-in. x 10-in. x 1-in. baking pan.
2. Bake at 350° for 25-30 minutes or until firm; bake longer if desired.

Chili & Cheese Ham Strata

Don't you just love it when you find a holiday recipe that can be folded into the everyday repertoire? This strata, layered with sourdough, cheddar and savory ham, is egg-cellent for Easter but just as wonderful for any other brunch!

—THERESA KREYCHE TUSTIN, CA

PREP: 20 MIN. + CHILLING • **BAKE:** 40 MIN.
MAKES: 8 SERVINGS

- 6 slices sourdough bread (1 inch thick)
- ¼ cup butter, softened
- 2½ cups (10 ounces) shredded cheddar cheese, divided
- 1 cup cubed fully cooked ham
- 1 can (4 ounces) chopped green chilies
- ¼ cup finely chopped onion
- 2 tablespoons minced fresh cilantro
- 5 eggs
- 1½ cups 2% milk
- ¼ teaspoon salt
- ¼ teaspoon ground cumin
- ¼ teaspoon ground mustard

1. Remove and discard crust from bread if desired. Butter bread; cube and place in a greased 13x9-in. baking dish. Sprinkle with 1¾ cups cheese, ham, chilies, onion and cilantro.
2. Whisk the eggs, milk, salt, cumin and mustard in a large bowl. Pour over the bread mixture; cover and refrigerate overnight.
3. Remove from the refrigerator 30 minutes before baking. Bake, covered, at 350° for 30 minutes. Uncover; sprinkle with remaining cheese. Bake 10-15 minutes longer or until a knife inserted in center comes out clean. Let stand 5 minutes before cutting.

Poppy Seed Pecan Muffins

Whenever I can carve out even a little free time, I love to bake. And after almost endless experimenting, I have to say that these muffins are my all-around favorites. They're easy to make, and the hint of orange peel just says spring to me.

—RUTH BOLDUC CONWAY, NH

PREP: 20 MIN. • **BAKE:** 15 MIN.
MAKES: 1 DOZEN

- ¼ cup butter, softened
- ¾ cup sugar
- 2 eggs
- 1 cup 2% milk
- ½ teaspoon grated orange peel
- 2 cups all-purpose flour
- 2½ teaspoons baking powder
- ½ teaspoon salt
- ¼ teaspoon ground nutmeg
- ½ cup chopped pecans
- ½ cup golden raisins
- 2 tablespoons poppy seeds

1. Cream butter and sugar in a large bowl. Add eggs, one at a time, beating well after each addition. Stir in milk and orange peel. In another bowl, combine the flour, baking powder, salt and nutmeg. Add to creamed mixture just until moistened. Stir in the pecans, raisins and poppy seeds.
2. Fill greased or paper-lined muffin cups two-thirds full. Bake at 400° for 15-20 minutes or until a toothpick comes out clean. Cool for 5 minutes before removing from pan to a wire rack. Serve warm.
PER SERVING *240 cal., 9 g fat (3 g sat. fat), 47 mg chol., 232 mg sodium, 35 g carb., 1 g fiber, 5 g pro.*

POPPY SEED PECAN MUFFINS

top tip — Easter Deviled Eggs

I once hosted a birthday brunch buffet for my 90-year-old uncle. Since the event took place close to Easter, I wanted to prepare colored eggs but worried about the mess all of those broken egg shells would leave. That's when I decided to shell the eggs before coloring them. Once the color was set, I cut the eggs in half to make pretty pastel deviled eggs. Served on a plate of fresh lettuce, they were the hit of the party.

—CAROL W. SPOKANE, WA

Alfredo-Pancetta Stuffed Shells

I thought up this recipe while I was driving home from work. The local paper started a new reader recipe feature, so I sent this in, and I was published! Warm up some bread, pour the Chardonnay, and enjoy.

—**TAMI VOLTZ** RUDOLPH, OH

PREP: 30 MIN. • **BAKE:** 35 MIN.
MAKES: 6 SERVINGS

- 12 uncooked jumbo pasta shells
- 4 ounces pancetta, finely chopped
- 1 teaspoon olive oil
- 1 package (6 ounces) fresh baby spinach
- 2 garlic cloves, minced
- ½ teaspoon crushed red pepper flakes
- 1 carton (15 ounces) part-skim ricotta cheese
- 2 tablespoons grated Parmesan cheese
- 1 egg yolk, beaten
- ¼ teaspoon pepper
- 1 jar (15 ounces) roasted garlic Alfredo sauce
- ½ cup shredded mozzarella cheese

1. Cook pasta shells according to package directions; drain and rinse with cold water.

2. Meanwhile, cook pancetta in oil in a large skillet over medium heat until crisp. Remove to paper towels, reserving drippings. Saute the spinach, garlic and pepper flakes in drippings until spinach is wilted.

3. Transfer spinach mixture to a small bowl. Add ricotta, Parmesan cheese, egg yolk and pepper; mix well.

4. Spread ½ cup Alfredo sauce into a greased 11-in. x 7-in. baking dish. Spoon ricotta mixture into pasta shells; place in baking dish. Pour remaining sauce over shells.

5. Cover and bake at 375° for 25 minutes. Sprinkle with mozzarella cheese. Bake 10-15 minutes longer or until cheese is melted. Top with pancetta.

APRICOT-GINGERSNAP HAM

Apricot-Gingersnap Ham

I've been told my Easter ham is as much a feast for the eyes as it is for the taste buds. The combination of apricot, brown sugar and gingersnaps usually ensures plenty of oohs and aahs!

—**MELANIE WOODEN** RENO, NV

PREP: 20 MIN. • **BAKE:** 2 HOURS
MAKES: 15 SERVINGS (3½ CUPS SAUCE)

- 1 spiral-sliced fully cooked bone-in ham (7 to 9 pounds)
- 1½ cups apricot preserves
- ½ cup packed brown sugar
- ⅓ cup Dijon mustard
- 1½ cups crushed gingersnap cookies (about 30 cookies)
- 3 cups chicken broth
- ½ teaspoon salt
- ¼ teaspoon pepper
- 3 tablespoons cornstarch
- ½ cup cold water

1. Line a shallow roasting pan with heavy-duty foil. Place ham on a rack in prepared pan. Cover and bake at 325° for 1½ hours.

2. Combine the preserves, brown sugar and mustard, reserving ¼ cup of mixture for sauce. Spread over ham. Press cookie crumbs onto ham.

3. Bake, uncovered, for 30-45 minutes longer or until a thermometer reads 140°. Remove meat to a serving platter and keep warm, reserving ⅓ cup of the drippings.

4. Combine the broth, salt, pepper, reserved ham drippings and reserved apricot mixture in a small saucepan. Combine cornstarch and water until smooth. Stir into saucepan. Bring to a boil; cook and stir for 2 minutes or until thickened. Serve with ham.

ALFREDO-PANCETTA STUFFED SHELLS

MUSHROOM & ASPARAGUS EGGS BENEDICT

Mushroom & Asparagus Eggs Benedict

This recipe is easy to make, but it looks sophisticated. I like to serve it with broiled grapefruit topped with brown sugar and ginger for breakfast, and a mixed green salad tossed with tomatoes and balsamic vinaigrette for brunch.

—**NADINE MESCH** MOUNT HEALTHY, OH

PREP: 25 MIN. • **COOK:** 25 MIN.
MAKES: 4 SERVINGS

- 12 fresh asparagus spears
- 3 teaspoons olive oil, divided
- 1 shallot, finely chopped
- 2 tablespoons butter, divided
- 2⅔ cups sliced baby portobello mushrooms
- 2½ cups sliced fresh shiitake mushrooms
- 1 garlic clove, minced
- ¼ cup sherry
- ½ cup heavy whipping cream
- ½ teaspoon salt
- 1 tablespoon minced fresh basil
- 1 tablespoon white vinegar
- 4 eggs
- 4 slices French bread (¾ inch thick), toasted
- ¼ teaspoon pepper
- 2 teaspoons balsamic vinegar

1. Saute asparagus in 1 teaspoon oil in a large skillet until crisp-tender; remove and keep warm.
2. Saute shallot in remaining oil and 1 tablespoon butter in the same skillet until tender. Add mushrooms and garlic; cook 4 minutes longer. Add sherry, stirring to loosen browned bits from pan. Stir in cream and salt. Bring to a boil. Cook and stir for 1-2 minutes or until slightly thickened. Stir in basil.
3. Meanwhile, place 2-3 inches of water in a large skillet with high sides; add white vinegar. Bring to a boil; reduce heat and simmer gently. Break cold eggs, one at a time, into a custard cup or saucer; holding the cup close to the surface of the water, slip each egg into water.
4. Cook, uncovered, until whites are completely set and yolks are still soft, about 4 minutes. With a slotted spoon, lift eggs out of the water.
5. Spread remaining butter over toast slices. Top each with asparagus, a poached egg and mushroom mixture. Sprinkle with pepper and drizzle with balsamic vinegar. Serve immediately.

Savory French Toast Bake

Spend just 15 minutes prepping this casserole the night before, and you'll have extra time to make a fruit salad and pour the coffee as it bakes.

—**PATRICIA NIEH** PORTOLA VALLEY, CA

PREP: 15 MIN. + CHILLING
BAKE: 50 MIN. + STANDING
MAKES: 10 SERVINGS

- 1 loaf (8 ounces) day-old French bread, cut into ½-inch slices
- 6 eggs, beaten
- 2 cups 2% milk
- 4 teaspoons Dijon mustard
- ½ teaspoon salt
- ½ teaspoon pepper
- ½ cup minced chives, divided
- 1½ cups (6 ounces) shredded Gruyere or Swiss cheese, divided

1. Arrange half of the bread slices in a greased 13-in. x 9-in. baking dish. In a large bowl, combine the eggs, milk, mustard, salt, pepper and ¼ cup chives.
2. Pour half of the egg mixture over bread; sprinkle with 1 cup cheese. Layer with remaining bread and egg mixture. Sprinkle with remaining cheese. Cover and refrigerate overnight.
3. Remove from the refrigerator 30 minutes before baking. Bake, uncovered, at 350° for 50-55 minutes or until a knife inserted near the center comes out clean. Let stand for 10 minutes before cutting. Sprinkle with remaining chives.

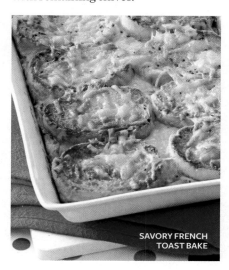

SAVORY FRENCH TOAST BAKE

PINEAPPLE SHRIMP TACOS
GRILLED STEAK & ONION TACOS
CHIPOTLE RANCH CHICKEN TACOS

Pineapple Shrimp Tacos

Taste the tropics with our cool and crispy take on shrimp tacos. Wrapping the shells in lettuce adds even more crunch, while keeping the tacos tidy after you take a bite.
—TASTE OF HOME TEST KITCHEN

START TO FINISH: 25 MIN.
MAKES: 4 SERVINGS

- 1 pound uncooked large shrimp, peeled and deveined
- 3 teaspoons olive oil, divided
- 1 large sweet orange pepper, sliced
- 1 large sweet red pepper, sliced
- 1 small onion, halved and sliced
- 1 cup pineapple tidbits
- 1 envelope fajita seasoning mix
- ⅓ cup water
- 8 corn tortillas (6 inches), warmed
- ½ cup shredded cotija or mozzarella cheese
- 8 large romaine lettuce leaves

1. Cook shrimp in 2 teaspoons oil in a large skillet over medium heat for 4-6 minutes or until shrimp turn pink; remove and keep warm.
2. In the same skillet, saute the peppers, onion and pineapple in remaining oil until tender. Add seasoning mix and water. Bring to a boil; cook and stir for 2 minutes. Return shrimp to the skillet; heat through. Spoon onto tortillas; top with cheese. Wrap lettuce around tortillas to serve.

Grilled Steak & Onion Tacos

Fire up the grill for soft tacos stuffed with zesty beef, sweet red onions and health-boosting avocado. Oh, yeah!
—TASTE OF HOME TEST KITCHEN

START TO FINISH: 30 MIN.
MAKES: 4 SERVINGS

- 1 beef top sirloin steak (1 to 2 pounds)
- 2 tablespoons taco seasoning
- 2 medium red onions, cut into ½-inch slices
- 2 teaspoons olive oil
- 8 flour tortillas (6 inches)
- 2 medium ripe avocados, peeled and sliced
  Sour cream, fresh cilantro leaves and lime wedges

1. Sprinkle steak with taco seasoning. Moisten a paper towel with cooking oil; using long-handled tongs, lightly coat the grill rack. Grill steak, covered, over medium heat or broil 4 in. from the heat for 6-8 minutes on each side or until meat reaches desired doneness (for medium-rare, a thermometer should read 145°; medium, 160°; well-done, 170°). Let stand for 5 minutes.
2. Meanwhile, brush onions with oil. Grill, uncovered, over medium heat for 3-4 minutes on each side or until tender.
3. Grill tortillas on each side until warm. Thinly slice steak. Top tortillas with steak, avocado and onions. Serve tacos with sour cream, cilantro and lime wedges.

Chipotle Ranch Chicken Tacos

Chop, chop...or not. These tacos are easy on the cook with ready-to-use produce, pico, dressing and cheese. Thinly slice the radishes and hot peppers, and your party is ready.
—TASTE OF HOME TEST KITCHEN

START TO FINISH: 20 MIN.
MAKES: 4 SERVINGS

- 2 cups shredded rotisserie chicken
- 2 cups frozen corn, thawed
- ¼ cup pico de gallo
- 8 taco shells, warmed
- 1 cup (4 ounces) shredded Monterey Jack cheese
- 1 cup coleslaw mix
- 6 radishes, thinly sliced
- ½ cup chipotle ranch salad dressing
- 3 jalapeno peppers, seeded and thinly sliced

1. Combine the chicken, corn and pico de gallo in a small microwave-safe dish. Cover and cook on high for 1-2 minutes or until heated through.
2. Spoon chicken mixture into taco shells. Top with the remaining ingredients.
NOTE *Wear disposable gloves when cutting hot peppers; the oils can burn skin. Avoid touching your face.*

MEXICAN MENU IDEAS

Make your next fiesta a success with these easy menu add-ons.

Beverages: lemonade, margarita, white sangria, wine or beer
Appetizers: quesadillas, nachos, guacamole, chili con queso or black bean soup
Side dishes: refried beans, grilled vegetables, Spanish rice or corn custard
Desserts: caramelized bananas over vanilla ice cream, fresh pineapple with toasted coconut and lime zest, Mexican flan or mango sorbet
Dessert drinks: Mexican hot chocolate or coffee with coffee liqueur, sugar, cinnamon and cream

Fresh Lime Margaritas
PAGE 306

MINTY TEA PUNCH

Minty Tea Punch

Forget sugary (and boring) soft drinks. For your next potluck, treat your family and friends to a refreshing homemade punch. Serve it up in mason jars with striped paper straws, and you'll really wow the crowd.

—**CRYSTAL JO BRUNS** ILIFF, CO

PREP: 15 MIN. + CHILLING
MAKES: 12 SERVINGS (¾ CUP EACH)

- 8 cups water, divided
- 12 mint sprigs
- 4 individual tea bags
- 1 cup orange juice
- ¼ cup lemon juice
- ½ cup sugar
    Ice cubes
    Orange and lemon slices, optional

1. In a large saucepan, bring 3 cups water to a boil. Remove from heat; add mint and tea bags. Steep, covered, 3-5 minutes according to taste. Discard mint and tea bags.
2. Stir in orange and lemon juices, sugar and remaining water. Transfer to a pitcher; refrigerate until chilled. Serve over ice; add orange and lemon slices if desired.
PER (¾-CUP) SERVING *43 cal., 0 fat (0 sat. fat), 0 chol., trace sodium, 11 g carb., trace fiber, trace pro.* **Diabetic Exchange:** *½ starch.*

Linda's Best Marinated Chicken

I have been using this grilled chicken recipe since I was 12 years old. It's so moist and delicious, it will melt in your mouth.

—**LINDA PACE** LEES SUMMIT, MO

PREP: 15 MIN. + MARINATING
GRILL: 40 MIN. • **MAKES:** 4 SERVINGS

- 1¼ cups olive oil
- ½ cup red wine vinegar
- ⅓ cup lemon juice
- ¼ cup reduced-sodium soy sauce
- ¼ cup Worcestershire sauce
- 2 tablespoons ground mustard
- 1 tablespoon pepper
- 3 garlic cloves, minced
- 1 broiler/fryer chicken (3 to 4 pounds), cut up

1. Place the first eight ingredients in a blender; cover and process until blended. Pour 2 cups marinade into a large resealable plastic bag. Add chicken; seal bag and turn to coat. Refrigerate 4 hours or overnight. Refrigerate remaining marinade.
2. Drain chicken, discarding marinade in bag. Grill chicken, covered, over medium heat 40-45 minutes or until juices run clear, turning occasionally and basting with reserved marinade during the last 15 minutes.

Basil Dill Coleslaw

I was introduced to basil when I married into an Italian family. I love the aromatic fragrance. It adds a unique flavor to this tasty slaw, which is a cool accompaniment to grilled meats.

—**JUNE CAPPETTO** SEATTLE, WA

START TO FINISH: 10 MIN.
MAKES: 6 SERVINGS

- 6 cups shredded cabbage or coleslaw mix
- 3 to 4 tablespoons chopped fresh basil or 1 tablespoon dried basil
- 3 tablespoons snipped fresh dill or 1 tablespoon dill weed

DRESSING
- ½ cup mayonnaise
- 3 tablespoons sugar
- 2 tablespoons cider vinegar
- 2 tablespoons half-and-half cream
- 1 teaspoon coarsely ground pepper

In a large bowl, combine cabbage, basil and dill. In a small bowl, whisk dressing ingredients until blended. Drizzle over cabbage mixture; toss to coat. Refrigerate until serving.
PER SERVING *138 cal., 11 g fat (2 g sat. fat), 7 mg chol., 87 mg sodium, 8 g carb., 1 g fiber, 1 g pro.* **Diabetic Exchanges:** *2 fat, 1 vegetable.*

Grilled Vegetable Platter

The best of summer in one pretty side dish! These veggies are pefect for entertaining. Grilling brings out their natural sweetness, and the easy balsamic marinade perks up their flavors.

—**HEIDI HALL** NORTH ST. PAUL, MN

PREP: 20 MIN. + MARINATING
GRILL: 10 MIN. • **MAKES:** 6 SERVINGS

- ¼ cup olive oil
- 2 tablespoons honey
- 4 teaspoons balsamic vinegar
- 1 teaspoon dried oregano
- ½ teaspoon garlic powder
- ⅛ teaspoon pepper
    Dash salt
- 1 pound fresh asparagus, trimmed
- 3 small carrots, cut in half lengthwise
- 1 large sweet red pepper, cut into 1-inch strips
- 1 medium yellow summer squash, cut into ½-inch slices
- 1 medium red onion, cut into wedges

1. In a small bowl, whisk the first seven ingredients. Place 3 tablespoons marinade in a large resealable plastic bag. Add vegetables; seal bag and turn to coat. Marinate 1½ hours at room temperature.
2. Transfer vegetables to a grilling grid; place grid on grill rack. Grill, covered, over medium heat 8-12 minutes or until crisp-tender, turning occasionally. Place vegetables on a large serving plate. Drizzle with remaining marinade.
NOTE *If you don't have a grilling grid, use a disposable foil pan. Poke holes in the bottom of the pan with a meat fork to allow liquid to drain.*
PER SERVING *144 cal., 9 g fat (1 g sat. fat), 0 chol., 50 mg sodium, 15 g carb., 3 g fiber, 2 g pro.* **Diabetic Exchanges:** *2 vegetable, 2 fat.*

LINDA'S BEST MARINATED CHICKEN
BASIL DILL COLESLAW
GRILLED VEGETABLE PLATTER

PATRIOTIC POPS

Patriotic Pops

My kids love homemade ice pops, and I love knowing that the ones we make are good for them. We whip up a big batch with multiple flavors so they have many choices, but these patriotic red, white and blue ones are always a favorite.

—**SHANNON CARINO** FRISCO, TX

PREP: 15 MIN. + FREEZING
MAKES: 1 DOZEN

- 1¼ cups sliced fresh strawberries, divided
- 1¾ cups (14 ounces) vanilla yogurt, divided
- 1¼ cups fresh or frozen blueberries, divided
- 12 freezer pop molds or 12 paper cups (3 ounces each) and wooden pop sticks

1. In a blender, combine 1 cup strawberries and 2 tablespoons yogurt; cover and process until blended. Transfer to a small bowl. Chop remaining strawberries; stir into strawberry mixture.

2. In same blender, combine 1 cup blueberries and 2 tablespoons yogurt; cover and process until blended. Stir in remaining blueberries.

3. Layer 1 tablespoon strawberry mixture, 2 tablespoons yogurt and 1 tablespoon blueberry mixture in each of 12 molds or paper cups. Top molds with holders. If using cups, top with foil and insert sticks through foil. Freeze until firm.

PER SERVING *45 cal., 1 g fat (trace sat. fat), 2 mg chol., 24 mg sodium, 9 g carb., 1 g fiber, 2 g pro.* **Diabetic Exchange:** *½ starch.*

Caribbean Grilled Ribeyes

I created this spicy-sweet steak with my father-in-law in mind. He loved it, and so did everyone else. It's especially good alongside seafood.

—**DE'LAWRENCE REED** DURHAM, NC

PREP: 10 MIN. + MARINATING
GRILL: 10 MIN. • **MAKES:** 4 SERVINGS

- ½ cup Dr Pepper
- 3 tablespoons honey
- ¼ cup Caribbean jerk seasoning
- 1½ teaspoons chopped seeded habanero pepper
- ½ teaspoon salt
- ½ teaspoon pepper
- 4 beef ribeye steaks (¾ pound each)

1. Place the first six ingredients in a blender; cover and process until blended. Pour into a large resealable plastic bag. Add steaks; seal bag and turn to coat. Refrigerate for at least 2 hours.

2. Drain steaks and discard marinade. Grill steaks, covered, over medium heat or broil 3-4 in. from heat for 4-6 minutes on each side or until meat reaches desired doneness (for medium-rare, a meat thermometer should read 145°; medium, 160°; well-done, 170°).

NOTE *Wear disposable gloves when cutting hot peppers; the oils can burn skin. Avoid touching your face.*

CARIBBEAN GRILLED RIBEYES

GRILLED CORN RELISH

Grilled Corn Relish

This colorful relish is a great way to get kids to eat their veggies. It's an instant upgrade for hot dogs.

—**ELLEN RILEY** BIRMINGHAM, AL

START TO FINISH: 25 MIN.
MAKES: 2 CUPS

- 1 large sweet red pepper
- 2 medium ears sweet corn, husks removed
- 5 tablespoons honey Dijon vinaigrette, divided
- 2 green onions, thinly sliced
- ½ teaspoon coarsely ground pepper
- ¼ teaspoon salt

1. Cut red pepper lengthwise in half; remove seeds. Grill red pepper and corn, covered, over medium heat 10-15 minutes or until tender, turning and basting occasionally with 3 tablespoons vinaigrette.

2. Remove corn from cobs and chop red pepper; transfer to a small bowl. Add green onions, pepper, salt and remaining vinaigrette; toss to combine.

PER (¼-CUP) SERVING *42 cal., 1 g fat (trace sat. fat), 0 chol., 157 mg sodium, 8 g carb., 1 g fiber, 1 g pro.* **Diabetic Exchange:** *½ starch.*

Bacon-Wrapped Hot Dogs

Here's a juicy, delicious and savory meal in a bun. I make it for picnics, barbecues and tailgate parties, and it always gets compliments. To transport, wrap the hot dogs in foil.

—**PETER HALFERTY** CORPUS CHRISTI, TX

PREP: 25 MIN. • **GRILL:** 10 MIN.
MAKES: 8 SERVINGS

- 12 bacon strips
- 8 cheese beef hot dogs
- 8 bakery hot dog buns, split and toasted
- ¼ cup chopped red onion
- 2 cups sauerkraut, rinsed and well drained
  Optional condiments: mayonnaise, ketchup or Dijon mustard

1. In a large skillet, cook bacon over medium heat until partially cooked but not crisp. Remove to paper towels to drain; cool slightly. Wrap 1½ strips of bacon around each hot dog, securing with toothpicks as needed (do not wrap tightly or bacon may tear during grilling).

2. Grill, covered, over medium heat or broil 4 in. from heat 6-8 minutes or until bacon is crisp and hot dogs are heated through, turning frequently. Discard toothpicks. Serve hot dogs in buns with onion and sauerkraut; top with condiments of your choice.

BACON-WRAPPED HOT DOGS

GIANT CUPCAKE PUMPKIN

Giant Cupcake Pumpkin

Make a smiley statement by decorating a whole tray of chocolate-spice cupcakes. Once everyone's seen the big picture, they can each take a treat.

—GENA LOTT OGDEN, UT

PREP: 35 MIN. • **BAKE:** 20 MIN. + COOLING
MAKES: 26 CUPCAKES

- 1 package spice cake mix (regular size)
- 1 cup solid-pack pumpkin
- 1 cup water
- 2 eggs
- 1 cup (6 ounces) miniature semisweet chocolate chips
- 2 cans (16 ounces each) vanilla frosting
- 1 teaspoon maple flavoring
  Orange food coloring
  Reese's pieces

1. Preheat oven to 350°. Line 26 muffin cups with paper liners.
2. In a large bowl, combine cake mix, pumpkin, water and eggs; beat on low speed 30 seconds. Beat on medium 2 minutes. Stir in chocolate chips. Fill prepared cups two-thirds full.
3. Bake 16-20 minutes or until a toothpick inserted in center comes out clean. Cool in pans 10 minutes before removing cupcakes to wire racks to cool completely.
4. In a large bowl, beat frosting and flavoring; tint frosting orange. Arrange cupcakes on a large platter, forming a pumpkin. Spread frosting over cupcakes. Decorate with Reese's pieces as desired.

Pumpkin Ice Cream Treat

Everyone will scream for pumpkin-y ice cream this Halloween. I like to have some in the freezer, ready for visitors.

—DIXIE TERRY GOREVILLE, IL

PREP: 15 MIN. + FREEZING
MAKES: 8 SERVINGS

- 1½ cups pumpkin pie filling
- ⅓ cup sugar
- 1 teaspoon vanilla extract
- 1 quart vanilla ice cream, softened
- 1 cup finely chopped pecans, toasted
  Graham cracker
  Thin licorice pieces

In a large bowl, mix pie filling, sugar and vanilla until blended. Fold in ice cream. Spread into a 9-in. round pan coated with cooking spray. Sprinkle pecans over the top in thin stripes, forming the vertical lines of a pumpkin shape. Add a graham cracker stem and licorice vines. Freeze, covered, 3-4 hours or until firm.

⑤INGREDIENTS
Wiggly Pumpkins

Pumpkin-shaped cookie cutters form these festive hand-held snacks. My grandkids love them.

—FRANCES POSTE WALL, SD

PREP: 45 MIN. + CHILLING
MAKES: 14-16 SERVINGS

- 2 packages (6 ounces each) orange gelatin
- 2½ cups boiling water
- 1 cup cold milk
- 1 package (3.4 ounces) instant vanilla pudding mix
  Candy corn
  Black licorice and/or gumdrops

Dissolve gelatin in water; set aside for 30 minutes. Whisk milk and pudding mix until smooth, about 1 minute. Quickly pour into gelatin; whisk until well blended. Pour into a greased 13x9-in. pan. Chill until set. Cut into circles or use a pumpkin-shaped cookie cutter. Just before serving, add candy eyes and mouths.

FAST FIX
Jack-o'-Lantern Pops

As soon as they see these pumpkin pops, your little goblins' faces will light right up.

—CLARA COULSON MINNEY
WASHINGTON COURT HOUSE, OH

START TO FINISH: 30 MIN.
MAKES: 6 SERVINGS

- 1 package (10½ ounces) miniature marshmallows
- 3 tablespoons butter
- ⅛ teaspoon salt
  Red and yellow gel food coloring
- 6 cups Rice Krispies
  Wooden pop sticks
  Miniature chocolate, green and yellow Tootsie Roll Midgees, as desired

Miniature green apple AirHeads bars
Black decorating gel or chocolate frosting, optional

1. In a large saucepan, combine marshmallows, butter and salt. Cook and stir over medium-low heat until melted. Remove from heat; tint orange with red and yellow food coloring. Stir in cereal.
2. With buttered hands, shape mixture into six pumpkins. Insert a wooden pop stick into each pumpkin.
3. Cut chocolate Tootsie Rolls crosswise in half; press one half into the top of each for stems. Cut AirHeads into thin strips; roll between hands to form vines. Press vines into pumpkins near stem. For leaves,
4. roll out green Tootsie Rolls on waxed paper to ⅛-in. thickness. With kitchen scissors, cut out leaves and attach to vines.
5. Add Jack-o'-lantern faces using decorating gel or additional Tootsie Roll cutouts made with yellow and chocolate Tootsie Rolls.

JACK-O'-LANTERN POPS

PUMPKIN TIRAMISU

Pumpkin Tiramisu

Tiramisu is a classic dessert that everyone enjoys. For an unbeatable fall flavor, try my version. It features a creamy pumpkin filling and sweet spices.

—HOLLY BILLINGS BATTLEFIELD, MO

PREP: 25 MIN. + CHILLING
MAKES: 16 SERVINGS

- 1½ cups heavy whipping cream
- 2 packages (8 ounces each) cream cheese, softened
- 1 can (15 ounces) solid-pack pumpkin
- ¾ cup milk
- ½ cup packed brown sugar
- 4 teaspoons pumpkin pie spice, divided
- 2 teaspoons vanilla extract, divided
- 1 cup strong brewed coffee, room temperature
- 2 packages (3 ounces each) ladyfingers, split
- 1 carton (8 ounces) frozen whipped topping, thawed
  Additional pumpkin pie spice

1. In a large bowl, beat cream until stiff peaks form; set aside. In another bowl, beat the cream cheese, pumpkin, milk, brown sugar, 1 teaspoon pie spice and 1 teaspoon vanilla until blended. Fold in whipped cream.
2. In a small bowl, combine coffee and remaining pie spice and vanilla; brush over ladyfingers. In a 3-qt. trifle dish, layer a fourth of the ladyfingers, pumpkin mixture and whipped topping. Repeat layers two times. Sprinkle with additional pie spice.
3. Cover and refrigerate for 4 hours or until chilled.

⑤ INGREDIENTS
Garlic Rosemary Turkey

Our whole house smells incredible while the bird is roasting, and my family can hardly wait to eat. The garlic, herbs and lemon are such simple additions, but they're all you really need to make this holiday turkey shine.

—CATHY DOBBINS RIO RANCHO, NM

PREP: 10 MIN. • **BAKE:** 3 HOURS + STANDING
MAKES: 10 SERVINGS

- 1 whole turkey (10 to 12 pounds)
- 6 to 8 garlic cloves
- 2 large lemons, halved
- 2 tablespoons olive oil
- 2 teaspoons dried rosemary, crushed
- 1 teaspoon rubbed sage

1. Preheat oven to 325°. Cut six to eight small slits in turkey skin; insert garlic under the skin. Squeeze two lemon halves inside the turkey; squeeze remaining halves over outside of turkey. Place lemons in the cavity.
2. Tuck wings under turkey; tie drumsticks together. Place on a rack in a shallow roasting pan, breast side up. Brush with oil; sprinkle with rosemary and sage. Roast 1 hour.
3. Cover turkey with foil; roast 2 to 2½ hours longer or until a thermometer inserted in thigh reads 180°. Baste turkey occasionally with pan drippings.
4. Remove turkey from oven. Let stand 20 minutes before carving. If desired, skim fat and thicken pan drippings for gravy. Serve with turkey.

⑤ INGREDIENTS FAST FIX
Simple Turkey Gravy

A classic from-scratch gravy recipe works for any roasted meat or poultry. Switch up the herbs to fit your preferences, or simply use what you have on hand.

—TASTE OF HOME TEST KITCHEN

START TO FINISH: 20 MIN.
MAKES: 16 SERVINGS (¼ CUP EACH)

  Turkey drippings
- 3 to 3½ cups chicken broth, divided
- ½ cup all-purpose flour
- ½ teaspoon dried thyme
- ½ teaspoon rubbed sage
- ½ teaspoon pepper

1. Pour turkey drippings and loosened browned bits from roasting pan into a 4-cup measuring cup. Skim fat, reserving 2 tablespoons. Add enough broth to the drippings to measure 3 cups.
2. In a large saucepan, whisk flour, ¾ cup broth and reserved fat until smooth. Add thyme, sage and pepper; gradually whisk in the drippings mixture. Bring to a boil, stirring constantly; cook and stir for 2-3 minutes or until thickened.

⑤ INGREDIENTS
Roasted Cauliflower & Brussels Sprouts with Bacon

This is a surefire way to get my husband to eat Brussels sprouts. Between the roasted flavor of the veggies and the crisp, smoky bacon, the delicious side dish will convert even the pickiest eater.

—LISA SPEER PALM BEACH, FL

PREP: 30 MIN. • **BAKE:** 20 MIN.
MAKES: 10 SERVINGS

- 2 pounds fresh Brussels sprouts, thinly sliced
- 1 pound fresh cauliflowerets (about 7 cups), thinly sliced
- ¼ cup olive oil
- 1 teaspoon freshly ground pepper
- ½ teaspoon salt
- 1 pound bacon strips, cooked and crumbled
- ⅓ to ½ cup balsamic vinaigrette

1. Preheat oven to 375°. In a very large bowl, toss Brussels sprouts and cauliflower with oil, pepper and salt. Transfer to two greased 15x10x1-in. baking pans.
2. Roast 20-25 minutes or until vegetables are tender. Transfer to a serving bowl. Just before serving, add bacon and drizzle with vinaigrette; toss to coat.

GARLIC ROSEMARY TURKEY
SIMPLE TURKEY GRAVY
ROASTED CAULIFLOWER
& BRUSSELS SPROUTS WITH BACON

FRUIT & NUT ANDOUILLE STUFFING
FRESH GINGER CRANBERRY RELISH
GOUDA MIXED POTATO MASH
GREEN BEANS WITH YELLOW-PEPPER BUTTER

"This flavor-packed stuffing recipe has had a spot on our Thanksgiving table for many years. It reminds us of home, family, and all the things that make the holiday season so special."

—KATHLEEN SPECHT CLINTON, MT

⑤ INGREDIENTS

Fruit & Nut Andouille Stuffing

PREP: 15 MIN. • **BAKE:** 25 MIN.
MAKES: 16 SERVINGS (¾ CUP EACH)

- ¼ **cup butter, cubed**
- 1 **pound fully cooked andouille sausage links or flavor of your choice, finely chopped**
- 1 **package (7 ounces) mixed dried fruit, chopped**
- 1 **cup chopped walnuts**
- ¼ **teaspoon pepper**
- 1 **package (14 ounces) seasoned stuffing cubes**
- 3½ **to 4 cups water**

1. Preheat oven to 325°. In a Dutch oven, heat butter over medium heat. Add sausage, dried fruit, walnuts and pepper; cook and stir 6-8 minutes or until sausage is lightly browned. Add stuffing cubes; toss to combine. Stir in enough water to reach desired moistness.
2. Transfer to a greased 13x9-in. baking dish. Bake 25-30 minutes or until heated through.

---

⑤ INGREDIENTS

Fresh Ginger Cranberry Relish

This tasty relish goes way beyond your Thanksgiving dinner plate. It's also great with chicken and pork, and will even perk up a ho-hum deli sandwich.

—MELODE WEINER PLYMOUTH, CA

PREP: 15 MIN. + CHILLING
MAKES: 5 CUPS

- 1 **large navel orange**
- 1 **medium lemon**
- 2 **packages (12 ounces each) fresh or frozen cranberries, thawed**
- 1 **cup sugar**
- ⅓ **to ½ cup coarsely chopped fresh gingerroot**

Cut unpeeled orange and lemon into wedges; remove any seeds. Transfer orange and lemon to a food processor; add remaining ingredients. Pulse until chopped. Transfer to a bowl; refrigerate, covered, overnight.

---

⑤ INGREDIENTS

Gouda Mixed Potato Mash

Can't decide what type of spuds to serve for Thanksgiving? Make both by preparing this casserole featuring Yukon Gold and sweet potatoes. Gouda cheese provides a rich flavor.

—SHELBY GODDARD BATON ROUGE, LA

PREP: 20 MIN. • **COOK:** 15 MIN.
MAKES: 12 SERVINGS (⅔ CUP EACH)

- 6 **medium Yukon Gold potatoes, peeled and cubed**
- 2 **medium sweet potatoes, peeled and cubed**
- ½ **cup 2% milk**
- 1 **cup (4 ounces) shredded Gouda cheese**
- 1 **teaspoon paprika**
- ½ **teaspoon salt**
- ½ **teaspoon pepper**

1. Place Yukon Gold and sweet potatoes in a Dutch oven; add water to cover. Bring to a boil. Reduce heat; cook, uncovered, 10-15 minutes or until tender. Drain; return to pan.
2. Mash potatoes, gradually adding milk. Stir in cheese, paprika, salt and pepper.

---

⑤ INGREDIENTS FAST FIX ▸

Green Beans with Yellow-Pepper Butter

Colorful, crunchy and buttery, these beans come together quickly and will be a hit at your holiday table. For a variation, sprinkle toasted pine nuts over the top just before serving.

—JUDIE WHITE FLORIEN, LA

START TO FINISH: 30 MIN.
MAKES: 12 SERVINGS

- 3 **medium sweet yellow peppers, divided**
- 2 **tablespoons plus ½ cup butter, softened, divided**
- ⅓ **cup pine nuts**
- 1 **to 2 tablespoons lemon juice**
- ½ **teaspoon salt**
- ¼ **teaspoon pepper**
- 2¼ **pounds fresh green beans**

1. Finely chop 1½ yellow peppers. In a large skillet, heat 2 tablespoons butter over medium-high heat. Add chopped peppers; cook and stir until tender.
2. Place pine nuts, lemon juice, salt, pepper and remaining butter in a food processor; process until blended. Add cooked peppers; process to blend.
3. Place beans in a Dutch oven and cover with water. Cut remaining 1½ peppers into thin strips; add to beans. Bring to a boil. Cook, covered, 5-7 minutes or until vegetables are crisp-tender; drain well. Add butter mixture and toss to coat.

❓ Did you know?

Cranberries are one of just a few commercially grown fruits that are native to the North American continent. About 1,000 growers in the United States and Canada provide most of the world's cranberries. The leading cranberry-producing states are Wisconsin, Massachusetts and New Jersey.

Basil & Sun-Dried Tomato Crescents

If your family is anything like mine, you may want to make a double batch of these crescents since they disappear so quickly. This is a low-fuss recipe that's meant to be shared.

—**MARA FLETCHER** BATESVILLE, IN

START TO FINISH: 30 MIN.
MAKES: 16 ROLLS

- 2 **tubes (8 ounces each) refrigerated crescent rolls**
- ⅔ **cup butter, softened**
- ½ **cup minced fresh basil**
- ¼ **cup oil-packed sun-dried tomatoes, patted dry and finely chopped**
- 1 **teaspoon garlic powder**

1. Preheat oven to 375°. Unroll each tube of crescent dough; separate dough into eight triangles. In a small bowl, mix remaining ingredients; spread over triangles.

2. Roll up and place 2 in. apart on ungreased baking sheets, point side down; curve to form crescents. Bake 11-13 minutes or until golden brown.

BASIL & SUN-DRIED TOMATO CRESCENTS

CHOCOLATE-NUT CARAMEL TART

Chocolate-Nut Caramel Tart

With just a few ingredients and in less time than you'd think, this sinfully rich tart is ready to go. It's a good recipe to have up your sleeve for any gathering.

—**KATHLEEN SPECHT** CLINTON, MT

PREP: 20 MIN. • **BAKE:** 15 MIN. + CHILLING
MAKES: 12 SERVINGS

- 1 **sheet refrigerated pie pastry**
- 1 **jar (13 ounces) Nutella, divided**
- 20 **caramels**
- ⅓ **cup heavy whipping cream**
- 1¾ **cups chopped macadamia nuts, toasted**
  Whipped cream, optional

1. Preheat oven to 450°. Unroll pastry into a 9-in. fluted tart pan with removable bottom. Press onto bottom and up sides of pan; trim pastry even with edge (discard or save trimmed pastry for another use). Generously prick bottom of crust with a fork. Bake 9-11 minutes or until golden brown. Cool completely on a wire rack.

2. Reserve 2 tablespoons Nutella for topping; spread remaining Nutella into cooled crust. In a small saucepan, combine caramels and cream; cook over medium-low heat until blended, stirring occasionally. Remove from heat; stir in macadamia nuts. Spread evenly over Nutella.

3. In a microwave, heat reserved Nutella until warmed; drizzle over filling. Refrigerate for 1 hour or until firm. If desired, serve the tart with whipped cream.

NOTE *To toast nuts, spread in a 15x10x1-in. baking pan. Bake at 350° for 5-10 minutes or until lightly browned, stirring occasionally. Or, spread in a dry nonstick skillet and heat over low heat until lightly browned, stirring occasionally.*

Apple-Gorgonzola Endive Salad

Curly endive is slightly bitter, making it a good match for sweet and crunchy apples. The dressing recipe came from my grandma, so it's extra special.

—**PAT FERJANCSIK** SANTA ROSA, CA

PREP: 20 MIN. + CHILLING
MAKES: 10 SERVINGS

- 1¼ **cups heavy whipping cream**
- ⅔ **cup red wine vinegar**
- 1 **teaspoon salt**
- 1 **teaspoon pepper**
- 5 **medium red apples, thinly sliced (about 5 cups)**
- 2 **cups (8 ounces) crumbled Gorgonzola cheese**
- 10 **cups torn curly endive**

In a large bowl, whisk the cream, vinegar, salt and pepper. Stir in apples and cheese. Refrigerate, covered, at least 1 hour. Serve apple mixture over endive.

Rocky Toffee Fudge

A hint of Kahlua gives grown-up taste to the classic combination of marshmallows and chocolate.

—TASTE OF HOME TEST KITCHEN

PREP: 10 MIN. + CHILLING
MAKES: 2½ POUNDS

- 1 teaspoon butter
- 1 can (14 ounces) sweetened condensed milk
- 2 cups (12 ounces) dark chocolate chips
- 1 cup (6 ounces) semisweet chocolate chips
- 1 cup miniature marshmallows
- ½ cup milk chocolate English toffee bits
- ⅓ cup Kahlua (coffee liqueur)

1. Line a 9-in.-square baking pan with foil. Grease foil with butter; set aside. Combine milk and chips in a large microwave-safe bowl. Microwave, uncovered, on high for 1 minute; stir. Cook 30-60 seconds longer, stirring every 30 seconds, or until chips are melted. Stir in the marshmallows, toffee bits and Kahlua.
2. Transfer to prepared pan. Cover and refrigerate for 2 hours or until firm. Lift fudge out of pan using foil. Gently peel off foil; cut fudge into 1-in. squares. Store in an airtight container.
NOTE This recipe was tested in a 1,100-watt microwave.

Crunchy Mint Fudge

Celebrate the season with old-fashioned fudge spiked with the flavors of spearmint and peppermint.

—TASTE OF HOME TEST KITCHEN

PREP: 10 MIN. + CHILLING
MAKES: 2½ POUNDS

- 1 teaspoon butter
- 1 can (14 ounces) sweetened condensed milk
- 2 cups (12 ounces) semisweet chocolate chips
- 1 cup Andes creme de menthe baking chips
- 1½ cups coarsely crushed candy canes, divided
- 1 teaspoon vanilla extract

1. Line a 9-in.-square baking pan with foil. Grease foil with butter; set aside. Combine milk and chips in a large microwave-safe bowl. Microwave, uncovered, on high for 1 minute; stir. Cook 30-60 seconds longer, stirring every 30 seconds, or until chips are melted. Stir in 1¼ cups candy canes and vanilla.
2. Transfer to prepared pan. Sprinkle with remaining candy canes; press down gently. Cover and refrigerate for 2 hours or until firm. Lift fudge out of pan using foil. Gently peel off foil; cut fudge into 1-in. squares. Store in an airtight container.
NOTE This recipe was tested in a 1,100-watt microwave.

Easy Holiday Fudge

A friend shared this quick and easy candy recipe with me. The holidays wouldn't be the same without it.

—IDA HILTY AMITY, OR

PREP: 10 MIN. + CHILLING
MAKES: ABOUT 2½ POUNDS

- 1 teaspoon butter
- 1 can (14 ounces) sweetened condensed milk
- 2 cups (12 ounces) semisweet chocolate chips
- 1 cup butterscotch chips
- 1 cup chopped pecans
- ½ cup raisins
- 1 teaspoon vanilla extract

1. Line a 9-in.-square baking pan with foil. Grease foil with butter; set aside. Combine milk and chips in a large microwave-safe bowl.
2. Microwave, uncovered, on high for 1 minute; stir. Cook 30-60 seconds longer, stirring every 30 seconds, or until chips are melted. Stir in the pecans, raisins and vanilla.
3. Transfer to prepared pan. Cover and refrigerate for 2 hours or until firm. Using foil, lift fudge out of pan. Gently peel off foil; cut fudge into 1-in. squares. Store in an airtight container.
NOTE This recipe was tested in a 1,100-watt microwave.

Snack Attack Fudge

Surprise! Salty snacks are stirred into homemade fudge for a taste the guys (and gals) will all go crazy for.

—TASTE OF HOME TEST KITCHEN

PREP: 10 MIN. + CHILLING
MAKES: ABOUT 2½ POUNDS

- 1 teaspoon butter
- 1 can (14 ounces) sweetened condensed milk
- 2 cups (12 ounces) milk chocolate chips
- 1 cup (6 ounces) semisweet chocolate chips
- 1 cup miniature pretzels, coarsley crushed
- ½ cup crushed ridged potato chips
- ½ cup Beer Nuts
- 1 teaspoon vanilla extract

1. Line a 9-in.-square pan with foil. Grease foil with butter; set aside.
2. Combine the milk and chocolate chips in a large microwave-safe bowl. Microwave, uncovered, on high for 1 minute; stir. Cook 30-60 seconds longer, stirring every 30 seconds, or until chips are melted. Stir in pretzels, potato chips, Beer Nuts and vanilla.
3. Transfer to prepared pan. Cover and refrigerate for 2 hours or until firm. Lift fudge out of pan using foil. Gently peel off foil; cut into 1-in. squares. Store in an airtight container.
NOTE This recipe was tested in a 1,100-watt microwave.

Did you know?

Cookie cutters filled with fudge make cute party favors for holiday guests. Line a flat shallow pan with buttered foil, then top with lightly buttered cutters. Pour the warm fudge mixture into the cutters and top with nuts, crushed candies or other toppings. Let the fudge stand until set, then decorate with icing or sprinkles if desired. Wrap the candy cutters in clear or colored cellophane and tie with colorful ribbon. Don't forget to attach a copy of the recipe!

SNACK ATTACK FUDGE

CRUNCHY MINT FUDGE

ROCKY TOFFEE FUDGE

CANDY BAR FUDGE REINDEER

EASY HOLIDAY FUDGE

Candy Bar Fudge Reindeer

This sweet butterscotch and peanut butter delight is as cute as a button.

—TASTE OF HOME TEST KITCHEN

PREP: 20 MIN. + CHILLING
MAKES: 2 DOZEN

- 1 teaspoon butter
- 1 can (14 ounces) sweetened condensed milk
- 2 cups (12 ounces) butterscotch chips
- 1 cup (6 ounces) peanut butter chips
- 2 Snickers candy bars (2.07 ounces each), chopped
- ¾ cup red and green milk chocolate M&M's
- 1 teaspoon vanilla extract
  M&M's minis and miniature pretzels

1. Line a 9-in.-square baking pan with foil. Grease foil with butter; set aside. Combine milk and chips in a large microwave-safe bowl.

2. Microwave, uncovered, on high for 1 minute; stir. Cook 30-60 seconds longer, stirring every 30 seconds, or until chips are melted. Stir in candy bars, M&M's and vanilla. Transfer to prepared pan. Cover and refrigerate for 2 hours or until firm. Lift fudge out of pan using foil. Gently peel off foil; cut fudge into 3-inch rows. Cut each row into eight triangles. Gently press M&M's minis into fudge for eyes and mouth; press in pretzels for antlers. Store in an airtight container.

NOTE *This recipe was tested in a 1,100-watt microwave.*

CHERRY BONBON COOKIES

Cherry Bonbon Cookies

You'll see these red and green bonbon cookies in my home every yuletide. They're a standard on my cookie tray.
—**LORI DANIELS** BEVERLY, WV

PREP: 20 MIN.
BAKE: 15 MIN./BATCH + COOLING
MAKES: 3 DOZEN

- 36 maraschino cherries
- 1 cup butter, softened
- 1½ cups confectioners' sugar
- 1 tablespoon 2% milk
- 3 teaspoons vanilla extract
- 2¾ cups all-purpose flour
- ¼ teaspoon salt

CHRISTMAS GLAZE
- 1¼ cups confectioners' sugar
- 1 to 2 tablespoons water
  Red and green liquid food coloring
  Colored sprinkles

CHOCOLATE GLAZE
- 1 cup confectioners' sugar
- 1 to 2 tablespoons water
- 1 ounce unsweetened chocolate, melted
- 1 teaspoon vanilla extract
- ½ cup chopped pecans or walnuts

1. Pat cherries dry with paper towels; set aside. In a large bowl, cream butter and confectioners' sugar until light and fluffy. Beat in milk and vanilla. Combine flour and salt; gradually add to creamed mixture and mix well.
2. Shape a tablespoonful of dough around each cherry, forming a ball. Place 2 in. apart on ungreased baking sheets. Bake at 350° for 14-16 minutes or until bottoms are browned. Remove to wire racks to cool.
3. For Christmas glaze, in a small bowl, combine confectioners' sugar and enough water to achieve a dipping consistency. Transfer half of the glaze to another bowl; tint one bowl green and the other red. Dip the tops of nine cookies in green glaze and nine cookies in red glaze, then decorate with sprinkles. Let stand until set.
4. For chocolate glaze, in a small bowl, combine confectioners' sugar and enough water to achieve dipping consistency. Stir in chocolate and vanilla. Dip the tops of remaining cookies in glaze, then sprinkle with nuts. Let stand until set.

⑤INGREDIENTS FAST FIX ▶

Frosty Peppermint Popcorn

Whether you need a quick gift idea or yummy munchies for movie night, we've got you covered with this peppermint twist on regular popped popcorn.
—**TASTE OF HOME TEST KITCHEN**

START TO FINISH: 10 MIN.
MAKES: 3½ QUARTS

- 3½ quarts popped popcorn
- ⅓ cup crushed peppermint candies
- ½ pound white candy coating

Combine popcorn and candies. Chop and melt candy coating; drizzle over popcorn-candy mixture. Toss to coat. Cool on waxed paper; break apart.

FAST FIX ▶

Sweet & Salty Snowmen

Kids have a blast creating different looks for their pretzel snowmen with candy scarves, buttons and top hats. If any are left over, they make cool table decorations posed in a glass filled with coconut snow. You can prop them with a bit of Styrofoam, too.
—**CAROL BERNDT** AVON, SD

START TO FINISH: 25 MIN.
MAKES: 8 SNOWMEN

- 8 pretzel rods
- 6 ounces white baking chocolate, melted
  Assorted candies: M&M's miniature baking bits, miniature chocolate chips, small gumdrops, jelly rings, Fruit by the Foot fruit rolls

1. Dip pretzel rods two-thirds of the way into melted white chocolate, or drizzle chocolate over pretzels with a spoon. Attach baking bits for buttons and noses and chocolate chips for eyes.
2. For hats, dip the bottom of a small gumdrop into chocolate and press onto a jelly ring; attach to the top of each pretzel.
3. Carefully stand snowmen by placing them upright in a tall glass or pressing the bottom of the pretzel rods into a 2-in.-thick piece of Styrofoam. For scarves, cut fruit rolls into thin strips; tie around snowmen.
NOTE *This recipe was tested with Chuckles jelly rings.*

CRANBERRY-PISTACHIO STICKY BUNS

"Looking for a fantastic brunch item? Then try these delicious sticky buns. They use frozen yeast roll dough and couldn't be simpler to make. The buns rise overnight in the refrigerator, so you just need to bake them the next morning." —**ATHENA RUSSELL** FLORENCE, SC

Cranberry-Pistachio Sticky Buns

PREP: 20 MIN. + CHILLING
BAKE: 30 MIN. • **MAKES:** 2 DOZEN

- 1 cup chopped pistachios
- ½ cup dried cranberries
- 1 teaspoon ground cinnamon
- 24 frozen bread dough dinner rolls, thawed
- ½ cup butter, cubed
- 1 cup packed brown sugar
- 1 package (4.6 ounces) cook-and-serve vanilla pudding mix
- 2 tablespoons 2% milk
- ½ teaspoon orange extract

1. Sprinkle the pistachios, cranberries and cinnamon in a greased 13-in. x 9-in. baking dish. Arrange rolls in a single layer on top.

2. In a small saucepan over low heat, melt butter. Remove from the heat; stir in the brown sugar, pudding mix, milk and extract until smooth. Pour over dough. Cover and refrigerate overnight.

3. Remove from the refrigerator 30 minutes before baking. Bake at 350° for 30-35 minutes or until golden brown. (Cover loosely with foil if top browns too quickly.) Cool for 1 minute before inverting onto a serving platter.

Cranberry Almond Coffee Cake

Cranberries add a delightful tartness to a coffee cake that has become a Christmas morning tradition for my family. I make my own almond paste to use when preparing this treat.

—ANNE KEENAN NEVADA CITY, CA

PREP: 20 MIN. **BAKE:** 45 MIN. + COOLING
MAKES: 9 SERVINGS

- ½ cup almond paste
- 6 tablespoons butter, softened
- ½ cup plus 2 tablespoons sugar, divided
- 3 eggs
- 1⅓ cups all-purpose flour, divided
- 1 teaspoon baking powder
- 1 teaspoon almond extract
- ½ teaspoon vanilla extract
- 2¼ cups fresh or frozen cranberries

1. In a small bowl, cream almond paste, butter and ½ cup sugar until fluffy. Add two eggs, one at a time, beating well after each addition. Combine 1 cup flour and baking powder; add to creamed mixture. Beat in the remaining egg and flour. Stir in extracts. Gently fold in cranberries.
2. Spread evenly into a greased 8-in.-square baking dish; sprinkle with remaining sugar. Bake at 325° for 45-55 minutes or until a toothpick inserted near the center comes out clean. Cool on a wire rack.

CRANBERRY ALMOND COFFEE CAKE

Christmas Cheese Balls

Christmas at our house just wouldn't be complete without these rich and savory cheese balls. Friends and family ask for them every year—and I can make three gifts from just one recipe.

—MARGIE CADWELL EASTMAN, GA

PREP: 20 MIN. + CHILLING
MAKES: 3 CHEESE BALLS

- 4 pkg. (8 ounces each) cream cheese, softened
- 4 cups (1 pound) shredded cheddar cheese
- 1 cup chopped pecans
- ¼ cup evaporated milk
- 1 can (4¼ ounces) chopped ripe olives, drained
- 2 garlic cloves, minced
- ½ teaspoon salt
  Minced fresh parsley, chopped pecans and paprika
  Assorted crackers

1. In a small bowl, beat cream cheese and cheddar cheese. Stir in the pecans, milk, olives, garlic and salt. Divide into thirds; roll each into a ball.
2. Roll one ball in parsley and one in nuts. Sprinkle one with paprika. Cover and refrigerate. Remove from the refrigerator 15 minutes before serving. Serve with crackers.

CHERRY-CHOCOLATE COCONUT MERINGUES

EAT SMART
Cherry-Chocolate Coconut Meringues

Dried cherries lend sweetness and texture to delicious, low-fat holiday cookies.

—MARY SHIVERS ADA, OK

PREP: 15 MIN.
BAKE: 25 MIN./BATCH + COOLING
MAKES: 3 DOZEN

- 3 egg whites
- ½ teaspoon almond extract
  Dash salt
- ⅓ cup sugar
- ⅔ cup confectioners' sugar
- ¼ cup baking cocoa
- 1¼ cups finely shredded unsweetened coconut
- ½ cup dried cherries, finely chopped

1. Place egg whites in a large bowl; let stand at room temperature for 30 minutes.
2. Add extract and salt; beat on medium speed until soft peaks form. Gradually add sugar, 1 tablespoon at a time, beating on high until stiff glossy peaks form and sugar is dissolved. Combine confectioners' sugar and cocoa; beat into egg white mixture. Fold in coconut and cherries.
3. Drop by rounded tablespoonfuls 2 in. apart onto baking sheets coated with cooking spray. Bake at 325° for 25-28 minutes or until firm to the touch. Cool completely on pans on wire racks. Store in airtight container.
NOTE *Look for unsweetened coconut in the baking or health food section.*
PER SERVING *42 cal., 2 g fat (1 g sat. fat), 0 chol., 10 mg sodium, 6 g carb., 1 g fiber, 1 g pro.* **Diabetic Exchange:** *½ starch.*

**Crystal Jo Bruns'
Polish Casserole**
PAGE 309

Easy Odds & Ends

Here's a round-up of irresistible baked goods, satisfying suppers, cocktail and dinner pairings, recipes that prolong the sun-kissed tastes of summer and more.

**Kathleen Smith's
Chicken Fajitas**
PAGE 307

**Jennifer Heasley's
Peanut Butter & Jelly Bites**
PAGE 301

**Samantha Pazdernik's
Family-Favorite Fried Chicken**
PAGE 302

Recipe Showdown

When daughters make over their **moms' favorite recipes**, everybody wins. Joan Hallford's **handy shortcut** gets apple crisp on the table faster than her mom's from-scratch version. And Emily Carney lightens up her mother's versatile quick bread.

MOM'S CINNAMON-APPLE CRISP

Mom's Cinnamon-Apple Crisp

I was fortunate when a dear friend shared this recipe with me more than 50 years ago. The sweet-smelling combination of apples, cinnamon, sugar and nutmeg has been a welcome aroma in my house ever since.

—**CLEO LIGHTFOOT** SOUTHLAKE, TX

PREP: 20 MIN. • **BAKE:** 40 MIN.
MAKES: 9 SERVINGS

- 6 **cups thinly sliced peeled tart apples**
- ½ **cup sugar**
- 1 **tablespoon all-purpose flour**
- ¼ **teaspoon ground cinnamon**
- 2 **tablespoons butter**

TOPPING
- 1 **cup all-purpose flour**
- 1 **cup sugar**
- 1 **teaspoon baking powder**
- ¼ **teaspoon ground nutmeg**
- ½ **cup cold butter, cubed**
- 1 **egg, lightly beaten**
  Vanilla ice cream, optional

1. Combine the apples, sugar, flour and cinnamon in a large bowl. Transfer to an 11-in. x 7-in. baking dish; dot with butter.
2. For topping, combine the flour, sugar, baking powder and nutmeg in another large bowl. Cut in butter until mixture resembles coarse crumbs. Stir in egg just until moistened; sprinkle over filling.
3. Bake, uncovered, at 375° for 40-45 minutes or until topping is golden brown and apples are tender. Serve warm with ice cream if desired.

Daughter's Apple Crisp

My mom's apple crisp is the best in all of Texas—honest! I tweaked it slightly, though, and now I spend less time in the kitchen and more time catching up with my spry 92-year-young mother.

—**JOAN HALLFORD** NORTH RICHLAND HILLS, TX

PREP: 10 MIN. • **BAKE:** 40 MIN.
MAKES: 9 SERVINGS

- 2 **cans (21 ounces each) apple pie filling**
- 2 **tablespoons butter**

TOPPING
- 1 **cup all-purpose flour**
- 1 **cup sugar**
- 1 **teaspoon baking powder**
- ¼ **teaspoon ground nutmeg**
- ½ **cup cold butter, cubed**
- 1 **egg, lightly beaten**
  Vanilla ice cream, optional

1. Place pie filling in an 11-in. x 7-in. baking dish; dot with butter. Combine flour, sugar, baking powder and nutmeg in a large bowl. Cut in butter until mixture resembles coarse crumbs. Stir in egg just until moistened; sprinkle over filling.
2. Bake, uncovered, at 375° for 40-45 minutes or until topping is golden brown and filling is bubbly. Serve warm with ice cream if desired.

DAUGHTER'S APPLE CRISP

2 teaspoons ground cinnamon
1 teaspoon baking powder
1 teaspoon baking soda
1 teaspoon salt
1 cup chopped walnuts or pecans

1. Whisk the sugar, oil, applesauce and eggs in a large bowl. Stir in 2 cups of A to Z ingredients of your choice and the vanilla. Combine the all-purpose and whole wheat flours, cinnamon, baking powder, baking soda and salt; stir into liquid ingredients just until moistened. Stir in nuts. Pour into two greased 8-in. x 4-in. loaf pans.

2. Bake at 325° for 50-55 minutes or until a toothpick inserted near the center comes out clean. Cool for 10 minutes before removing from pans to wire racks.

A to Z Ingredients

Apples, peeled and shredded

Applesauce

Apricots (dried), chopped

Banana (ripe), mashed

Carrot, shredded

Coconut

Dates, pitted and chopped

Dried plums, pitted and chopped

Figs (dried), chopped

Grapes (seedless), chopped

Oranges, peeled and chopped

Peaches, peeled and chopped

Pears, peeled and chopped

Pineapple (canned), crushed and drained

Pumpkin, canned

Raisins

Raspberries, fresh or frozen

Rhubarb, chopped fresh or frozen

Strawberries, chopped fresh or frozen

Sweet potatoes, cooked and mashed

Zucchini, shredded

"We love this recipe around my house because we can change it from one day to the next on a whim. Just throw whatever fruit is in season into the mix, and you've got a tailor-made treat!" —**CHRISTINE SAXE** ADA, MI

Mom's A-to-Z Bread

PREP: 20 MIN. • **BAKE:** 50 MIN. + COOLING
MAKES: 2 LOAVES (12 SLICES EACH)

1½ cups sugar
1 cup canola oil
3 eggs
2 cups A to Z ingredients (choose from list at right)
3 teaspoons vanilla extract
3 cups all-purpose flour
2 teaspoons baking powder
2 teaspoons ground cinnamon
1 teaspoon baking soda
1 teaspoon salt
1 cup chopped walnuts

1. Combine the sugar, oil and eggs in a large bowl. Stir in 2 cups of A to Z ingredients of your choice and the vanilla. Combine flour, baking powder, cinnamon, baking soda and salt; stir into liquid ingredients just until moistened. Stir in walnuts. Pour into two greased 8-in. x 4-in. loaf pans.

2. Bake at 350° for 50-55 minutes or until a toothpick inserted near the center comes out clean. Cool for 10 minutes before removing from pans to wire racks.

Daughter's A-to-Z Bread

I love my Mom's A-to-Z Bread, but the original recipe was a bit heavy on sugar and oil for my family. My version lowers the sugar and fat but retains all the flavor folks rave about!

—**EMILY CARNEY** GRAND LEDGE, MI

PREP: 20 MIN. • **BAKE:** 50 MIN. + COOLING
MAKES: 2 LOAVES (12 SLICES EACH)

1 cup sugar
½ cup canola oil
½ cup unsweetened applesauce
3 eggs
2 cups A to Z ingredients (choose from list at right)
1 tablespoon vanilla extract
2 cups all-purpose flour
1 cup whole wheat flour

Fun Foods

Stir up some fun with these **delightful treats** sure to please the kid in all of us. Perfect for lunch-box bites, after-school snacks and movie-night munching, these **irresistible cuties** have got your nibbling needs covered.

Island Breeze Popcorn

Be warned: This sweet-and-savory take on popcorn is highly addictive.
—**TASTE OF HOME TEST KITCHEN**

START TO FINISH: 10 MIN.
MAKES: 3½ QUARTS

- 3½ quarts popped popcorn
- ⅓ cup butter, softened
- 2 teaspoons curry powder
- 1 teaspoon sugar

- **Toasted coconut**
- **Almonds**
- **Golden raisins**
- **Salt**

Combine butter, curry powder and sugar. Microwave until butter is melted; stir. Drizzle over popcorn; toss. Sprinkle with coconut, almonds, raisins and salt.

Peanut Butter Lover's Popcorn

Here's a fun way to jazz up popcorn. For an over-the-top peanut butter treat, prepare it with Reese's peanut butter bits instead of M&M's.
—**TASTE OF HOME TEST KITCHEN**

START TO FINISH: 10 MIN.
MAKES: 3½ QUARTS

- 1 cup sugar
- 1 cup honey
- 1 cup peanut butter
- 3½ quarts popped popcorn
- M&M's
- Miniature pretzels

Bring sugar and honey to a boil in a heavy saucepan over medium heat, stirring constantly. Boil for 5 minutes, stirring constantly. Remove from heat. Stir in peanut butter. Pour over popcorn; toss. Cool on waxed paper. Add M&M's and pretzels.

ISLAND BREEZE POPCORN
PEANUT BUTTER LOVER'S POPCORN

Peanut Butter & Jelly Bites

My friend is an avid runner. After I heard that she craved a peanut butter and jelly sandwich during a race, I whipped up these easy-to-carry bites for her.

—JENNIFER HEASLEY YORK, PA

PREP: 25 MIN. • **BAKE:** 15 MIN. + COOLING
MAKES: 2 DOZEN

- **4 ounces cream cheese, softened**
- **½ cup strawberry jelly, divided**
- **2 tubes (8 ounces each) refrigerated seamless crescent dough sheets**
- **½ cup creamy peanut butter**
- **1 cup confectioners' sugar**
- **5 tablespoons 2% milk**

1. Preheat oven to 350°. In a small bowl, beat the cream cheese and ¼ cup of jelly until smooth. Unroll each sheet of crescent dough into a rectangle. Spread each with half of the filling to within ½ in. of edges. Roll up jelly-roll style, starting with a long side; pinch seam to seal. Cut each roll widthwise into 12 slices; place slices on parchment paper-lined baking sheets, cut side down.

2. Bake 12-15 minutes or until golden brown. Cool on pans 2 minutes. Remove to wire racks to cool.

3. In a small bowl, beat peanut butter, confectioners' sugar and milk until smooth. Drizzle over rolls; top with remaining jelly.

FAST FIX
Hamburger Cookies

My husband loves peppermint patties, and our son is crazy for vanilla wafers. So I put the two together to make a cool cookie that looks just like a burger.

—JULIE WELLINGTON YOUNGSTOWN, OH

START TO FINISH: 30 MIN.
MAKES: 20 COOKIES

- **½ cup vanilla frosting**
  Red and yellow paste or gel food coloring
- **40 vanilla wafers**
- **20 peppermint patties**
- **1 teaspoon corn syrup**
- **1 teaspoon sesame seeds**

Place ¼ cup frosting in each of two small bowls. Tint one red and the other yellow. Spread yellow frosting on the bottoms of 20 vanilla wafers; top with a peppermint patty. Spread with red frosting. Brush tops of the remaining vanilla wafers with corn syrup; sprinkle with sesame seeds. Place over red frosting.

HAMBURGER COOKIES

Deep-Fried Delicious

Fry up some **classic comfort foods** with the **winning recipes** you'll find here. To keep fried foods hot and fresh, drain the food on paper towels, then place on a pan in a 200° oven.

MAPLE-BACON DOUGHNUT BITES

Maple-Bacon Doughnut Bites

These delicious bite-size treats are ready in minutes, and they'll disappear in a flash. And don't relegate the deep-fried goodness to the breakfast nook. I've never had anyone turn these down, no matter the time of day.

—**CHELSEA TURNER** LAKE ELSINORE, CA

PREP: 20 MIN. • **COOK:** 5 MIN./BATCH
MAKES: ABOUT 2 DOZEN

- 1½ **cups all-purpose flour**
- ½ **cup sugar**
- 2 **teaspoons baking powder**
- ½ **teaspoon salt**
- 1 **egg**
- ½ **cup 2% milk**
- 1 **tablespoon butter, melted**
  Oil for deep-fat frying

GLAZE
- 1 **cup confectioners' sugar**
- 3 **tablespoons maple syrup**
- 1 **tablespoon 2% milk**
- 1 **teaspoon vanilla extract**
- 7 **maple-flavored bacon strips, cooked and crumbled**

1. In a large bowl, whisk flour, sugar, baking powder and salt. In another bowl, whisk egg, milk and melted butter until blended. Add to flour mixture; stir just until moistened.
2. Heat oil to 350° in an electric skillet or deep fryer. Drop tablespoonfuls of batter, a few at a time, into hot oil. Fry 3-4 minutes or until golden brown, turning often. Drain on paper towels.
3. In a small bowl, mix confectioners' sugar, maple syrup, milk and vanilla until smooth. Dip warm doughnuts into glaze; sprinkle tops with bacon.

Family-Favorite Fried Chicken

I was never impressed with the fried chicken recipes I'd tried, but then I started to experiment and came up with one that my whole family loves. Once you taste it, you'll know why.

—**SAMANTHA PAZDERNIK** BRECKENRIDGE, MN

PREP: 20 MIN. • **COOK:** 10 MIN./BATCH
MAKES: 4 SERVINGS

- 1 **cup all-purpose flour**
- ½ **cup dry bread crumbs**
- 2 **tablespoons poultry seasoning**
- 1 **tablespoon paprika**
- ½ **teaspoon dried parsley flakes**
- ¼ **teaspoon salt**
- ¼ **teaspoon onion powder**
- ¼ **teaspoon garlic powder**
- ¼ **teaspoon pepper**
- 3 **eggs**
- 1 **broiler/fryer chicken (3 to 4 pounds), cut up**
  Oil for deep-fat frying

1. In a shallow bowl, mix the first nine ingredients. In a separate shallow bowl, whisk eggs. Dip chicken pieces, one at a time, in eggs; coat with flour mixture.
2. Heat oil to 375° in an electric skillet or deep-fat fryer. Fry chicken, a few pieces at a time, 4-5 minutes on each side or until golden brown and juices run clear. Drain on paper towels.

FAIMLY-FAVORITE FRIED CHICKEN

Fiery Potato Chips

Chili powder and cayenne pepper turn these chips into seasoned crowd-pleasers.
—SUE MURPHY GREENWOOD, MI

PREP: 15 MIN. + SOAKING
COOK: 5 MIN./BATCH • **MAKES:** 10 CUPS

- 4 **medium unpeeled potatoes**
- 4 **teaspoons salt, divided**
- 4 **cups ice water**
- 1 **tablespoon chili powder**
- 1 **teaspoon garlic salt**
- 1 **teaspoon dried parsley flakes**
- ¼ to ½ **teaspoon cayenne pepper**
  Oil for deep-fat frying

1. Using a vegetable peeler or metal cheese slicer, cut potatoes into very thin lengthwise strips. Place in a large bowl; add 3 teaspoons salt and ice water. Soak for 30 minutes; drain.
2. Place potatoes on paper towels and pat dry. In a small bowl, combine the chili powder, garlic salt, parsley, cayenne and remaining salt; set aside.
3. In an electric skillet or deep fryer, heat oil to 375°. Cook the potato chips in oil in batches for 2-3 minutes or until deep golden brown, stirring frequently.
4. Remove with a slotted spoon; drain on paper towels. Immediately sprinkle with reserved seasoning mixture. Store in an airtight container.

CARROT FRITTERS

FAST FIX ▶
Carrot Fritters

Crispy and mild-flavored, these fritters get snatched up quickly. If there are any left over, they reheat well for a snack the next day.
—SUSAN WITT FAIRBURY, NE

START TO FINISH: 30 MIN.
MAKES: 20 FRITTERS

- 1 **cup all-purpose flour**
- 1 **teaspoon salt**
- 1 **teaspoon baking powder**
- 2 **eggs**
- ½ **cup milk**
- 1 **teaspoon canola oil**
- 3 **cups shredded carrots**
  Oil for deep-fat frying

1. In a large bowl, combine the flour, salt and baking powder. Whisk the eggs, milk and oil; stir into dry ingredients just until moistened. Fold in carrots.
2. In an electric skillet or deep-fat fryer, heat oil to 375°. Drop batter by 2 tablespoonfuls into hot oil; press lightly to flatten. Fry until golden brown, about 1-2 minutes on each side. Drain on paper towels.

top tip

Garden-Fresh Fritters

No matter how much garden zucchini and yellow squash I cook, I'm still looking for ways to use it up. One of my favorite simple recipes is to beat an egg with milk, salt, pepper and enough flour to make a batter. I dip slices of fresh squash into the batter and deep-fry them. They're wonderful with chicken or steak.
—GRACE L. ALVIN, TX

FIERY POTATO CHIPS

Dynamic Duos

Pair up these **popular entrees** with a hand-picked side dish or custom beverage, and you're on your way to a memorable dinner. These pairings are **great for company**.

Pizza in a Skillet

I love the versatility of this recipe. I was starving when I first came up with it, and my fridge was nearly bare. The result was a quick-fix pizza that cooks in the skillet with a crispy, cracker-thin tortilla crust. Toss on whatever toppings you happen to have on hand.

—**CARA COBB** ABBEVILLE, GA

START TO FINISH: 30 MIN.
MAKES: 2 SERVINGS

- ⅓ **cup thinly sliced onion**
- ⅓ **cup thinly sliced green pepper**
- 2 **teaspoons olive oil, divided**
- 1 **cup sliced mushrooms**
- 2 **flour tortillas (6 inches)**
- 28 **slices pepperoni**
- 1 **cup chopped tomatoes**
- ¾ **cup shredded Mexican cheese blend or cheddar cheese**
  Crushed red pepper flakes, optional

1. Saute onion and green pepper in 1 teaspoon oil in a large skillet until crisp-tender. Add mushrooms; cook 2 minutes longer. Remove and keep warm.

2. Lightly brown one tortilla in ½ teaspoon oil in the same skillet. Turn over; top with half of the pepperoni, tomatoes, onion mixture and cheese. Cover and cook until cheese is melted, about 2 minutes. Sprinkle with pepper flakes if desired. Repeat for second pizza.

Layered Italian Soda

Italian sodas are fun, and your gang will love them. Try making the sodas with differently flavored syrups, or even topping off each glass with a shot of whipped cream and a cherry.

—**TASTE OF HOME TEST KITCHEN**

START TO FINISH: 5 MIN.
MAKES: 2 SERVINGS

- ¼ **cup black currant or blackberry flavoring syrup**
- ½ **cup orange juice**
- 1⅓ **cups carbonated water, chilled**

Place 2 tablespoons syrup in each of two tall glasses. Layer each glass with ¼ cup orange juice and ⅔ cup carbonated water, slowly pouring down inside of tilted glass to keep layers separated. Serve immediately.
NOTE *This recipe was tested with Torani brand flavoring syrup. Look for it in the coffee section.*

PIZZA IN A SKILLET
LAYERED ITALIAN SODA

top tip — Vegetarian Pizza Ideas

Top your pizza crust with one of these satisfying combos:

- Pesto, tomatoes, artichoke hearts, black olives and feta cheese
- Mashed black beans, red onion, bell peppers, jalapenos and pepper Jack cheese
- Roasted red pepper puree, mushrooms and fresh mozzarella cheese
- Marinara sauce, fresh spinach and basil, kalamata olives, mozzarella and feta cheese

ROASTED LIME CHICKEN
MOSCOW MULE

Roasted Lime Chicken

The hints of lime that infuse this juicy chicken make it the most-requested dish at family dinners.

—KATHY MARTINEZ SPRING VALLEY, CA

PREP: 20 MIN. + MARINATING
BAKE: 2 HOURS + STANDING
MAKES: 6 SERVINGS

- ½ cup Dijon mustard
- ¼ cup lime juice
- ¼ cup soy sauce
- 2 tablespoons minced fresh parsley or 2 teaspoons dried parsley flakes
- 2 tablespoons minced fresh rosemary or 2 teaspoons dried rosemary, crushed
- 2 tablespoons minced fresh sage or 2 teaspoons rubbed sage
- 2 tablespoons minced fresh thyme or 2 teaspoons dried thyme
- 1 teaspoon white pepper
- 1 teaspoon ground nutmeg
- 1 roasting chicken (6 to 7 pounds)
- 4 medium limes, cut into wedges

1. Combine the first nine ingredients in a small bowl. Cover and refrigerate ¼ cup marinade; pour remaining marinade into a 2-gallon resealable plastic bag. Add the chicken; seal bag and turn to coat. Refrigerate for at least 4 hours.

2. Drain chicken and discard marinade. Place lime wedges inside the cavity. Tuck wings under chicken; tie drumsticks together. Place chicken breast side up on a rack in a shallow roasting pan. Brush reserved marinade over chicken.

3. Bake at 350° for 2 to 2½ hours or until a thermometer inserted in thigh reads 180°, basting occasionally with pan juices. Cover loosely with foil if chicken browns too quickly. Let stand for 15 minutes before carving.

⑤INGREDIENTS FAST FIX

Moscow Mule

Here's an old-time cocktail that was popular in the 1940s and '50s. It's traditionally served in a copper mug with plenty of ice.

—TASTE OF HOME TEST KITCHEN

START TO FINISH: 5 MIN.
MAKES: 6 SERVINGS

- 2 cups ginger ale, chilled
- 2 cups ginger beer, chilled
- ⅔ cup lime juice
- 1¼ cups vodka
  Ice cubes

Combine the ginger ale, ginger beer, lime juice and vodka in a pitcher. Serve over ice.

FAST FIX
Fresh Lime Margaritas

This basic margarita recipe is easy to modify to your tastes. Also try mixing it in the blender for a frosty creation. For berry-flavored margaritas, substitute frozen strawberries for some of the ice.

—TASTE OF HOME TEST KITCHEN

START TO FINISH: 15 MIN.
MAKES: 4 SERVINGS

- 4   lime wedges
- 1   tablespoon kosher salt
- ½   cup tequila
- ¼   cup Triple Sec
- ¼   cup lime juice
- ¼   cup lemon juice
- 2   tablespoons superfine sugar
- 1⅓ cups crushed ice

1. Using lime wedges, moisten rims of four glasses. Holding each glass upside down, dip rim into salt; set aside.

2. In a pitcher, combine the tequila, Triple Sec, lime juice, lemon juice and sugar; stir until sugar is dissolved. Serve in prepared glasses over crushed ice.

FAST FIX
Pork 'n' Pepper Tacos

As a proud native of the Lone Star State, I love the spicy food that's indigenous to Texas. But since both my husband and I have hectic schedules, I need dishes that are quick to prepare. Omit the jalapenos for friends who prefer milder foods.

—JACQUIE BALDWIN RALEIGH, NC

START TO FINISH: 30 MIN.
MAKES: 8 TACOS

- 2   pounds boneless pork, cut into thin strips
- 3   tablespoons canola oil
- 1   medium onion, chopped
- 2   medium jalapeno peppers, finely chopped
- 1   tablespoon chili powder
- ½   teaspoon salt
- ¼   teaspoon pepper
- 8   taco shells, warmed
      Shredded lettuce, shredded cheddar cheese, chopped tomato and salsa

1. Saute pork in oil in a large skillet until lightly browned. Add onion and jalapenos; cook 5 minutes longer.
2. Stir in seasonings. Reduce heat; cover and cook for 5-10 minutes or until meat and vegetables are tender, stirring occasionally.
3. Serve in taco shells with lettuce, cheese, tomato and salsa.

NOTE *Wear disposable gloves when cutting hot peppers; the oils can burn skin. Avoid touching your face.*

FRESH LIME MARGARITAS
PORK 'N' PEPPER TACOS

CHICKEN FAJITAS

PER SERVING *246 cal., 8 g fat (1 g sat. fat), 66 mg chol., 628 mg sodium, 15 g carb., 3 g fiber, 29 g pro.* **Diabetic Exchanges:** *3 lean meat, 1 starch, 1 fat.*

EAT SMART ⑤INGREDIENTS FAST FIX

Avocado Tomato Salad

This salad is terrific with Mexican food and makes a super appetizer on toasted baguette. The recipe combines tomatoes and avocados, a source of healthy fat.

—**GINGER BUROW** FREDERICKSBURG, TX

START TO FINISH: 15 MIN.
MAKES: 6-8 SERVINGS

- 4　cups chopped tomatoes
- ½　cup chopped green pepper
- ¼　cup chopped onion
- ½　teaspoon salt
- ⅛　teaspoon pepper
- 2　medium ripe avocados, peeled and cubed
- 1　tablespoon lime juice

In a large bowl, combine the tomatoes, green pepper, onion, salt and pepper. Place the avocados in another bowl; sprinkle with lime juice and toss gently to coat. Fold into tomato mixture. Serve immediately.

PER SERVING *134 cal., 10 g fat (2 g sat. fat), 0 chol., 215 mg sodium, 11 g carb., 5 g fiber, 2 g pro.* **Diabetic Exchanges:** *2 vegetable, 2 fat.*

EAT SMART

Chicken Fajitas

This is the best fajita recipe I've tried. The servings are hearty, but they're so good, we never have trouble finishing them.

—**KATHLEEN SMITH** PITTSBURGH, PA

PREP: 15 MIN. + MARINATING
COOK: 15 MIN.
MAKES: 2 SERVINGS

- ¼　cup lime juice
- 1　tablespoon reduced-sodium soy sauce
- 2　teaspoons canola oil
- 1　garlic clove, minced
- ½　teaspoon salt
- ½　teaspoon chili powder
- ½　teaspoon cayenne pepper
- ¼　teaspoon pepper
- ½　teaspoon liquid smoke, optional
- 2　boneless skinless chicken breast halves (4 ounces each)

FILLING
- 2　teaspoons canola oil
- 1　medium onion, julienned
- ½　small sweet red or green pepper, julienned
- 1　teaspoon reduced-sodium soy sauce
- ½　teaspoon lime juice
- 4　fat-free tortillas (6 inches), warmed
  Salsa and sour cream, optional

1. In a large resealable plastic bag, combine the first eight ingredients; if desired, add liquid smoke. Add chicken; seal bag and turn to coat. Refrigerate at least 2 hours.
2. Drain chicken and discard marinade. Moisten a paper towel with cooking oil; using long-handled tongs, rub on grill rack to coat lightly. Grill chicken, covered, over medium heat or broil 4 in. from heat for 4-6 minutes on each side or until a thermometer reads 165°.
3. In a large nonstick skillet, heat oil over medium-high heat. Add onion and red pepper; cook and stir 5-7 minutes or until tender. Stir in soy sauce and lime juice.
4. Cut chicken into thin slices; add to vegetables. Serve with tortillas and, if desired, salsa and sour cream.

AVOCADO TOMATO SALAD

Shepherd's Pie

When you need a real meat-and-potatoes fix, try this satisfying casserole. It combines creamy mashed potatoes with a hearty meat filling. Your favorite barbecue sauce gives the dish extra tang.

—CINDY KLISKEY PEPPERELL, MA

PREP: 25 MIN. • **BAKE:** 25 MIN.
MAKES: 2 CASSEROLES (8 SERVINGS EACH)

- 5 **pounds potatoes (about 10 medium), peeled and cubed**
- 2 **pounds ground beef**
- 2 **large onions, chopped**
- 2 **garlic cloves, minced**
- 2 **cans (15½ ounces each) whole kernel corn, drained**
- 1½ **cups barbecue sauce**
- 2 **packages (8 ounces each) cream cheese, softened**
- ¼ **cup butter, cubed**
- 1 **teaspoon salt**
- ¼ **teaspoon pepper**
- 2 **cups (8 ounces) shredded cheddar cheese**

1. Place potatoes in a stockpot and cover with water. Bring to a boil. Reduce heat; cover and cook for 10-15 minutes or until tender.

2. Meanwhile, cook the beef, onions and garlic in a Dutch oven until meat is no longer pink; drain. Stir in corn and barbecue sauce.

3. Drain potatoes; mash with cream cheese, butter, salt and pepper. Spoon meat mixture into two greased 13-in. x 9-in. baking dishes. Spread mashed potatoes over tops; sprinkle with cheese. Cover and freeze one casserole for up to 3 months.

4. Bake the remaining casserole, uncovered, at 350° for 25-30 minutes or until bubbly.

TO USE FROZEN CASSEROLE *Thaw in the refrigerator overnight. Remove from the refrigerator 30 minutes before baking. Bake, covered, at 350° for 1¼ hours or until bubbly. Uncover; bake 5-10 minutes longer or until heated through and cheese is melted.*

Sweet-Sour Lettuce Salad

This easy salad dressing is refreshing and slightly sweet. It compliments fresh lettuce and crisp bacon bits quite nicely.

—LOIS FETTING NELSON, WI

START TO FINISH: 10 MIN.
MAKES: 8 SERVINGS

- ½ **cup sugar**
- ¼ **cup vinegar**
- 2 **tablespoons water**
- ¾ **cup half-and-half cream**
- 8 **cups torn salad greens**
- 6 **bacon strips, cooked and crumbled**

In a jar with tight-fitting lid, combine the sugar, vinegar and water; shake until sugar is dissolved. Add cream; shake well. Just before serving, toss greens, bacon and dressing in a large bowl.

SHEPHERD'S PIE
SWEET-SOUR LETTUCE SALAD

"When I first made this dish, my 2-year-old liked it so much that he wanted it for every meal. You can use any pasta shape that will hold the sauce."
—CRYSTAL JO BRUNS ILIFF, CO

Polish Casserole

PREP: 25 MIN. • **BAKE:** 45 MIN.
MAKES: 2 CASSEROLES (6 SERVINGS EACH)

- 4 **cups uncooked penne pasta**
- 1½ **pounds smoked Polish sausage or kielbasa, cut into ½-inch slices**
- 2 **cans (10¾ ounces each) condensed cream of mushroom soup, undiluted**
- 1 **jar (16 ounces) sauerkraut, rinsed and well drained**
- 3 **cups (12 ounces) shredded Swiss cheese, divided**
- 1⅓ **cups 2% milk**
- 4 **green onions, chopped**
- 2 **tablespoons Dijon mustard**
- 4 **garlic cloves, minced**

1. Cook pasta according to package directions; drain and transfer to a large bowl. Stir in the sausage, soup, sauerkraut, 2 cups cheese, milk, onions, mustard and garlic.

2. Spoon into two greased 8-in. square baking dishes; sprinkle with remaining cheese. Cover and freeze one casserole for up to 3 months. Bake the remaining casserole, uncovered, at 350° for 45-50 minutes or until golden brown and bubbly.

TO USE FROZEN CASSEROLE *Thaw in the refrigerator overnight. Remove from the refrigerator 30 minutes before baking. Bake, uncovered, at 350° for 50-55 minutes or until golden brown and bubbly.*

(5) INGREDIENTS | FAST FIX

Tangy Zucchini Saute

You don't have to go to great lengths to zip up zucchini, as this recipe tastefully proves. You can serve up our savory creation in a jiffy.
—TASTE OF HOME TEST KITCHEN

START TO FINISH: 30 MIN.
MAKES: 6 SERVINGS

- 4 **medium zucchini, halved lengthwise and sliced**
- 1 **medium onion, chopped**
- 2 **tablespoons olive oil**
- 2 **garlic cloves, minced**
- 1 **teaspoon Italian seasoning**
- ½ **teaspoon salt**
- ¼ **teaspoon pepper**
- 1 **to 2 tablespoons white balsamic vinegar**

1. In a large skillet, saute zucchini and onion in oil until tender, about 10 minutes.

2. Stir in the garlic, Italian seasoning, salt and pepper; cook 1 minute longer. Add vinegar; saute for 1-2 minutes or until liquid is evaporated and zucchini is evenly coated.

Summer's Bounty

Preserve the **sun-kissed flavors** of summer with the reader recipes you'll find here. Brimming with summer berries, garden basil and crisp fresh-picked veggies, this resource will **keep the sun shining** well into the dark, cool months.

BASIL BUTTER

(5) INGREDIENTS
Freezer Sweet Corn

With this preparation the corn stays crisp-tender, so I can enjoy it any time of the year. I received this recipe from my daughter's mother-in-law, who lives on a farm in Iowa.

—JUDY OUDEKERK ST. MICHAEL, MN

PREP: 30 MIN. • **COOK:** 15 MIN.
MAKES: 3 QUARTS

- 4 quarts fresh corn (cut from about 20 ears)
- 1 quart hot water
- ⅔ cup sugar
- ½ cup butter, cubed
- 2 teaspoons salt

In a stockpot, combine all ingredients; bring to a boil. Reduce heat; simmer, uncovered, 5-7 minutes, stirring occasionally. Transfer to large shallow containers; cool, stirring occasionally. Freeze in resealable plastic freezer bags or freezer containers, allowing headspace for expansion.

FREEZER SWEET CORN

(5) INGREDIENTS
Basil Butter

I make this tasty butter during the growing season and freeze it for later use. It's wonderful for sauteing veggies, on top of grilled meats, tossed into pasta or spread on homemade bread.

—EMILY CHANEY PENOBSCOT, ME

PREP: 15 MIN. + CHILLING
MAKES: 1 CUP

- 1½ cups loosely packed fresh basil leaves
- 1 cup butter, softened
- 1 teaspoon seasoned pepper
- 1 teaspoon lemon juice
- ½ teaspoon garlic salt

1. Place basil in a food processor; pulse until chopped. Add remaining ingredients; process until blended.
2. Transfer to a sheet of plastic wrap; shape into a log. Refrigerate up to one week or wrap securely and freeze for longer storage. Unwrap and slice to use with seafood, poultry, vegetables, pasta and bread.

Pickled Bell Peppers

Everyone around here knows me for this colorful, tasty dish. I serve it with a lot of meals, especially our weeknight cookouts.
—**HEATHER PRENDERGAST** SUNDRE, AB

PREP: 20 MIN. + CHILLING
MAKES: 4 CUPS

- **2** each medium sweet red, yellow and green peppers, cut into 1-inch pieces
- **1** large red onion, thinly sliced
- **2** teaspoons mixed pickling spices
- **½** teaspoon celery seed
- **1** cup sugar
- **1** cup cider vinegar
- **⅓** cup water

1. In a large glass bowl, combine peppers and onion. Place pickling spices and celery seed on a double thickness of cheesecloth. Gather corners of cloth to enclose seasonings; tie securely with string.
2. In a small saucepan, combine sugar, vinegar, water and spice bag. Bring to a boil; boil 1 minute. Transfer spice bag to pepper mixture. Pour vinegar mixture over top. Cool to room temperature. Refrigerate, covered, 24 hours, stirring occasionally.
3. Discard spice bag. Refrigerate pickled peppers up to 1 month.

FREEZER CUCUMBER PICKLES

PICKLED BELL PEPPERS

(5) INGREDIENTS
Freezer Cucumber Pickles

When I first started to make these crunchy pickles, I wasn't sure if freezing cucumbers would actually work. To my surprise, they came out perfectly. Now I share them with friends and neighbors.
—**CONNIE GOENSE** PEMBROKE PINES, FL

PREP: 20 MIN. + FREEZING
MAKES: 10 PINTS

- **4** pounds pickling cucumbers, sliced
- **8** cups thinly sliced onions (about 8 medium)
- **¼** cup salt
- **¾** cup water
- **4** cups sugar
- **2** cups cider vinegar

1. Divide cucumbers, onions, salt and water between two large bowls. Let stand at room temperature 2 hours. Do not drain.
2. Add 2 cups sugar and 1 cup vinegar to each bowl; stir until sugar is dissolved. Transfer to ten 1-pint freezer containers, leaving 1-in. headspace for expansion; freeze up to 6 weeks.
3. Thaw pickles in refrigerator 8 hours before using. Serve within 2 weeks of thawing.

FREEZER RASPBERRY SAUCE

⑤ INGREDIENTS

Freezer Raspberry Sauce

This is a great topping for ice cream and, since it's thicker than sweetened berries, it's nice over sponge cake and shortcake, too. My family loves it over waffles, along with a dab of plain yogurt.
—**KATIE KOZIOLEK** HARTLAND, MN

PREP: 20 MIN. + STANDING
MAKES: 4 PINTS

- **10 cups fresh raspberries, divided**
- **3 cups sugar**
- **1 cup light corn syrup**
- **1 package (3 ounces) liquid fruit pectin**
- **2 tablespoons lemon juice**

1. Rinse four clean 1-pint plastic containers and lids with boiling water. Dry thoroughly. Crush 6 cups raspberries, 1 cup at a time, to measure exactly 3 cups; transfer to a large bowl. Stir in sugar and corn syrup; let mixture stand 10 minutes, stirring occasionally.

2. In a small bowl, mix liquid pectin and lemon juice. Add to raspberry mixture; stir constantly for 3 minutes to evenly distribute pectin. Stir in remaining whole raspberries.

3. Immediately fill all containers to within ½ in. of tops. Wipe off top edges of containers; immediately cover with lids. Let sauce stand at room temperature for 24 hours or until partially set. Refrigerate sauce for up to 3 weeks or freeze for up to 12 months.

4. Thaw frozen sauce in refrigerator before using.

⑤ INGREDIENTS

Orange Blueberry Freezer Jam

This quick jam lets me savor the taste of fresh-picked blueberries no matter the season, but I have to fight off my kids, who start eating the berries right away.
—**MARK MORGAN** WATERFORD, WI

PREP: 25 MIN. + STANDING
MAKES: 4 CUPS

- **2½ cups sugar**
- **1 medium orange**
- **1½ cups fresh blueberries, crushed**
- **1 pouch (3 ounces) liquid fruit pectin**

1. Rinse four clean 1-cup plastic containers with lids with boiling water. Dry thoroughly.

2. Preheat oven to 250°. Place the sugar in a shallow baking dish; bake 15 minutes. Meanwhile, finely grate 1 tablespoon peel from orange. Peel and chop orange.

3. In a large bowl, combine blueberries, warm sugar, grated peel and chopped orange; let stand 10 minutes, stirring occasionally. Add pectin; stir constantly for 3 minutes to evenly distribute pectin.

4. Immediately fill all containers to within ½ in. of tops. Wipe off top edges of containers; immediately cover with lids. Let stand at room temperature until set, but not longer than 24 hours.

5. Jam is now ready to use. Refrigerate up to 3 weeks or freeze up to 12 months. Thaw frozen jam in refrigerator before serving.

ORANGE BLUEBERRY FREEZER JAM

SURPRISE RASPBERRY JAM

⑤INGREDIENTS

Surprise Raspberry Jam

I've made this jam for years and no one has been able to guess the secret ingredient—tomatoes!

—**ELIZABETH BAKER** BIRDSBORO, PA

PREP: 15 MIN. • **COOK:** 35 MIN. + STANDING
MAKES: ABOUT 5½ CUPS

- 5 **cups chopped peeled fresh tomatoes**
- 4 **cups sugar**
- 1 **tablespoon lemon juice**
- 2 **packages (3 ounces each) raspberry gelatin**

1. Rinse three 1-pint plastic containers with lids with boiling water. Dry thoroughly.

2. In a large saucepan, combine tomatoes, sugar and lemon juice. Cook and stir over high heat until boiling. Reduce heat; simmer, uncovered, 25 minutes. Remove from heat. Skim foam if needed. Add gelatin; stir until completely dissolved.

3. Immediately fill containers to within ½ in. of tops. Cool to room temperature, about 1 hour. Wipe top edges of containers; cover with lids. Let stand at room temperature 3 hours or until set, but not longer than 24 hours.

4. Jam is now ready. Refrigerate for up to 3 weeks or freeze for up to 12 months. Thaw frozen jam in refrigerator before serving.

Don't ditch those last dabs and dribbles! They're culinary gold after a spell in the deep freeze.

❶ CHOPPED ONIONS Simply freeze chopped onions in water; before cooking, thaw, drain and stir into just about anything.

❷ CHIPOTLE PEPPERS IN ADOBO SAUCE Thaw, then puree or chop and toss into chili, salsa and marinade for smoky heat.

❸ LEMON AND LIME JUICE Freeze fresh juice so it's ready when you need a touch of tart.

❹ YOGURT Pop a couple of frozen cubes into a blender with juice to make dynamite smoothies.

❺ TOMATO PASTE Freeze what's left in the can so you'll always have what you need for a savory sauce.

❻ TEA Plain old ice cubes dilute pitchers of iced tea as they melt. Use frozen tea cubes instead.

❼ PUREED BUTTERNUT SQUASH Stir it into soups, stews and sauces as they simmer for a richer flavor and creamy texture.

❽ PESTO Speed up prep time of pasta, crostini and more. Thaw the cubes in the fridge first.

❾ CHICKEN BROTH Freeze this kitchen essential by the tablespoon so you know just how much to add.

❿ HERBS For a burst of flavor, freeze herbs in water, then thaw and drain before using.

⓫ COFFEE Brew a full-flavored iced coffee drink, or add a kick to desserts, gravy and more.

⓬ BERRIES Add to smoothies and baked goods, or thaw and sprinkle on yogurt for a tastier breakfast.

⓭ TOMATO JUICE Keep these on hand for chilis, stews and drinks.

⓮ WINE Punch up a meal by putting a cube or two in pretty much any savory sauce you create.

Easy Meal-in-Ones

Nothing beats a **tasty one-dish dinner** for easy cooking and quick clean-up. Here's a trio of **family-pleasing favorites** to carry you through mealtime with panache.

"So simple but so good, this saucy pasta dish is always well received. I love that I can prepare it in no time on a weeknight, but it tastes like I worked hard on it all day. A sprinkle of fresh basil adds just the right sweetness." **—SUSAN HEIN** BURLINGTON, WI

CHICKEN & SPINACH MOSTACCIOLI

Chicken & Spinach Mostaccioli

PREP: 20 MIN. • **COOK:** 15 MIN.
MAKES: 4 SERVINGS

- 8 ounces uncooked mostaccioli
- ½ cup coarsely chopped sun-dried tomatoes (not packed in oil)
- 1 cup boiling water
- 3 tablespoons butter
- 1 large onion, thinly sliced
- 2 garlic cloves, minced
- 2 tablespoons all-purpose flour
- 2¼ cups chicken broth
- 1 cup half-and-half cream
- 3 cups coarsely chopped fresh spinach
- 2 cups cubed cooked chicken breast
- ¼ teaspoon salt
- ⅛ teaspoon pepper
  Thinly sliced fresh basil

1. Cook mostaccioli according to package directions for al dente. Meanwhile, in a small bowl, combine tomatoes and boiling water; let stand 5 minutes. Drain.

2. In a Dutch oven, heat butter over medium heat. Add onion and garlic; cook and stir 4-5 minutes or until tender. Stir in flour until blended; gradually whisk in broth and cream. Bring to a boil, stirring constantly; cook and stir 2 minutes or until thickened. Stir in spinach, chicken, drained tomatoes, salt and pepper.

3. Drain mostaccioli; add to the pan. Cook until heated through and the spinach is wilted, stirring occasionally. Sprinkle with basil.

Beef and Orzo Skillet

Not only does this recipe make tasty use of leftover brisket, it also cooks in just one pot, making cleanup a cinch.
—MARGIE WILLIAMS MT. JULIET, TN

PREP: 15 MIN. • **COOK:** 25 MIN.
MAKES: 5 SERVINGS

- 1 cup halved fresh mushrooms
- 2 celery ribs, thinly sliced
- 1 medium sweet yellow pepper, cut into 1-inch pieces
- 1 medium onion, chopped
- 1 tablespoon olive oil
- 2 cans (14½ ounces each) fire-roasted diced tomatoes, undrained
- 2 cups cubed cooked beef brisket
- 1 cup beef broth
- ¾ cup uncooked orzo pasta
- ½ cup barbecue sauce
- 1 teaspoon dried oregano

Saute the mushrooms, celery, pepper and onion in oil in a Dutch oven until tender. Stir in the remaining ingredients. Bring to a boil. Reduce heat; cover and simmer for 15-20 minutes or until pasta is tender.

BEEF AND ORZO SKILLET

Spring Pilaf with Salmon & Asparagus

Celebrate the best of spring in one fabulous dish. Fresh asparagus, carrots, lemon and chives complement leftover cooked salmon in this simple entree.

—STEVE WESTPHAL WIND LAKE, WI

PREP: 15 MIN. • **COOK:** 30 MIN.
MAKES: 4 SERVINGS

- 2 **medium carrots, sliced**
- 1 **medium sweet yellow pepper, chopped**
- ¼ **cup butter, cubed**
- 1½ **cups uncooked long grain rice**
- 4 **cups reduced-sodium chicken broth**
- ½ **teaspoon salt**
- ¼ **teaspoon pepper**
- 2½ **cups cut fresh asparagus (1-inch pieces)**
- 12 **ounces fully cooked salmon chunks**
- 2 **tablespoons lemon juice**
- 2 **tablespoons minced fresh chives, divided**
- 1 **teaspoon grated lemon peel**

1. Saute carrots and yellow pepper in butter in a large saucepan until crisp-tender. Add rice; cook and stir for 1 minute or until lightly toasted.
2. Stir in the broth, salt and pepper. Bring to a boil. Reduce heat; cover and simmer for 20 minutes. Stir in asparagus. Cook, uncovered, 3-4 minutes longer or until rice is tender.
3. Stir in the salmon, lemon juice, 1 tablespoon chives and lemon peel; heat through. Fluff with a fork. Sprinkle with remaining chives.

General Recipe Index

This handy index lists every recipe by food category, major ingredient and/or cooking method, so you can easily locate recipes to suit your needs.

✓ *Recipe includes Nutrition Facts*

||||||||||||||||||||||||||||||||||||||||||||||||||||||||||||||||||||||||||||||||||||||||

**TACO BUBBLE PIZZA
PAGE 179**

BREAKFAST SKEWERS
PAGE 91

FAVORITE CHILI CHEESEBURGERS
PAGE 225

QUICK CHERRY
TURNOVERS
PAGE 61

**CURRIED BEEF PITAS
WITH CUCUMBER SAUCE
PAGE 116**

**GRILLED PINEAPPLE PORK
& VEGETABLES
PAGE 76**

CREAMY HAM & CORN SOUP
PAGE 45

CHICKEN & APPLE SALAD WITH GREENS
PAGE 120

RAVIOLI WITH SAUSAGE
& TOMATO CREAM SAUCE
PAGE 23

BERRY MINI CHEESECAKES PAGE 268

CHICAGO-STYLE BEEF ROLLS
PAGE 194

CANTONESE SWEET AND SOUR PORK
PAGE 205

**VEGETABLE ORZO SOUP
PAGE 73**

MARGHERITA PITA PIZZAS
PAGE 175

BUFFALO SLOPPY JOES
PAGE 33

Alphabetical Recipe Index

This handy index lists every recipe in alphabetical order so you can easily find your favorites.

✓ *Recipe includes Nutrition Facts*

BUSY-DAY CHICKEN FAJITAS
PAGE 188

CHICKEN & SPINACH MOSTACCIOLI
PAGE 314

**GARBANZO-STUFFED MINI PEPPERS
PAGE 104**

LOADED POTATO SALAD
PAGE 235

MOJITO MARINATED FRUIT
PAGE 228

**PORK QUESADILLAS WITH FRESH SALSA
PAGE 136**

SMOKED SAUSAGE JAMBALAYA PAGE 47